EARLY CULTU
OF MAINLAND
SOUTHEAST ASIA

EARLY CULTURES
OF MAINLAND
SOUTHEAST ASIA

CHARLES HIGHAM

For Tony and Eileen Higham
My Parents

Acknowledgements

First published in USA in 2002 by
Art Media Resources, Ltd.
1507 South Michigan Avenue
Chicago, IL 60605 USA
Tel: 312-663-5351
Fax: 312-663-5177
E-mail: info@artmediaresources.com
www.artmediaresources.com

British Library Cataloguing-in-Publication Data.
A catalogue record for this book is available from
the British Library.

ISBN 1 58886 028 0

Editor and Publisher Narisa Chakrabongse
Design Supadee Ruangsakvichit
Production Supervision Paisarn Piemmettawat

The rapid progress of research into the prehistory of
mainland Southeast Asia over the past decade has
quickly dated my previous synthesis, The Archaeology of
Mainland Southeast Asia. With the encouragement of
Narisa Chakrabongse, I have prepared a new book
which will, I hope, fill a growing gap in the literature.
I am most grateful to her, as well as her colleagues
Paisarn Piemmettawat and Supadee Ruangsakvichit at
River Books, for their constant support and advice.
During several meetings in London to review the layout
of this book, Hansjörg Mayer provided many most
helpful and sensitive suggestions.

Archaeology is dependent on teamwork, and I
record my thanks to all my colleagues who, over the
past 30 years, have made it possible to consider a
synthesis of such a large area. There are now so many,
that it would almost take another book to name them
all. However, I would like to thank in particular my
co-director Rachanie Thosarat, who worked with me at
Khok Phanom Di, Nong Nor, Ban Lum Khao, Ban Non
Wat and Noen U-Loke, and Amphan Kijngam, my
co-director at Ban Na Di.

I have been most fortunate in the generosity of
colleagues who have contributed photographs to
augment this volume: Dr. V. Pigott and the Thailand
Archaeometallurgy Project, Dr. P. Sørensen,
Dr. G. Albrecht, Dr. A. Reinecke, Dr. R. Mourer,
Dr. H. Loofs-Wissowa, Dr. A. Källén, Dr. Patrizia Zolese,
Dr. Nguyen Viet, Dr. Thongsa Sayavongkhamdy,
Dr. M. Stark, Dr. P.-Y. Manguin, Dr. D. O'Reilly,
Dr. R. Ciarla, Dr. F. Rispoli, Dr. Yasushi Kojo, Dr. Ian
Glover, Dr. J.-P. Pautreau, Dr. N. Chang and
Professor D. Anderson. I thank them all for their
contribution to this book. Leslie O'Neill of the
Anthropology Department, University of Otago,
prepared the maps of Southeast Asia, and I thank him
for his cooperation.

Printed and bound in Thailand by
Amarin Printing and Publishing Public Co. Ltd.

Contents

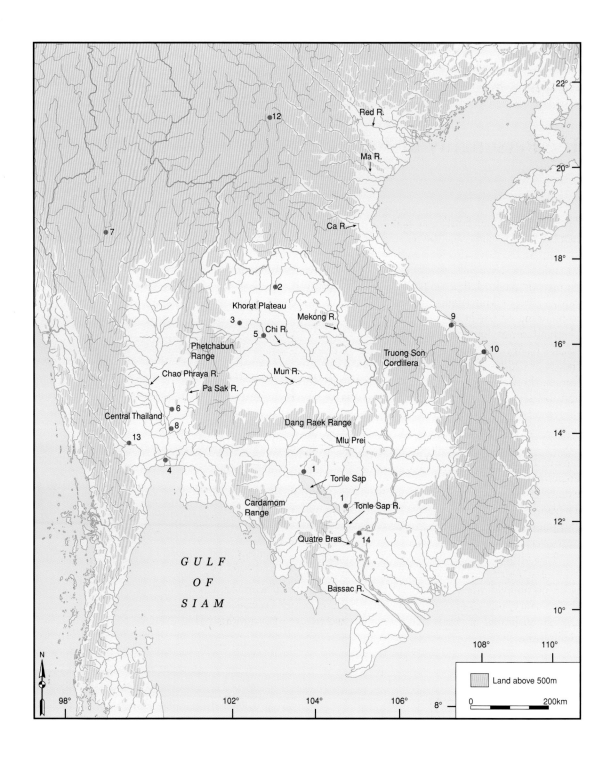

Red R.

Ma R.

Ca R.

● 12

● 7

● 2

Khorat Plateau

Mekong R.

● 3

5 ● Chi R.

● 9

Phetchabun
Range

● 10

Truong Son
Cordillera

Chao Phraya R.

Mun R.

Pa Sak R.

● 6

Central Thailand

● 8

Dang Raek Range

● 13

Mlu Prei

● 4

● 1

Tonle Sap

Cardamom
Range

1

Tonle Sap R.

Quatre Bras

14

GULF

OF

SIAM

Bassac R.

108°   110°

8°

Land above 500m

0   200km

N

98°   102°   104°   106°

22°

20°

18°

16°

14°

12°

10°

Chapter One

The Personality of Southeast Asia

The archaeology of Southeast Asia has for long lain in the shadows cast by its two giant neighbours, India and China. The very name once applied to the area, Indo-China, reflects subservience. Colonial attitudes also brought a particular flavour to interpretations of the prehistoric past. Madeleine Colani, accustomed to the vibrant Aurignacian or Magdalenian cultures of her native France, found little to recommend the late hunter-gatherer societies of Viet Nam. George Cœdès described the late prehistoric inhabitants of Southeast Asia as having a very low level of culture (Cœdès 1968). Writing in the early 1960s, Grahame Clark described the area as a "kind of funnel, through which people have spread over Indonesia, Melanesia and further afield" (Clark 1962: 201). This approach was sharply reversed between 1968 and 1980 by claims that Southeast Asia witnessed not only the world's earliest agriculture, but also the oldest Bronze Age and first use of iron (Solheim 1968, 1972, Gorman and Charoenwongsa 1976). Such notions are in danger of becoming engrained in the literature. Turnbaugh *et al.* (1999: 406), for example, described how rice cultivation originated in "Northern Thailand..... including the sites of Ban Chiang and Non Nok Tha", and publish a map showing the spread of rice cultivation in a northward direction into China.

This unsatisfactory situation calls for a judicious review of Southeast Asian prehistory in the light of much recent research. We will find no evidence for such early agriculture or metal working. On the contrary, one can trace a consistent pattern, which culminated in the establishment at Angkor of one of the world's great pre-industrial civilisations.

Defining Southeast Asia

Like a concertina, mainland Southeast Asia has no fixed form. It could logically encompass all the territory between the Yangzi and the Chindwin rivers. The Holocene rise in sea level has drowned extensive tracts which formerly belonged to the mainland. This book will concentrate upon the central or core region of Southeast Asia,

Opposite:
1. Angkor, 2. Ban Chiang, 3. Non Nok Tha, 4.Bangkok, 5. Khon Kaen, 6. Lopburi, 7. Chiang Mai, 8. Ayutthaya, 9. Hue, 10. Da Nang, 11. Samrong Sen, 12. Dien Bien Phu, 13. Kanchanaburi, 14. Kampong Cham.

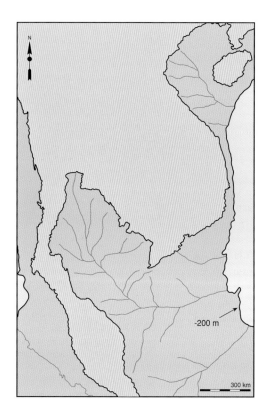

The reconstructed coastline at the height of the Ice Age 15,000 years ago reveals how much low-lying coastal land was lost with the subsequent rise in the sea level.

which is defined as the valleys of three great rivers, the Red, Chao Phraya and the Mekong, but will incorporate where appropriate, the prehistory of Yunnan, Guangxi and Guangdong (known collectively as Lingnan), as well as recent advances in Burma.

Whatever the variable, Southeast Asia exhibits diversity. It could be argued for instance, that we are dealing with a subtropical monsoon area, and at a very general level, this is true. But the impact of the monsoon is tempered by numerous local factors. Proximity to the sea, altitude and relationship to the uplands affect the amount of rainfall, the duration of the dry season and for some regions, even the existence of one. The Southeast Asian landscape has undergone a series of profound changes over the period covered by this book, which prehistorians ignore at their peril. The seas which now separate the mainland from the islands of Sumatra, Java and Borneo are uniformly shallow, rarely exceeding 36 metres in depth. The sea bottom still reveals the channels of drowned rivers. Geomorphological studies undertaken in the Strait of Melaka and the South China Sea (Tjia 1980) have revealed a rapidly rising sea level. According to Geyh, Kudrass and Streif (1979), 10,000 before present (BP) the sea level was between 40-60 metres below its modern level, exposing an immense area of low-lying terrain traversed by the extensions of the Chao Phraya and Mekong rivers. Between 8,000-6,000 BP, the sea level rose from -12.8 to +1.2 metres relative to the present coast, and subsequent raised beaches dating between 5,000-4,000 BP reveal a sea level between 2.5 and 5.8 metres higher than at present.

The reduction in sea level to the current shore began about 4,000 years ago, and was accompanied by minor oscillations. During the period of elevated levels between c. 7,000-1,000 BP, areas which now comprise the Chao Phraya, Mekong and Red River lowlands were shallow extensions of the sea. Takaya (1969) has shown that during this period, clay laid down under brackish water attained a depth of up to 14 metres in the vicinity of Bangkok. These changes altered the personality of Southeast Asia. Ten thousand years ago, it comprised extensive mountain chains and a vast region of low-lying marshy land across which snaked several major rivers and numerous tributaries. Five millennia later, the latter had all but disappeared and with it, an entire chapter of Southeast Asian prehistory.

We can pick up the thread of coastal settlement only when the sea level stabilised and then began to fall, revealing once again a low-lying riverine landscape but by now, covered by a mantle of marine clay. The three major river valleys we can recognise today for their concentrations of population are truncated versions of their ancestral channels, but each has built up a substantial delta in the recent past. Indeed, the Mekong is now adding to its delta at the rate of 80 metres per annum as deforestation has led to increased soil erosion. Dobby (1967) has recognised a series of regions determined on the basis of their landscape. These fall into two major groupings, river systems and their associated flat, flood-prone valleys and the intervening uplands. The former group incorporates Central Thailand and the Chao Phraya delta, the valleys and deltas of the Red, Ma and Ca rivers, and the lower Mekong and Tonle Sap plains. To these, one should add the flood plains of the Mun and Chi rivers on the Khorat plateau, both tributaries of the Mekong. All three valleys share a marked seasonality in water flows. This reflects the seasonal nature of the rainfall in their respective catchments and in the case of the Mekong, the coincidence between the onset of the rainy season and the spring melt of snow in the Himalayas. The rivers regularly break their banks and flood huge areas before branching into their respective deltas. Such floods deposit silt over a broad area and where not too deep, permit the growth of 'floating' rice, a variety with a long stalk and rapid growth rate. The floods also create natural levées behind which there is commonly a swamp forest where floodwaters rest. The Mekong has its minimum flow in February. In 1949, this attained 1,700 cubic metres/second (cumecs). The maximum flow seven months later was 34,000 cumecs, carrying 10,200 kg of silt per second. Such is the spate that the waters of the Mun River cannot enter the Mekong, and at the Quatre Bras, where the Mekong, Tonle Sap, Bassac and Lower Mekong rivers come together, the water volume is so great, that the Tonle Sap River reverses direction and

The Mekong River at Kampong Cham in Cambodia seems as large as an inland sea.

Rainfall and wind patterns change with the season of the monsoon. Left: In May, the prevailing wind moves from the southwest, bringing moist wind to the coast of the Gulf of Siam. The lower Mekong Valley and coastal Viet Nam suffer from a rain shadow effect. Right: Rainfall in the dry season is controlled by the flow of air from Eastern Asia. While relatively damp in coastal Viet Nam, it is dry for months on end in the interior.

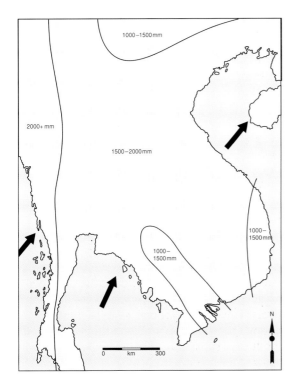

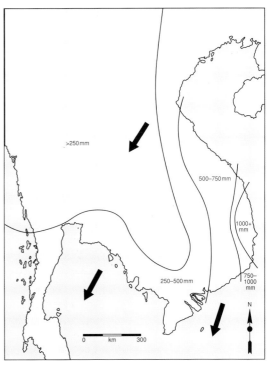

The Tonle Sap, or Great Lake of Cambodia, acts as a giant safety valve for the Mekong River in spate during the rainy season. The course of the linking Tonle Sap River alters to flow back into the lake, greatly expanding its size. With the dry season, the flow reverses to drain the lake.

Four rivers come together at the Quatre Bras, or Four Arms. In this view, temporary houses crowd the bank at Phnom Penh in Cambodia. The Tonle Sap River and upper Mekong are on the left hand side, the Bassac and lower Mekong on the right.

Right: Looking south from Phanom Rung in Northeast Thailand, the Dang Raek escarpment rises on the horizon. Beyond lie Cambodia and Angkor.

Left: The foothills of the Truong Son Cordillera rise in the distance above the coastal plain in Northern Viet Nam.

backs up into the Tonle Sap Lake. This Great Lake then increases its dry season area fourfold, thereby alleviating floods in the delta country below the Quatre Bras. In the absence of such a unique safety valve, the Red and Chao Phraya rivers habitually experienced more extreme and rapid flooding. In the latter area, this problem has been checked by the construction of dams, canals and pumping stations. The Red River also flows in part through canals, and is constrained by the construction of linear embankments.

These three river systems are bounded by uplands. The Red River delta is ringed on all but its eastern margin by rugged sandstone and limestone hills. The Truong Son Cordillera lies between the coast and the Mekong River, and historically served as the frontier between the Khmer and the Chams. The Dang Raek escarpment divides the Khorat Plateau from the North Cambodian plain, while a broad corridor between the Dang Raek and Cardamom ranges provides ready access from Cambodia to the Chao Phraya valley. The latter is again ringed by hills. To the west, lies a further old granite and limestone karstic mountain chain which today separates the Thai and the Burmese. The northern mountains comprise a very old and much folded and eroded system of shales, schists and limestone. On the eastern margins lies the Phetchabun range, a natural barrier between the Chao Phraya plains and the Khorat plateau. It is often said that the plains and mountains provide the basic contrast between two distinct modes of human adaptation. It should also be noted that the relief itself is a determinant in the patterns of rainfall and vegetation.

The whole area is subject in varying degrees to the sharply seasonal wind patterns that underlie the monsoonal regime. Between October and April the wind flows from the northeast, but it reverses in May to bring air from the southwest. The impact of these changing wind patterns varies with location and altitude. The Cardamom, Phetchabun and western ranges of Thailand receive much rainfall with the southwest monsoon, whereas the Chao Phraya and Tonle Sap plains and the Khorat plateau lie in respective rain shadows. The Truong Son cordillera attracts more rain than the coastal plains of Viet Nam and the Red River delta lying to the east. Indeed, the monsoon rains which bring moisture to the Truong Son range become the hot and dry 'Lao' wind when they enter the rain shadow which lies to the east. Paradoxically therefore, though these areas produce much rice, there is often insufficient rainfall and the farmers rely on river floods and their annual discharge of silt. This problem is exacerbated by the unpredictability of the rainfall and uncertain timing for the commencement of the monsoon rains. Thus between 1914-25, the wet season in Northeast Thailand lasted a minimum of 174 and a maximum of 236 days per annum. The predominantly northeastern wind pattern which establishes itself in October-November brings cooler temperatures and rain to the eastern fringes of the Truong Son range. The Red River delta experiences low cloud cover, extensive

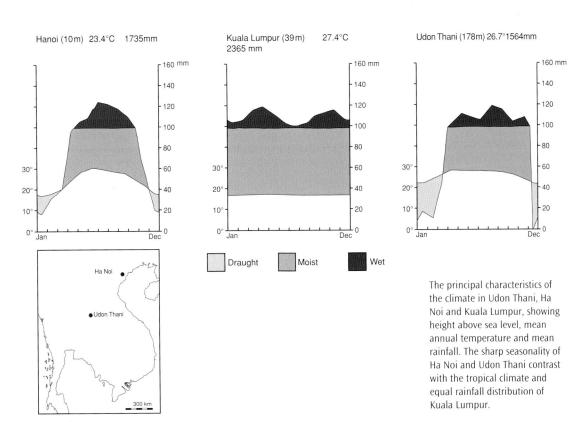

The principal characteristics of the climate in Udon Thani, Ha Noi and Kuala Lumpur, showing height above sea level, mean annual temperature and mean rainfall. The sharp seasonality of Ha Noi and Udon Thani contrast with the tropical climate and equal rainfall distribution of Kuala Lumpur.

drizzle and cool weather. The Truong Son Range now induces a rain shadow in the lands to the west, and during this long dry season, the plains west of the Mekong experience hardly any precipitation, cloudless skies, and a combination of cool nights and hot days. The uplands, however, are less affected and experience an abbreviated dry season.

Holdridge (1967) has employed relief, altitude and drainage in his analysis of the natural vegetation cover. Subsidiary variables include exposure to the wind and the ground water regime. In his terminology, distinct associations of plant and animal communities are known as 'life zones', several of which affect patterns of human adaptation. In one of his study areas, located in the vicinity of Khon Kaen in Northeast Thailand, he found that under about 400 m, dry deciduous forest cover predominated, merging over that altitude, with a subtropical wet forest. The conversion from one to the other was also identified in the Lopburi and Chiang Mai areas. The distribution of the deciduous forest is linked with a sharply seasonal availability of water, and hence a capacity to withstand drought. The dipterocarp trees are well adapted to this habitat, shedding leaves during the dry season. As a result, there is no permanent canopy of evergreen trees to screen the ground from the direct impact of rain, and grasses and shrubs flourish. This habitat favours grazers, such as the deer, wild cattle and elephant, provided there is regular access to water and salt licks. It is also much easier for people to modify this habitat through dry-season burning. Above 400 metres in areas with over 2,000 mm of rain a year, we find a new configuration, with its plant communities merging and ultimately taking on the form of canopied rainforest. Since the ground is screened from sun and rain, there is little grass growth and large herbivores are rare. Only the opportunistic and omnivorous pig thrives at ground level. Where there are favourable cleared enclaves, one finds rhinoceros, gaur, banteng, elephant and the sambar deer. The canopies, however, sustain a varied arboreal fauna within which squirrels and civets find a regular food supply. In the absence of an attenuated dry season, the rigours of a long period of aridity do not present a problem for human settlement.

This sub-tropical wet forest in turn gives way at about 1,000 metres to a subtropical lower montane wet forest, in which evergreen oaks and chestnuts appear. Hitherto, this elevated habitat has not yielded data on prehistoric settlement. Two further life zones are particularly significant, and emphasise the considerable diversity of environments that were settled in prehistory. These are the mangrove habitat of the sheltered coasts, and the swampy environment of the deltas and deeply flooded river plains. The former is a pioneer community of plants that colonises the mudflats exposed to regular tidal flows. Plants are restricted

With rising altitude in northern Thailand, one encounters canopied rainforest.

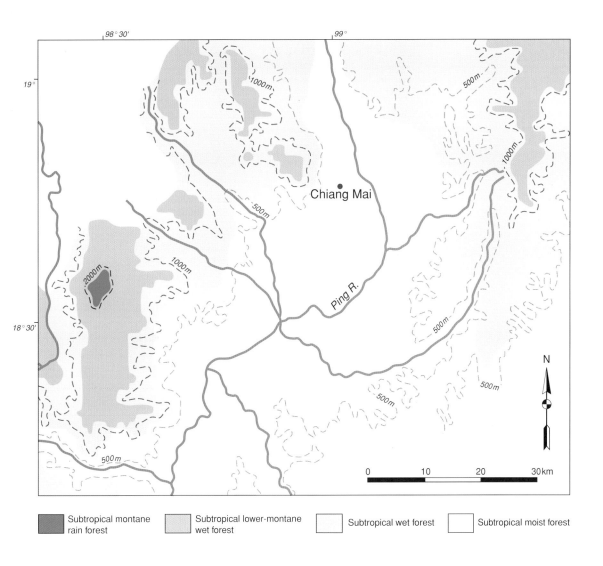

Subtropical montane rain forest

Subtropical lower-montane wet forest

Subtropical wet forest

Subtropical moist forest

to a few salt-tolerant species, and exposure to salt water reduces the number of mammals to those which feed off intertidal resources, such as crabs and shellfish at or near ground level, and the nectar and fruits of the mangroves themselves. Mammals include otters, macaques, pigs and bats. The deltas and flood plains are too wet for dense woodland to form and include large open areas of reeds and swampy grasses well adapted to the rhinoceros, water buffalo and swamp-deer.

Such broad divisions into life zones leave only the most generalised impression of the complex mosaic of plant and animal communities within which human societies operated. Upland areas, largely under evergreen varieties of forest, are to be found in Western Thailand, the Northern highlands of Thailand comprising the valleys of the Ping, Nan and Yom rivers, the Cardamom mountains, the highlands north and west of the Red River delta, and the Truong Son range. Lowlands with variable swamp or deciduous forest, or mangrove associations include the Chao Phraya plains and the Pa Sak valley, the Chao Phraya delta, Khorat plateau, the deltas of the Red and Mekong rivers, the

The life zones in the Chiang Mai study area as proposed by Holdridge (1967). Note the close relationship between altitude and vegetation.

Estuarine mangroves such as these, at the mouth of the Saigon River, are one of the three richest habitats known, in terms of bio-productivity.

Tonle Sap plains and the coastal plains of central Viet Nam. There is considerable scope for local variety and not least, for human influence on the habitat.

Aspects of Diversity

From a political point of view, there has never been uniformity in Southeast Asia. The closest approach to overall control over the three rivers came with the kingdom of Angkor between AD 1000-1300, and French colonial rule (from the 1890s until 1954). The former however, never ruled the Red River valley and the latter's control excluded Thailand. Today, each valley has its own political apparatus. The valley of the Chao Phraya has been Thai for at least seven centuries. The lower Mekong is Khmer and has been for at least two millennia and the Red River is the heartland of the Vietnamese. Each is distinct linguistically and when we encounter the subject of linguistics, diversity is at its most apparent. The visitor to a market place in the uplands of Northern Thailand could within minutes, hear at least three separate languages being spoken.

For the prehistorian, present language distributions are both a lead and a pitfall for an understanding of the prehistoric period. This situation results from the possibility of a stable population being influenced by exposure to an alien language to the point of adopting it, as well as the possibility of the replacement of a language as a result of expansion and friction by a dominant group. Thus the replacement of Cham by Vietnamese reflects military pressure and expansion by the latter (Bayard 1979, Shorto 1979).

For some parts of Southeast Asia, there are inscriptions which indicate that with the development of early states, three of the major languages of the area were present. In the Chao Phraya valley, some of the early inscriptions were written in Mon, a language closely related to the Khmer found in the inscriptions of the Tonle Sap plains and the Mekong valley. Along the coast of central Viet Nam, inscriptions are in Cham and north of the Ca River, albeit without supporting inscriptions, the language spoken in later prehistory was probably Vietnamese. Lebar *et al.* (1964) recognise four major language groups in Southeast Asia today. The Sino-Tibetan need not detain us for long, as the upland speakers of this group such as Lahu, Lisu, Akha and Yao are small immigrant groups which have entered the area during the last few centuries. The older groups are Thai, Austroasiatic and Austronesian.

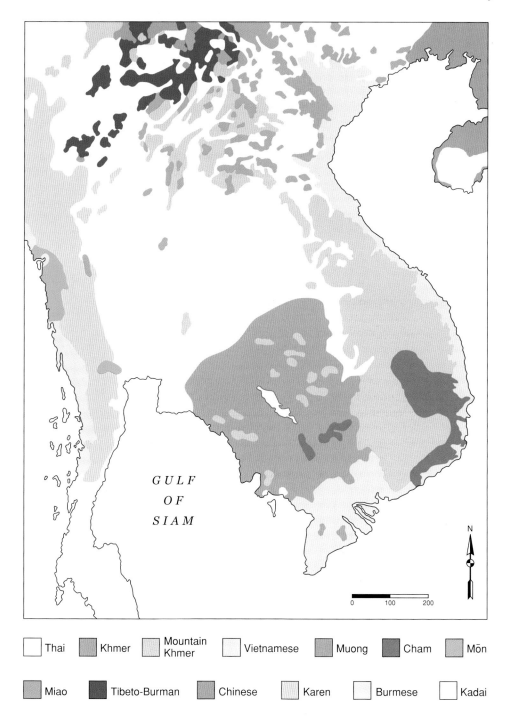

| Thai | Khmer | Mountain Khmer | Vietnamese | Muong | Cham | Mōn |

| Miao | Tibeto-Burman | Chinese | Karen | Burmese | Kadai |

The Thai language probably has a time depth of less than a millennium in Thailand itself, and represents movement into the area from southern China. Bayard (1979) has suggested that this might have taken the form of small groups of warrior nobles and their retainers moving into the Chao Phraya valley, an area which had for at least a millennium previously, been occupied by Mon speakers. Mon is an Austroasiatic language whose affinities lie with Khmer and

The current distribution of the main language families spoken in Southeast Asia.

The first European visitors to Angkor were amazed by its size and splendour. The discovery of the Angkor Wat bas reliefs brought home the splendour of this Southeast Asian civilisation. Here, we see the army of Angkor: infantry, elephants and chariots.

Hundreds of *apsaras*, divine maidens, awaited the arrival of King Suryavarman II at Angkor Wat.

Vietnamese. The Cham language is quite distinct, being Austronesian. Its closest affinities lie with the languages spoken in Borneo, and its time depth on the mainland before about AD 400 is unknown. It is likely to have a more recent history than the widely distributed languages of the Austroasiatic group. Some variants of Khmer, Cham and Vietnamese are found in the uplands, where there is some evidence that Austroasiatic languages preceded Thai. Thus the Khmu, an upland group in central Laos, are referred to by the Lao (Thai group) as their 'older brothers' in the area. The Yumbri, a surviving group of hunter-gatherers in upland Northern Thailand, are also probably Austroasiatic in terms of language, although the duration of their hunting and gathering there is not yet defined. Most languages spoken by the inhabitants of the Truong Son cordillera are of Khmer affinities, though upland Cham groups are found in the southeastern area.

While parts of Southeast Asia have been subjected to colonial rule, there has never been overall colonisation. The Han occupied the Red River valley in the first century AD, and the Chinese stayed there for nearly a millennium. They stopped their southward expansion however, at the Truong Son cordillera. The French occupied the same area during the 19th century, and added Cambodia, Laos and Cochin China, but their presence was for a far shorter period. Thailand has never been subjected to colonisation, and this distinction accounts for a further index of variability, namely the history and extent of prehistoric research.

Europeans in Southeast Asia: From Antiquarianism to Archaeology

The replacement of speculation on the past by scientific enquiry took place in Europe during the course of the 19th century. In Southeast Asia, there was no such development, and in due course, European workers laid the foundations of archaeological investigations. Contact between the indigenous kingdoms of Southeast Asia and Europeans, in contrast to visits by Roman entertainers and explorers like Marco Polo, followed the Bull promulgated by Pope Alexander VI, which divided the world between Spain and Portugal; Spain took the Americas and Portugal, the lands beyond Africa. Portuguese policy was to take strong points as foci for trade, with Macao and Goa as centres for China and India. For Southeast Asia, they chose Melaka. This involved forcible seizure by d'Albuquerque in 1509. The Sultan of Melaka was then a vassal to the king of Siam, so wisely d'Albuquerque sent an emissary, Duarte Fernandez, to the Court of Ayutthaya to report on the event. Thereby in 1511, diplomatic contact was established between the Portuguese and the Kingdom of Siam. Portugal soon became a political and economic force. A commercial treaty was concluded in 1516, and two decades later, 170 Portuguese were employed as royal body-guards. In 1538, 300 Portuguese were settled at Pattani, and by the end of the century, a Jesuit priest had his own ministry in Ayutthaya.

The early Portuguese missionaries marvelled at the size and splendour of Angkor Wat, built in the first half of the 12th century. (Courtesy Paisarn Piemmattawat)

Portuguese interest in Southeast Asia saw the first European appreciation of the abandoned sacred cities of the Angkorian civilization. The first published accounts of Angkor reflect visits by Portuguese missionaries or merchants between 1550-1570. F. Marcello de Ribadeneyra (1601) established a long tradition of disbelief in the achievements of the indigenous inhabitants when he wrote:

> "We suppose that the founders of the kingdom of Siam
> came from the great city which is situated in the middle
> of a desert in the kingdom of Cambodia. There are the
> ruins of an ancient city which some say was built by
> Alexander the Great or the Romans, it is amazing that no
> one lives there now, it is inhabited by ferocious animals,
> and the local people say it was built by foreigners".

The same conclusion was reached by Bartolome L. de Argensola (1609):

> "One finds in the interior within inaccessible forests, a
> city of six thousand houses, called Angon. The monuments
> and roads are made of marble, and are intact. The
> sculptures are also intact, as if they were modern. There
> is a strong wall. The moat, stone lined, can admit boats.
> The bridges are supported by stone giants. Where the
> canals end, one sees the vestiges of gardens. The perimeter
> of a lake in the area surpasses 30 leagues. There are
> epitaphs, inscriptions, which have not been deciphered.
> And in all this city, when the natives discovered it, there
> were no people, no animals, nothing living. I confess I
> hesitate to write this, it appears as fantastic as the
> Atlantis of Plato. A learned man supposed these to be the
> works of Trajan."

The early 17th century was a period of intense commercial rivalry. By 1605-1610, the Japanese were serving as body-guards to Siamese King

"The bridges are supported by stone giants." Portuguese missionaries encountered this southern gate to Angkor Thom, the city of Jayavarman VII, in the late 16th century.

Right: "The perimeter of a lake in the area surpasses 30 leagues." Early visitors to Angkor were amazed by the size of the massive Western Baray or reservoir, which is 8 km in length and a thousand years old.

Ekat'ot-Sarot at his court in Ayutthaya, and a Japanese visitor to Angkor between 1623-1636 made the earliest known plan of the great temple mausoleum of Angkor Wat (Péri 1923). In 1609, 16 Siamese were sent as envoys to the court at the Hague, and a few years later, Erik Van Wuystoff was travelling up the Mekong on an exploratory trading mission. His interests were in hides, pepper and gold in exchange for which he supplied cotton cloth (Garnier 1871). On 17 September 1612, Lucan Antheuniss presented the Thai King with a letter from James I of England, and the English were granted a cantonment at Ayutthaya between the Dutch and the Japanese. Antheuniss then set in train inland exploration by despatching Samuel Driver to Chiang Mai (Hutchinson 1940). The same century saw the French interest quicken, not just in commercial terms, but also in military activity. In 1664, a Catholic mission was established at Ayutthaya, and priests were active in the provinces.

One early French embassy to the Thai court of Ayutthaya included S. de la Loubère. The 1687 treaty he helped conclude with King Narai had a commercial intent. The French obtained a trading monopoly over the tin of Phuket and the cession of an island trading base at Mergui. De la Loubère wrote a detailed account of his visit and it contains the impressions of a cultivated European mind on a variety of issues. They may be the earliest speculations on the geomorphology of the area, and the origins of the inhabitants. His theories on origins were based on linguistic evidence, for he observed the presence of two languages, the vernacular Thai and the court language of Pali. He wrote:

> "As for what concerns the origine of the Siameses, it would be difficult to judge whether they are a single people, directly descended from the first men that inhabited the countrey of Siam, or whether in the process of time some other nation has not also settled there, notwithstanding the first inhabitants. The principal reason of this doubt proceeds from the Siameses understanding of two languages viz. the vulgar, which is a simple tongue consisting almost wholly of monosyllables, without conjugation or declension, and another language, which I

*have already spoken of, which to them is a dead tongue
known only by the learned, which is called the Balie
tongue, and which is enricht with the inflexions of words,
like the languages we have in Europe." (de la Loubère
1693).*

He also recorded perhaps the earliest archaeological and cultural-
historical observation when he wrote:

*"They do likewise daily discover pits anciently dug; and
the remains of a great many furnaces which are thought to
be abandoned during the ancient wars of Pegu." (de la
Loubère 1693: 10).*

He noted too, the nature of the soil. With considerable accuracy,
he commented that:

*"(the soils) are not stony; it being difficult to find a flint,
and this makes me believe of the country of Siam, that
some have reported of Egypt, that it has been gradually
formed of the clayish earth which the rain waters have
carried down from the mountains....it is therefore this
mud descending from the mountains, that is the real cause
of the fertility of Siam, wherever the inundation extends
itself." (De la Loubère 1693: 15).*

The same commercial and missionary interest which brought
Europeans to Ayutthaya likewise brought them to the Annamese
Court at Hue. It must be recalled that the ancient kingdom of the
Chams had been overwhelmed by the Vietnamese expansion from the
Red River delta. By the 19th century, the Vietnamese had also seized
the Mekong delta and were pressing hard against the southeastern
flank of Cambodia. The Emperor in Hue therefore, held sway over a
tract largely equivalent to modern Viet Nam. In contrast to the
situation in Thailand, the French resolved to take parts of Viet Nam
by force. The initial pretext for conflict was local disapproval of
missionary activity. This lead to a punitive French expedition against
Tourane (Da Nang) in 1847, and on
August 31st, 1858, a concerted attack
was mounted by four vessels and 2,500
men under the command of Admiral
Rigault de Genouilly. Having seized the
port and its environs, the French
occupied Saigon and proceeded with the
colonisation of Cochin China. Four years
later, after much bloodshed and
resistance, three provinces and trading
rights were ceded to France by Emperor
Tu Duc. In 1866, an expedition under
Captain Doudart de Lagrée (1883)
retraced the voyage of Van Wuystoff up

On 31 August, 1858, Admiral
Rigault de Genouilly with four
vessels under his command and a
force of 2,500 men attacked Da
Nang, seen here in the distance,
and set in train the colonisation
of Viet Nam. American marines
assaulted this beach a century
later.

the Mekong to explore the possibility of opening trade links with Western China (Garnier 1871, Osborne 1975). When it became apparent that such contacts were better served by using the Red River passage, the French turned their attention to Tonkin. They raised their flag in Hanoi for the first time in 1873. This did not pass without the most spirited and enduring resistance until the turn of the century. The establishment of a protectorate was accomplished at a heavy price involving brutal repression, but by 1900, they had established control over Viet Nam and imposed colonial rule. This was combined with their domination over Cambodia, which had been in effect since 1884, and of the Kingdom of Laos, which had been taken over in 1893.

It was during this progressive annexation of their various colonies, that the French scholar Henri Mouhot (1864) undertook the first dedicated scientific European exploration of Southeast Asia. He embarked from London in April 1858, and died in Laos in November, 1861. Although principally concerned with plant, animal and invertebrate species, his observations extended to the customs of the indigenous inhabitants and their origins. He died with his work incomplete, but his journals survived. They permit us to appreciate the intensity of his research and depth of his insight. Like de la Loubère, Mouhot was a keen observer of the countryside. Of the plain flanking the Chao Phraya River he wrote:

> "the first glance, one distinguishes what was formerly the bed of the sea, this great plain having taken the place of an ancient gulf; proof of which is afforded by numerous marine shells, many of which I collected in a perfect state of preservation." (Mouhot 1864 vol. 1: 128).

His journeys took him to the Great Lake (Tonle Sap) of Cambodia, and thence to the monuments of Angkor. He spent several weeks there, recording both the dimensions of each major structure and noting the folklore concerning their origins. He refused to provide definitive interpretations of the monuments which confronted him, and his comments were reserved:

> "Until some learned archaeologist shall devote himself to this subject, it is not probable that ought but contradictory speculations will be promulgated." (Mouhot 1864 vol. 2: 20).

Mouhot's journal when published in 1864 attracted much interest. It was clear that the new colonies had a rich archaeological heritage, such that by the 1870s, fieldwork at such sites as Samrong Sen in Cambodia was being reported locally and in Metropolitan France (Corre 1879). This realisation encouraged the new

The village of Samrong Sen lies next to the Sen River. This view was taken in 1970, but it would have changed little since the 1870s, when French administrators and scientists first realised its prehistoric foundations. Henri Mansuy excavated there a century ago and found a deep sequence and rich prehistoric past.
(Courtesy Dr. R. Mourer)

administration to found the École Française d'Extrême Orient. Under the inspiration of Paul Doumer and members of the Academie d'Inscriptions et Belle Lettres in Paris, the School was promulgated in 1898 on the model of the existing French schools in Athens, Rome and Cairo. The founding regulations, published on 15 December, 1898, specified a permanent archaeological mission to explore the archaeology and philology of the Indochinese peninsula. Stress was given to the history of monuments and idioms, and to contribute to the scholarly study of neighbouring regions, not least India and China. The foundation director, Louis Finot, was charged with the establishment of a museum and a library, and the furtherance of archaeological and philological research. Finot was fortunate in his choice of early research appointees, and his team entered what we can in retrospect, recognise as the Golden Age of archaeological research in Southeast Asia. Paul Pelliot was a foundation member, appointed in 1899. A brilliant student of Chinese and aged only 26 when he joined the school, he worked on the historical geography of the area through the analysis of Chinese texts (Pelliot 1902). His contributions were seminal and remain the principal source in a western language, for the early institutions of Southeast Asian states. Henri Parmentier was appointed in July, 1900 and more than any other, laid the foundations for our appreciation of the historic monuments of Indo-China. His paper in volume 2 of the Bulletin de l'École on excavation procedures remains a model of common sense and in many ways, ahead of its time even in European contexts. He noted for example, that:

Left to right, Victor Goloubew, Louis Finot, an un-named Khmer and Henri Parmentier at Ta Prohm, Angkor. Goloubew was well known for his research at Angkor, Finot was the first director of the École Française d'Extrême Orient, and Henri Parmentier was one of the first research appointees at the École.

> *"An excavation is not an amusement, as is generally considered, but a scientific pursuit, very delicate because if badly executed, it means the destruction of an historic document."*

Parmentier put theory into practice. He was responsible for recording all the known monuments of the Chams, as well as the early and later Khmer. His reports were accompanied by his own drawings, photographs and maps showing the location of all the sites. A third early appointee was Capt. E. Lunet de Lajonquière. Seconded from the army, he was charged with the mission of locating and describing all the monuments, inscriptions and statues, as well as reporting on their condition and need for conservation. His task was undertaken before Parmentier commenced his own fieldwork, and his report was published in 1902 (Lunet de Lajonquière 1902). It comprises one of the first scholarly analyses of historic sites in Southeast Asia, for he included part of Thailand in his survey area.

The Bayon, the temple mausoleum of Jayavarman VII at Angkor, is embellished with evocative bas-reliefs. Here, we can see an army on the march.

A family with a wooden cart follows the army. The Bayon, Angkor.

In this scene from the Bayon, a crocodile and fish are seen below a naval battle on the Great Lake.

In addition to this widespread and intensive archaeological research, Finot himself was continuing the French tradition of Sanskrit studies by translating the inscriptions which were now being found in increasing numbers. In 1902, for example, he reported on two new inscriptions of the Cham king Bhadravarman (Finot 1902). Together with his predecessors, M.A. Barth and A. Bergaigne, and his successor George Cœdès, Finot was instrumental in establishing the dynastic sequences of early Cambodia and Champa (Barth 1885, Bergaigne 1893, Cœdès 1937-1954) The wide range of interests which made up these early studies is revealed in the School's third bulletin, which was issued on a quarterly basis during 1903. It included a further analysis of an inscription, this time a stela raised under Jayavarman VII in Vientiane, which revealed the wide extent of the Khmer Realm in the 13th century AD. Henri Parmentier reported on his excavation at the great Cham centre of Dong Duong. There was also a report on the Chams, and a consideration of a visit to Tonkin in 1626 by the Portuguese. A reproduction of the bas reliefs of Angkor Thom by Dufour and Carpeaux (1910) was reported in the same volume. The representations of battle scenes, involving ballistae mounted on elephants, reached a wide audience, and stressed the deep fund of information present in this medium. Perhaps the most significant contribution to this issue however was Pelliot's work on the ancient state of Funan, assembled on the basis of Chinese documentary references. This tour-de-force of historic scholarship laid the foundations for all later attempts to establish the location and nature of the earliest state in Southeast Asia. At a more practical level, we find that the museum building was now complete and the galleries filling, while the library acquisitions were already being catalogued. A Congress of Orientalists attracted 128 scholars.

The 1904 bulletin contains a significant reference to the foundation of a scholarly society in Thailand. On February 26th of that year, a meeting of 39 interested people held at the Oriental Hotel in Bangkok

After eight centuries, the farm cart in use has hardly changed from that seen on the bas reliefs of the Bayon.

resolved to found a society "for the investigation and encouragement of arts, sciences and literature in relation to Siam and neighbouring countries". It also aimed to publish scholarly papers, form a library and maintain an ethnographic museum. The Siam Society, as it was named, has always been enthusiastically patronised by the royal family, and the first paper on the foundation of Ayutthaya was presented by Prince Damrong. Its interests have been broad, but archaeology has been prominent since the society's foundation. Indeed, at the first annual general meeting held on 7 April, 1904, Colonel Gerini stressed the importance of archaeology and inscriptions, and encouraged those living outside Bangkok to send details of new discoveries to the society. This precept was followed, for the third meeting heard a paper on the antiquities of the Mun Valley. By the end of the first year, the membership list had increased four-fold over those attending the inaugural discussion. The interest in archaeology is further shown by W.W. Bourke's communication in 1905, which described archaeological remains from peninsular Thailand. He referred to the number of beads of Indian origin found at Krabi, and suggested an Indian origin for the mine shafts for the extraction of tin ore identified on Phuket Island (Bourke 1905).

Although the Siam Society brought together scholars interested in a wide range of disciplines, it lacked state funding and never employed its own archaeological research staff. However, on 27 March 1911, King Rama VI commanded the foundation of the Fine Arts Department, and entrusted it with responsibility for cultural heritage, including archaeology. This has been manifested in the curation of historic buildings, conservation of artefacts, the provision of museums and encouragement of proper archaeological excavations (FAD 2000).

The École Française has always been supported by the French taxpayer, and during the 56 years of its direction of affairs within the Indochinese Union, it was able to mount and maintain major research programmes. Its director also controlled access to research opportunities. This had two effects. Archaeology in the French Colony bounded ahead compared with that in Thailand, while most research was undertaken by French archaeologists. One searches in vain for any training of or participation by Vietnamese, Khmer or Laotians. The history of archaeological enquiry reached a fulcrum with the defeat of French forces in Viet Nam and subsequent involvement of Cambodia in armed conflict. Until the mid 1950s, the school with its headquarters

Wilhelm G. Solheim II played a prominent role in developing Southeast Asian prehistory, beginning in the 1950s.

in Hanoi, maintained a steady stream of fundamentally important reports. The foundations were laid for a proper appreciation of the Khmer and Cham civilizations. The late Bronze Age and Chinese occupation of the Red River delta were explored through archaeological remains, while in the surrounding uplands, Colani and Mansuy were excavating caves yielding the remains of hunter gatherers known collectively as 'Hoabinhian'. Mansuy (1902) at Samrong Sen and Lévy (1943) in the Mlu Prei area, examined open prehistoric occupation sites and anticipated by up to 80 years, the discovery of similar sites at Non Nok Tha and Ban Chiang in Northeast Thailand. Along the raised shorelines of Viet Nam, Patte (1925) identified coastal occupation sites, commonly referred to as kitchen middens. Even before the second world war, Paris (1929, 1931) was describing the canals visible from the air along the marshy lowlands of the Mekong delta. Research continued unabated during the Japanese occupation, and it was during the second world war that Malleret excavated at the great port city of Oc Eo, and was able to show that the site was once part of the Funan Civilization earlier identified from Chinese texts by Pelliot. Perhaps the outstanding contribution to knowledge of this mature era in the history of the École Française however, was the compilation by George Cœdès, the director, of all the Sanskrit inscriptions known from mainland Southeast Asia. Each inscription was set out first in its original language, and then translated into French before being considered in its historic and cultural perspective. It will always remain a basic source of information on the early civilisations of the area.

The situation changed dramatically with Vietnamese independence. Ho Chi Minh placed much emphasis on archaeological research and the authorities turned to the Soviet Union for the necessary training of archaeologists. The Musée Louis Finot in Hanoi became the National Museum, and the Vietnamese Institute of Archaeology took over the central organising role of the École Française. Despite problems imposed by the absence of facilities, the research undertaken has greatly expanded our knowledge of the prehistoric period in Viet Nam. Even during the height of the American bombing, excavations continued, and with the assistance of the radiocarbon dating laboratories in China, East Germany and New Zealand, a chronology for the later prehistoric cultures began to emerge. The picture now is one of immense vigour, largely devoted to the identification of the prehistoric origins of the Vietnamese people.

The development of archaeology in Thailand has taken a different course. The Thais themselves have been to the fore in the analysis of art history and monuments of early Thai civilisations, but the prehistoric period was silent until the first few foreign fieldwork programmes. Two early contributions were stimulated by the second world war. Van Heekeren, a Dutch archaeologist, was despatched as a prisoner of war to labour on the railway line in Kanchanaburi province. He identified prehistoric stone implements there and after the war, returned for further investigations under less demanding constraints. Williams-Hunt served with the Royal Air Force, and became interested through aerial photography, in the circular mounded sites of

The excavation of Khok Charoen by William Watson and Helmut Loofs-Wissowa opened a new chapter in prehistoric Thai research. Here, the 1967 excavation season nears completion.
(Courtesy Dr. H.H.E. Loofs-Wissowa)

Above left: The excavation of Ban Kao in 1961 was the first major prehistoric excavation to be undertaken in Thailand. It was directed by Danish archaeologist Per Sørensen.
(Courtesy Dr. Per Sørensen)

Left: The burials at Khok Charoen belong to the Neolithic period, and were only just below the present surface.
(Courtesy Dr. H.H.E. Loofs-Wissowa)

Northeast Thailand. These concentrate in the valley of the Mun River, and were the subject of an exploratory paper (Williams-Hunt 1950). A third early figure was Quaritch-Wales, whose interests were mainly art historical. He examined many of the large early historic town sites and excavated several before and after the second world war.

Prehistoric research in Thailand received two major stimuli during the 1960s. The first was a series of large excavations which revealed inhumation cemeteries in association with a range of complete artefacts. Sørenson at Ban Kao pioneered these discoveries, when he excavated a cemetery with human inhumation burials associated with complete pottery vessels and stone axes (Sørensen and Hatting 1967). He introduced and applied techniques of excavation long since perfected in Denmark. Watson and Loofs-Wissowa (Watson 1979, Watson and Loofs-Wissowa 1967) identified an important cemetery at Khok Charoen and Bayard's excavations at Non Nok Tha in 1966 and 1968 added bronze to the repertoire of finds and hinted at a far earlier start to metallurgy in Thailand than had hitherto been considered (Bayard 1972). The excavations of Ban Chiang in 1974-5 under the direction of Gorman and Charoenwongsa added a further landmark because it was conceived as a joint programme between the University of Pennsylvania and the Thai Fine Arts Department, with particular emphasis being given to the training of young Thai archaeologists. This and subsequent training programmes have led to the establishment of Thai archaeologists in institutional bases, not

least the Fine Arts Department and the University and Museum systems. Their contribution in terms of fieldwork and analysis now exceeds by far, that of visiting foreign workers.

Yet problems remain. Archaeology in Cambodia, always a focal area, began promisingly with a training programme for students at the Royal University of Fine Arts, undertaken by Roland and Cecile Mourer at Laang Spean in 1968-9. The nightmare of the Khmer Rouge then intervened, and only recently have training programmes begun again. The Viet Nam war made joint research and communication difficult or impossible. To these formidable obstacles, one must add the problems of synthesis in a region where much basic information is now available only in local languages. Nevertheless, great strides have been and continue to be made.

The Basic Cultural Framework

It is now possible to describe a widespread pattern to the prehistory and early history of Southeast Asia. It can be divided into five interlinked phases. The earliest involved two distinct adaptations by hunters and gatherers. One saw the occupation of the interior uplands by small and probably mobile groups. Their remains are widely represented in the forefront of caves and are generally known as Hoabinhian, after the Vietnamese province where they were first described. The second involved the occupation of the coastline. Estuaries are one of the richest habitats known in terms of biological vigour, particularly when linked with mangrove forests. Many prehistoric settlements survive on the old raised beaches formed during periods of higher sea level. Recent excavations in such sites have uncovered the remains of large, permanent and rich hunter-gatherer communities.

The transition to rice cultivation took place in the middle reaches of the Yangzi Valley, probably within the period 8000-6000 BC. The establishment of agricultural villages there appears to have stimulated population growth as the new subsistence base took hold. By 5000 BC, settlements were established in the lower Yangzi Valley and during the early third millennium BC, we can identify intrusive occupation of southern China. By exploiting the river routes, rice cultivators reached the Red River valley, the Khorat Plateau and Central Thailand during the period 2500-2000 BC. If linguistic evidence is taken into account, the new settlers would have spoken early Austroasiatic languages and intruded into Burma and Eastern India at about the same time. This critical period in Southeast Asia will be described as the Neolithic. It involved the occupation of the inland tributary valleys where rice cultivation was undertaken together with the raising of domestic cattle and pigs, the hunting of the local fauna, as well as fishing and collecting. The intrusive societies interacted with the long-established hunters and gatherers, and at one or two coastal settlements, we find evidence for exchange of goods and ideas between the two. The latter, however, did not survive for long after the establishment of the Neolithic.

The Neolithic period was of short duration. A few late sites in Viet Nam and Lingnan include exotic imported jades and bronzes which originated in the Shang civilization of China. Such contact might well have brought the knowledge of bronze casting, for from about 1500 BC, a distinctive Southeast Asian Bronze Age can be recognized. Sites with similar casting technology are found from Hong Kong and the adjacent mainland west to Viet Nam, Cambodia, Thailand and Burma. Southeast Asia has some high-quality deposits of copper ore, and rich sources of tin. A series of excavations in the copper mines and the villages they serviced now make it possible to assess the social as well as the technological correlates of metallurgy.

The Bronze Age lasted a bare millennium before we encounter the first evidence for iron forging. The origins of iron smelting are not known, but the dating of the earliest iron, in the mid first millennium BC, is similar to that for the Warring States Period of China. It would be surprising if the advent of iron in both areas were unrelated. A local innovation in Central Thailand, or contact with India, might also have occurred, for the Iron Age of Southeast Asia differed regionally. In areas open to the imperial ambitions of the Han Dynasty, there was a rapid rise of powerful chiefdoms followed by an equally fast demise with incorporation as Chinese commanderies, or provinces. Beyond the imperial boundaries, Iron Age societies reveal indigenous and increasingly complex structures, a rapid growth of population, and participation in a growing international trade network.

By AD 100-200, it is possible to identify the rise of an early state in the Mekong Delta. This trend gathered pace in the valleys of the Mekong and Chao Phraya rivers, and the coastal plains of Viet Nam. Agrarian states firmly based upon local traditions emerged under leaders who adopted aspects of Hinduism and Buddhism, and Sanskrit names. This Indic veneer to an essentially indigenous growth of civilisation characterised the states of Angkor, of Dvaravati in Central Thailand and of Champa in Viet Nam. These, or at least their descendants, were to encounter the European merchants, colonialists and missionaries described above.

Rice farming is the mainstay of the Southeast Asian society. Here, farmers transplant rice in front of the massive Western Baray at Angkor. Their fields lie within the ancient 8th century city of Banteay Choeu.

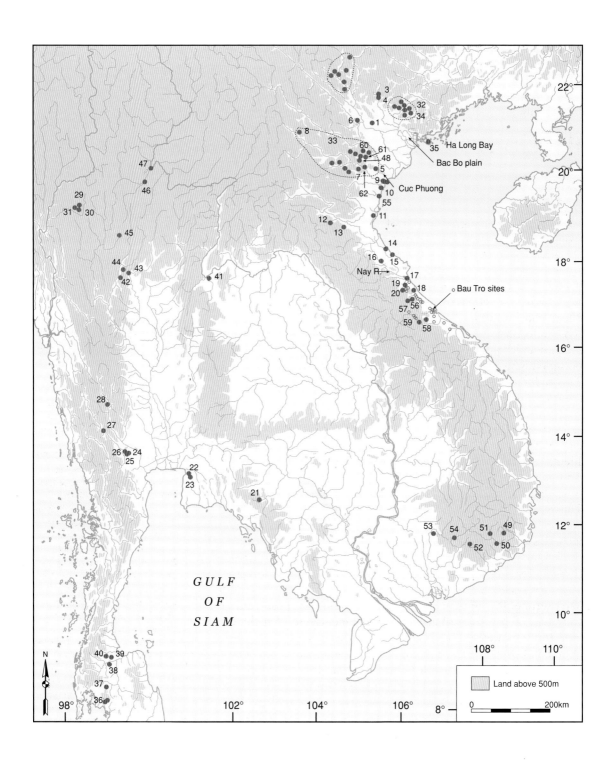

3
4
32
34
Ha Long Bay
6
1
35
8
33
Bac Bo plain
60
61
48
5
7
9
Cuc Phuong
62
10
55
11
12
13
14
16
15
Nay R→
17
19
18
20
Bau Tro sites
57
56
59
58
47
46
29
31
30
45
44
43
42
41
28
27
26 24
25
22
23
21
53
54
51
49
52
50

GULF

OF

SIAM

N

22°

20°

18°

16°

14°

12°

10°

8°

98°

102°

104°

106°

108°

110°

Land above 500m

0   200km

Chapter Two

Hunters and Gatherers

Hunting and gathering in Southeast Asia is not an extinct lifestyle. Even among the most specialised rice farming communities, there remains a vigorous tradition of collecting wild food resources. Fish for example, are an essential ingredient in the diet. Shellfish are collected and, though drastically reduced during the last century, wild animals are still hunted and trapped. The remoter forests of North and Peninsular Thailand sustain groups that rely entirely upon food collection.

A detailed appreciation of the hunter-gatherer societies which occupied Southeast Asia during the past 40,000 years is not possible. This is due to the probable destruction or loss of sites as a result of sea level fluctuations and the changes in the landscape involved. The rise in sea level would have submerged coastal hunter-gatherer settlements throughout the drowned Sunda shelf. The layer of marine clay that blanketed the drowned landscape is up to 14 metres thick. Identifying submerged settlements is currently an impossible task. To this problem we may add the likely destruction or at best covering of lowland sites by a mantle of alluvial silt laid down by floodwaters. This process would have been greatly accelerated by the major land clearance and resultant exposure of soils to intense rains, which increases the pace of sedimentation.

The recovery of upland settlement sites is far simpler, particularly those under rock shelters. The major river systems of Southeast Asia, as we have seen, are separated by uplands which include a limestone-karst terrain. It is in such areas, where elevation has protected sites from natural processes of erosion and sedimentation, that the first indications of a widespread occupation by hunter-gatherers were obtained. Given the range of environments in question, and the time span involved, it is reasonable to expect local variations in the characteristics of hunter-gatherer societies. This might involve regional distinctions in terms of the pattern and form of material artefacts, as well as in subsistence activities, and preferred burial practices. Not least, it is quite possible that, where some local groups were conservative, others were innovative. It is for example, within local hunter-gatherer societies that one might seek the initial moves towards the modification of the environment involved in early agriculture and the domestication of animals.

Opposite:
The distribution of the principal hunter-gatherer sites mentioned in the text. 1. Co Loa, 2. Ha Giang culture, 3. Mieng Ho, 4. Nguom, 5. Con Moong, 6. Son Vi, 7. Lang Bon, 8. Hang Pong 1, 9. Da But, Con Co Ngua, Go Trung, 10. Hoa Loc, 11. Quynh Van, 12. Tham Hoi, 13. Hang Chua, 14. Phoi Phoi, 15. Phai Nam, 16. Nui Dau, 17. Bau Tro, 18. Dong Hoi, 19. Yen Lac, Xom Tham, Xom Thon, Hang Tran and Hang Doi, 20. Kim Bang, 21. Laang Spean, 22. Khok Phanom Di, 23. Nong Nor, 24. Khao Talu, 25. Ment Cave, 26. Heap Cave, 27. Sai Yok, 28. Tham Ongbah, 29. Spirit Cave, 30. Banyan Valley Cave, 31. Steep Cliff Cave, 32. Bac Son sites, 33. Classic area of Hoabinhian sites, 34. Ha Lung, 35. Cai Beo, 36. Lang Rongrien, Moh Khiew, 37. Khao Thao Ha, 38. Buang Baeb, 39. Khao Khi Chan, 40. Pak Om, 41. Chiang Khan, 42. Khao Pah Nam, 43. Ban Don Mun, 44. Ban Mae Tha, 45. Pha Chang, 46. Tham Pra, 47. Chiang Saen, 48. Dieu Cave, 49. Lac Xuan, 50. Ta Hin, 51. Ta Lieng, 52. Doi Giang, 53. Doan Van, 54. Nout Lieng Kra, 55. Doi Than, Con Ruom, 56. Duc Thi, 57. Khe Toong, 58. Hang Doi, 59. Ban Rac, Dakrong and Lao Bao, 60. Sung Sam, 61. Xom Trai, 62. Bat Mot.

Hunter gatherers are best considered in the four areas which have seen the most intensive research. The first covers the mountain spine and coasts of Viet Nam. The uplands of northern Thailand have also seen much research. The third area comprises the Gulf of Siam and its surrounding uplands and finally, peninsular Thailand and adjoining parts of Malaysia have been investigated.

The Truong Son Cordillera and the Coast of Viet Nam

It was in 1906, shortly after the foundation of the École Française, that the first site revealing evidence for a prehistoric hunter-gatherer group was excavated at Tham Khoach. Subsequently, Madeleine Colani and Henri Mansuy laid the foundations for detailed prospecting and excavations. Before considering the sites and the evidence now available for this important stage in the sequence of events there, it is necessary to outline some of the principal features of the environment. Today, the area pivots on the intensely settled and farmed Bac Bo plain. During much of the period under review, the Red River would have had a greater distance to travel than at present before reaching the coast, due to a lower sea level. It may well have been that the marshy flood plain was settled by groups of hunter gatherers. If so, then no evidence survives, because the sites would lie under alluvial deposits which have steadily accumulated with regular inundations. Where the terrain is elevated, and in particular where human habitation occurred under the protection of rock shelters, evidence for hunter-gatherer settlement is abundant. The survival of much undisturbed vegetation on the upland hills of Cuc Phuong gives some idea of the habitat during the early prehistoric period under review. The moist and cool winds which flow across the Bac Bo plain from November until March-April rule out an extended dry season even at low levels. Consequently, there is a dense, canopied rainforest, with the upper branches reaching up to 45 metres above ground surface. Further sub-canopies occur at 30 and 20 m. The area is well watered, and there are numerous short streams which flow into the Ma River.

The continuous prograding of the coastline with the advance of the Red River delta, allied with sedimentation following flooding, has meant that no relevant sites have been found along the delta coastline itself. Both to the north and the south of the delta, however, prehistoric coastal settlements have been identified. These are usually located on raised beaches which represent the shoreline from about 6,000-3,500 BP. There are also sites on some of the islands which stud Ha Long Bay. Over the past eighty years, the prehistoric sites in this diverse area have been successively subdivided into regional groups defined

The upland of Cuc Phuong overlooks the coastal plain. It is home to many Hoabinhian cave sites.

Ha Long Bay was a scene of intensive hunting, gathering and fishing.

largely on the basis of similarities or differences in material culture. With the advent of radiocarbon dating, it has been possible to order them within a chronological framework.

The inland groups with their associated chronologies are called Nguom (older than 23,000 BP), Dieu (from 30,000 BP), Son Vi (*c.* 23,000-13,000 BP), Hoabinhian (*c.* 18,000-BP and Bacsonian (*c.* 10,000-BP). The Dieu industry, best represented at Dieu Cave, is characterised by the striking of flakes from the parent stone core (Nguyen Gia Doi 1999). Radiocarbon dates indicate an age of at least 30,000 years BP, and then a continuation into the Holocene period. Early occupation has also been identified at the rock shelter of Mieng Ho, and the cave of Nguom in the uplands of Bac Thai Province (Quang Van Cay 1995). Excavations at the latter in 1980-2 uncovered two layers stratified under Son Vi material, characterised by small stone scrapers and points, as well as some pebble core tools (Ha Van Tan 1997, Reinecke 1998, Trinh Nang Chung 1998). The stratigraphic and chronological relationships between the last three cultures are best demonstrated at Con Moong, a rock shelter within the Cuc Phuong upland. The lowest of the three levels contains stone tools of Son Vi type. Stone assemblages from the 140 Son Vi sites comprise quartz pebbles flaked along one surface to create a working edge. This meant that much of the original surface of the cobble remained in place. Ha Van Tan (1976) has distinguished, apart from the flakes which result from the manufacture of stone tools, four main types of artefact. One is the large quartzite cobble with a transverse cutting edge, which he feels were used as choppers and/or scrapers. The second has a cutting edge on the longitudinal edge of the tool. These side choppers or scrapers normally make up the majority of implements found in Son Vi sites. There are also a few implements with flaking on two working surfaces and lastly, pebbles with flaking along only one edge, termed 'round-edged pebbles'. Vu The Long (1977) has analysed the animal remains from Con Moong, and found a considerable number of shellfish, as well as evidence for hunting a range of mammals including pig, large and small deer and civet cats.

Stone tools from the hunter gatherer sites of Bac Bo. Top row, Son Vi flaked tools. Middle row, Hoabinhian sumatralith, axe and short axe from Hang Tam. Lowest row, Bacsonian polished axe.

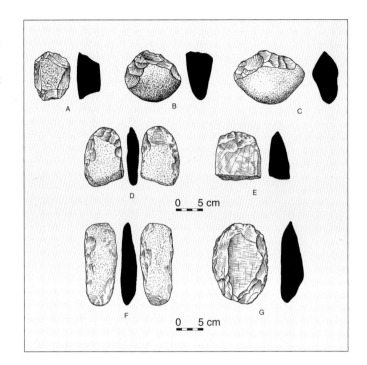

There are a few caves, such as Con Moong, which reveal the Son Vi industry underlying the next stage, that called Hoabinhian. Ha Van Tan (1997) has suggested that the Son Vi industry developed progressively into the Hoabinhian, but that there were regions where the former persisted. The majority of the Son Vi sites are found on elevated terrain above the Bac Bo plain in Vinh Phu province. Under such circumstances, the survival of organic remains representing food debris or charcoal suited to radiocarbon dating is ruled out. This situation only stresses the importance of the finds from Con Moong and the cave of Pong One, located near the headwaters of the Ma River. At this second site, the stone industry characteristic of Son Vi has been found mixed with characteristic early Hoabinhian material. This suggests that the Hoabinhian originated in an earlier Son Vi context. The two available radiocarbon dates from Pong One, as well as those from Son Vi, suggest that this transition was underway by about 11,000-12,000 BP. According to Nguyen Duc Tung and Pham Van Hai (1979), the pollen record for the Bac Bo plain witnessed a transition at that juncture, from a hot and dry to a hot and moist climate, a change which may have been associated with the rapid rise in the post-Pleistocene sea level. Nguyen Viet, however, has pointed out that the set of dates from Xom Trai suggest that the Hoabinhian was in being by 16,000-18,000 BP.

In Tay Nguyen to the south, a local variant of the Son Vi culture has been identified at Doi Giang, Ta Lieng, Lac Xuan and Ta Hin. These open sites are found in close conjunction with intermontane springs or streams, and reveal a similar material culture to their northern counterparts (Pham Duc Manh 1995).

The Hoabinhian

The subsequent Hoabinhian incorporated a more complex stone industry first recognized by Colani (1927) during fieldwork in the eastern margins of the Truong Son Cordillera. Her excavations in about twenty rock shelters concentrated in the province of Hoa Binh, hence the adoption of the term 'Hoabinhian' to describe them. Colani noted that the people had a hunting and food-gathering economy, made flaked stone tools from river cobbles and hunted animal species which survive to this day. She concluded that the assemblages were relatively recent, and certainly after the end of the Pleistocene period. Sung Sam is a typical Hoabinhian rockshelter, located about 100 metres above the valley floor. The occupation layers there reach a depth of 1.4 metres, and excavations by Tran Quoc Vuong in 1974 encountered stone tools, animal bones and the remains of shellfish collected from the nearby stream bed.

The stone implements centre on a tool known as the sumatralith. This was made by removing flakes from one side of a river cobble. Modification of such river pebbles by flaking forms the basis of the Hoabinhian stone working tradition. The range of tools was limited. Apart from the sumatralith, which is also known as a unifacial discoid, there is the simple removal of a row of flakes along one edge of a pebble to form a cutting edge. More common are 'short axes', artefacts modified to form a convex cutting edge at one end. Since the recovery of flakes which were probably removed when sharpening a blunt implement are not uncommon, it is considered likely that such 'short' axes reflect either a continuous process of sharpening or the accidental breaking of a sumatralith. It is also apparent from the bruised surfaces of some pebbles, that they were used for crushing or pounding without any prior modification. Although stone artefacts are the most abundant, there was also a vigorous bone industry, as evidenced at the Da Phuc rock shelter. Most of the 105 bone tools found there comprise points or awls.

The Hoabinhian cave of Xom Trai has yielded a set of radiocarbon determinations in the range of 16,000-18,000 BP.

Above left: The Hoabinhian cave of Sung Sam, excavated by Tran Quoc Vuong in 1974. It was occupied about 10,000 years ago. (Courtesy Dr. Nguyen Viet)

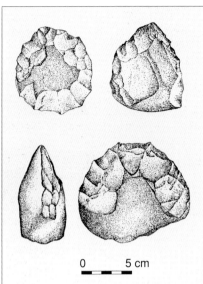

Typical Hoabinhian flaked stone tools are found over an extensive area of Southeast Asia.

The characteristic Hoabinhian site comprises a small rock shelter giving access to both the dissected limestone uplands and the nearby stream. Food remains include shellfish, fish, and hunted mammals. Vu The Long's (1977) analysis of the Con Moong fauna for example, revealed the presence of wild cattle and water buffalo, rhinoceros, forest birds and both water turtle and land tortoise. Many freshwater bivalve and gastropod shellfish were also recovered. Excavations at the Hoabinhian cave of Xom Trai have also yielded, for the first time in a Vietnamese Hoabinhian context, the remains of rice. This site is located only about 15 metres above the surrounding plain, and has been meticulously excavated by Nguyen Viet. The basal two metres were undisturbed and yielded a wide array of Hoabinhian stone implements in association with carbonised plant remains and shellfish. The radiocarbon dates suggest, as has been noted, that occupation was under way by 16,000 years ago.

Despite the passage of seven decades since Colani undertook her fieldwork, it is still possible to sift useful information from her reports. Not least, it is important to analyse the location of the individual sites relative to major geographical features such as rivers, minor tributaries and hills. Her original work in the vicinity of the regional centre of Hoa Binh involved the excavation of several sites, and her reports were, for their time, of the highest quality (Colani 1927). She observed the depth of the stratigraphy and the development of stone technology through the successive layers. The basal contexts at such sites as Sao Dong contained large flaked stone implements, while the first, very rare polished stone tools made their appearance in the intermediate horizon. The stone itself was exotic to the region, suggesting that early polished implements were obtained through exchange. Pottery, she noted, was found only in the latest layers.

The same approach was adopted in her work on the sites in the Ma River valley. She described eight rock shelters, all of which yielded Hoabinhian material culture (Colani 1930). These shelters commanded elevated ground above the margins of the tributary streams. Lang Bon is one such site, situated only 40 metres above sea level, but still safely above the Ma flood plain. Colani also reported the presence of shellfish, crabs and water turtles, the present river being only 200 metres from the cave. The bones and teeth of rhinoceros, carnivores and deer were also found. The same general points can be made of the more southerly group of sites, about 80 km north of Dong Hoi in the valley of the Nay River. Two rock shelters, Yen Lac and Kim Bang, lie on opposite sides of the river, at the junction of the flood plain and the limestone massif. Yen Lac is characteristically small, measuring only 25 by 6 m. Deer, gastropod and bivalve shellfish were excavated, but no stratigraphy was noted there. Recent fieldwork has identified further rockshelters at Duc Thi, Xom Tham, Xom Thon, Khe Toong, Hang Tran and

This large Hoabinhian Cave, known as Bat Mot, was discovered by Madeleine Colani. It is located in the Ma Valley of northern Viet Nam.

Hang Doi, and three open sites at Ban Rac, Dakrong and Lao Bao (Reinecke *et al.* 1999). Open Hoabinhian sites have also been identified at Doan Van and Nout Lieng Kra, in the Central Highlands of Tay Nguyen Province, thus extending the area of this group significantly (Pham Duc Manh 1995).

Burials are rare in Hoabinhian contexts. A major exception is Lang Cao, where Colani (1927) found about 200 skulls within an area of only 25 square metres. They were propped up by stones, with few associated limb bones, but no grave goods. The crania were buried some time after death within a reserved area. If the social group responsible was mobile for some of the year, then this cave may represent a central focus for the burial of the dead whose remains were returned there at some interval after death. This particular rite differs from that represented at Hang Dang and Moc Long caves, where the dead were buried in a crouched position, covered in red ochre and associated with stone tools.

The Hoabinhian rock shelters were occupied from about 18,000 BP. During the ensuing millennia, we can discern two major changes in material culture: the advent of grinding and polishing the working surfaces of stone tools, and the manufacture of fired pottery vessels. It is important to recognise that during the currency of the Hoabinhian, and the initial trends towards polishing stone tools and making pottery, the coast was some distance from the present shore, and any prehistoric settlement there has been lost through subsequent inundation. That contact with coastal groups occurred however, is evident from the finding of marine shells in inland sites.

This view of Lac Bon Cave was taken by Madeleine Colani during her pioneer fieldwork in northern Viet Nam. It had been occupied by Hoabinhian hunter-gatherers.

The Bacsonian

Bac Son province, north of the Red River, was a second location for research into early hunter-gatherers. Excavations by Henri Mansuy and Madeleine Colani recovered ground and polished stone implements. These have traditionally been set apart from those of the Hoabinhian, and named Bacsonian after the province where they were first discovered. There is no general agreement among Vietnamese prehistorians on the relationship between the Hoabinhian and Bacsonian groupings, although regionality in stone-working traditions could reasonably be expected.

Thus, there is some technological evidence for the succession from flaking to early edge grinding. Both at Bo Lum and Bo Nam caves, Ha Van Tan confirmed earlier findings by Mansuy (1924) that polishing was applied to the cutting edges of what are, for all intents and purposes, flaked Hoabinhian sumatraliths. Neither site, however, yielded any pottery, suggesting that the technique of polishing was under way there before a ceramic industry. A shell from Bo Nam has been radiocarbon dated to about 8,000 years ago, but a specimen from

Bo Lum has yielded a radiocarbon date 2,000 years earlier. The latter seems extremely early and needs confirmation from further determinations. The same problem applies to dates from a level at Tham Hai cave containing evidence for edge-grinding. This, again, has been dated in the vicinity of 9,500 years ago. Of course, there is no reason why edge polishing should not belong to this early horizon, nor is there any interdict on an earlier trend to polishing in one region over another. In terms of stratigraphic succession in a given region, however, we can again turn to Con Moong, where polished implements are found in level three, above the layers containing characteristic Hoabinhian flaked tools.

Hoang Xuan Chinh (1984) has argued for the development of edge-ground implements within a Hoabinhian context, and has pointed out the importance of this technological development. Not least, he has suggested that it involves the conversion of a hand-held flaked stone tool into a hafted polished axe. The latter is considerably more efficient, particularly in forest clearance and wood working. He has also pointed out the existence, in such sites as Xom Trai, of large hoe-like implements which under microscopic examination, reveal scars suggestive of use in working soil.

Nguyen Van Hao (1979) has considered the later occupation deposits of the Bacsonian phase, dating to the seventh millennium BP at Ha Lung Cave. Cord-marked pottery was common by this period, which now overlaps that when the sea level reached its post-Pleistocene maximum, and it becomes possible to consider coastal as well as inland settlement sites.

Coastal Groups in Viet Nam

There is a long tradition of coastal archaeology in Viet Nam, and currently, Ha Van Tan recognises several early groupings of sites which he calls 'cultures'. Their individuality and distinctiveness is based on their regional distribution, and the typology of pottery and stone artefacts. All reveal a marine economy, and most contain burials interred in a flexed, seated position associated with grave goods. It is usually the abundance of pottery and polished stone axes, adzes and 'hoes' which have convinced the Vietnamese that they are dealing with an agriculturally-orientated society. The biological remains of domestic plants and animals are, however, rarely mentioned.

The Cai Beo culture is represented only at the eponymous site, situated on the island of Cat Ba, 40 km from the present shore of the gulf of Bac Bo. The sequence commences with a stone tool assemblage with strong Hoabinhian affinities, while the layer in question also contains pottery fired at a low temperature, and decorated with basketry impressions. The second layer includes a shouldered axe of a type found occasionally by Colani in Hoabinhian contexts, as well as incised and cord-marked pottery. The early parts of this assemblage have provided a radiocarbon date of c. 4500 BC. The final assemblage includes shouldered, polished axes and adzes of a type paralleled in the sites of the Ha Long culture. The importance of Cai Beo then, lies in the documented development incorporating polished stone axes, of a Hoabinhian-inspired stone technology to one which the Vietnamese prehistorians describe as Neolithic. A report on the associated biological material should be most revealing.

Analogous sites are known from Thanh Hoa province. During the 1930s, Patte (1932) excavated the shell midden of Da But. This 5-metre-thick settlement covered an area of only 1,500 square metres, and to judge from the faunal remains, was located in the vicinity of an estuary and salt marshes. Patte recovered polished stone axes markedly similar to those of the inland hunter-gatherer sites. There are also spindle whorls, stone net sinkers, much pottery and twelve burials inhumed in a flexed position. Grave goods included round-based pottery vessels, shell jewellery, stone axes and red ochre. Recent Vietnamese excavations have revealed evidence for domestic activities in the form of hearths, ceramics and the remains of hunted animals (Bui Vinh 1991). There is also a radiocarbon determination of 4500-5000 BC from a layer 70 cm below the site's surface.

As the sea level fell away from Da But, so settlement followed the receding shoreline. Con Co Ngua is slightly larger than Da But, and the biological remains indicate the same marine adaptation. However, occupation here continued after a change from marine to more inland conditions dated to about 3500 BC, at which point we find stone hoes in addition to the bones of the pig and water buffalo. Ceramics belonging to the Da But tradition were recovered in 1977 during excavations at the still later site of Go Trung. The stone axes are distinct from those of Bau Tro, having an ellipsoid cross section. Net sinkers were found, together with the remains of sea fish.

The Bau Tro 'culture', called after a site first examined by the French archaeologist, Étienne Patte (Patte 1924), remains one of the best documented. Bau Tro is a small site set among sand dunes. Three lenses of shell midden interspersed with sand comprise a three metre-deep sequence. One of the middens is notably thicker than the other two, and *Placuna*, an oyster-like marine bivalve is the dominant species. Other food remains include cockles, fish and turtle. The stone industry involved the manufacture and sharpening of polished stone adzes. The shouldered variety dominates, but there are also rectangular examples. The rejuvenation of adzes by removing flakes is evidenced by the recovery of flakes of stone bearing a polished surface. Several

Doi Than, a site formerly located on the coast of Viet Nam, but now many kilometres inland.

The shell mound of Con Ruom, which has been assigned to the Quynh Van culture.

types are found, including shouldered and quadrangular specimens. The pottery is in the main, decorated with cord-marked impressions, though some have incised decoration and lines of circular indentations. Stone rings and beads are encountered, as well as possibly the earliest evidence for interment of the dead in jars (Reinecke 1998). The evidence from Bau Tro indicates a marine adaptation by a people who probably occupied the area for three successive but fairly brief periods within the period 2500-2000 BC. They were well familiar with the use of ceramic containers and polished stone-cutting implements. The value of intensive site surveys has been fully demonstrated by Reinecke and his Vietnamese associates, who have added a further 27 Bau Tro culture sites to the inventory since 1997. These are found on the old raised beaches beyond the present shore (Reinecke *et al.* 1999).

Perhaps the best insight into the cultural development of this group, however, comes from Phoi Phoi and Phai Nam (Ha Van Tan 1977). The main changes are seen in the increasing predominance of polished, shouldered adzes and the appearance of polished 'hoes' attaining at least 30 cm in length. At Phai Nam, however, despite the parallels in pottery with that from Phoi Phoi, more of the shouldered adzes were polished. Whereas Ha Van Tan (1980) considers that this reflects a difference in chronology, it could equally be the result of Phai Nam being a site wherein stone adzes were roughed out before being exchanged or completed elsewhere. That such specialisation in the manufacturing process occurred, is shown at Nui Dau, where adze roughouts were found (Ha Van Tan 1976). A similar absence of polishing characterised the stone assemblage of Quynh Van. About 20 sites are known, including Con Ruom, clustering behind the present coast in Nghe An and Ha Tinh provinces. Two radiocarbon dates from the uppermost horizon of Quynh Van suggest that later occupation there is dated to the 3rd millennium BC. Since the site is about 6 metres thick, initial occupation may have been considerably earlier. Thirty-one flexed inhumation burials have been recovered. Agriculture has been mooted there, but the evidence is based on the presence of pottery and a polished-stone industry rather than any diagnostic plant or animal remains. Closer to the present shore, one finds sites ascribed to the Thac Lac culture. Doi Than is one such site. It covers only about 0.5 ha, and during the six weeks of excavations there, Cao Xuan Pho recovered an enormous amount of pottery decorated with infilled bands. The stratigraphy of the site incorporates shell lenses interspersed with more general cultural fill. Cultural remains include shouldered adzes, grinding stones, arrowheads and stone bracelets. It is thought to date between 3000-2000 BC.

Further south, we encounter the enigmatic site of Bau Du, which was located in an estuarine environment. It comprises a series of shell middens containing the remains of shellfish, and the bones of deer, monkey and rhinoceros. Crabs, fish and turtle are also abundantly represented (Ha Van Tan 1997). Although dated as late as 3000-2500 BC, no pottery, nor polished stone tools were encountered, and the stone tool industry has a strong Hoabinhian flavour. If this was not a specialised site for initial stages in flaking stone implements, it reflects a marked regionality in these coastal groups of Northern Viet Nam. Indeed, the early coastal Vietnamese 'Neolithic' as a whole is an enigmatic entity. In the absence of detailed appraisals of settlement patterns, biological data and palaeo-environments, we are left with the unsatisfactory situation of being asked to accept the presence of agriculture on the basis of pottery and polished stone axes rather than on the subsistence activities of the people in question. In due course, the recovery of biological material and establishment of a chronological framework will assist greatly in the formulation of models which bring together the coastal and inland settlement into a coherent relationship

Excavations at Doi Than have revealed lenses of shellfish, representing exploitation of the coast.

The Hunter-Gatherer Occupation from Peninsular Thailand to the Gulf of Siam

Several Hoabinhian cave sites are now known in peninsular Thailand, including Pak Om, Khao Khi Chan, Buang Baeb and Khao Thao Ha (Shoocondej 1996). Excavations at the huge cavern of Lang Rongrien, in Krabi Province of Thailand, have provided the longest and most important hunter-gatherer sequence available on the mainland of Southeast Asia. Radiocarbon determinations from the lower contexts of Anderson's excavations in 1983 indicated settlement between 38,000-27,000 years ago. During this period, corresponding to the extreme cold of the late Pleistocene in higher latitudes, the sea level was lower than at present, and the coast was located at least 30 km from the cave. Brief visits by hunter-gatherers have left the remains of their hearths, stone tools and the animals they hunted. The local chert was used as a source for manufacturing flaked knives, scrapers and chopping tools. The lower layers at Lang Rongrien were found after Anderson removed what looked like the stony bedrock of the cavern, only to find that it had formed through roof fall. Underneath lay the remains of earlier occupation.

Lang Rongrien during the course of the excavation by Douglas Anderson.

After the removal of rock fall at Lang Rongrien, Anderson encountered layer 8, which dates back into the Pleistocene Period. (Courtesy Professor Douglas Anderson)

View over the karst terrain from Sakai Cave.

Right: A section through the cultural sequence at Sakai Cave reveals hearths. The lowest layer accumulated about 10,000 years ago.

Excavations in progress at Sakai Cave in 1993.

A Mani forest camp near Sakai Cave, southern Thailand.

Cay, a Mani hunter, is gluing the mouth piece of a blowpipe for hunting.

An abandoned Mani camp at La Yuan Pueng rockshelter in March 1994. Apart from the bones of hunted animals, hearths and stone tools, little would survive to document their stay.

Above left: A group of Mani hunter-gatherers encamped at La Yuan Pueng rockshelter in southern Thailand, Satun Province.

Left: The Mani painted on the walls of this rockshelter in January 1996. (All photographs of Sakai Cave and the Mani courtesy Dr. Gerd Albrecht)

The upper layers at Lang Rongrien contain a Hoabinhian stone industry, while at the nearby site of Moh Khiew, Pookajorn (1992) has identified not only evidence for Hoabinhian hunter gatherers, but also four human graves one of which appears to have involved a seated, crouched position matched in the Vietnamese sites described above. Grave goods included flaked stone tools and quartz pebbles.

Further to the south in Trang Province, Albrecht and colleagues from Germany and Silpakon University have not only excavated the large cavern of Sakai, but also visited and recorded the Mani, surviving hunter-gatherers in this region (Albrecht *et al.* n.d.). This unique opportunity even involved the analysis of the remains of Mani occupation on the surface of the cave floor. It was found that the seasonal rhythm of the monsoon encourages settlement in the airy and cool rain forest during the dry season, while the shelter afforded by rock shelters make them more attractive during the rains. The social groups in either case were small, measured in the teens in one case with 12 adults and five children, and the area under occupation covered about 40 square metres. The Mani exploit a similar range of animals as during the remote prehistoric past, including gibbons, macaques, squirrels and a range of fish and shellfish. Their shelters comprise small huts fashioned from bamboo, leaves and tree bark which would leave few if any archaeological traces. However, hearths containing stones and raised on clay supports are used, and these would survive.

The excavations within Sakai cave itself incorporated a cultural build up about two metres deep and dating up to 10,000 years ago. It included a number of hearths, while the material remains were dominated by stone flakes. No evidence for polished stone tools or pottery vessels was encountered. The faunal remains reflect hunting in a canopied forest: the bones of gibbons and macaques, squirrels and civets predominate. The prehistoric hunter-gatherers also collected freshwater shellfish, and a few marine shellfish must have come to the cave from at least 30 km away.

The Chao Phraya Valley

In many respects, the environment of the Chao Phraya valley and the surrounding uplands matches that of Bac Bo. During much of the period under review, the sea level was considerably lower, which meant that the Chao Phraya's passage to the sea was much longer, and there were more extensive tracts of lowland. With the rise in sea level, the river valley was truncated, and a window opened on prehistoric coastal settlement through the analysis of sites located on raised beaches. The river valleys are likewise surrounded by uplands, within which there are rock-shelters containing the remains of hunter-gatherer occupation. Such sites have been identified in the valleys of the Kwae Yai and Kwae Noi rivers in Kanchanaburi province, Thailand. The first research was undertaken at the caves of Sai Yok and Tham Ongbah by a Danish expedition. The stone artefacts reveal marked similarities to those found in the Hoabinhian caves of Bac Bo. Such is the degree of similarity, that the term Hoabinhian has become a general one to encompass sites across the face of Southeast Asia and beyond.

Our knowledge of Hoabinhian hunter-gatherer adaptation to the western hills which fringe the Chao Phraya Valley has been enlarged by Pookajorn's excavations at four further rock shelters (Pookajorn 1981). All are located on the slopes of low limestone hills that command the terraces of the Kwae Noi River. They were probably located in an area of deciduous woodland, and the research undertaken has greatly expanded our knowledge of hunter-gatherer groups there. The richest material and best evidence for chronology came from Khao Talu. This cave has several distinct chambers one of which had been used as a burial area in later prehistory. Many stone beads, polished adzes and broken potsherds as well as fragments of human bone were found, but unfortunately the whole area had been looted. Under this layer, and within a 3-metre-deep section of the adjacent chamber, at least three earlier living floors were found intact. The excavators found the characteristic sumatraliths, as well as flaked points, picks, scrapers and hammer stones. The associated faunal material was rare in the lowest occupation layer, and much bone was so fragmented that identification to species was ruled out. Among the larger species, the sambar deer, pig deer, cattle, pig and muntjak were present. There were also a few tiger bones and the remains of freshwater shellfish, turtle and frog. By screening all excavated material, Pookajorn recovered fragments of gourd and nut palm. The earliest hunter-gatherer occupation has been dated, on the basis of two radiocarbon dates, to about 10,000 years ago, while the latest period of occupation followed four thousand years later. By that period, cord-marked and incised pottery was found in association with the stone implements which in all levels, reveal marked similarities with the flaked stone industries of the Bac Bo Hoabinhian.

Ment Cave is only 30 metres from Khao Talu. A 1.6-metre-thick horizon of prehistoric occupation material was found there. The stone artefacts included scrapers, side choppers and sumatraliths, and these were associated with a rich assemblage of animal, shell and plant remains. In addition to the species represented at Khao Talu, there were remains of crocodile, birds, a canid and the goral. Excavations at Heap Cave revealed a similar sequence to that from Khao Talu. There were four successive living floors, all associated with a characteristic stone industry and assemblage of animal species. Only in the uppermost were pieces of pottery recovered. No radiocarbon dates are available yet, but the chronology is expected to match that from Khao Talu. Nearby Petch Kuha cave contained one

The pottery from Laang Spean reveals a wide range of decorative styles.

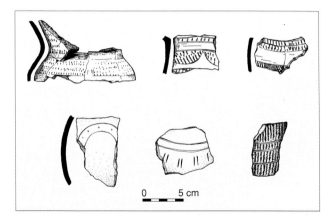

0   5 cm

The cave of Laang Spean lies on top of the Phnom Teak Trang in Western Cambodia. Excavations there by Roland and Cecile Mourer in 1968-70 uncovered important Hoabinhian remains.

The excavation of Laang Spean was undertaken in conjunction with the collection of pollen samples to reconstruct the ancient environment. (Courtesy Dr. Roland Mourer)

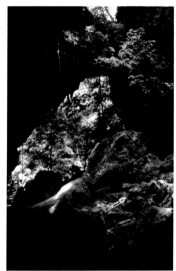

A view from the gloomy interior of Laang Spean.

Middle: The arch at Laang Spean gives the site its name, 'Bridge Cave'.

Far right: Excavations at Laang Spean in 1968. (Courtesy Dr. Roland Mourer)

living floor, but no pottery was encountered. The excavations at these four sites reinforces the idea that hunter-gatherer societies in the western Thai uplands practiced broad spectrum hunting, gathering and foraging over a period spanning at least nine millennia.

Further research into hunter-gatherer occupation of this area has been undertaken at the cave of Laang Spean, or 'Bridge Cave'. It is located 150 metres above sea level, on a limestone hill in the valley of the Stung Sangker. Excavations by Roland and Cecile Mourer encountered five successive cultural levels, all of which provided evidence for the material culture, subsistence activities and environment of the hunter-gatherers who lived there. The cave is located about 400 km east of the sites just described in the Kwai Noi valley, and 100 km northeast of the present shore of the Gulf of Siam. The excavators took a series of pollen samples from the archaeological deposits, which revealed that the environs of the cave were probably under forest. It was also noted that fern spores and grass pollen were found, and it is likely that it was blown to the cave from the surrounding lowlands.

Radiocarbon dates from the successive layers indicate that the initial settlement took place about 9,000 years ago, and that the successive later occupation events took place about 4000, 2000 and 500 BC and AD 1000. The lowest layer contained a few flakes of stone, and is not as rich as that laid down during the second occupation, when short axes, scrapers and sumatraliths were encountered. This same level also revealed increasing quantities of cord-marked and paddle-impressed potsherds. The pottery in the succeeding cultural level was also associated with stone flakes and core tools, but was much more complex in terms of shape and decoration. One of the features noted, was the presence of ring-footed bases and a curvilinear ornament comprising bands infilled with impressed dots imparted with a serrated implement, like the edge of a bivalve shell. Cultural levels four and five have provided some stone flakes and pottery, but the details are not yet available. Most of the stone found is in the form of flakes removed in the manufacture of core tools, indicating local production. Moreover, unlike the situation in Bac Bo, no edge ground or hafted polished axes were found (Mourer and Mourer 1970).

The evidence for subsistence is abundant. Turtle remains, crab claws and shellfish indicate the exploitation of lakes and streams. There are many bones from birds, snakes, reptiles and fish. Among the large species, there are the remains of rhinoceros, deer, cattle and monkey. It has often been noted, that such hunter-gatherer groups exploited a wide spectrum of available food resources. Mourer (1977) however, is adamant that there is no biological evidence at Laang Spean for agriculture.

A view into Spirit Cave during the excavations by Chester Gorman.

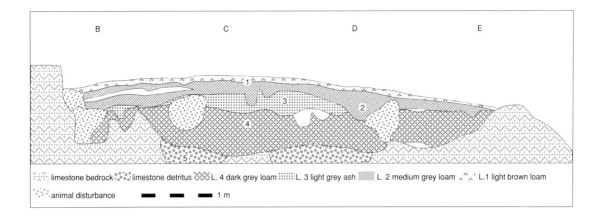

animal disturbance ▬ ▬ ▬ 1 m

The section through the rock shelter of Spirit Cave.

A Hunting and Gathering Tradition in the North Thai Uplands

During the mid 1960s, Chester Gorman initiated a research programme in the uplands of northern Thailand, to illuminate a local hunter-gatherer pattern and identify possible changes towards plant cultivation. The rugged limestone crags and valleys of his study area are cut by swiftly-flowing streams. His first excavation took place at Spirit Cave, which is located on a hillside overlooking the Khong Stream. The cave commands a fine view over the valley and surrounding hills which, even during the dry season, are covered by a canopied evergreen forest. Kuchler and Sawyer (1967) described the valley floor vegetation in this region as a dense cover of tall canopy trees dominated by dipterocarps and teak, a sub-canopy of medium trees with vines, with grasses and bamboo at ground level. Ascending from the valley floor to the cave, we encounter a transition to a forest with two distinct canopies. *Dipterocarpus costatus* and *Mosinda angustifolia* are important in each layer, but there is much more open ground cover. This vegetation pattern surrounds the cave, located about 650 metres above sea level, and up to the ridge tops at 750 m. Within reach of the cave, however, there are ridges and summits under a pine-mixed oak forest with a dense, grassy ground cover. Thus, the site falls within Holdridge's sub-tropical wet forest. Recently-deposited alluvium covers the narrow Khong Stream valley, while the hill slopes comprise either limestone outcrops, or pockets of red, limestone-derived soils. None of these is currently cropped in the vicinity of Spirit Cave, but they are favoured for horticulture where they occur within easy reach of modern Shan villages.

The distribution of animal species today integrates with these three vegetational resource-zones. The river and its margins sustain the otter and fishing cat, and a wide range of shellfish and fish. The canopied forest harbours the main arboreal animals, which include the langur, macaque and gibbon, a range of civets, squirrels, small cats and the clouded leopard. Terrestrial species are thinly distributed, but comprise deer, pig, wild cattle, serow, goral and their predators, the leopard and tiger. Formerly, rhinoceros and elephant were present.

Spirit Cave comprises a complex of three small rock shelters, all of which contain prehistoric occupation. The middle one had the deepest stratigraphical sequence and it was there that excavation commenced during the middle months of 1966 (Gorman 1972, 1977). Gorman divided the cave floor into metre squares and his excavations followed the indications of cultural stratigraphy. Progress was slow, because all material excavated was passed through screens in order to recover microscopic plant remains. Despite pits and hollows reflecting animal disturbances, it was possible to recognise a stratified series of layers, some with superimposed hearths.

The first occupants scooped out shallow depressions, laid sticks in a radial manner like spokes of a wheel, and lit their fires. This activity was followed by a build-up of cultural material: stone artefacts, food remains and further ashy lenses. This layer was homogeneous across the excavated area, and may well represent intermittent occupation over a lengthy period. The next layer included hearths overlying patches of soil burnt by their heat. The greatest depth of build-up took place in the middle part of the shelter, which contrasts with the superceding layer two. The latter was thickest towards the cave mouth and again comprised a maze of hearths, charcoal lenses and pits dug into layer three. The surface of layer two was so compacted by subsequent occupation that the distinction between it and layer one was particularly clear. Moreover, several pottery sherds were found on the trampled surface. One hearth on the surface of layer two was associated with two small quadrangular adzes, and several small, slate knives were also found. The uppermost and latest cultural layer was relatively thin, but is found across the excavated area.

The occupation lasted between about 9000 and 5500 BC. All the stone artefacts found in layers two, three and four correspond with the several forms found in Bac Bo Hoabinhian sites. We find the unifacial discoids, grinding stones and flakes that bear signs of edge damage. The surfaces of all the grinding stones recovered bear traces of crushed red ochre or iron oxide, fragments of which are found at the site. About a third of the flakes had been used, for microscopic examination revealed thin striations running both along the worked surfaces and vertical to them Gorman and White's (1979) analysis suggests that they result from sharpening the tool by removing flakes from the working edge. A group of small calcite blades also have abrasions and striations. Their function is hard to document, but they may have been used to fashion wooden implements. The large unifacial discoids bear many small stepped flake scars along their edges suggesting use in battering or crushing.

The surface of layer two saw the advent of pottery, quadrangular stone adzes and small, slate knives. Characteristic flaked stone tools continued in use however, and some were even found lying on the surface of the rock shelter when Gorman first visited it. The AMS radiocarbon dating technique has been applied to an organic coating in one of these pot sherds, and result suggests a date in the 2nd millennium BC.

The screening undertaken at Spirit Cave led to the collection of a microfauna which complements the larger animal bones found and

The author excavating at Banyan Valley Cave in 1970.

described at most other hunter-gatherer sites where such a procedure was not undertaken. Moreover, the retention of all fragments of bone made it possible to outline aspects of behaviour such as cooking techniques and animal processing. The assemblages from each level are extremely fragmentary and many of the large limb bone fragments bear the traces of battering. The close conjunction of unifacial discoids with such comminuted bone fragments at the related site of Steep Cliff Cave hints strongly that they were used, among other tasks, in food preparation. Intense charring on broken bone surfaces further suggests that the meat adhered to the bone during cooking or drying over an open fire.

Many species were brought to Spirit Cave. Although a sharp half-hour climb from the Khong Stream, the occupants included the valley bottom in their territory, for each layer contains fish bones, as well as freshwater crab claws. Shellfish too, were taken to the shelter from the stream bed, and both otter and fishing cat bones are found. Arboreal animals predominate. Among primates, the langur and macaque are most common, but the gibbon and slow loris are also present. Other small arboreal mammals include the banded palm civet, the elusive marten, the flying squirrel and small squirrels of the genus *Callosciurus*. Then there are small terrestrial mammals, such as the bamboo rat, badger and porcupine and the agile leopard cat. The sambar deer and pig are the only reasonably large mammals found at Spirit Cave.

The faunal assemblage is interesting not only for what it contains, but for what is absent. Thus, we find no evidence for the dog, which is not surprising given the absence from Southeast Asia of a native wolf. Dogs are particularly useful in hunting large ground-dwelling animals such as wild cattle, rhinoceros, pig and deer. While it is not contested that all those species can be obtained by other means, such as spear-traps, it is possible that their rarity reflects the hunting techniques employed. Indeed, anyone who has lived in the canopied jungle of upland Northern Thailand cannot fail to be impressed by the number of animals adapted to the upper tree cover. Obtaining squirrels, langurs and the marten would have been greatly facilitated by a system of traps or light, accurate projectile points. Traps, too, could have been effective in securing the smaller ground dwelling mammals such as the rat, badger and porcupine.

The recovery of plant remains was one of the most important aspects of the excavations at Spirit Cave. Yen (1977) has recognised about 22 genera and has reconstructed their possible uses. *Canarium* seed fragments are the most numerous. All were smashed, probably to obtain the edible kernels. Three samples of betel nut were found in layers one and two, which suggest that this widespread stimulant was in use at least towards the end of the occupation period. The kernels of butternut and fruit of the Euphorbiaceae are particularly interesting because they are a source of poison. Poison-tipped projectile points would help account for the presence of the bones of elusive arboreal mammals. Seven fragments of bamboo stem indicate interest in this valuable plant. Yen has noted that *Canarium* and *Madhuca* are exploited by the Shan for their resins and gums, substances valuable in hafting composite implements, and coating pottery vessels to improve water retention. The genera *Prunus* (almond), *Terminalia* and *Castanopsis* were all represented by seed shells or kernels in layer three, and probably evidence food collection in the surrounding forests. Thus far, the plants described grow in the present forest in northern Thailand. We can now turn to a group of plants currently cultivated in the area, fragments of which were found at Spirit Cave. Layers two and three yielded the remains of bottle gourd. This plant may be eaten or, when mature, used as a container. Some identifications remain tentative. Nine specimens looked like peas, but their condition makes it difficult to rule out the possibility that they are palm kernels. Two bean-like seeds were found in layers two and four respectively but precise identification is not possible.

Banyan Valley Cave is just visible through the trees. The field in the foreground has been cleared to cultivate opium poppies.

This assemblage demonstrates that the occupants of the cave exploited a range of local plants with a variety of potential uses. Some are still used for food, others as condiments and stimulants. Then there are sources of poison, gum and resin. Indeed, any survey of hunter-gatherer occupation of the evergreen forest habitat following the research at Spirit Cave must acknowledge the broad spectrum of resources, and intimate acquaintance of the occupants with the plant and animal world around them. The Spirit Cave assemblage, however, added to the questions surrounding such societies by raising new issues.

Among these was the possibility that the leguminous plants and nuts were cultivated. Were this the case, then the occupants of this site would rank among the earliest plant cultivators known. In prehistoric research, one site imparts only limited information. Hence the concern for locating a number of sites in order to reconstruct a settlement pattern. Spirit Cave may represent but one facet of a given group's activities, in the same way that a temporary summer encampment would only give a partial picture of a transhumant pastoral society. Gorman therefore returned to Mae Hongson in 1972 to seek further sites and by excavation, resolve some of the problems posed above. In the event, two further caves were excavated.

Banyan Valley Cave

New excavations began at Banyan Valley Cave, about 30 km east of Spirit Cave. It is located beside a permanent stream just as it cascades into a cleft in the limestone bluff. It is hemmed in by precipitous slopes and the canopied evergreen forest. The hillside has a series of caverns, that yielding prehistoric remains being considerably broader and deeper than Spirit Cave. A test square excavated during April

Stone artefacts from Banyan Valley Cave. Left to right, a stone projectile point, a flaked axe and a sumatralith or unifacial discoid.

5 cm

5 cm

1972 revealed stratified occupation layers with hearths, just like those at Spirit Cave. The uppermost contained cord-marked pottery and several fragments of rice husk. A larger excavation was underway by December of the same year.

The impression gained during excavation, was that the sequence and contents of the layers were similar to those at Spirit Cave. Screening also yielded numerous small animal bones and fragments of plants. The same range of stone tools was present, and the upper layers provided a sample of pottery, similar bifacially-worked slate knives and quadrangular edge-ground adzes. More rice husks were present in the upper layer and a sophisticated tanged stone projectile point unlike anything else found in a like context was found. Reynolds (1992), in a report based on Gorman's original records, has stressed the contrast between a Hoabinhian industry in the lower two layers, and the changes in the uppermost.

Examination of the pottery fragments in the laboratory has shown that cord marking was the preferred decorative technique. In some cases, the cord marking was restricted to bands with narrow undecorated strips between them. In others, irregular striations were cut at right angles across a sherd otherwise completely cord marked. As vertical cord marking approached the rim on a third specimen, it gave way to a band of burnishing. Apart from the presence of the burnished wares similar to those from Spirit Cave, there were a few examples with meandering incised lines set in pairs, enclosing a row of dots impressed with a sharp pointed implement. While showing parallels with Spirit Cave, the Banyan Valley assemblage seemed more variable, and possibly represented a later time span.

The animal bones from Banyan Valley correspond in most respects to those from Spirit Cave, but also indicate some intriguing differences. Fish and crab are present, but the fish are smaller. The stream at Banyan Valley, while adjacent to the cave itself, is considerably smaller than that near Spirit Cave. The same range of small arboreal and terrestrial mammals recurs, but one fragmentary bone could well come from a dog. Given the absence of wolves from which to domesticate this animal, this specimen could conceivably come from a wild jackal or cuon, a domesticated form of jackal or possibly a domesticated dog obtained through exchange or contact with an intrusive, but alien group of people. At present, one cannot choose between these alternatives. It is, however, interesting that nearly all the large herbivores native to Northern Thailand were recognised among the bones, including the rhinoceros, wild cattle, the muntjak or barking deer, pig deer, mouse deer and serow.

Yen's analysis of plant remains shows that many match those from Spirit Cave. *Canarium* seeds, bamboo, cucumber and gourd fragments, together with the same possible legume seeds point to an interest in local plant resources. The discovery of 110 rice husks however, added a new dimension, and these have been analysed by Yen to ascertain whether or not they come from a wild or cultivated form, or from one documenting early trends towards a domesticated variety. In order to clarify this issue, Yen collected 128 samples of wild and cultivated rice grains. His comparative analyses suggested that the prehistoric sample probably comes from a wild source. Only husks were found at the site, many of which were fractured. By experimenting with tools similar to the grinding stones found there, Yen was able to replicate the breakage pattern when removing the grain.

At the time of excavation, it was anticipated that the site was contemporary with Spirit Cave. The pottery and stone axes looked of similar style and tradition, and the unifacial discoids were virtually identical. Both displayed a broad-ranging food quest in a forested, riverine habitat. The dates' however, were much later than expected. The lower levels yielded dates of about 3500 BC, but the uppermost was as late as about AD 900. The site thus assumes a particular interest, because it demonstrates the long currency of hunting and gathering in the uplands of Northern Thailand.

Steep Cliff Cave

Steep Cliff Cave is a narrow shelter on a precipitous slope. Excavations in 1973 revealed a thick bone midden dominated by large animals, but also containing the remains of small, arboreal creatures such as the Himalayan striped squirrel, a tiny animal weighing under 50 gm, which lives in the middle and upper tree canopy. Macaques and langurs are again present, as well as the red giant flying squirrel, which nests in tall trees or in clefts on cliff faces. The slow loris is mainly nocturnal and arboreal. The excavation provided almost a thousand fragments of water turtle or woodland tortoise carapaces. Fish bones are absent, however, and only one fragment of crab claw was found. This site is a long walk from the nearest permanent water. Given this situation, it is remarkable that the larger species include the remains of five water buffalo. Indeed, the thick bone midden, which represents one of the cultural layers, includes the bones of three wild cattle, two water buffalo, seven sambar deer, four muntjak, two pig deer, two pigs and 600 fragments of turtle or tortoise carapace. It may be significant, that the two fragments of canid bone from the site were also found in this midden. The tiger, leopard and clouded leopard are rarely represented.

A detailed examination of the mammal bones should provide details for the pattern of exploiting large animals. Consider the problems facing a group about to remove the meat and other

The excavation of Steep Cliff Cave.

valuable commodities, such as the hide, sinew and select bones or antler, from an animal weighing up to a ton. The Hidatsa Indians skinned buffalo where it was killed, discarded bones of the extremities which yielded little meat, and took only choice cuts, the tongue and kidneys back to their base camp for consumption, leaving only those bones that bore little meat, such as the skull and limb extremitites. The Mani hunters of southern Thailand today literally fillet the entire skeleton at the kill site, and remove only the meat.

All the major bones of the heavy bovids (cattle and buffalo) and of the sambar deer were found at Steep Cliff Cave. Skull fragments, teeth, vertebrae and even hoof bones were no rarer than the more favoured bones if meat alone was the objective of butchery. This situation is the more remarkable, because access to the site from any direction is precipitous, it is far removed from the favoured environment for at least the water buffalo, if not for wild cattle and deer as well. Moreover, most bones were smashed and charred. Even compact and robust bones bore the marks of heavy and persistent battering. It may well be that dismembered limbs were manhandled to Steep Cliff Cave, further butchered and the meat dried.

If this is the case, then the people involved also obtained canarium seeds and seeds resembling the pea or the palm, both of which are found in the thick bone midden. Pepper vine seeds, almond shells, bamboo and bean-like remains occur in other levels which are not dominated by concentrations of bone.

Radiocarbon dates for Steep Cliff Cave fall within the range 5500-3500 BC. The three caves thus form a sequence of occupation, beginning at about 9000 BC at Spirit Cave and ending a thousand years ago at Banyan Valley. This sequential aspect in the dating is bound to affect any interpretation of this hunting-gathering tradition in Northern Thailand, because it is necessary to seek differences between the sites that might reflect the course of cultural change. It would for example, be feasible to propose that, following a period of concentration on small game animals and forest foraging, the occupants of the Northern Thai uplands increased their hunting repertoire to include the larger herbivores, and finally augmented their subsistence base with the collection of wild rice. We are, however, dealing with a large area and only three excavated sites. We have no information to illuminate activities away from rock shelters, if only because such dry shelters protect cultural remains from decay and erosion. A reasonable objective under such circumstances, is to define common factors in each site as consistent aspects of the north Thai hunter-gatherer complex, particularly given local environmental features. At the same time, it is felt desirable to explain changes that occurred with time, to define any apparent historical trends.

All sites reflect a generalised subsistence economy in which plants, reptiles, fish, crabs, shellfish, land snails, and small forest mammals were sought. While the three caves differ in their physical setting, at least Spirit and Banyan Valley caves were still within evergreen wet canopied forest with access to water. They also reveal an interest in bamboo, and yield a common range of unifacial discoids probably used to process animal remains and fashion wooden implements. They employed twine, poison and resinous gum which, together with bamboo, remain to this day the constituents of composite trapping, snaring and hunting implements.

The discovery of possible leguminous plant remains at Spirit Cave, prompted a claim that they could well have come from a domesticated species (Solheim 1970). This notion formed the basis of claims that Northern Thailand was an area in which the cultivation of plants occurred at a very early date. It is now felt that the early plant remains from that site are too few, and so tentatively identified, that a more cautious interpretation is necessary. Broad spectrum foraging was the mainstay of subsistence at the three sites. Certain forest plants may have been favoured by the removal of their competitors, but this is a widespread phenomenon among plant gatherers, and does not constitute the same potential for major cultural changes as does the domestication of rice.

There are many more Hoabinhian sites in the hills of northern Thailand. Those in the Mae Chaem Valley, which flows into the Ping River south of Chiang Mai, have been examined by Santoni et al. (1986). A Hoabinhian stone industry has been found at, for example, the Pha Chang rock shelter, but no pottery or ground stone tools were encountered. Some of the red painted forms on the cave walls might also belong to this period. Moreover, fieldwork at Doi Kam in Chiang Rai province has identified stone chopping tools which in all likelihood, result from Hoabinhian occupation of an open site (Maleipan 1992). A similar, open site has been found at Chiang Saen, on the bank of the Mekong River (Natapintu and Phommanodch 1990).

The excavated caves in northern Thailand reveal how broad spectrum hunter-gatherers occupied elevated rock shelters for part if not all of their activities. If the opinions of modern hill tribes are sought, this pattern of settlement would have lessened the impact of spirits and in particular, those appearing under the guise of the lowland malarial mosquito. The lengthy occupation in the uplands manifested by the transient use of rock-shelters poses the possibility that these foragers attained a position of equilibrium with their environment. Much recent research has shown that, far from being concerned over food supplies, hunter-gatherers, even those surviving under harsh marginal conditions, spend relatively little time engaged in the food quest. Sahlins (1972) has described hunter-gatherers as "the original affluent society". While such groups may be poor in material goods, their ideological and spiritual lives are often more complex than the modern city dweller's. Archaeological research has shown that some hunter-gatherers have survived and maintained their way of life over very long periods of time. We have seen that the Mani remain hunting and gathering to this day. The Australian Aborigine has an ancestry stretching back over 50,000 years. During that time, there

The coastal site of Nong Nor comprised a cultural layer dominated by shellfish.

have been periods of adjustment to cope with fluctuations in climate, and to accommodate new peoples and ideas. When the first European explorers described the way of life of the Inuit, the buffalo hunters of the Great Plains and even the inhabitants of Terra del Fuego, they were witnessing the product of many millennia of successful adaptation by hunter-gatherer societies. The question posed is not so much how hunter-gatherers survived for so long, but rather why some of them adopted agriculture and stock raising at all.

When we consider the characteristics of the hunter-gatherers in Northern Thailand, we find a long term adaptation to the subtropical wet, evergreen forest. One characteristic of this forest type is the insulating effect of the upper tree canopy. Humidity and the temperature range at ground level are far more stable than under deciduous cover, or following forest clearance. Of course in monsoonal conditions, there is a dry season, but its impact is dulled and its duration decreased in the higher altitude wet monsoon forest. Operating in such an environment was facilitated by a succession of available foods. While the hardest time of the year was undoubtedly the end of the dry season, there were still the stream resources and game animals to exploit. Indeed, Gorman (1971) has shown that the shellfish at Spirit Cave were collected in both the wet and dry seasons. Such a changing mosaic of food sources, an economy without specialisation or reliance on any given plant or animal, and even any specific technique of food procurement, is held to favour long-term stability. This is further supported if hunter-gatherer groups were small and accustomed to move as the occasion demanded. It is a tenable proposition that their broad spectrum subsistence in this remote place continued to at least AD 900 and survives to this day in the forests of southern Thailand.

Coastal Settlement Round the Gulf of Siam

There have been two excavations of prehistoric hunter-gatherer sites behind the present shore of the Gulf of Siam. Nong Nor was occupied for a brief period measured in months rather than years, around 2450 BC. It was identified during the course of an intensive site survey in 1990, and excavated over three seasons in the ensuing years. By test pitting the margins of the site, it was estimated that it covered about 700-1000 square metres, of which 50 per cent was uncovered (Higham and Thosarat 1998a).

Boyd (1998) has examined the sediment sequence in the vicinity of the site, and has reconstructed an environment dominated by a series of indented marine embayments. When projected onto his reconstructed coast during the late third millennium BC, we find that Nong Nor and many similar sites were located on the protected shore, which allowed the occupants shelter while giving unfettered access to the open sea.

The contour of the occupation site at Nong Nor can be seen in the section through the site.

The only hunter-gatherer burial at Nong Nor was that of a woman interred, in a seated and crouched position, under a group of pottery vessels.

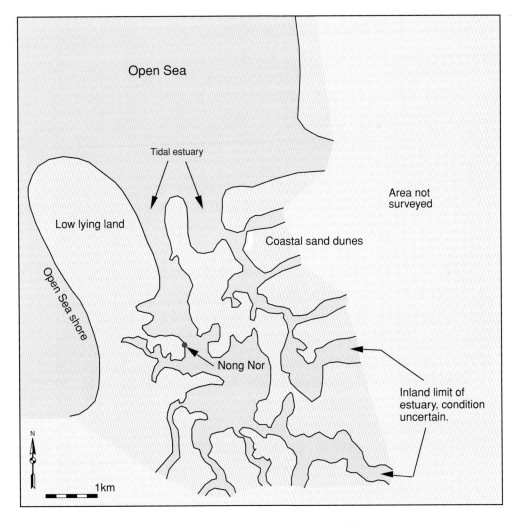

The reconstructed coastline in the vicinity of Nong Nor 4,500 years ago. It reveals that the site was located on the edge of a marine inlet. Such information is made possible by the fieldwork of geomorphologists.

Nong Nor comprises a shell midden varying in thickness from a few centimetres on the eastern margin to 60 cm in the centre. The dominant shell species is *Meretrix lusoria*, a cockle adapted to sandy beaches. On detailed examination, however, the inhabitants undertook a wide range of activities other than collecting shellfish. Many varieties of fish were represented among the faunal remains, including tiger and bull sharks. They also hunted marine mammals, such as the dolphin, and the large eagle ray. Few land animals are represented, however, and the bones recovered were nearly all worked into artefacts. The shell midden contained many hearths and ash spreads. Some of the latter may have been used for firing ceramic vessels, since pottery sherds were relatively common. Indeed, several complete pottery vessels were found over a woman buried, as in Viet Nam, in a crouched seated position. Her grave goods included a pebble used for burnishing the surface of the clay vessels before firing, to impart a sheen to the surface. Clay anvils used to shape pottery vessels were recovered, showing beyond doubt that the hunter-gatherers of Nong Nor made burnished and incised pottery vessels at the site. They also used polished stone adzes.

No evidence for cultivation or the raising of domestic animals was found. A marine inlet, fringed in all likelihood by mangrove forest, was not a location in which one would expect rice to grow, due to the impact of the tides on the salinity of available water. All the evidence available points to a marine adaptation, in which dolphins, fish and shellfish were consumed. The thin occupation layer, lack of any evidence for periodic abandonment and the small size of the site all point to a small population and brief period of occupation. Perhaps, during the course of a seasonal occupation, the pottery vessels were made for cooking, storage and in at least the one case identified, for use as mortuary offerings to the dead.

Khok Phanom Di

Khok Phanom Di, the second hunter-gatherer site to be opened by excavation, is a large (about 5 ha) mound now situated some 22 km from the present shore of the Gulf of Siam and about 14 km north of Nong Nor. It was occupied between about 2000-1500 BC. Five centuries of occupation witnessed several periods of environmental change, but there can be little doubt that the first settlers were attracted by the broad estuary and abundant potting clay. The estuary provided inexhaustible supplies of food, and the river facilitated trade.

The 1984-5 excavation involved a 10 by 10 metre square, located centrally on the mound. The choice of so large an area was taken in the light of smaller test squares at the site, which revealed a very deep and complex stratigraphic sequence up to 8 metres deep. It was particularly hoped to identify spatial aspects of behaviour, particularly given the discovery of inhumation burials. In order to record the precise location of all artefacts in an area of 100 square metres, a

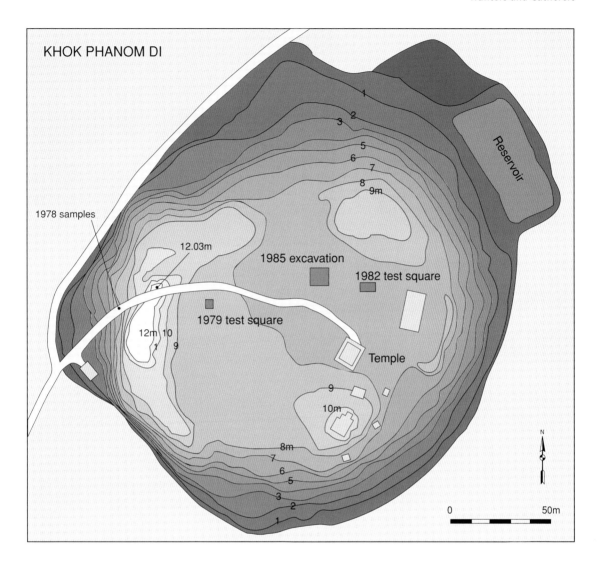

KHOK PHANOM DI

Reservoir

1978 samples

12.03m

1985 excavation

1982 test square

1979 test square

Temple

12m 10

8m

N

0   50m

The plan of Khok Phanom Di, showing the areas excavated.

Left: Khok Phanom Di is the large tree-covered mound on the skyline.

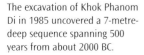

The excavation of Khok Phanom Di in 1985 uncovered a 7-metre-deep sequence spanning 500 years from about 2000 BC.

Right: The excavation of Khok Phanom Di took place in a 10 by 10 metre square, protected from rain and sun by a large roof.

computer was employed to ascertain the depth below datum and co-ordinates based on four measurements taken from each of the four corners of the square to the item being recorded. Excavations proceeded over a period of seven months, and produced a wealth of finds which open a new dimension in our understanding of the coastal hunter-gatherers of Southeast Asia.

The lowest layer, almost 7 metres below the present mound surface, included much ash, which gave it a distinctive grey colour. The artefacts relate to fishing, the manufacture of pottery vessels, and, probably, forest clearance and wood working. Adzes, for example, were plentiful and show evidence of heavy use. The clay anvils and burnishing stones, 21 of which were found in a cache dug into the natural substrate along with an anvil and three adzes, evidence a pottery industry. Bone stylus points, thought to have been used for decorating pottery vessels, are also present from the earliest context. *Lates calcarifer*, a fish which comes into estuaries to spawn, was represented, along with crabs of the mangrove and muddy river margins. The midden laid down in layer 11 was dominated by muddy shore and mangrove species. Some hunting is revealed by the presence of bones from species known to inhabit mangroves – the macaque and pig. One deer bone was found, but the dog was absent. Some fragments of rice chaff were found in a layer which might well have accumulated very rapidly. No burials were associated with it. The material culture and subsistence in this first occupation phase are virtually a mirror image of Nong Nor.

Layer 10 is a thick accumulation of midden lenses, ash spreads, rows of post holes representing former wooden structures, some with the wood still in place, hearths rich in charcoal, pits containing organic refuse and areas where redeposition through water action formed thin lenses. It incorporates graves ascribed to the first three mortuary phases (MP), and will be described beginning with the deposits containing the six graves in MP1 (5.88 to 6.51 metres below datum). Most artefacts continue unchanged from layer 11, with two additions: the first bone awls and clay netweights. However, Vincent (2001) has found that significant changes took place in the ceramic tradition, which might indicate the presence of newcomers into the

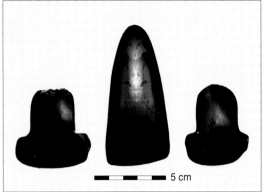

community. Marine and mangrove species again predominate, including many marine fish, shellfish and crabs.

Deposits accumulated to a depth of 29 cm between the latest grave of the first MP and the earliest of MP2. During this period, the nature of the build up remained unchanged. We encounter at least one substantial midden deposit in which *Anadara* valves dominate numerically. There is also a linear row of five hearths, while fishhooks, burnishing stones, net weights and clay anvils recur. The abundant evidence for burning might reflect local firing of the pottery vessels. The MP2 graves were distributed in clusters, with intervening spaces filled by pits and midden deposits. The distribution of a thick shell midden complements the grave clusters, and its linear edges and right-angled turns suggests that it accumulated against rigid structures, such as the wooden walls of collective tombs. This midden contained over 137,000 shellfish, most adapted to the mangrove and muddy intertidal waters. Apart from this midden, there was a change in the nature of the deposits associated with MP2. In place of ash spreads and hearths, we find circular pits containing bivalve shellfish, many of which were unopened. Postholes indicate the presence of structures in the vicinity of, and possibly round, the grave clusters. While the adzes, burnishing stones, anvils and awls continued as before, there were also two innovations. All the bone harpoons came from this part of the site, and a single shell knife, thought to have been used in harvesting a grass, such as rice, were found. There was also an increase in the number of fishhooks and clay netweights.

The faunal remains reveal continuity in the presence of a few pig and macaque bones, but we also find the first presence of the otter and the dog. The latter is exotic to South-East Asia, and can only have been introduced in the company of human communities. The pattern of inhuming the dead with the head pointing to the east continued, but there were many more burials, with individuals set out in clusters. Men had strong upper body musculature, while virtually all women display evidence of child bearing. However, anaemia was widespread amidst very high infant mortality.

Much energy was expended on mortuary ritual. Bodies were covered with red ochre, wrapped in a shroud fashioned from sheets of asbestos, and laid on a wooden bier. Pottery vessels were expertly

Polished stone adzes made from imported stone were common at Khok Phanom Di, and many were sharpened to the point that they were virtually too small to be of further use.

Above left and below: Fish hooks and harpoons were made of bone, and used for fishing and, probably, hunting marine mammals.

This infant from the second mortuary phase, like so many others at Khok Phanom Di, died at birth.

Burial 150 at Khok Phanom Di belongs to mortuary phase 1. The 2.5 year old child was buried in a crouched position with no grave goods. The infant had suffered from severe anaemia which probably contributed to early death.

A row of postholes from basal Khok Phanom Di must represent some form of structure.

From left to right, burials 91, 113 and 99 at Khok Phanom Di. Burial 91 was a man who died when about 45 years of age. He had strong upper body musculature and had enjoyed a healthy childhood, but suffered from very worn teeth. Burial 113, a woman who lived to about the same age, had lost many of her teeth and suffered from degeneration of the knee bones. Burial 99 was a 6-9 month old. Does this group represent a prehistoric family?

Right: Burial 147 of mortuary phase 1 at Khok Phanom Di contained the remains of a young man who died when aged about 19 years. He had no grave goods, but was the tallest person encountered. He lay 6 metres below the present surface of the mound.

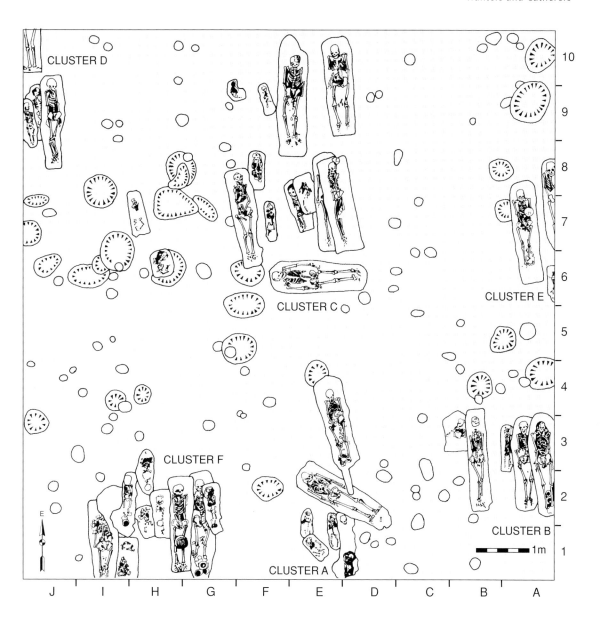

CLUSTER D

CLUSTER C

CLUSTER E

CLUSTER F

CLUSTER A

CLUSTER B

1m

J I H G F E D C B A

The distribution of graves during Mortuary Phase 2 at Khok Phanom Di.

Wood has survived in this posthole at Khok Phanom Di.

Ash spreads such as this one probably accumulated as a result of firing pottery vessels

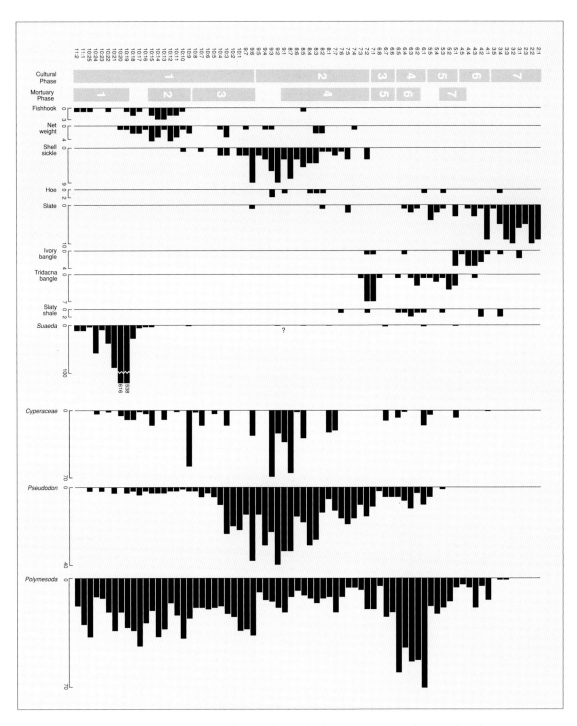

The sequence at Khok Phanom Di reveals many changes in the environment and the material culture over a span of five centuries.

made, brilliantly burnished and incised with complex designs. One man was found with about 39,000 shell disc beads, and shell beads in barrel and funnel forms were found with many burials. Cowrie shells included in one grave are almost certainly exotic, and bangles were fashioned from fish vertebrae. Other grave offerings included the teeth of rhinoceros and muntjak, a stone adze, a fishhook and the stones used to burnish pottery vessels. The range of grave goods

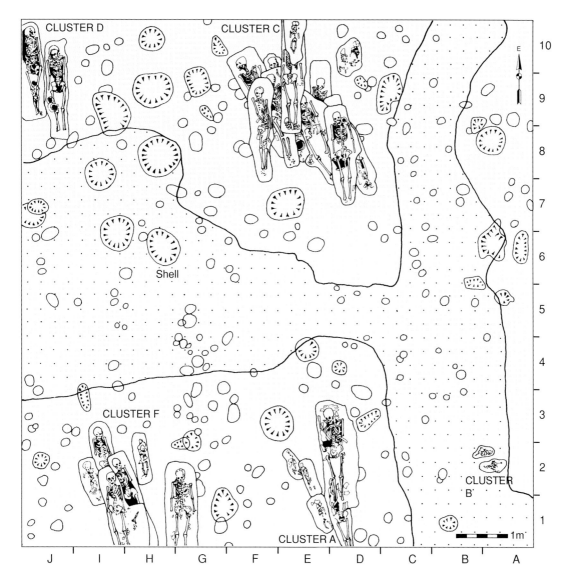

CLUSTER D

CLUSTER C

Shell

CLUSTER F

CLUSTER B

CLUSTER A

E

10
9
8
7
6
5
4
3
2
1

J   I   H   G   F   E   D   C   B   A

1m

echoes some of the activities suggested by Tayles (1999) as possible correlates of bone degeneration: making pots and paddling canoes. No clear differences have been detected in the mortuary rituals and grave goods found with men and women, although some individuals stand out on the basis of either their barrel beads, or association with shell beads and pottery vessels.

During MP3, which followed directly from MP2, the singular shell midden known as lens 2 first tapered off in size, and then ceased. The stratigraphic sequence included many postholes, pits, and lenses containing ash and charcoal. Artefacts included burnishing stones and clay anvils. Only one fishhook was recovered, and net-weights became rare. The first leucogranite hoe was encountered, along with several more shell knives. Human faeces from burial 67 contained domesticated rice remains, while burial 56 provided food residue from the lower abdominal area which comprised fish bones, scales, and rice chaff. During this phase, there was a fall in the

The distribution of graves during Mortuary Phase 3 at Khok Phanom Di.

The manufacture of pottery vessels was undertaken at Khok Phanom Di throughout its occupation. Many were of the highest quality, and were placed in graves of the deceased as mortuary offerings to the dead.

Ceramic anvils from Khok Phanom Di were used to shape pottery vessels. Many have what look like ownership marks.

number of shellfish adapted to clean subtidal and intertidal marine sand, offset by a rise in the species which occupy landward mangroves. It seems that the site was being distanced from the mouth of the estuary, and that siltation was affecting shellfish beds. Half way through this mortuary phase, there were hints of impending environmental changes, as the freshwater fish and shellfish began to increase at the expense of marine species.

Just over half of all graves contained infants or children. Males continued to develop strong upper bodies, indeed they were taller and more robust than at any other phase. But anaemia still affected health. The grave goods included shell disc beads, pottery vessels some of which were burnished and incised with complex designs, burnishing stones and a fish vertebra bangle.

One man was buried with four unique items: a nautilus shell, fish skeleton, shark fin spine and a small stone chisel. There are also hints that men and women were beginning to be accorded different burial offerings. A man was interred with a turtle carapace ornament, and a woman with a clay anvil. This set a pattern to be followed in later phases. It is also intriguing to note that, as shellfish of the clean intertidal conditions fell away in frequency, so the number of disc beads in burials declined. Three early MP3 graves had respectively 1,500, 859 and 1,260 such beads, but later MP3 graves had none. The decline continued into MP4.

Vincent's (2002) exhaustive study of the ceramic artefacts has pinpointed a vital transition in the middle of MP3, from one ceramic tradition to another. New sources of clay and temper were preferred, and there were subtle changes in the form and decoration of the pottery vessels. This might mean that people with potting skills, almost certainly women, were entering the community from other settlements which shared the same basic ceramic tradition.

Mortuary activity virtually ceased during the accumulation of layer 9 over a depth of 34 cm. During this period, several midden, ash and charcoal lenses were deposited, and their distribution followed that of the earlier major midden. This suggests that existing mortuary structures belonging to MP3 remained in place and influenced the location of later deposits. During layer 9, shellfish from clean coralline subtidal and intertidal conditions were no longer present and estuarine species also declined, to be compensated for by a continued rise in shellfish adapted to freshwater habitats. This

This group of mortuary phase 4 graves incorporates two men, a woman and a child.

Burial 24 from mortuary phase 4 contained the remains of a 25- year-old man who probably suffered from anaemia, but lived an active life leading to strong muscle development. He was interred with a splendid turtle carapace ornament.

Right: Burial 45, from mortuary phase 4 at Khok Phanom Di, contained the remains of a woman who lived into her mid forties. She enjoyed a physically active life, involving consistent work with her hands and arms.

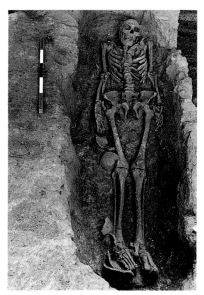

change is matched by the distribution of fish and crab remains, those adapted to freshwater taking the place of earlier species coming from marine or lower estuarine conditions. We also find the first representation of the water buffalo and small deer, but macaques and pigs continued to predominate. The first pygmy cormorants and pelicans were found, birds adapted to rivers and marshes. The last crocodile bone was found in lower layer 9. There appears too, to have been a change in fishing strategy, for fishhooks were no longer in evidence and netweights were rare. While adzes, burnishing stones and anvils were still found, shell knives surged in numbers.

MP4 corresponds with a period when freshwater conditions prevailed. Several stone hoes were found, and numerous shell knives. An ostracode from this context is from a species adapted to freshwater conditions, such as a rice field. Freshwater fish and crabs again rose in frequency compared with marine or mangrove species.

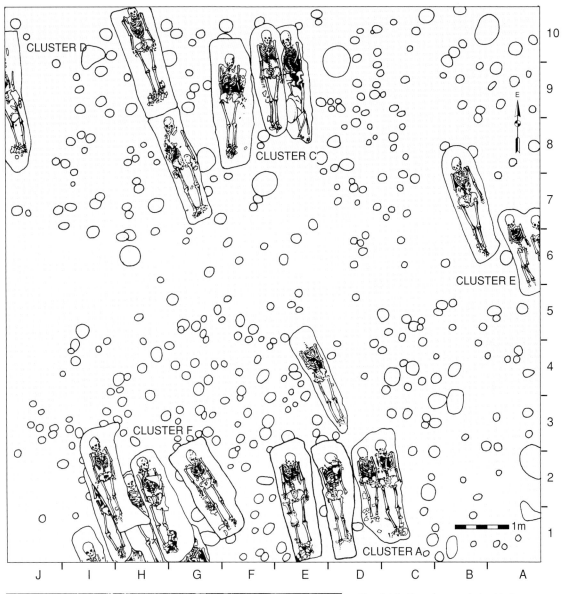

CLUSTER D

CLUSTER C

CLUSTER E

CLUSTER F

CLUSTER A

1m

J   I   H   G   F   E   D   C   B   A

The distribution of graves during Mortuary
Phase 4 at Khok Phanom Di.

Left: The excavation of Khok Phanom Di
during the uncovering of mortuary
phase 4 graves.

It is possible that burning, resulting in a series of ash lenses, preceded the renewal of the tradition of interring the dead in clusters during MP4, and within the mortuary area, we find a number of postholes, but markedly fewer pits. The burials, while still in their traditional clusters, were now less crowded in on each other, and were provided with individual graves. The trend towards distinguishing between males and females by the provision of turtle carapaces for the former, and anvils for the latter, was strengthened. Other grave goods included pottery vessels, now bearing less ornamentation, burnishing stones, and a single fishhook. Shell disc beads were rare compared with MP2 and early MP3. The human remains reveal a number of profound changes. Infant mortality fell, but child mortality rose. Four of the five dead children had suffered from severe anaemia. The rise in infants surviving to childhood would have involved a greater investment in child rearing, and probably a reduction in the number of births through greater spacing between pregnancies. There was a reduction in sexual dimorphism: men were now smaller, lived shorter lives and lacked the powerful upper body musculature of their forebears. Tooth wear declined in both sexes. Whereas tooth wear had caused most abcess formation in MP2-3 in males, caries was responsible in MP4. It seems highly likely that the diet involved less abrasive food and more rice

Only 15 cm of cultural deposit accumulated between the last burial of MP4 and the interment of burial 15, which belongs to MP5. Both the environment and the mortuary ritual, however, underwent major changes. There was a reversal to coastal, mangrove conditions, while interment in clusters ceased, and three people, a woman and two infants, were buried in an area not hitherto used for this purpose. These graves were large and the dead were richly endowed with grave goods. The woman was interred wearing garments encrusted with over 120,000 shell disc beads and she wore new forms of jewellery made from tridacna, such as discs, bangles and almost 1,000 large I-shaped beads. She was also accompanied by ten complete pots, some of novel form. An anvil with an ownership mark and two burnishing stones had been placed beside her right ankle, the former being made of clay from an exotic source (Vincent 2002). It is also likely that the woman, who died in her mid thirties, was a potter, for her wrist musculature was well developed, and her body was covered by clay cylinders thought to have been intended for conversion into pottery vessels. The infant buried in an adjacent grave was also interred with a range of novel shell jewellery, fine pots and a miniature clay potter's anvil with an identical ownership mark. A second infant was found within two large, impressively decorated pots, and the remains of a very rich male just intruded into the excavation area. The narrow stratigraphic band associated with MP5 burials saw the advent of land snails, indicating that the site was now joined to dry land. Mason (1991) has suggested that this was a delayed impact of an environmental change which occurred earlier in the sequence. This period also lacked any shellfish from the clean coralline habitat to which tridacna is adapted suggesting that the new range of shell jewellery was exotic. Ivory bangles were found for the first time,

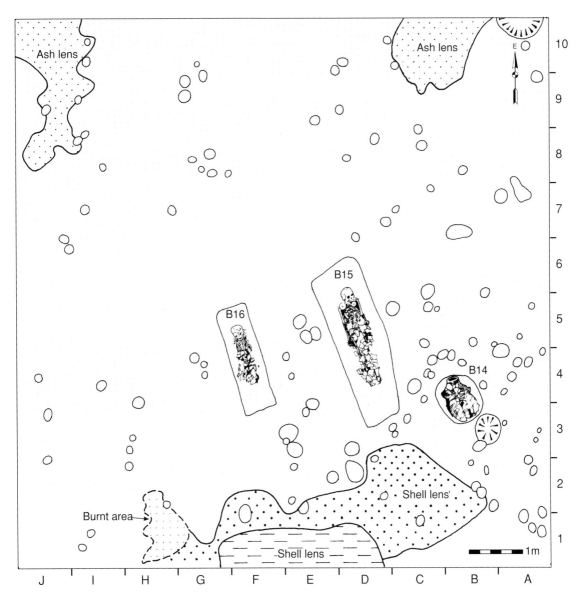

The distribution of graves during Mortuary Phase 5 at Khok Phanom Di.

Below left and right: A new range of exotic jewellery, including beads, ear ornaments, bangles and discs was introduced at Khok Phanom Di during the fifth mortuary phase.

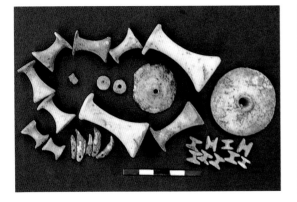

Burial 15 from Khok Phanom Di was found within a remarkably large and deep grave. The body was covered with clay cylinders thought to have been destined for conversion into pottery vessels. The smaller grave contained the remains of a later female, burial 4, who also had a clay anvil and burnishing stones beside the lower legs.

Above right: When burial 4 from Khok Phanom Di was removed, she was found directly over the grave of a headless male.

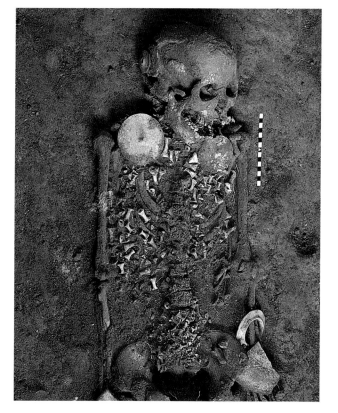

Burial 15 from Khok Phanom Di was also accompanied by several expertly-made ceramic vessels of novel form.

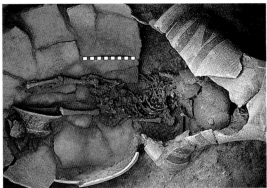

although not with burials. The last shell knife was found just before the start of MP5.

The earliest MP6 burials followed with little interval from MP5 and under continuing marine conditions. The mortuary ritual now involved investment in substantial mortuary structures. A raised building with clay wall foundations and a clay plastered floor contained three rich interments. A contemporary row of burials just to the west was housed within a wooden structure, with far fewer grave goods. A more marine or at least brackish water habitat seems to have continued into the currency of MP7, the final phase, which is represented only by a handful of graves. The wall of the earlier clay mortuary structure remained in place while in layer 4 sandy deposits accumulated. Several pits were dug within the layer, and they contained faunal remains which included many marine species of fish, shellfish and the mangrove crab. This was a relatively thin layer which represents the last period in which the inhabitants exploited a marine habitat. We cannot demonstrate a period of site abandonment with the end of layer 4, but it is a possibility. With layers 3 and 2, which are undated, the excavated area was used as a pottery workshop. We find many clay anvils and burnishing stones, as well as cylinders of unfired clay thought to represent an early stage in the forming of pots, and a dump of clay. But other activities were also indicated by material remains. A new form of small awl was present in abundance, as well as bone stylus points, much worked antler and numerous slate bangles.

Ivory is also relatively abundant. Faunal remains include the first major occurrence of bovid bones, but trapping was also undertaken, with the otter and various civets being identified. Small deer, either muntjak or pig deer, increased in numbers, and at the top of layer 2, netweights reappeared. Potsherds were more abundant than at any other period of occupation. The impression is one of occupation by a community which continued to hunt, trap and fish, within a more forested habitat, obtained exotic raw materials through exchange and manufactured pottery vessels from the local clay.

The superposition of clusters over time, and continuity in the basic mortuary ritual, has encouraged the excavators to construct a hypothetical series of genealogies. This exercise has been supported by bone abnormalities found in successive 'generations' of the same

The largest pottery vessels found at Khok Phanom Di enclosed the remains of this infant, whose grave lay beside that of burial 15.

Left: The exposure of burial 15 revealed a woman interred with over 120,000 shell beads, two horned discs and shell ear ornaments.

Burial 16 from Khok Phanom Di, an infant aged about 15 months at death, lay in a large grave adjacent to burial 15. The infant was buried with thousands of shell beads, beautiful pottery vessels, an exotic shell bangle and a miniature clay anvil beside the ankles.

cluster, but requires testing, if possible, by the analysis of DNA. We do not know, for example, whether a man and woman interred next to each other in association with infants were related by descent or by marriage. These genealogies are particularly durable in the case of cluster C and F and are used as a vehicle for exploring the history of this community over four or five centuries.

During MP2 and 3, the inhabitants had access to an estuary with rich food resources, and every opportunity for maritime or riverine exchange. That this occurred is suggested by the different wear on the teeth of men when compared with the women, and the strong upper body musculature of the former. While there was an abundance of food, and little if any incentive to experiment with domestication of plants or animals, the community suffered very high infant mortality. Their remains reveal poor overall health and in particular, anaemia associated with a blood disorder. This is an inherited condition which will often prove fatal to the newly born. Some of the family clusters failed to survive for more than a few generations, and this could be due to such high mortality. Most adults died before the age of 40 years, and many succumbed in their twenties.

Estuaries are subject to rapid and unpredictable change. This can result from slight oscillations in sea level, rapid sedimentation, and

the movement of rivers to new and often distant channels. There is consistent evidence for a change to fresh water conditions beginning in the middle of MP3, and continuing through MP4. At the same time, a new clay source was used, the form and decoration of pottery vessels changed, and the people began to use large granite hoes, and fashion shell knives. Examination of the wear on these knives suggests use in harvesting grasses, such as rice (Higham T. 1993). These changes were accompanied by new mortuary rituals. Men were now interred with large ornaments fashioned from turtle shells, while women were often associated with the clay anvils used to shape pottery vessels. Long distance travel by boat might have been less frequent, for men and women now had a similar pattern of tooth wear, and men were less robust. The accumulating evidence is compatible with a period of marked change during which rice was cultivated locally.

This period did not last for long. With MP5, the biological indicators point to a reversion to marine conditions. Freshwater shellfish declined as those of the mangroves increased. Granite hoes and shell knives were no longer encountered. Yet this was a period of spectacular change in mortuary wealth. We can gain particular insight into this development through a consideration of burial 15. This woman had strongly-muscled hands and forearms, and was interred with large and richly-ornamented pottery vessels, together with an anvil and two burnishing stones. She lay under a pile of clay cylinders destined for conversion into pottery vessels. Her grave goods are of unparalleled abundance: she wore an upper garment embroidered with 120,000 disc beads, and necklaces comprising almost a thousand large I-shaped shell beads and five pierced carnivore canines. Two horned shell discs lay on her chest, and she wore shell ear ornaments and a heavy shell bangle. Among the most intriguing burials at this site lay beside this large and elaborate grave. It contained the remains of a 15-month-old infant disposed in an identical manner. Clay cylinders again covered the body, there were over 12,000 disc beads and 200 of the I-shaped form, a shell bangle and most intriguingly, a miniature clay anvil placed, as with the adjacent woman, by the right ankle. Burial 43, which was only partially in the excavated area, was a male aged about 30 at death accompanied by over 56,000 disc beads, 435 I-beads, two heavy

The woman in burial 15 from Khok Phanom Di was interred with her ceramic anvil and two burnishing stones in a shell container.

Left: One of the novel pottery vessels which accompanied burial 15 from Khok Phanom Di. (maximum width 32 cm)

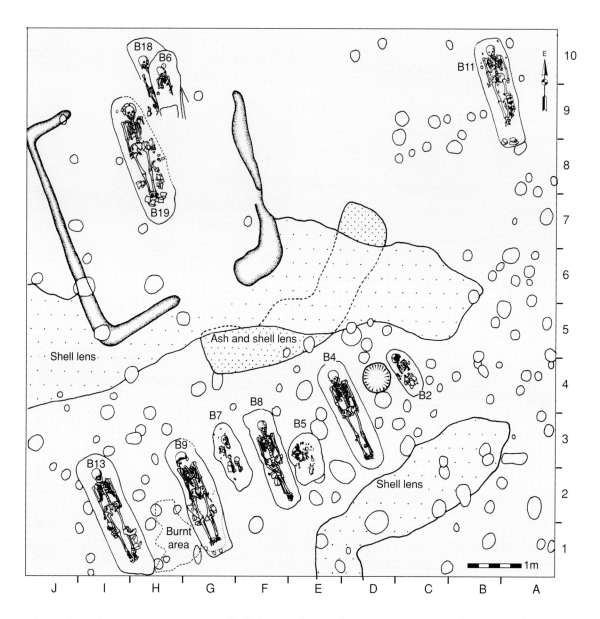

exotic shell discs and a turtle carapace ornament but no anvil or burnishing stone.

Exotic imports, such as tridacna shell jewellery, ivory and slaty shale now appeared. There was also much emphasis on a dead woman as a potter. It seems highly likely that such accumulated wealth involved exchange, in which women participated as specialists in the manufacture of pottery vessels. The presence of a miniature anvil with an infant further suggests that girls began to learn their skills at a tender age.

Although not as wealthy as their immediate predecessors, MP6 burials showed continuing changes in mortuary ritual against a background of marine conditions. Two women and a child were buried within a rectangular, raised mortuary structure with clay wall foundations. One woman died after a relatively healthy life, when in

Above and opposite:
The distribution of graves during Mortuary Phases 6 and 7 at Khok Phanom Di.

B12

Raised platform

Plastered floor

Walls

CLUSTER 1

B3

B1

Red soil
lens

Shell lenses

1m

J   I   H   G   F   E   D   C   B   A

her mid 20s. The other was about 42 years old at death and was in poor health with degeneration of the spine, and evidence for the heavy use of her shoulders. Both were accompanied by a clay anvil, while the younger woman and the child had burnishing stones as well.

This chamber lay to the east of a second, contemporary group of burials confined within the foundations of a large wooden mortuary structure. There were two women and two men, together with four infants. They were much poorer, in terms of mortuary wealth, than their contemporaries in the raised building to the east, but one of the women was found with an anvil and two burnishing stones, and another had eight such stones. There is an interesting possibility that these two contrasting groups represent a richer and a poorer social group, but a larger area would need to be uncovered to explore this further.

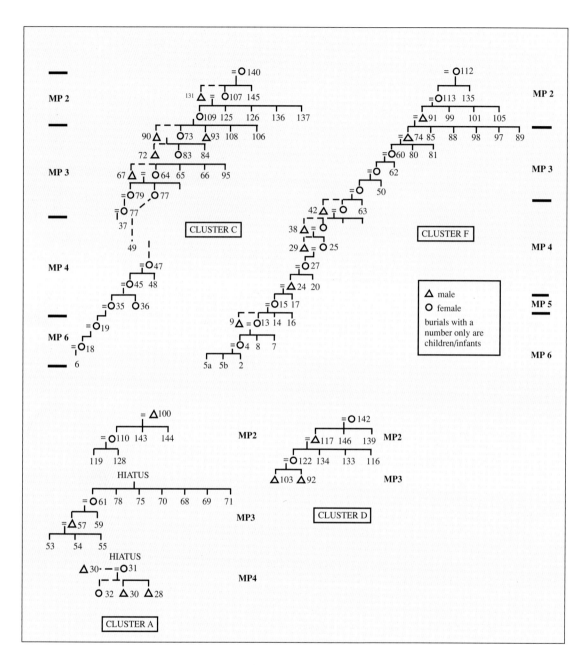

These hypothetical genealogies from Khok Phanom Di were reconstructed on the basis of the grave clusters being superimposed over time.

Quite apart from illuminating the history of coastal hunter gatherers over a period of 500 years, the excavation of Khok Phanom Di enables a review of a most important issue in Southeast Asian prehistory, the origin and spread of rice agriculture. Fifteen years ago, research on this issue in southern China had hardly begun and the possibility of influence from that quarter, although proposed by Sørensen, was not being further considered. Several attempts had been made to identify a transition to rice cultivation in Southeast Asia. Gorman had looked in the uplands, Penny in the piedmont zone (Penny 1984). Both foundered for lack of supporting evidence. The excavation of Khok Phanom Di sought to test the hypothesis

With mortuary phase 6 at Khok Phanom Di, a rich woman was interred within a raised mortuary structure with clay wall foundations.

Left: The grave for the infant burial 16 at Khok Phanom Di was far too big for the tiny body it contained. The bones were very well preserved.

that it had been a focus for the transition to rice agriculture. This originated firstly in the fact that earlier excavations had uncovered the remains of rice in deep layers. Second, the first radiocarbon dates obtained by Damrongkiat Noksakul suggested initial occupation by the 5th millennium BC. Finally, the great depth of the site suggested a long period of occupation.

The hypothesis, that rice cultivation in this part of Southeast Asia had an origin in coastal communities, whence it spread inland with a growing population, has not been supported by the results of the excavations. There is no evidence for rice in any form in the first occupation phase at Nong Nor. Khok Phanom Di, according to the radiocarbon dates from the 1984-5 excavation, was not as early as thought, initial settlement being in the vicinity of 2000 BC. Fragments of rice, and exotic pottery sherds containing rice remains, have been found throughout the sequence. Thompson (1996) has shown that it was of a cultivated variety, but this does not prove local cultivation. Our assessment of the environment of Khok Phanom Di during MP1-3 suggests a salt water estuary backed by mangroves and salt flats. This is not conducive to rice cultivation. It is, however, possible that the hunter-gatherers of this site obtained rice from inland farming communities by exchange. Only during the fourth mortuary phase did the environment permit rice

Directly in front of the mortuary structure at Khok Phanom Di, a row of burials was contained within a wooden building represented by post foundations.

cultivation, and it was during this period that we find hoes, harvesting knives, and a change in the physical attributes of the people. This was followed by a reversion to marine conditions and, to judge by the splendour of the burials, a surge in exchange activity.

Khok Phanom Di is, in this interpretation, a site which documents interaction between a community of hunter-gatherers with deep ancestral roots in the rich, warm estuarine habitat of Southeast Asia, and newly-established farming communities in their exchange orbit. It reveals what one could reasonably expect from any reading of the literature on more recent coastal hunter-gatherer groups, a society which grew to be wealthy and socially graded, on the basis of controlling and participating in long-distance exchange. While the pottery vessels made by the woman in burial 15 were probably made by her own hand, her profusion of shell ornaments came from afar, and signalled her high social attainment.

The People of Khok Phanom Di

The excellent preservation of the human skeletal remains has opened a window on changing patterns of health, diet and activities undertaken at Khok Phanom Di (Tayles 1999). The health of a prehistoric population over time can be approached on the basis of a number of skeletal indicators. Age at death is one of the most significant, and can be determined through the eruption patterns in the teeth and physical changes in bone structure. The diet can be considered by examining tooth wear, while periods of physical stress may leave their mark in the presence of lines of growth cessation, or poor dental development. Although there are numerous pathogens and diseases in tropical and subtropical areas that can afflict human populations, few leave unequivocal traces in the skeleton. However, anaemia leads to changes in bone morphology, while recurrent use or stress induces osteoarthritis in the affected joints. There is also the possibility of identifying fracture patterns.

Fully 41% of the population died at or soon after birth, and over half failed to reach adulthood. There was a general decline in mortality among individuals aged from five to 19, but a third died when aged between 20 and 39 years, and a mere 7% lived beyond the age of 40. Community leaders must have been very young. The average height for women was 1.54 m, while that for men was 1.62m.

Such general figures are of limited value, for the human remains at Khok Phanom Di incorporate changes over time. Tayles's comprehensive description of the sample shows, for example, that a two-year-old from MP1 suffered from anaemia, while the adults had experienced growth disruptions when young. Yet solid bone mass among the adults reflects an adequate diet. There were only six burials in this first phase, but 56 individuals comprise MP2, 31 failing to attain 12 months of age. This is a high proportion indeed, and must have placed great emotional and physiological stress on the women. Each of the eleven women and eight men who reached adulthood had suffered ill health during infancy or childhood. There was also a marked incidence of joint degeneration: all men examined suffered problems with their shoulder joints and over half also experienced problems with their backs, feet, ankles, knees and hands. Women suffered degeneration in the knees, and elbows. There were also differences between men and women on the basis of their dentition. Whereas almost one in five female teeth displayed caries, only 5% of male teeth were carious. These differences suggest a sexual division of labour and possibly diet. The degeneration of the shoulders in men might have been caused by such an activity as canoeing or at least taking boats out to sea, while absences from the base community by men would almost inevitably have involved a different diet.

High infant mortality continued into MP3, with 20 of the 42 individuals dying at birth, and three surviving only for a few months. All the 19 adults had experienced a disruption in their growth when young, and at least three suffered from anaemia. The same pattern of joint degeneration was found as in the previous phase, suggesting similar activities, while men were taller and more robust than before or after. Twelve of the adults suffered caries. An extra insight into health and diet during this phase has come from two rare sources. Burial 67 contained the skeleton of a man who died when in his mid thirties. Like his male contemporaries, he suffered considerable degeneration in his shoulder joints. Faecal remains were recovered from his grave, and these provide an intimate insight into his diet, for they contained cultivated rice chaff and fish bones. There was also a helminth egg probably from the giant liver fluke *Fasciolopsis buski*. This unpleasant parasite is common in low-lying areas where flooding can cause faecal contamination. Those afflicted may expect to suffer from diarrhoea, a loss of appetite and malnutrition. He also ingested hair, identified as coming from humans, mice and probably rats, and a beetle of a species commonly found in rice stores. It appears that there was a low level of food hygiene at Khok Phanom

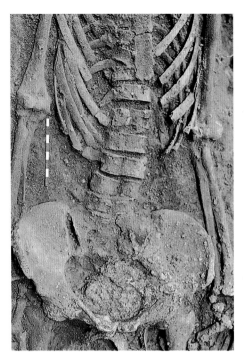

Above and right: The food remains found in the abdominal area of this small woman included rice chaff and the bones of freshwater fish.

Di. This receives confirmation from the remains of partially digested food found in the pelvic area of burial 56, that of a woman who died in her mid forties. She was the smallest adult recovered, suffered many periods of ill health as a child and grew to be anaemic, with poor muscular development. She had consumed rice and complete fish, including bones and scales. Sting ray teeth were also present, and the remains of a mite which lives in leaf litter. If the mite had not entered the grave after interment, its presence suggests that food was eaten from the ground.

There were marked changes with the fourth mortuary phase. Infant mortality declined sharply, with only two fatalities among the newly born, and two deaths of infants aged under a year. There was also a marked reduction in shoulder joint problems among the men, linked with less robust growth overall and a reduction in the size differences between the sexes. Unlike the preceding phases, some adults failed to reveal any traces of growth disturbances when young, and male and female tooth wear were now similar. These changes could result from any of a series of causes, but it is hard not to single out a relationship with the changes in the environment and economy during this phase. The increase in freshwater indicators and presence of hoes and harvesting knives suggest that people were now growing their own rice, and spending less time away from the home settlement. This hypothesis receives some support from the dental evidence. Carious teeth were now far less frequently encountered. Domett (1999) has found that with increasing reliance on rice, Bronze Age people display fewer caries than in the early phases at Khok Phanom Di. She has ascribed this to the beneficial effects of a diet of rice which, unlike maize, is demonstrably not cariogenic.

With phases 5 and 6, which it is recalled saw a return to more saline, marine conditions, the number of teeth with caries rose to 29%, compared with only 8% during phase 4. While a neat correlation between caries and rice consumption is not in question, this trend does suggest at least a different diet. Infant and child mortality also returned to the levels experienced before MP4 and Tayles has

This outstanding decorated vessel came from the latest burial phase at Khok Phanom Di (maximum width, 20 cm).

suggested that the reduced stature of males and females in the last phases of the cemetery reflect a decline in the health of children.

Hunters and Gatherers: Summary

There were two major aspects to hunter-gatherer societies in Southeast Asia. One is coastal, the other inland. We only know of the former when the sea level formed raised beaches beyond the present shore. Many sites are now known, from Viet Nam to the Gulf of Siam. Estuaries are particularly rich in naturally-replenished food sources, and encourage permanent occupation. Even the earliest sites reveal pottery making, while the dead were interred by preference in a seated, crouched position. Khok Phanom Di is a late hunter-gatherer site, which documents interaction with intrusive, inland rice farmers. It is possible to document and provide explanations for the series of environmental, social and economic changes which took place over a period of about 20 generations.

By contrast, the inland hunter-gatherers are known almost exclusively from occupation remains in rock shelters. This provides only a partial glimpse of their way of life, for they must surely also have occupied many open sites as well. The evidence from rock shelters suggests a broad-spectrum foraging and hunting tradition, involving only brief periods of occupancy. Faunal remains reveal a pattern of hunting, trapping, fishing, and collecting. As might be anticipated, plants were collected for a variety of purposes. Some late contexts suggest that these hunters and gatherers were familiar with pottery vessels, and used polished stone implements. Few groups, however, survived for long the arrival of lowland agricultural communities in the late third millennium BC.

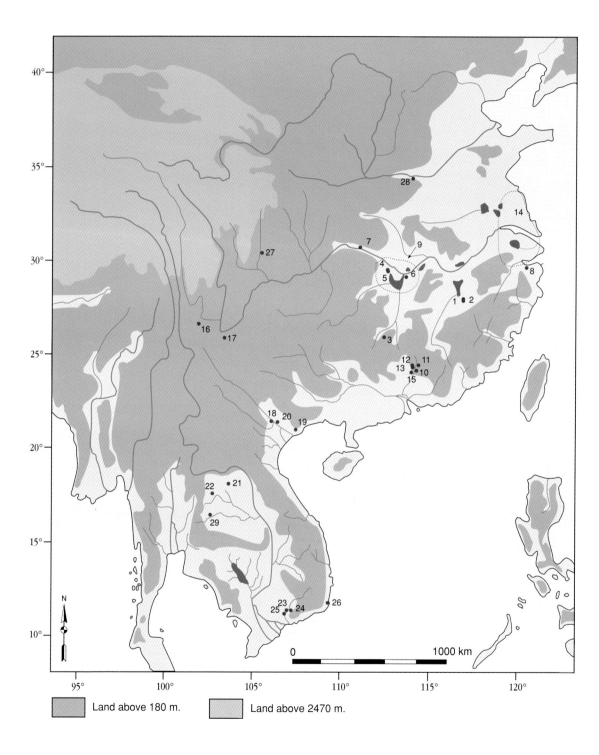

Land above 180 m.   Land above 2470 m.

Chapter Three

The Neolithic Settlement of Southeast Asia

The origins of rice cultivation represent one of the most vital and influential changes in the history of Southeast Asia. It is so central an issue, that during the past three decades, a series of research endeavours have sought the transition to rice agriculture within Southeast Asia itself. Gorman's excavations at Spirit and Banyan Valley caves provided speculative fuel for local origins. Penny proposed and tested a model for rice domestication in the piedmont zone, while Higham and Thosarat set their excavation of Khok Phanom Di within a model for this key innovation in the coastal environment. All three have foundered for lack of supportive evidence. In the meantime Sørensen's prescient suggestion that rice farmers expanded into Southeast Asia from an ultimate homeland in China was largely disregarded (Sørensen 1972).

Concentrated research in the middle reaches of the Yangzi River valley between the eastern end of the Three Gorges and Lake Poyang, together with a growing body of linguistic evidence, have required a return to the basic elements of Sørensen's hypothesis. Increasing insight into factors which might have stimulated plant and animal domestication underline the potential importance of environmental and cultural stress. It is hard to identify either in the hot, languid conditions of the tropical estuary, with its fecund provision of food, or the canopied forests of the interior of Southeast Asia. As one moves to the north, however, we find that the climate of the Yangzi Valley underwent a series of profound changes incorporating the end of the Pleistocene ice age and the oscillations in temperature and rainfall which characterised the early Holocene. Recent evaluations of pollen spectra and faunal assemblages there reveal a climate 4-10° C cooler and much drier between 20,000 and 15,000 BC (Higham and Lu 1998). Rainfall was probably 1000 mm per annum below its present level of 1,600 mm, accounting for the predominance of drought resistant plants in the pollen spectra. From 15,000 to about 13,700 years BP, the climate moderated, encouraging the spread of oak and pine, elm and willow but thereafter, and until 10,000 BP, there was a reversal to cold conditions described across Eurasia as the Younger Dryas period. Thereafter, it again became warmer and moister. Broad-leaved trees colonised the valley and the fauna became subtropical. Increased rainfall fed rivers and lakes, and wild rice spread from refugia.

Opposite:
The location of the main early sites with evidence for rice cultivation in China and Southeast Asia.
1. Diaotonghuan,
2. Xianrendong, 3. Yuchanyan,
4. Bashidang, 5. Pengtoushan,
6. Fenshanbao, 7. Chenbeixi,
8. Hemudu, 9. Area of the Tangjiagian culture, 10. Shixia,
11. Xincun, 12. Chuangbanling,
13. Niling, 14. Area of the Liangzhu culture,
15. Nianyuzhuan,
16. Baiyancun, 17. Dadunzi,
18. Phung Nguyen, 19. Trang Kenh, 20. Lung Hoa, Xom Ren,
21. Ban Chiang, 22. Non Nok Tha, 23. Cu Lao Rua, 24. Cau Sat,
25. Ben Do, 26. Xom Con,
27. Sanxingdui, 28. Erlitou,
29. Ban Non Wat.

It is against this environmental kaleidoscope that we can measure the significance of recent finds from deep excavations in the caves which fringe the lacustrine lowlands. The sequence at Diaotonghuan, for example, spans the later Pleistocene into the early Neolithic period. This cavern overlooks a small, swampy basin (Zhao Zhijun 1998). The excavators have identified 16 sequential zones of occupation, and recovered samples of rice phytoliths, the hard silica bodies found in the rice plant. There was, for example, a surge in the numbers of rice glume phytoliths in zone G, which is tentatively dated to the terminal Pleistocene. These are seen as evidence for the collection of wild rice during the mild phase which characterised that period. Rice phytoliths were extremely rare during zone F, which corresponds to the Younger Dryas cold phase. However, rice was again abundantly represented during zone E, which is thought to date between 10,000-8,000 BP. About half the sample conforms with a domestic variety of rice. This context also provided the first evidence for pottery in the form of very crude, sometimes cord-marked vessels which could well have been made in order to cook rice.

A lack of reliable radiocarbon dates makes this a tentative framework, but it gains support from similar sequences in other caves. Xianrendong is located only 800 metres from Diaotonghuan, and again has a lower Palaeolithic occupation under a Neolithic horizon containing rice phytoliths. Yuchanyan also overlooks low-lying wetlands, and has provided a sample of fish, turtle and mammalian bone as well as rice husks said to be transitional to the domestic form. Potsherds from this site are dated in the vicinity of 12,500 BP (Yuan Jairong and Zhang Chi 1999). Bashidang is a village site which covers about three hectares. Its lower layers date to about 8,000 BP, and excavations in 1993-7 uncovered waterlogged deposits which had preserved over 15,000 rice grains. These have been ascribed to a cultivated variety (Pei Anping 1998). Water caltrop and lotus, both of which can easily be propagated in marshes and lakes, were also abundantly represented in this settlement, together with hunted and probably domestic animals, pottery vessels, wooden spades and pestles, the foundations of pile dwellings and over 100 human burials. Bashidang is similar in many respects to the settlement of Pengtoushan, 20 km to the southwest. Here, we again encounter a cemetery in which the dead were interred with complete pottery vessels and exotic stone ornaments. The clay used for making pots was tempered with rice chaff. There are also the remains of houses, and every sign of a successful adaptation to the rich resources offered in the middle Yangzi lake land. Two radiocarbon determinations obtained from the rice used as a tempering agent are 6420-6990 and 5780-6380 BC (Crawford and Chen Shen 1998).

This accumulating body of evidence indicates that the Yangzi Valley was one of the very few areas in Eurasia that witnessed a Neolithic Revolution, the transition from hunting and gathering to agriculture. Population growth is a recurrent characteristic of sedentary agricultural communities. As settlements grow, there is a strong incentive for a group to move and found a new community. This appears to have followed the establishment of such sites as

Pengtoushan and Bashidang. Fenshanbao, which was occupied within the period 8000-7500 BP, lies east of Lake Dongting, and excavations have revealed 50 burials and pottery tempered with rice. To the west, we find agriculture spreading upstream to Chenbeixi in the Three Gorges. In an easterly direction, the famous site of Hemudu was a base for lakeside rice cultivation by 7000 BP.

This sequence has a strong bearing on the Neolithic settlement of Southeast Asia, because it is now possible to trace the expansion of agricultural communities progressively further to the south. Several rivers provide access from the Yangzi Valley to the rich hot lowlands of Lingnan. The Gan and Xiang rivers flow north to Lakes Poyang and Dongting, while the Bei flows south. Au Ka-fat (1993) has described close similarities, in terms of the temper, form, decoration and colour, between the pottery of the Tangjiagan culture of Hunan, and many sites in Guangdong. Evidence for the establishment of rice farmers is, not unexpectedly, in the headwaters of the Bei River, where the sites Shixia, Xincun, Chuangbanling and Niling date from the early third millennium BC. Shixia in its earliest phase, included a cemetery in which grave goods included jade *cong* (tubes) of deep ritual significance in the Liangzhu culture to the north, as well as bracelets, pendants and split rings. The subsequent Nianyuzhuan culture sites reflect a further spread of agricultural settlement, but began to encounter and interact with rich hunter-gatherer groups commanding the delta of the Zhu River.

The Bei is just one of the rivers which ultimately connects the Yangzi Valley with Southeast Asia. In general, they flow south and radiate out from a hub in the eastern Himalayan foothills. From east to west, they include the Red, Mekong and Chao Phraya systems. Further to the west, this configuration is repeated in the form of the Irrawaddy, Chindwin and Brahmaputra rivers. Given the dense canopied forests that would then have dominated the lowlands of Southeast Asia, the rivers were the principal arteries for communication and movement.

Yunnan is a key area for documenting any expansionary movement of this nature, because it has links with the Yangzi, Mekong and Red rivers. Baiyancun is a site which lies within striking distance of all three. It has a deep stratigraphic sequence, involving over four metres of accumulated cultural material. The initial settlement has been dated to between 2400-2100 BC, and excavations over an area of 225 square metres have revealed the remains of eleven houses and a cemetery. Many of the human remains were found with no cranium, and grave goods were also absent, but the pottery from this phase was decorated with a distinctive series of patterns, incorporating parallel incised lines infilled with impressions (YPM 1981). The nearby site of Dadunzi is rather later, the single radiocarbon date suggesting a mid second millennium BC occupation. House plans were noted, often superimposed over earlier structures, and 27 burials were encountered. Adults were

Phung Nguyen sites are located in the rolling hills above the confluence of the Red and Black rivers

buried in extended positions with no preferred orientation, and infants were interred in mortuary jars. The style of pottery decoration matched that found earlier at Baiyancun.

The Red River links Yunnan with the rolling lowlands of Bac Bo, a region that had sustained maritime and inland settlements for millennia before the first farmers were established. Although the status of subsistence activities during the currency of the inland 'Hoabinhian' and coastal Da But and Cai Beo groups is in doubt, there is no question that hunting-gathering and fishing were mainstays. The situation is much clearer for the third millennium BC, and one of the principal tasks for the future lies in documenting the articulation between the late hunter-gatherer groups and those in which rice cultivation and animal husbandry were undeniably established. The latter sites dominate the Middle Country, an area of rolling lowlands dissected by minor tributaries of the Red River. It is studded with archaeological sites and much research has been devoted to them.

The earliest agricultural settlements take their name from Phung Nguyen, a site which has been extensively investigated. There are relatively few radiocarbon dates for this sequence. The Phung Nguyen phase probably belongs from the late third to the mid second millennium BC. The recent research at Co Loa has revealed initial settlement during this phase, from about 2000 BC (Lai Van Toi

The distribution of Phung Nguyen sites in Bac Bo.
1. Phung Nguyen, 2. Lung Hoa,
3. Doi Giam, 4. Xom Ren,
5. Go Bong.

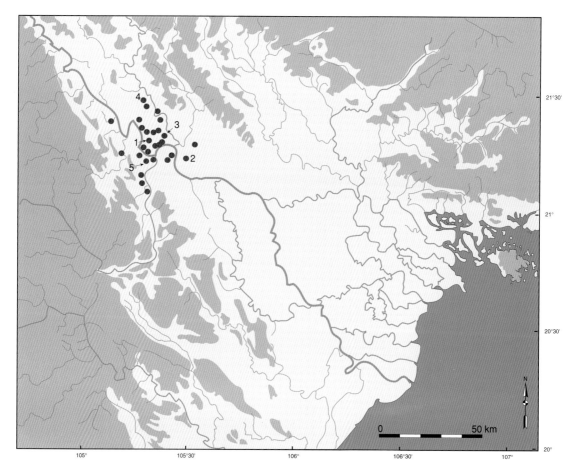

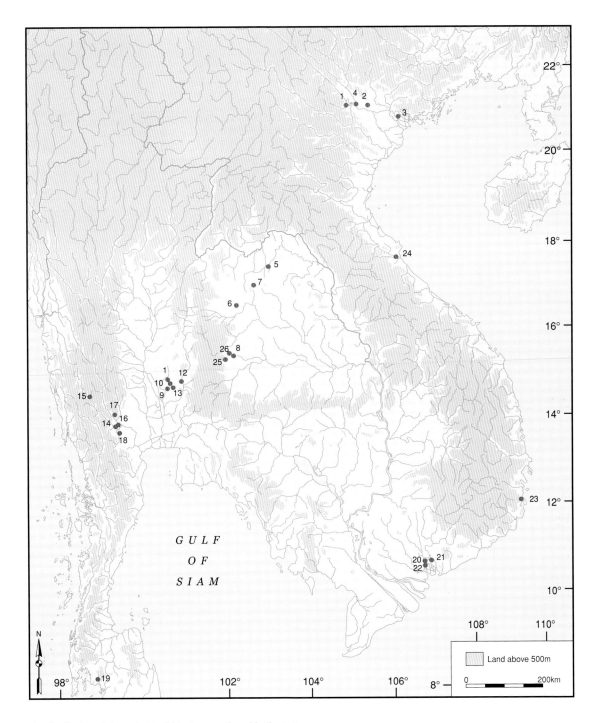

The distribution of the main Neolithic sites mentioned in the text.
1. Phung Nguyen, 2. Co Loa, 3. Trang Kenh, 4. Lung Hoa, 5. Ban Chiang,
6. Non Nok Tha, 7. Ban Phak Top, 8. Ban Lum Khao, 9. Ban Tha Kae,
10. Non Pa Wai, 11. Ban Phu Noi, 12. Khok Charoen, 13. Huai Yai,
14. Ban Kao, 15. Sai Yok, 16. Nong Chae Sao, 17. Han Songchram,
18. Rai Arnon, 19. Lang Rongrien, 20. Cu Lao Rua, 21. Cau Sat,
22. Ben Do, 23. Xom Con 24 Con Nen, 25. Ban Sanuan, 26. Ban Non Wat.

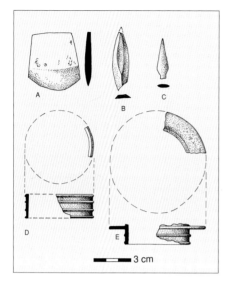

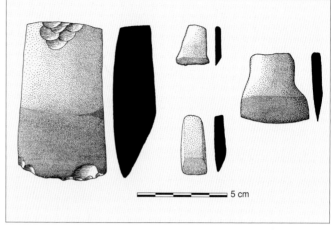

The stone adzes from Phung Nguyen were abundant and variable in size and form.

The material culture from Phung Nguyen includes many stone artefacts such as axes, bracelets and arrowheads. A. stone axe, B-C. stone projectile points, D-E. stone bracelets.

1999). Most settlements are found above the confluence of the Red and Black rivers. They cover between 1-3 ha, and are found on slightly elevated terrain near small stream confluences. The principal excavated site is at Phung Nguyen itself (Hoang Xuan Chinh and Nguyen Ngoc Bich 1978). It covers 3 ha, of which 3,960 square metres have been excavated. The stratigraphy, as in most Phung Nguyen sites, is shallow, barely exceeding 1 metre in depth. Excavations commenced in 1959, and were followed by two further campaigns.

All this activity provided a large sample of most interesting material culture. No trace of bronze was recovered, but there was a substantial sample of ceramic, bone and stone artefacts. Spindle whorls attest to a weaving industry, and bone harpoons suggest some form of hunting. The stone adzes take a variety of forms. Only four of the shouldered variety were found, compared with 777 examples of a quadrangular form, some of which were sharpened so consistently that they are broader than they are long. When one adds stone adze fragments for which the shape is indeterminate, 1,138 adzes or adze fragments were recovered. There are also 59 small stone chisels, some with cutting edges only 10 mm wide. Almost 200 whetstones were found. They bore grooves that result from sharpening the stone adzes and chisels. Stone projectile points were rarer. Three reach the dimensions of a spear point, the remainder are more likely to be tanged arrowheads.

The inhabitants of Phung Nguyen also fashioned stone rings mostly in nephrite. The total sample of 540 specimens has been sub-divided into eight types based on the shape of the cross-section. Most are rectangular, but some are much more complex, having a range of ribs and flanges. While some are large enough to rank as adult bracelets, others have small diameters and were either designed for children or perhaps for display as earrings. Stone beads were also made, most being tubular and measuring up to 1.3 cm in length.

There was also a vigorous tradition of working clay. There are pellet-bow pellets and clay net-weights, but most attention was accorded the manufacture of clay vessels. It is on the basis of changing decorative styles, that the Vietnamese archaeologists have designated phases to this culture. The earliest, called after the site of Go Bong, is characterised by incised parallel bands infilled with rows of impressions imparted with a pointed implement. The favoured motif is in the shape of an 'S' meander. The second sub-phase incorporates a range of designs based according to Ha Van Tan (1980) on 'geometric asymmetry'. Incised bands infilled with dentate impressions alternate with bands left blank, to form a series of most attractive design fields. This form of decoration has clear parallels with the Yunnan Neolithic sites of Baiyancun and Dadunzi.

The late Phung Nguyen style of pottery is found at the site of Trang Kenh, near Haiphong. Nguyen Kim Dung's excavations there have revealed a sophisticated workshop for the manufacture of nephrite bracelets and beads, involving working chisels, drill points, saws and grinding stones (Nguyen Kim Dung 1990, 1998). The radiocarbon dates suggest that the workshop dates to about 1650-1500 BC, but the introduction of craft skills in working nephrite and jadeite ornaments represents a key link with the Chinese Neolithic. The bangles from Phung Nguyen are the product of highly-skilled lapidaries. The value attached to stone jewellery and weaponry is also in evidence at Lung Hoa, a second late Phung Nguyen site characterised by deep graves, some cut over 5 metres into the ground and equipped, as in the Lingnan Fubin culture, with ledges (Hoang Xuan Chinh 1968). Two graves include stone bracelets, beads and earrings as well as ceramic vessels as mortuary offerings. One *ge* halberd is particularly interesting, because it matches those found in southern China and north into the early urban states at Sanxingdui and Erlitou. The *yazhang* jade blade is also a central feature of the latter two assemblages, and specimens have been recovered from Phung Nguyen and Xom Ren. Even at this late stage in the expansion and establishment of Neolithic communities in Southeast Asia, contact was maintained with the increasingly complex societies of the Yangzi and Huanghe rivers (Ha Van Tan 1993).

Archaeological fieldwork in the uplands north of the Red River has resulted in an appreciation that Neolithic sites were not confined to the relatively open terrain above Viet Tri. The Lo River, for example, attracted intrusive settlements characterised by a range of stone adze forms, stone bangles and a ceramic industry. These sites, known collectively as the Ha Giang culture, might well have been sources for the high quality stone found in such profusion at the many Phung Nguyen settlements (Bui Vinh 1995). Further south, recent excavations at the coastal late Neolithic site of Con Nen have

0   5 cm

The pottery vessels from Phung Nguyen sites incorporate a wide range of incised designs of considerable complexity.

yielded tubular stone beads, stone bangles and adze heads, decorated potsherds and tubular ceramic feet for pottery vessels. The settlement of Central Viet Nam during the late Neolithic period is a major area of future research.

The Mekong Valley

The Mekong River provides a direct link between the headwaters of the Yangzi River and the extensive lowlands of the Khorat Plateau and Cambodian plains. Neolithic remains were discovered in the 19th century at Samrong Sen. After its passage through the dissected uplands of Laos, the plains stretch invitingly to the south, access being provided by a network of tributaries. A site survey along these river courses in 1990-1 revealed many small settlement mounds which provided samples of the same black, pattern-incised pottery as was found at Baiyancun and in the Phung Nguyen sites. The absence of a major

Artefacts from the excavation of Con Nen by the German Archaeological Institute and University of Hue. 1-9 stone beads, 10 stone bangle, 11-13 stone adze heads, 14 stone, with drill holes. 15-21 pottery sherds, 22 tubular ceramic foot. (Courtesy Dr. Andreas Reinecke)

excavation at any one of these sites, and the rarity of radiocarbon determinations from secure contexts, remains a major lacuna in our knowledge of this vital Neolithic period, one made all the more pressing by the ravages inflicted by looters.

The transition to agriculture in this region may be considered through this archaeological record, as well as the study of cores taken from natural swamp or lake deposits. The latter incorporate pollen and other plant remains that provide a picture of changing vegetation patterns in the past. These can be dated through the radiocarbon method, and thus calibrated with information gained through excavation of prehistoric sites. Lake Kumphawapi is an extensive, shallow lake in Udorn Thani Province chosen as the focus for an intensive site survey in 1980-1. The objective of this exercise, was to locate as many sites as possible in a study area specifically chosen to incorporate all the landforms typical of the plateau as a whole. These range from the lacustrine soil on the margins of the lake and so through the ascending elevations to the low, middle and high terraces. By studying aerial photographs, extensive walking, inspecting natural and artificial exposures of the soil and talking to villagers, many prehistoric sites were identified and three, excavated. Several of these sites provided the same black incised and impressed pottery characteristic of Baiyancun and Phung Nguyen (Wichakana 1984).

The lake sediments have subsequently been cored and studied for their changing pollen and phytolith frequencies (Penny et al. 1996, Kealhofer 1996, 1997). The study of pollen is handicapped by the difficulty of distinguishing between that of rice and other grasses.

However, increasingly wet conditions were noted from about 4500-3700 BC, and marked changes compatible with increasing rice cultivation over the last 2,000 years. The phytolith core covered the period from 12,000-4500 BC. Kealhofer noted evidence for burning from the late Pleistocene through to the end of the sequence, some if not all of which might be the result of hunter-gatherer activity. Burning facilitates hunting by freshening grass growth, and also makes it easier to collect yams and other plants when the covering vegetation is cleared. No compelling evidence was encountered for the establishment of agricultural communities up to 4500 BC, when the records for phytoliths

ceased. White (1997), however, has described a peak in carbon fragments and reduction in tree pollen in one of these cores, dated to the fifth millennium BC. She then stressed that, if this change signals "the base of the Ban Chiang cultural tradition", then it would place the establishment of intrusive agricultural communities two millennia earlier than I have suggested as being consistent with the archaeological evidence.

These pots from Samrong Sen in Cambodia are very similar to those excavated from the Khorat Plateau Neolithic sites. Hitherto unpublished, these vessels are in the collections of the Lyon museum in France, and were recovered from Samrong Sen during the 19th century.

Such episodes of burning and a reduction in forest cover are not unusual in Southeast Asian pollen spectra. At least three were present in the vicinity of Khok Phanom Di. Maloney (1991) sensibly noted several possible causes. Natural conflagrations are not uncommon in this area at the end of the long dry season. Hunter-gatherers employ fire to modify their environment. Until settlements dating to the fifth millennium are identified, the chronology of initial Neolithic settlement is best discussed on the basis of available data.

Four sites provide some insight into the chronology of early Neolithic settlement. Ban Chiang has been the subject of much controversy over claims for very early settlement, and the inception of bronze and iron working (Gorman and Charoenwongsa 1976). This site has been excavated on several occasions, the 1974-5 seasons being best known because they provided the data for the present chronology. Initial attempts to obtain an internally-consistent dating framework foundered due to contradictions and problems over the provenance of the charcoal being dated. The new AMS dating technique now enables minute fragments of rice chaff from burial pots to be dated, and the first results have greatly clarified a difficult situation. There are two determinations from early Neolithic burial ceramics. One has provided a date of 2190-1880 BC, the other is 2050-1500 BC. These are not the earliest burials in the site, but the style of the pottery vessels is closely similar those from the initial mortuary phase, making it unlikely that initial settlement is earlier than about 2300 BC. Only a very small proportion of the site has been excavated, and earlier burials might well be present, but on current evidence, these dates may be cited as the best provenanced and earliest contexts for the Neolithic of the Khorat Plateau. One of

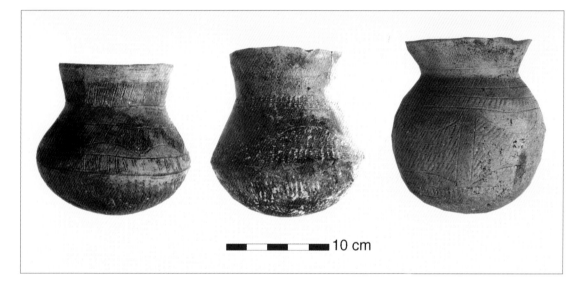

10 cm

These complete late Neolithic vessels were recovered at Ban Sanuan, in the upper Mun Valley, Northeast Thailand. They bear typically Neolithic incised designs.

Top and top right: Burial 44 at Ban Chiang 1974 contained Neolithic black, incised pottery vessels as grave offerings.

the comforting aspects of this pair, is their conformity with the slightly earlier determinations from Lingnan and Yunnan.

Non Nok Tha is if anything, even more difficult to interpret. It also underpinned claims for bronze technology in the fourth millennium BC (Solheim 1968). Excavated by Bayard in 1966 and 1968, it was found to be a cemetery with a cultural stratigraphy barely a metre deep. Bayard himself has stressed the internal inconsistencies and different chronological frameworks which could be compatible with the initial radiocarbon determinations (Bayard 1971, 1972, 1972a). Again, however, the AMS technique has been employed. The earliest phase is known as Early Period 1, and there are two determinations. One is 2307-1858 BC, the other is 1770-1310 BC. Either the initial settlement took place at about the same time as at Ban Chiang, or the site was first occupied in the middle centuries of the second millennium BC.

Ban Phak Top is located about 25 km southwest of Ban Chiang. Had the site not been completely destroyed by looting, it would have ranked as one of the most important of this period in Southeast Asia. The pottery vessels for sale there in 1974 were spectacular examples of the black incised style so characteristic of the Neolithic period.

These pots came from the small Neolithic site of Non Kao Noi in Northeast, Thailand.

Above left: The small excavation at Non Kao Noi revealed Neolithic burials with pottery vessels and green stone ornaments.

Left: The site of Ban Phak Top yielded many superb incised pottery vessels, but all complete examples came from looters.

Schauffler (1976) excavated a small square and submitted a radiocarbon sample interpreted as pre-dating the first occupation there. The resulting date is about 2500 BC. The lowest cultural level has a date of 2000 BC, and level 8 has three dates of between 1000-1500 BC. Excavations at Ban Lum Khao in 1995-6 encountered a Bronze Age cemetery, stratified over an initial occupation phase that yielded the familiar black incised and impressed pottery style. This site lies in the upper Mun Valley, and the five determinations for this first occupation phase suggest initial settlement by about 1500 BC. A few miles upstream, a small mound known as Ban Sanuan was found in 1999 to contain burials and pottery vessels of undoubted Neolithic affinities. Sadly, it was removed by a bulldozer before proper investigations could proceed.

There appears to be a consistent pattern to these radiocarbon determinations. On present evidence, the Neolithic period on the Khorat Plateau lasted for about a eight centuries, from 2300-1500 BC. This might well change with the course of future research, for it is stressed that earlier sites might now lie entombed under later, redeposited sediments.

Unfortunately, we know very little of the Neolithic settlement of the Khorat Plateau beyond its probable date, and the fact that early settlers introduced the inhumation burial rite, in which the dead were interred with mortuary offerings: pottery vessels, animal bones and personal ornaments. At Non Kao Noi for example, excavations in 1980 revealed a group of inhumation burials, one of which was

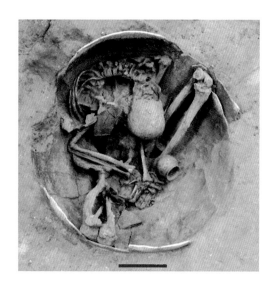

Burial 28 at Ban Non Wat. An adult was placed in a huge lidded pot, accompanied by a small cup and a bivalve shellfish. The pot was richly ornamented with incised and painted designs. (Scale 20 cm)

accompanied by three incised pottery vessels, while another included beads of an exotic green stone. No radiocarbon dates are available due to the lack of datable material (Higham and Kijngam 1984).

About ten Neolithic graves were found at the base of the 1974 excavation at nearby Ban Chiang but the absence of a final report means that we know little of this period.

The 1974 excavation uncovered 20 burials within part of a Neolithic cemetery, all but one coming from the second mortuary phase. Douglas (1996) has identified eight as adult females, four adult males and a further adult of unknown sex. Seven infants or children were also found, of which three died when aged less than three years and the balance, between the ages of three and ten years. Four women had an average height of 1.55m, while two men stood, on average, 1.65 metres tall.

Further insight into subsistence and the environment is provided by the excavation of Ban Lum Khao. The earliest occupation has been dated to about 1500 BC. It comprises a thin layer and several pits, but no burials. The contents of each pit were subjected to flotation to recover all the organic remains, and a very large sample of bones was recovered. The mammalian remains include bones from the water buffalo so large as to fall well within the range for wild rather than domestic animals. One pit contained the bones from 11 Eld's deer, as well as an adult sambar deer and a muntjak. There were also bones from the pig and domestic dog. A second pit also included the bones of three water buffalo and deer, but also over 100 carapace fragments from turtles. Fish were remarkably abundant. One pit contained 348 individuals, another 283 and a third, 130. *Anabas testudineus*, the doctor fish, was the most abundant. It occupies rivers, streams and marshes and remains a favoured food fish in this area today. *Ophicephalus striatus* is also abundant. This fish survives the dry season by sinking into soft mud in dried out streams or lake beds, and can grow up to a metre in length. Indeed, the size of the fish from basal Ban Lum Khao far exceeds those seen in the area today. Taken in conjunction with the large hunted water buffalo and deer, it seems probable that the first occupants of Ban Lum Khao, and probably the other Neolithic sites from the upper Mun Valley, entered a pristine environment not previously exploited by human groups.

Burial 16 at Ban Non Wat was accompanied by beautifully decorated pottery vessels. (Scale 10 cm)

The excavation of Ban Non Wat in 2002 encountered a second Neolithic settlement and cemetery, in which the dead were interred with outstanding pottery vessels. The largest of these, with a diameter of about 80 centimetres, contained the seated skeleton of an adult, associated with a small cup and a bivalve shell. Removal of the lid revealed that the shoulder of this pot had been decorated with fine incised designs highlighted with burnished and red-painted bands. No similar burial has been found in Southeast Asia. There were also three graves laid out on a north to south axis, each containing fine vessels ornamented with incised designs again highlighted with red paint or impressions. The radiocarbon dates for these burials may well lie in the first half of the second millennium BC.

The Chao Phraya Plains

Just north of Lopburi, the monotony of the flat flood plain of the Chao Phraya River is relieved by hilly outcrops which include veins of copper ore. This area has attracted intensive research over the past twenty years, including a site survey in which Mudar (1995) identified a series of sites which, on the basis of surface finds, are probably Neolithic. Kealhofer (1997) has examined the Holocene vegetation history of this key area on the basis of two cores, one taken from an old river channel adjacent to the prehistoric site of Ban Tha Kae, and the second from an old flood plain meander 15 km to the north. Riverine cores are more representative of the drainage basin as a whole than those taken from lake sediments, due to the likelihood of redeposition. The samples date from the late 7th millennium, and apart from a hiatus in the old river channel sequence from 4000-3000 BC, continue into the late prehistoric period. Rice phytoliths and carbon were found from the beginning of the river channel sequence, and from about 3700 BC in the Tha Kae spectrum. There are, however, insufficient rice phytoliths to distinguish wild from domestic specimens. Both sequences reveal a sharp increase in carbon at about 2500 BC, and at Tha Kae, evidence for agriculture is particularly evident from about 2000 BC. These results indicate human modification of the environment virtually from the start of the sequences, with major changes consistent with agriculture in the period 2500-2000 BC. There is also, however, the possibility of some form of agricultural activity by about 3700 BC.

Archaeological excavations in this area have so far failed to identify any occupation prior to 2500-2000 BC. At Non Pa Wai, Pigott *et al.* (1997) have uncovered a 75 cm-deep occupation layer rich in the remains of pottery sherds, stone adzes and marine shell jewellery. The pottery was decorated with the incised and impressed designs, but there was also a new and localised style in which the pots were formed within baskets which leave an unmistakable surface texture christened 'elephant hide' ware. Sixteen Neolithic burials were also found, grave goods including pottery vessels, stone adzes and marine shell jewellery. To judge from the faunal remains recovered in this early context, the site lay within a low-lying and swampy habitat.

A Neolithic cemetery was found under and to the north of the main mound at Non Pa Wai.

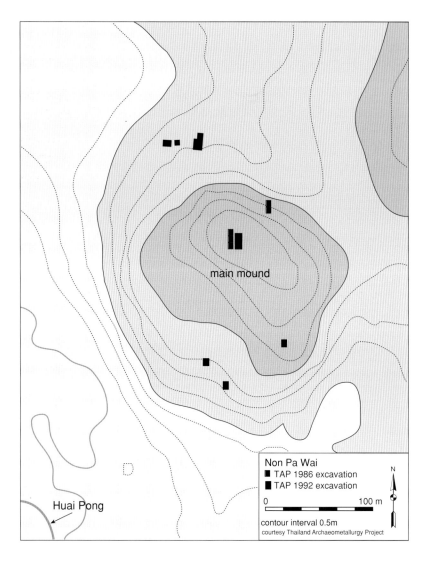

Non Pa Wai
■ TAP 1986 excavation
■ TAP 1992 excavation
0   100 m
contour interval 0.5m
courtesy Thailand Archaeometallurgy Project

main mound

Huai Pong

N

In his study of these human remains, Agelarakis (1997) has identified the remains of five women, three men, four children aged between three and seven years, and a newly born infant. Only one individual, a man, survived into his 30s and there was relatively high mortality among those still in their teens. Health was not good. Eight out of ten displaying appropriate evidence suffered childhood stress. However, the dental wear revealed a diet of well-prepared food compatible with an agricultural community.

Ban Tha Kae is located a few kilometres north of Lopburi, and to judge from aerial photographs, must once have been a large, late prehistoric moated settlement of great regional significance. Sadly it has been quarried for road fill and savaged by looters, and only a tiny part survived for scientific enquiry. The initial occupation matches in many respects, that of early Non Pa Wai. There are burials with red slipped and black incised and impressed pottery styles, along with shell beads, bivalve shells, bangles and earrings. Siripanish (1985) has described the motifs and forms of several pottery vessels recovered

Tha Kae, Section D, Burial 2. A red-ware high-pedestalled bowl with scale pattern impressed decoration in the form of meandering motifs. (Courtesy Dr. Roberto Ciarla and Dr. Fiorella Rispoli)

Left: Excavating a Neolithic burial at Non Pa Wai, at the surface of the outlier site. (Courtesy Dr. Vincent Pigott)

Below: Two mortuary vessels from Neolithic graves at Non Pa Wai. Left, a red ware tall necked jar with a small pedestal and meandering motifs on the shoulder. Right, a red ware tall necked jar with 'elephant-hide' impressions. Both date to about 1800-1600 BC. (Courtesy Dr. Roberto Ciarla and Dr. Fiorella Rispoli)

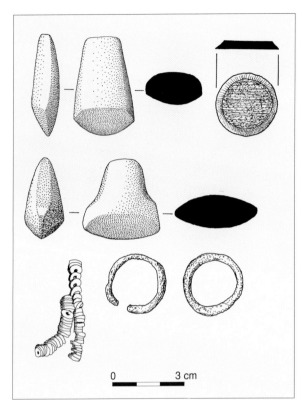

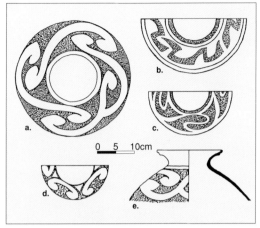

The pottery vessels from Ban Tha Kae show a wide variety of design motifs. Some look remarkably similar to examples from late Khok Phanom Di.

Ban Tha Kae was occupied from the Neolithic to the Iron Age. Its material culture includes stone adzes, shell beads and, top right, the central core resulting from the manufacture of a shell bangle.

Right: Ban Tha Kae, Section D, Burial 2. Neolithic – *ca*. 1800-1600 BC. (Courtesy Dr. Roberto Ciarla and Dr. Fiorella Rispoli)

from earlier excavations at this site, and these include incised and impressed decoration in the form of snakes and possibly stylised humans, the latter being paralleled in late graves at Khok Phanom Di. The local manufacture of marine shell bangles also provides evidence for exchange contact with coastal groups (Ciarla 1992).

Rispoli (1997) has undertaken a regional study of the decoration to be found on pottery vessels from these early Neolithic sites and has identified four main categories. The first is now familiar, the black burnished ware with incised and impressed designs. The potters also applied a thick red slip to the rims and necks of some vessels, or applied red painted designs. Elephant hide ware was also recognized, but it has a very limited distribution. The recovery of such ceramics during site surveys suggests a dense distribution of sites in the eastern margins of the Bangkok Plain north of Lopburi, particularly where springs emerge from the surrounding foothills. Thus Neolithic burials, associated with impressive mortuary vessels and stone and shell jewellery, have been revealed at the site of Non Mak La. Excavations there in 1994 by Vincent Pigott and Andrew Weiss encountered an unusual pottery vessel in the form of a cow, and two burials in a cruciform pattern. Infants were often interred in ceramic vessels.

Above and above left: The Neolithic burials at Non Mak La included marine shell ornaments.

Left: Two Neolithic burials from Non Mak La, one being laid over an earlier interment, but at a different orientation. (Courtesy Dr. Vincent Pigott)

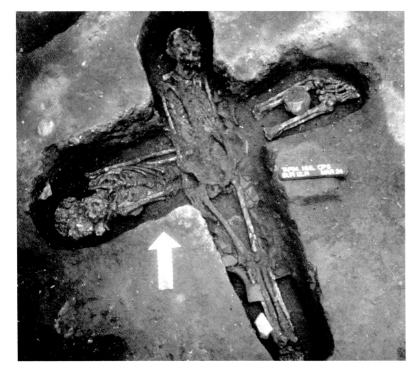

Definition of the main styles of Neolithic pottery in this area on the basis of these excavations have made it possible for Mudar (1995) to ascribe broad-band dates to a series of sites identified during her survey of the Lam Maleng Valley. This valley drains into the Lopburi River, and is located just to the north of Non Pa Wai. There are two major soil types, a lower grumosol which today yields a single crop of rice per annum, and an upper or high terrace soil not suited to rice, but sufficiently fertile for maize and beans. Mudar identified 20 sites with Neolithic pottery styles, all but three of which were located on the high terrace. The lower tract in the valley bottom attracted only three sites. Mudar has suggested that the earliest agriculturalists in the valley avoided the lower terrace, with its good soils for inundation rice cultivation in favour of dry land crops such as non-inundation rice, millet or root crops. This hypothesis needs to be tested through excavation.

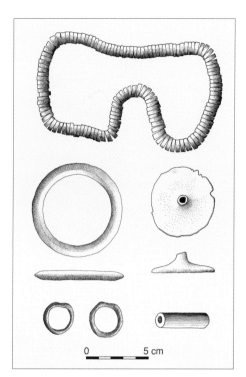

Examples of shell artefacts from Khok Charoen. There must have been considerable exchange with coastal communities, such as Khok Phanom Di.

Khok Charoen

Khok Charoen is located at the junction of two small streams, on an ecotone between the Phetchabun Range and the Pa Sak flood plain. Trial soundings in 1966 revealed five inhumation burials accompanied by pottery vessels and polished stone adzes, so the following year, William Watson and Helmut Loofs-Wissowa commenced a major excavation programme. Ultimately, almost 400 square metres were excavated and 44 burials uncovered. Natural soil was encountered at a depth of just over a metre. The burials follow a widespread pattern of being extended inhumations with an array of grave goods. Ho (1984) has concluded that there is a considerable differential in wealth between graves, the richest being accompanied by 19 pottery vessels, stone beads, 10 shell and nine stone bracelets and many small shell disc beads. Other burials were less well endowed, though shell disc beads were found in the pelvic areas of some skeletons and small, trapezoid polished stone adzes were common. Pottery vessels include examples with incised and impressed decoration recalling those from Tha Kae, Ban Chiang and Non Pa Wai. Others were cord marked and red slipped. Much of the shell used to make ornaments has a marine origin, trochus being used for bracelets, ear ornaments and possibly finger rings, and conus for small rings which Ho feels could have been worn on the fingers. No radiocarbon dates are available. Some of the shell jewellery recalls the forms recovered at Khok Phanom Di, a situation similar to that of the site of Huai Yai, in which H-shaped shell beads virtually identical with those found first in Khok Phanom Di during mortuary phase 6.

Excavations commence at Khok Charoen in 1966, under the direction of William Watson and Helmut Loofs-Wissowa. The site was discovered when a charcoal pit seen in the left foreground revealed human bones.

William Watson in white shirt shows visiting scouts the excavation of Khok Charoen in 1966. (Courtesy Dr. Helmut Loofs-Wissowa)

Right :
The restored collapsed, four-legged vessel from burial 9 during the 1968 season at Khok Charoen. (Courtesy Dr. Helmut Loofs-Wissowa)

The pottery vessels from the graves of Khok Charoen are variable in form. They include footed bowls, shallow bowls, cord-marked globular vessels and a large, cylindrical pot bearing incised decoration quite similar to that from later contexts at Khok Phanom Di.

Above left: Many of the Neolithic burials at Khok Charoen were fragmentary, and associated with broken pottery vessels.

Burial 24 at Khok Charoen, with pottery vessels and many stone bracelets.

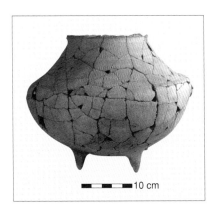

The excavation of a burial from Khok Charoen with multiple shell bracelets. (Courtesy Dr. Helmut Loofs-Wissowa)

The site of Khok Charoen lies in the centre of the picture, with the Petchabun Range in the background.

Helmut Loofs-Wissowa recording a burial at Khok Charoen.

Burials 24 and 38 at Khok Charoen.

A cord-marked globular vessel with a limestone adze in a burial from Khok Charoen.

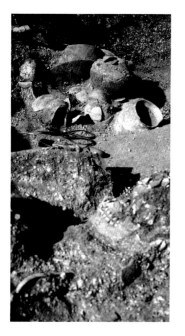

Left: A burial with many pottery vessels as grave goods from Khok Charoen.

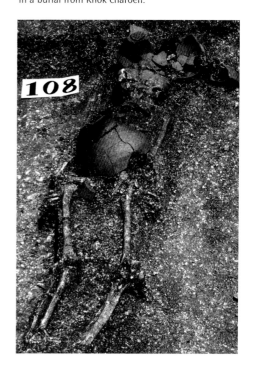

Right: Burial 4 at Khok Charoen was associated with several pottery vessels.

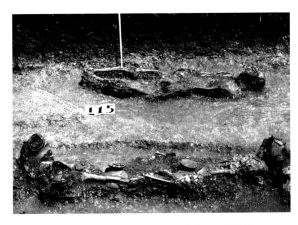

Burials 6, in the foreground, and 2 at Khok Charoen in the 1968 season.

Ham Parker at Khok Charoen. He also worked at Non Nok Tha and Non Nong Chik.

General view of the 1968 excavation at Khok Charoen.

A collapsed, four-legged vessel in burial 9, Khok Charoen.

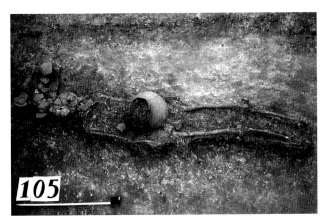

A burial associated with several pottery vessels at Khok Charoen.

A very rich burial at Khok Charoen, with a row of pottery vessels by the head. (Courtesy Dr. Helmut Loofs-Wissowa)

A Buddhist ceremony to bring peace to the spirits of the dead at Khok Charoen.

A section at Khok Charoen, emphasising the shallow nature of the deposits.

An aerial view of Khok Charoen during the 1970 season of excavations.

A Neolithic burial at Khok Charoen with a complete pottery vessel as a mortuary offering.

At the end of the excavation of Khok Charoen in 1970. (Courtesy Dr. Helmut Loofs-Wissowa)

The excavation of Ban Kao in 1961-2 was a pioneer programme which uncovered one of the largest exposures of a Neolithic site in Southeast Asia.

Ban Kao

The Bang site near the village of Ban Kao was the first Neolithic site to be examined in detail in this area. It lies in Kanchanaburi Province, near two tributaries that flow into the Khwae Noi River. It is not large, covering only 8,000 square metres, of which 400 were excavated in 1961-2 (Sørensen and Hatting 1967). A total of 42 inhumation graves were opened. Sørensen divided them into two groups, early and late Neolithic, on the basis of their depth below the surface, and the form of the pottery vessels found as mortuary offerings. However, one grave is intermediate between the two, and suggests a continuous use of the cemetery. The radiocarbon determinations suggest that this period falls between 2300 and 1500 BC. There is some evidence for patterning in the burials. Where it is possible to determine the sex of a skeleton, it seems that men and women were interred in pairs, women being found orientated with the head to the northwest, and men in the opposite direction. Only one infant interment was found, which surely means that either young and fragile bones did not survive, or that they were buried elsewhere. Early phase bodies were buried with pottery vessels and stone adzes, while the later burials incorporated richer sets of grave goods, including more pottery vessels, adzes, shell disc beads, the bones of young pigs, freshwater bivalve shells and stone beads.

Burial 11 from Ban Kao. Notice the necklace of shell beads and the bivalve shell to the right of the skull. This woman, who died when aged about 30 years, belongs to the Late Neolithic phase at Ban Kao. (Courtesy Dr. Per Sørensen)

Burial 2, an Early Neolithic grave from Ban Kao contained a woman aged about 35-40 years at death. She was interred with four pottery vessels and four stone adzes, one of which can be seen on the chest.

Right: Burials 6, in the foreground, and 7 from the Late Neolithic phase at Ban Kao. The former is a female aged about 45 years at death, the latter is a male aged under 30 years. Note the many pottery vessels associated as grave offerings.

The shell necklace from burial 11 at Ban Kao. The large beads are of nephrite or jade, and the larger has a length of 5.1 cm.

These unfinished stone bangles indicate manufacturing activity at Ban Kao. (Courtesy Dr. Per Sørensen)

Sørensen (pers. comm.) has pointed out the close similarity between the shell beads of burial 11 and those from Khok Phanom Di.

The importance of this site goes well beyond the number of the graves, and the quality of complete mortuary assemblages. Sørensen brought meticulous excavation procedures to the excavation of the Bang site, and the occupation remains allow insight into the daily activities of the inhabitants (Sørensen 1972). Stone bangles were manufactured there, and the bone fishhooks and clay netweights reflect the role of fish in the diet. There are shell knives and stone sickles, probably used to harvest rice. Spindle whorls evidence a textile industry and the whetstones were probably used to sharpen stone adzes.

The Bang site produced a wide range of pottery forms, the most distinctive being a carinated bowl raised on tripod feet. Similar forms have been found over a very wide area from Kanchanaburi south to peninsular Malaysia. Sørensen has noted their presence at Sai Yok, and at the site of Nong Chae Sao, where two burials were found under what may well be the remains of a domestic building. Shoocondej (1996) has described this pottery assemblage at Han Songchram and Rai Arnon, while far to the south, parallels have been

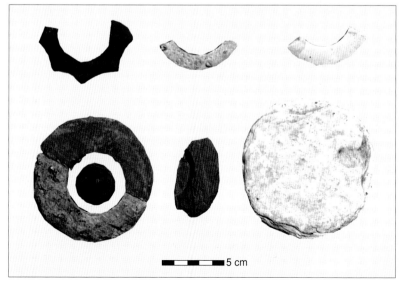

5 cm

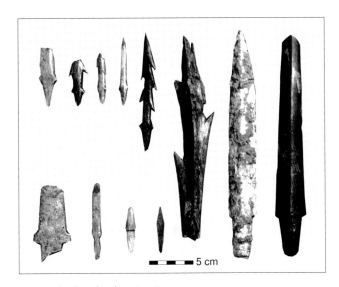

Bone projectile points from Ban Kao.

Bone was widely used at Ban Kao for a variety of implements, including points and fish hooks.

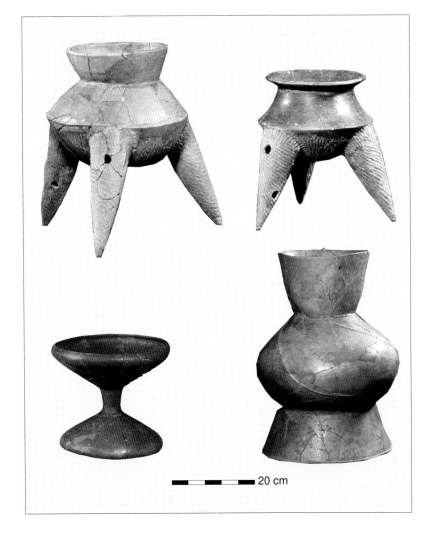

Top two, bowls raised on tripod feet are a hallmark of the Early Neolithic at Ban Kao.
Below left, an Early Neolithic type 3 goblet from Ban Kao.
Below right, a type 8 vessel from the Early Neolithic phase at Ban Kao, burial 13. (Courtesy Dr. Per Sørensen)

Stone adzes were regular mortuary offerings at Ban Kao.

found at upper layers of the Lang Rongrien rock shelter and at Jenderam Hilir on the western coastal plain of Malaysia. Leong (1991) has suggested that the latter site, dated from the later third millennium, represents the intrusion of agriculturalists.

The Lower Mekong and its Hinterland

Although the excavation of prehistoric sites in the Lower Mekong area has a history of over a century, only recently has the cultural sequence of the area assumed a structure of its own. In 1963, Malleret could only describe the known prehistoric settlements in the most general terms. Cu Lao Rua, better known is the Isle de la Tortue, was the best documented, having been described as early as 1888 by Cartaillhac. Excavations ensued in 1902 and 1937, and a local businessman assembled a collection of artefacts from the site. These included shouldered and quadrangular adzes, much pottery and stone bracelets, pendants and polishers.

Pham Duc Manh (2000) has advanced a four-fold division of later prehistory in the Dong Nai valley of which the first belongs to the Neolithic period. This he dates within the period 2500-2000 BC. The sequence begins with the site of Cau Sat, which is characterised by shouldered adzes and stone arm rings with a rectangular or trapezoid cross-section. The pottery from this site includes pedestalled bowls and tall jars with a flat base (Hoang Xuan Chinh and Nguyen Khac Su 1977). The second phase incorporates sites described by Fontaine (1972), of which Ben Do is best known. Pham Van Kinh (1977) has described the many large-shouldered adzes from this site. The shouldered form is much more abundant than adzes with a quadrangular cross-section and no shoulder.

There is further possible evidence for Neolithic settlement up the coast of southern and Central Vietnam. The Xom Con site, for example, has yielded round-based and pedestalled pottery decorated with incised and infilled designs, in addition to polished stone adzes and barbed bone points. Inland, there are sites of similar age and parallel material culture designated the Bien Ho culture (Nguyen Khac Su 1995).

The Neolithic: Summary

The past 15 years have seen a transformation in our understanding of the Neolithic in Southeast Asia. There is now a convincing sequence of cultural change leading from late Pleistocene hunters and gatherers directly into early rice farmers in the middle Yangzi lake land. This is tied in with environmental changes, which permit a reasonable, testable model for agricultural origins. The second advance has involved the study of language. Today, languages within the two major branches of the Austroasiatic family are distributed from eastern India to Viet Nam, and south to the Nicobar Islands (Diffloth 1994). There are strong grounds for suspecting that the inhabitants of much of Lingnan also formerly spoke Austroasiatic languages (Norman and Mei 1976). The distribution of these languages is patchy: in many parts of Southeast Asia, we find Thai, Burmese or Austronesian languages which in all probability, represent recent intrusions into what was once a more contiguous bloc. Reid (1994) has recently identified structural parallels between the Nicobarese sub-group of Austroasiatic, and Austronesian languages. This, he has written, suggests a common origin. Now, Austronesian languages are spoken from Easter Island to Malagasy, and from New Zealand to Taiwan. They represent a major expansion of peoples, in the main by maritime routes. The oldest Austronesian languages are to be found on the island of Taiwan.

The search for a common homeland from which both language families emerged thus has a centre of gravity in, or more probably beyond, Taiwan. The new archaeological evidence can now contribute to this issue, by specifying the origin of rice agriculture, and providing a logical platform for the expansion of human groups sharing a common ancestry. It is thus possible to trace the progressive establishment of farming groups south from Taiwan and ultimately, into the islands of Southeast Asia and the greater Pacific. These people spoke early Austronesian languages. It is proposed that on the mainland, there was a like expansion by those whose languages developed into the present members of the Austroasiatic family. Thus, we can pinpoint agricultural village communities expanding downstream to Hemudu, and southward to Shixia. In Yunnan, we find Baiyancun and down the Red, Mekong and Chao Phraya rivers, there are the settlements of Phung Nguyen, Ban Phak Top and Non Pa Wai. In this context, it is important to note that there are cognate

Burial 6, a close up of the Late Neolithic female cranium, showing two adzes and freshwater bivalve shells. (Courtesy Dr. Per Sørensen)

words to describe rice and aspects of its cultivation from Munda languages, west to Vietnamese.

This model can be tested. One new and potentially important avenue lies in the study of ancient DNA. Support would be forthcoming if, for example, it could be shown that the early settlers of Non Pa Wai, or Ban Kao, shared similar genetic sequences to the prehistoric inhabitants of the Yangzi Valley. The dog in Southeast Asia is first found in archaeological contexts at about the same time as the first agricultural settlements. A study of the cranial structure of early dogs has shown a clear relationship with the wolf (Higham *et al*. 1980). There are no native wolves in Southeast Asia, and the domestic dog is thus most likely to have been introduced. DNA studies might or might not link early prehistoric dogs with the Chinese wolf. There are burning episodes and rice phytoliths in Southeast Asian lake and river cores which have been dated well before the third millennium. White (1997) has suggested that those from Lake Kumphawapi reflect local agriculture two millennia prior to its first archaeological presence in the area. This possibility, if it is ever validated archaeologically, would not run counter to the proposed model, but would provide for an earlier intrusion than is currently documented.

The emerging pattern, rooted in firm archaeological evidence, reveals a pan Southeast Asian settlement by farming communities. We can now recognise shared decorative styles on the surface of pottery vessels from Central Thailand, to Yunnan and Bac Bo. The available chronological evidence, and we need much more, places this move within the period 2500-2000. The pottery from Ban Kao to peninsular Malaysia, however, contrasts in terms of style and form with this grouping, although there was clearly some contact, and the basic economy and mortuary traditions are similar. Sørensen (1972) proposed an expansionary movement from China to account for the fully formed establishment of Neolithic groups in the Ban Kao area. He further identified the Salween River valley as a possible expansionary route. It is not impossible that there were related movements as part of the same phenomenon.

This model is not one that can expect general acceptance or approval. It resembles the early views of Heine-Geldern (1932), in accounting for the settlement of Southeast Asia by different groups defined on the basis of language and material culture. Naturally, languages can change, and styles of material culture evolve for reasons other than migration. This is one reason why the above model is advanced for critical review and testing with further research. At present, it harmonises better with the available evidence than any other, and lies comfortably with a similar and related model advanced by Renfrew (1987) to account for the present distribution of Indo-European languages. It is certainly more convincing than the situation fifteen years ago, when we were still seeking, without success or any useful leads, a local transition to rice farming within Southeast Asia.

In reality, however, the situation between 2500-1500 BC was probably much more complex than the model might suggest at first site. Any intrusive group entering Southeast Asia would have

Late Neolithic pottery vessel from Ban Kao.
(Courtesy Dr. Per Sørensen)

encountered long-established hunters and gatherers. Those able to
live permanently in rich coastal habitats made pottery vessels, and
used polished stone adzes. They hunted marine mammals and went
out to sea to take large fish, and probably to exchange valuables,
such as marine shell jewellery. Two such hunter-gatherer sites on the
former shore of the Gulf of Siam date to the period when inland
agricultural villages were being established. When comparing the
material remains found at Khok Phanom Di and such inland sites as
Non Pa Wai, Ban Tha Kae and Khok Charoen, one is struck by
similarities. There are parallels in the motifs incised and impressed
onto pottery vessels, and virtually identical forms of shell ornaments.
There is no doubt that exchange relationships were forged between
both groups, and this might well have involved men or women
moving permanently from one to the other. At Khok Phanom Di, we
find that rice was consumed virtually from initial settlement despite
the most unresponsive environment for its local cultivation. During
the fourth mortuary phase, it was probably locally grown as
freshwater conditions prevailed. The succeeding phase saw
individuals accumulating unparalleled wealth, expressed as shell
jewellery and fine ceramics, as trading relations burgeoned.

It seems that some, at least, of the inland villages were small,
no more than 0.8 ha at Ban Kao, and smaller still at Non Kao Noi.
As might be expected, the settlers chose to live near well-watered
tributary streams, where wild and cultivated rice could flourish.
However we should not overestimate the importance of rice. There
are many wild plants, such as yams, which can contribute to the
diet, and the forests described by early European visitors teemed
with game. The rivers and lakes likewise supplied an abundance of
fish and shellfish. Food, to judge from the few human remains
found, was readily available. Yet the health and life expectancy of
people entering a hot, low-lying environment doubtless harbouring
malarial mosquitoes were low. Over time, trade links in high quality
stone for adzes and ornaments, and in marine shell for jewellery
developed and the Neolithic societies survived and expanded. At or
shortly after 1500 BC, these trade routes were conduits for
introducing the knowledge of copper smelting and alloying and thus,
establishment of the Southeast Asian Bronze Age.

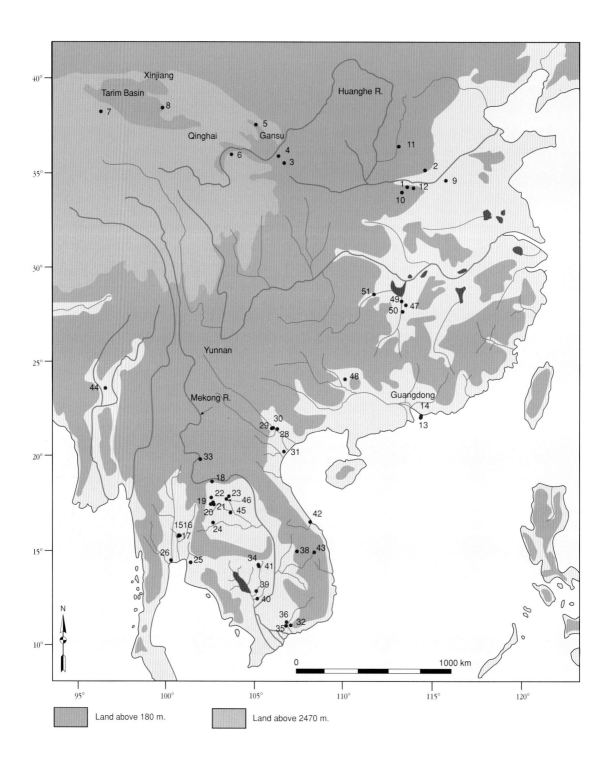

Chapter Four

The Bronze Age

An article published in 1968 claimed that bronze artefacts at the site of Non Nok Tha on the Khorat Plateau dated to the fourth millennium BC. Eight years later, claims for equally early dates were made on the basis of radiocarbon determinations from the site of Ban Chiang (Solheim 1968, Gorman and Charoenwongsa 1976). If validated, these would project Southeast Asia not only as one of the few locations for an indigenous development of metallurgy, but also as the earliest. These claims, however, have not been confirmed, and must be set aside. The AMS dating of rice chaff used as a ceramic temper in specimens from both sites has shown that the earliest bronzes were being cast within the period 1500-1000 BC.

It is necessary to adopt a broad stance when investigating the origins of this bronze-working tradition, a stance which will lead us north into China and then to the broad expanse of the Eurasian steppes. Given the splendour of the Chinese Bronze Age, seen in the output of the Shang Dynasty workshops at Zhengzhou and Anyang, it might seem strange that the earliest bronze castings in China come from the remote western provinces. Linduff (2000) has described sites of the Majiayao and Machang cultures in Gansu, Qinghai and Xinjiang which include cast and forged copper knives and other tools dated between 2740-1900 BC. This third millennium bronze industry in far western China was maintained in the Qijia culture. This comprises a series of agricultural villages dated between 2300-1800 BC, several of which have been excavated. At Qinweijia, for example, two burial areas were uncovered, the dead being accompanied by pottery vessels, needles, polished stone adze heads and pigs' mandibles (GATIA 1975). Some graves overlie storage pits, which contained a few objects in bronze and copper. An axe and a ring are of leaded bronze, a disc is of copper (Sun Shuyun and Han Rubin 1981). The industry appears fully fledged, for the axe was cast in a stone mould and hardened by annealing. Excavations at Dahezhuang have opened a substantial area of burials and house remains (GATIA 1974). The burials were on the same orientation as at Qinweijia, and contained similar bone implements, pottery vessels and pigs' jaws. One pot also contained millet, and millet was also found adhering to a copper knife found beside one of the houses. Copper-based knives, chisels, awls and rings have also been recovered (Chang 1986).

Opposite:
The distribution of the principal early Bronze Age sites in China and Southeast Asia:
1. Zhengzhou, 2. Anyang, 3. Qinweijia, 4. Dahezhuang, 5. Huangniangniangtai, 6. Gamatai, 7. Gumugou, 8. Huoshaogou, 9. Pingliangtai, 10. Wanchenggang, 11. Taosi, 12. Meishan, 13. Kwo Lo Wan, Shek Pik, 14. Tung Wan Tsai, 15. Non Pa Wai, 16. Non Mak La, 17. Nil Kham Haeng, 18. Phu Lon, 19. Non Pa Kluay, 20. Non Nong Chik, 21 Non Nok Tha, 22. Non Praw, 23. Ban Na Di, Ban Chiang, 24. Ban Lum Khao, 25. Nong Nor, 26. Khok Phlap, 27. Ob Luang, 28. Dong Dau, 29. Thanh Den, 30. Go Mun, 31. Hoa Loc, 32. Hang Gon, 33. Luang Prabang, 34. Mlu Prei, 35. Cu Lao Rua, 36. Doc Chua, 37. Bung Bac, 38. Pleiku, 39. Samrong Sen, 40. Long Prau, 41. O Yak, O Nari, O Pie Can, 42. Binh Chau, 43. Lung Leng, 44. Nyaunggan, 45. Ban Chiang Hian, 46. Ban Muang Phruk, 47. Changsha, 48. Yinshanling, 49. Yiyang, 50. Shaoshan, 51. Baihewan.

Huangniangniangtai has provided 32 copper-based items, including knives, awls, chisels, and a possible hairpin. While the knife and three awls analysed by Sun Shuyun and Han Rubin (1981) were of unalloyed copper, a mirror from the related site of Gamatai included 9.6% of tin.

The Siba culture of the same region dates between 1900-1600 BC. Huoshaogou is the best documented of these sites, incorporating 312 excavated burials set out in five groups. Grave goods include gold and bronze earrings, bronze knives, daggers, spearheads and socketed axes.

These bronzes are earlier than those of the Central Plains of China and several scholars have forwarded convincing evidence for a western origin. Kislenko and Tatarintseva (1999) have noted that the Afanasievo culture of the Irtysh, Ob and Yenesei valleys is an intrusive element east of the Urals, and may well represent an eastward movement of people belonging to the Yamnaya culture. The latter, which concentrates west of the Urals and dates in its earliest phase to about 3500 BC, is significant not only for the presence of copper-based metallurgy, but also for the presence of domestic horses and wheeled carts (Anthony 1998). The potential of transport by horse, and the movement of heavy goods through the use of baggage trains, would have opened wide vistas for the settlement of the steppes. This move east is a likely explanation for the thick distribution of Afanasievo sites.

Most Afanasievo sites are cemeteries, in which the dead were interred in the main with pottery vessels but occasionally one encounters copper beads, and gold and silver ornaments, as well as the remains of horses, sheep and cattle. Graves, singly or in groups, were ringed by a stone wall or stones set in a circle. The greatest density of sites lies in the copper-rich Minusinsk Basin in the middle reaches of the Yenesei Valley (Okladnikov 1990). It is claimed that the form of the crania of these people matches that found to the west, and was of Europoid affiliations. The metal industry became much more sophisticated in the succeeding Okunevo sites, for by now copper was being alloyed, and cast into knives, awls, fishhooks and bangles. The presence of tin suggests that the rich deposits of the Rudny Altai were by now exploited.

An Zhimin (1998) has considered the expansion of copper-based industries further east still, into the eastern margin of the Tarim Basin, as being evidence for contact of one form or another with the Afanasievo culture. Demonstrating this would stress the impact of horse transport during the Steppe Bronze Age. The Gumugou cemetery of the Könchi River valley is a key site in appreciating the chronology and cultural affiliations of the Tarim Basin Bronze Age. During the early period, dated between 2000-1500 BC, grave goods include copper, bone and jade ornaments, together with wheat grains. Gumugou is renowned for the survival of a wide range of organic remains which, if one takes the most likely set of radiocarbon results, date in the vicinity of 1700-1500 BC. Kuzmina (1998) has described the recovery of 42 graves lined with wood, in which the dead lay on a bed of twigs and birch bark. Barber's (1998) investigation of the clothing has revealed a tradition based on sheep's wool, in which the fabric was tailored on a loom rather than cut and stitched. One woman wore a cap and a woven woollen wrap. Boots and trousers have also survived. Extraordinarily, the plaid twills from this cemetery are similar to fragments from far to the west at Hallstatt in Austria. She has suggested that these two distant groups inherited the same textile tradition from a common source. Further details of the Gumugou burial rituals hint at an origin in the Afanasievo culture, including the provision of animal remains and the enclosing of the graves by a fence. Similar copper-based knives, awls, bracelets and earrings are also found. There is also convincing evidence, in the form of the remains of domestic goats, sheep, cattle and wheat, that the Gumugou economy incorporated agriculture and stock raising, in association with hunting and gathering. The preferred location of this and related sites was along the oases where rivers flowed from the surrounding mountains into the arid Tarim Basin.

These sites cast serious doubts on an indigenous origin for the Chinese bronze tradition. An Zhimin (1998) has noted the western parallels in copper and bronze working, and the strategic location of the Qijia sites adds weight to the possibility that horse transport across the steppes in the third millennium BC brought not only speakers of an Indo-European language, but also the technological expertise developed in the west.

The first rare bronze artefacts east of Gansu occur in a series of settlements ascribed to the Longshan culture. These feature a major innovation in settlement archaeology, for they were surrounded by stamped-earth walls. Pingliangtai, for example, incorporates a walled

The northern part of the Khorat Plateau contains many Bronze Age sites. The distribution reflects those areas that have been surveyed intensely. Many more settlements would be found with further research.
1. Lake Kumphawapi, 2. Non Nong Chik, 3. Non Nok Tha, 4. Don Klang, 5. Non Praw, 6. Non Kluay, 7. Ban Na Di, 8. Ban Phak Top, 9. Ban Chiang.

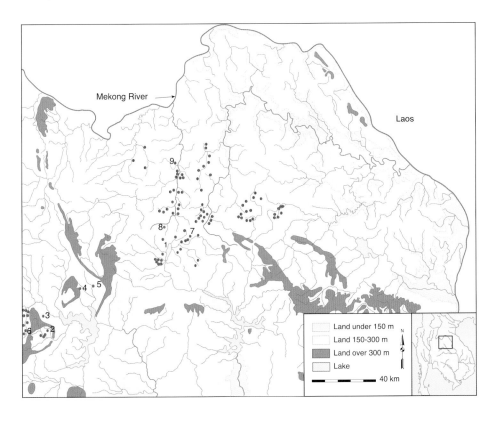

area of 5 hectares entered through gateways on the northern and southern walls, within which lies an inner enclosure 185 metres square. One pit contained what might be the remains of a copper-based artefact. At Wanchenggang, the defences enclose an area of 0.75 of a hectare, and the walls contain further foundations of stamped earth which incorporate what are probably sacrificial skeletons. A fragment of a bronze vessel from a late pit could well date to the early second millennium BC. Mortuary remains from this period are best represented in the sample of over 1,000 graves excavated at Taosi (Shaanxi-ATIA 1980). The trends to increasing social complexity seen in the preceding phases were further intensified: nine of the graves, all those identified being male, were exceptionally rich, offerings including jade rings and axes, and a wooden drum covered in crocodile skin (Pearson and Underhill 1987). Eighty graves fall into a middle category in terms of wealth, while the large number of remaining interments contained few, if any, offerings. Only one bronze object, part of a bell with 1.5% of tin, was recovered. Meishan has furnished domestic house foundations as well as two fragments of crucible, enough to confirm that a knowledge of bronze casting, which was to dominate the material culture of this area in due course, was entering the Yellow River Valley.

Once established, the bronze industry of the Xia and Shang dynasties took on its singular and essentially Chinese pattern. Vessels were cast in piece moulds to satisfy court ritual requirements, leading to individual vessels weighing over 800 kg. The Shang Dynasty cast a long shadow, for we find that typical jade halberds and *yazhang* blades, as well as the occasional bronze, found their way into northern Viet Nam and Lingnan. At this precise juncture in the prehistoric sequences of the Hong Kong area and Bac Bo, we find the first local bronze castings in bivalve moulds. Schofield (1975) found six such moulds for casting socketed axes at Shek Pik on Lantao Island, Hong Kong, in 1937 (Meacham 1975). Further axe moulds, which could easily belong to any one of several assemblages in Northeast or Central Thailand, were found at Kwo Lo Wan (Meacham 1993). These have been dated to between 1300 and 1000 BC. A further axe mould comes from Tung Wan Tsai, associated with dates between 1700-925 BC (Rogers *et al.* 1995). Chau Hing-Wah (1993) has equated the Bronze Age in this area with his fifth cultural phase, dated from 1500 BC. Meacham's review of the available radiocarbon determinations also suggests that the Bronze Age in this area should be dated within the period 1600-800 BC (Meacham 1999)

There are two alternative interpretations of this extensive body of data. Either we can see the origins of the Southeast Asian Bronze Age as being part of a continuum, which began in the Near East and progressively expanded across the steppes to the Gansu Corridor and into China. From there, knowledge of copper smelting and alloying would have spread south along well-established routes of exchange to Lingnan and so Southeast Asia. In due course, further expansion would see the knowledge of bronze reach the islands of Southeast Asia, and New Guinea. The second alternative would involve the local discovery of the properties of copper and tin ore, and their

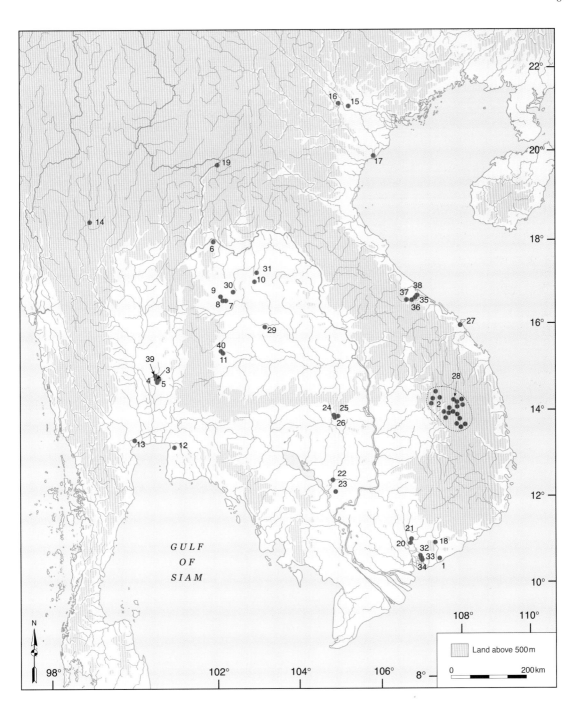

enhancement through alloying, coincidentally at the very time when
Neolithic societies were being exposed to imports and, presumably,
ideas, which originated in one of the most sophisticated of early
states.

Whether of exotic or local origin, knowledge of how to smelt
ores of copper and tin to make bronze and cast this alloy seems to
have spread very rapidly along the Neolithic exchange routes. We find
similar bronze artefacts and casting technology from Hong Kong and

Above: Surapol Natapintu at the entrance to a copper mine in the Khao Wong Prachan Valley.

Top right: The inselbergs of the Khao Wong Prachan Valley are rich in copper ore.

Top left: The stratigraphy of Non Pa Wai saw a deep layer of bronze processing debris on top of a Neolithic habitation area. (Courtesy Dr. Vincent Pigott)

the coast of Guangdong to Yunnan, into Bac Bo, down the Mekong Valley and into Central Thailand. The transition from the Neolithic into the Bronze Age occurred, as far as can be judged at present, within local and long-established communities. In many cases, for example, mortuary rituals remained the same and the same settlements were occupied. Bronze was cast into forms hitherto available only in stone, shell or bone, namely small axes, fishhooks, bracelets and arrowheads.

This transition is well represented at the site of Non Pa Wai in the Khao Wong Prachan Valley, Central Thailand. Radiocarbon dates reveal that copper smelting at Non Pa Wai began in the period 1500-1000 BC. Pigott, Weiss and Natapintu (1997) have described how the debris of copper smelting accumulated over an earlier Neolithic settlement during a period of at least seven centuries. This industrial deposit reached a maximum depth of some three metres, and spread over five hectares by the time the site was abandoned. Only 500 metres away, the site of Non Mak La, also with Neolithic and Bronze Age occupations, might well have been the home for those who used Non Pa Wai as their industrial base.

The Bronze Age sequence has been divided into two Periods (2A and 2B), although in this valley, the term Bronze Age tends to be misleading for virtually all the artefacts recovered were made of copper, not bronze. Two technological phases which coincide with the Bronze Age sequence have been identified. The first involved the exploitation of easily won superficial deposits of oxidic copper ores. Rich in copper and low in impurities, the ores were crushed into manageable pieces, and charged in ceramic crucibles in which smelting took place. The skeletal remains of metal workers from this first phase were found in graves cut down into the underlying Neolithic layer. One contained the skeleton of a man who died when over 25 years of age. His grave goods included a pair of ceramic moulds designed for casting a large socketed axe, a palette and handstone for grinding red ochre, pottery and a shell ear ornament.

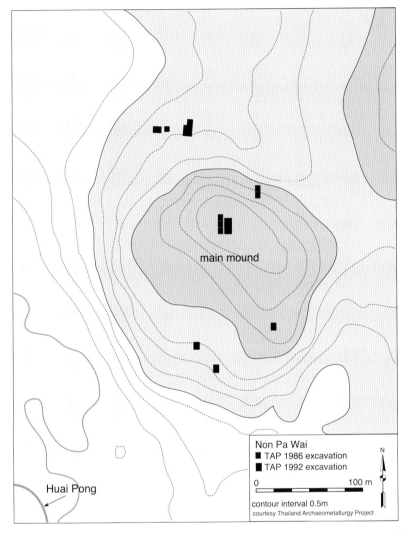

Non Pa Wai
■ TAP 1986 excavation
■ TAP 1992 excavation

0   100 m

contour interval 0.5m
courtesy Thailand Archaeometallurgy Project

Huai Pong

main mound

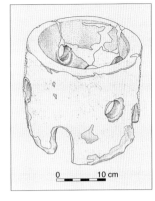

Above: The re-assembled furnace
chimney from Nil Kham Haeng
was used to facilitate copper
smelting.

Left: The Khao Wong Prachan
Valley and the Lopburi Plain,
showing the main distribution
of prehistoric and mining sites.

Burial 5 from Non Pa Wai square
A is known as 'the grave of the
metal worker'. The man, aged
over 25 years at death, was
interred with ceramic moulds for
casting a socketed axe.
(courtesy Dr. Vincent Pigott)

A second burial incorporated similar moulds, as well as
a copper fishhook. A third grave contained a young
skeleton with a copper socketed axe and a disk of red
ochre, and a fourth burial included pottery vessels,
bangles of exotic shell and marble, a whetstone and a
piece of copper. Red ochre was regularly used in
mortuary ritual, and was readily available at the massive
iron ore deposit at nearby Khao Tab Kwai which had
outcrops of copper ore as well.

   The convenient superficial sources of oxidic copper
ores were soon depleted. As the process of mining and
following the ore leads continued, however, miners
extracted more and more ores containing both oxides and
sulphides. Increasing use of these mixed ores, and
changing methods of smelting and casting, signal the
transition from Period 2A to 2B at Non Pa Wai. By 1000
BC, we find intense production at the site, again in
crucibles but now increasingly associated with portable

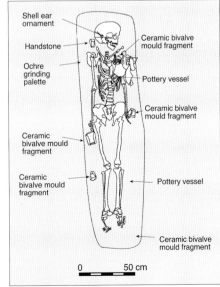

Shell ear
ornament

Handstone

Ochre
grinding
palette

Ceramic
bivalve mould
fragment

Ceramic
bivalve mould
fragment

Ceramic bivalve
mould fragment

Pottery vessel

Ceramic bivalve
mould fragment

Pottery vessel

Ceramic bivalve
mould fragment

0   50 cm

The iron ore deposit of Khao Tab Khwai, a major source of ochre for communities in the Khao Wong Prachan Valley, and also a source of copper ore.

Aerial view of the Khao Wong Prachan Valley. The site of Non Pa Wai is seen as a dark oval on the left edge of the image.

Stratigraphic section of Non Pa Wai, showing the white tufa bedrock at the bottom, then dark deposit of the Neolithic period. This is overlain by the deep industrial deposit that accumulated during the Bronze Age. Neolithic interments can be seen in the dark soil deposit.

A period 2A burial at Non Pa Wai, showing a copper socketed axe and a disc of red ochre.

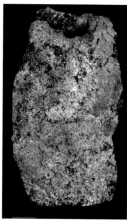

A large ceramic copper smelting crucible from Non Pa Wai, with the remains of slag that has bubbled over the rim. Scale 2 cm.

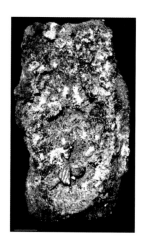

The interior surface of the same ceramic smelting crucible from Non Pa Wai, showing vitrification from the smelting process. (Courtesy Dr. Vincent Pigott)

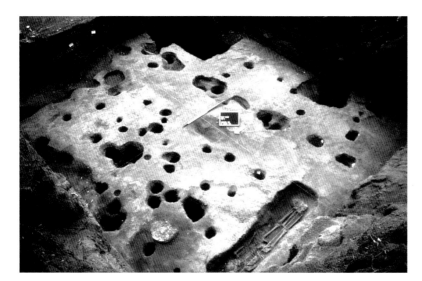

furnace chimneys. The latter, positioned over the smelting crucibles and charged with ore and charcoal, admitted draughts of air, perhaps a natural blast from prevailing winds or possibly via piston bellows to drive the smelting temperature to around 1250° C. Much of the resulting sulphide-rich metal was then poured into various moulds to produce small portable ingots destined, it is thought, for exchange.

Naturally, very few such ingots have survived the passage of time, but to judge from the extent of smelting debris at Non Pa Wai – over 50,000 ingot moulds were recovered from a tiny fraction of the site – output must have been considerable. Given the significant volume of ingots produced, it is suggested that their exchange ranged well beyond the local area and perhaps across greater Southeast Asia. Some ingots, however, were recovered during excavations at neighbouring Non Mak La, a large settlement and cemetery site which was, beyond reasonable doubt, the home base for those who mined in the local ore deposits and smelted at Non Pa Wai. That peoples at these sites engaged in distant exchange transactions is shown by the presence of tridacna, a shell adapted to clean, coral waters.

Nil Kham Haeng is a second major smelting site in the valley, located only three kilometres from Non Pa Wai. Copper production continued at this site for about 800 years, from *ca.* 1100-300 BC thus overlapping with that at Non Pa Wai for several centuries. The earliest activity corresponds to Period 2B at Non Pa Wai, while the later of Nil Kham Haeng's two main periods incorporated the transition into the Iron Age. Apparently mixed ores were being smelted here from the initial occupation. Increasingly lower quality ores required labour-intensive crushing in order to boost copper output during the smelting operation, which now involved ceramic-lined bowl furnaces cut into the ground, and covered by a portable furnace chimney. The latter were considered so important, it seems, that they were on occasion incorporated as mortuary offerings. Stratigraphically, Nil Kham Haeng is most unusual in

Andy Weiss, the Assistant Director, mapping at Non Pa Wai with an EDM total station.

Left: Non Pa Wai, showing a living surface, and burial 4.

An ingot mould from Non Pa Wai, scale 2 cm.

Excavations are in progress at Non Pa Wai. (Courtesy Dr. Vincent Pigott)

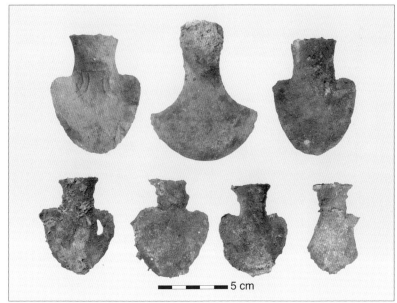

5 cm

Nil Kham Haeng, operation 3, revealing a finely-stratified matrix of crushed slag and ore.

Right: The output from the Khao Wong Prachan copper mines included many socketed implements, including axes. (Courtesy Dr. Vincent Pigott)

A mine gallery entrance on Phu Kha in the Khao Wong Prachan Valley, the closest source to Nil Kham Haeng. (Courtesy Dr. Vincent Pigott)

its fine succession of lenses made up of crushed ore and slag. These lenses were probably the result of redeposition of the crushed debris by monsoon rains. There were also burials, evidence for the manufacture of stone and shell bangles and faunal remains, in addition to the vast concentration of industrial debris in an area of more than 3 hectares. Nil Kham Haeng, as a production site, appears to have been inhabited continuously.

Much of the production at Nil Kham Haeng went into small, very thin socketed implements of unknown function. One of the burials included 60 as grave goods. As we shall see, bronze only became truly abundant in mortuary rituals during the Iron Age. Nil Kham Haeng was a centre for continuing copper production into the Iron Age, and again, must have supplied considerable quantities of copper for an extensive exchange network.

While the Khao Wong Prachan Valley was a major copper producing centre, it was not the only source for copper during the Bronze Age in Thailand. In Northeast Thailand at Phu Lon, Natapintu and Pigott investigated a copper-mining complex strategically placed to take advantage of the Mekong River as a conduit for access to and distribution of copper ores and bronze (Natapintu 1988). Here, the actual mining shafts have been explored, the stone mauls used to extract the ore and a ceramic vessel still lying within (Pigott and Weisgerber 1998). Charcoal from one adit furnished a radiocarbon determination of 830-590 BC. At Phu Lon, the Pottery Flat excavation revealed a substantial accumulation of crushed ore host rock, containing within evidence of some smelting activity, including malachite ore, slag and fragments of small ceramic crucibles, but only two casting moulds. Of particular interest are the crucibles, apparently used for the production of bronze. Analysis of the crucibles by Vernon (1996-7, 1997) indicates that they share not only the same shape as those known from village sites on the Khorat

A view from the copper mine of Phu Lon, looking north to the Mekong River during the dry season.

A view of the copper mining complex at Phu Lon, Thailand. It was the scene of intense prehistoric activity.

Excavations on the Pottery Flat at Phu Lon, with co-director Surapol Natapintu. A large deposit of crushed ore/slag can be seen in the foreground.

The 'Pinnacle' at Phu Lon, heart of the copper mining complex, under investigation.

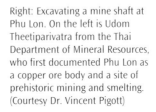

A mining maul from Phu Lon. Note the spalling from heavy use in mining and /or ore crushing. Hard and durable igneous cobbles were selected from the banks of the Mekong River. Scale 5 cm.

A ceramic pedestalled vessel from Phu Lon Pinnacle Mine 3. It is red slipped, and typical of the 1st millennium BC. Scale 5 cm.

Right: Excavating a mine shaft at Phu Lon. On the left is Udom Theetiparivatra from the Thai Department of Mineral Resources, who first documented Phu Lon as a copper ore body and a site of prehistoric mining and smelting. (Courtesy Dr. Vincent Pigott)

A mining gallery at the Phu Lon copper mining complex. (Courtesy Dr. Vincent Pigott)

An excavated mine shaft at the base of the pinnacle at Phu Lon.

Right: Part of a stone bivalve mould for casting a socketed implement, from the Pottery Flat excavation at Phu Lon. Note the inscribed cross on the exterior.

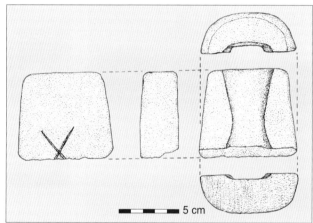

Examples of ceramic bivalve moulds from Non Pa Wai. The central mould was for casting a socketed implement, but those on the right and left are enigmatic. Note the marks on the exterior surfaces.

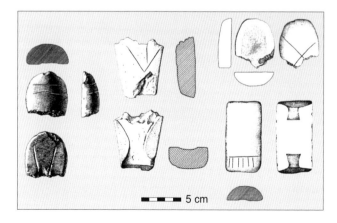

Cattle effigy pots have been found at Huai Yai and Non Nok Tha. (Courtesy Surapol Natapintu)

Plateau such as Ban Chiang and Ban Na Di, but remarkably they share the same technology of their manufacture as well. This suggests strong ties downstream along the Mekong with the Khorat Plateau villages which quite likely sought copper at deposits like Phu Lon in the ore-rich Phetchabun region to the west. Evidence at Phu Lon suggests that over time, and probably seasonally, different groups

This burial from Huai Yai contained H-shaped shell beads of identical form to those from Khok Phanom Di during mortuary phase 6.

Above left: Phu Noi, northern trench 1. Grave furniture from Bronze Age burial 8. (Courtesy Dr. Roberto Ciarla and Dr. Fiorella Rispoli)

perhaps on mining expeditions (marked by the distinct ceramic assemblages left behind) were exploiting this rich source of copper ore (Pigott 1998). While one radiocarbon determination suggested initial activity at Phu Lon within the period 1750-1425 BC, most of the mining and ore processing at the site flourished during the first millennium BC, again lasting well into the Iron Age.

There are almost certainly more mining and smelting complexes remaining to be discovered in Southeast Asia. Excavations in the two so far explored have immeasurably advanced our understanding of the Bronze Age, for we now have a feel not only for the technical skills involved, but also the social dimensions of mining communities (Knapp *et al.* 1998). Essentially, the mortuary data from the Khao Wong Prachan Valley disclose metal workers interred with the tools of their trade, just as the potters of Khok Phanom Di were found with theirs. Numerous ceramic moulds from Non Pa Wai (and a stone mould at Phu Lon), for example, bear what look like ownership marks, but it must also be noted that the production of copper did not involve increased social distinctions but rather a cooperative communal endeavour (White and Pigott 1996). Nor was the use of stone replaced by the coming of copper and bronze. In her survey in the Lam Maleng Valley, to the north of the Khao Wong Prachan Valley, Mudar (1995) identified 49 sites which correspond, in terms of pottery styles, to the Bronze Age. Of these, at least a quarter revealed evidence for the exploitation of local stone for the manufacture of ornaments, such as the bangles which recur in lowland cemeteries.

It is now also possible to follow the exchange routes, from mines to the communities that converted copper ingots and high quality stone into a range of ornaments, tools and weapons. At Ban Phu Noi, north of the Khao Wong Prachan Valley, Natapintu (1997) encountered a dense concentration of 32 burials in a square measuring only 5 by 3 metres. The inhumations were divided into three phases, although superpositions and a similar mortuary ritual suggest continuous use of this area as a cemetery. Ciarla and Rispoli (pers. comm.) have opened further areas and found that the cemetery belongs within the Bronze Age. The three graves of the first phase uncovered by Natapintu were richly endowed with grave goods. Burial 26 incorporated six pots, a stone adze, a bone fishhook on the

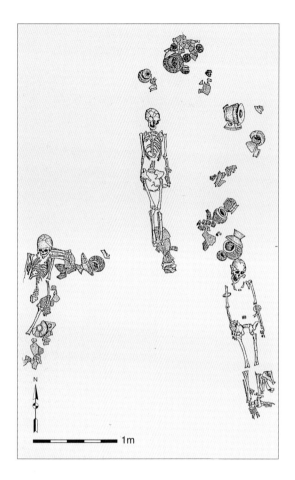

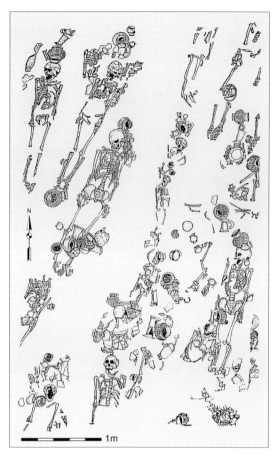

The burials from Phu Noi mortuary level 1.

Right: The burials from Phu Noi mortuary levels 2 and 3.

chest, shell, turtle carapace and ivory bangles and beads of deer antler and shell. The forelimb of a pig had been placed beyond the feet. Burial 25 was interred with ten pottery vessels as well as shell disc beads, and a stone bangle that had been broken in antiquity and repaired by boring holes still containing a fibrous cord. A marble bangle, ivory ear ornament and freshwater bivalve shell were associated with the intact part of burial 24.

Burials of the second and third mortuary phases had the head pointing to the northeast and due largely to the crowding of interments alongside and over each other, few were found intact. Grave goods continued to include pottery vessels, including a new form of high-pedestalled dish. Marine shell jewellery, chlorite and marble beads, stone bangles, bivalve shells and pigs' fore limbs were also associated, while turtle carapace discs with a central perforation recall those found with males in the later phases at Khok Phanom Di. Bronze Age graves have also been found by Ciarla and Rispoli over the Neolithic layers at Ban Tha Kae. Grave goods seen widely over Southeast Asia were recovered: pottery vessels, freshwater bivalve shells and shell disc beads.

Phu Noi, Northern Trench 2. General view of the bedrock with burials and post-holes cut into it, from the excavation of Ciarla and Natapintu.

Phu Noi, Northern Trench 3. General view of the Bronze Age necropolis during the excavation by Ciarla and Rispoli.

Phu Noi, Northern Trench 3. General view of the Bronze Age cemetery during the excavation by Ciarla and Rispoli.

Tha Kae, Op.1, square A quadrant b, burial 4. This Bronze Age burial was furnished with two pedestalled bowls decorated by red painted motifs, a fresh water bivalve shellfish and a string of tiny disk-shaped shell beads.

Phu Noi, Northern Trench 3. General view of the Bronze Age cemetery during the excavation by Ciarla and Rispoli. (Courtesy Dr. Roberto Ciarla and Dr. Fiorella Rispoli)

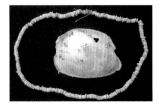

Tha Kae, Op.1, square A quadrant b, burial 4. The bivalve shell and disc beads which accompanied the dead.

■■■■ 5 cm

Tha Kae, Op.1, square A quadrant b, burial 4. A red slipped pedestalled bowl used as a mortuary offering.

Right: Tha Kae, Op.1, square A quadrant b. Looking down to the level of Early Bronze Age postholes (1500-1000 BC). On the far left of the image (east) is the Iron Age burial 1.
(Courtesy Dr. Roberto Ciarla and Dr. Fiorella Rispoli)

Non Nok Tha

In Northeast Thailand, Non Nok Tha, a small mound located 120 km south of the Phu Lon copper mines, lies at the confluence of two small streams set within an extensive tract of low terrace sandy loam soil. About two km to the southwest, the land rises to the sandstone ridge which comprises part of an upland known as Phu Wiang. The rise in altitude incorporates the transition from a moist deciduous to a wetter, evergreen forest.

Test excavations undertaken in 1965 revealed the presence of inhumation burials associated with whole pottery vessels and bronze artefacts. Encouraged by these associations, full-scale excavations were undertaken during 1966 and again in 1968. Proper dating of the bronzes was a principal objective, although the recovery of a large sample of human skeletons, intact pottery vessels and biological remains would lay the foundations of a proper understanding of the area's prehistory. These excavations confirmed that the site had served as a cemetery, but some post-hole patterns also suggested the layout of prehistoric houses. The deposits were little more than a metre deep, but the intercutting and superposition of burials made it possible to obtain a sequential series. Wherever possible, excavations followed the actual cultural layers rather than arbitrary levels of consistent thickness determined by the excavator. This allowed Bayard (1971) to sub-divide the occupation into successive soils and occasional periods of erosion. No less important was the determination of layers from which graves were cut. This allowed the establishment of successive phases of site use.

An examination of the changing artefact typology, the orientation of individual graves and succession worked out from intercutting grave pits are the bases for a sub-division of the sequence into early, middle and late periods. The early period (EP) had three constituent phases, the middle period (MP) eight, and the late period, six. The three are

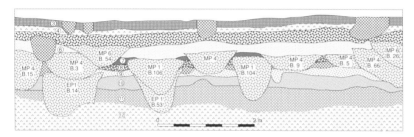

technologically distinct and only the first two concern us. The first was devised to represent the earliest graves of the 1966 excavations. Pottery was distinctive and there was a marked rarity of bronze objects. Indeed, only one item, an axe, was found. The grave in question was assigned to a late EP context. The middle period saw an increase in the amount of bronze, together with evidence in the form of crucibles, casting spillage and moulds, that metal implements were locally cast.

Initial attempts to date the sequence foundered for lack of internal consistency and difficulties in relating often very small quantities of charcoal to the event being dated. A cemetery of intercutting and superimposed graves is a very difficult site to date through conventional radiocarbon methods if no *in situ* charcoal is available. Fortunately this problem has been solved by the AMS dating technique. The new determinations make it clear that the Bronze Age graves fall within the period 1400-900 BC.

From its initial use as a cemetery, the burial rite involved extended inhumation in a grave between 40 and 90 cm deep. Adults as well as children were buried with a range of grave goods which normally comprised pottery vessels, stone adzes, shell-disc beads disposed in strings round the waist and the bones of animals. There are few exotic offerings. Of 87 well provenanced and relatively complete burials encountered, only five were accompanied by shell beads, and there were two shell bracelets. Bronze artefacts were very rare: one axe in a late EP context, and three in MP interments. Five burials in the latter phase incorporated bronze bracelets. Pottery vessels were the commonest grave offering, but the number of local or exotic examples is not known.

Above and above left: This grave from Non Nok Tha contained the skeleton of a man with a bronze socketed axe on his chest.

Above far left: The excavation of Non Nok Tha nears completion.

Left: The section through the site of Non Nok Tha.

Three mortuary pots from Bronze Age graves at Non Nok Tha. The tallest is 15cm high.
(Courtesy Dr. Donn Bayard)

Burial 8 belongs to the Early Period (EP). The child was interred with three pottery vessels. The rear limbs and jaw of a young pig were placed on the child's chest and the remains of an adult dog lay beyond the feet. Burial 14 contained the bones of a child. Four cord-marked vessels were placed in the grave but the body was also covered with a sheet of broken sherds which, it seems, were deliberately smashed over the body. Two rows of shell disc beads lay round the child's pelvis, a further two beads were found on the skull and a bone spatula was found over the left thigh. After the interment, the burial ritual included the placing of an entire pig and the forelimb of a cow round the child's head. The fore and rear limb bones of a pig were found on the child's shoulders and ankles, possible evidence for a pig skin shroud that covered the body before funerary urns were smashed and the grave filled. This technique has been encountered also at the Bang site, Ban Kao. Another complete pig's skeleton was found in burial 16, with three funerary urns and a concentration of beads in the area of the pelvis. While animal bones were common in the graves, they were not always found. Thus, an adult was interred with a stone adze and six vessels but no animal remains.

Apart from slight changes in the typology of pottery vessels, EP2 presented similar features. Graves tended to be shallower with one part of the excavation area containing only child burials and another with one exception, adult interments. Burial 112 contained a child's skeleton with four pottery vessels, three stone adzes and a shell under the right knee. The tusk of a young pig had been placed on the chest. In burial 90 of EP3, the first bronze implement was recovered over the chest of an adult male. This socketed axe was made of a 14% tin bronze. Round-based, cord-marked pots were found, one immediately next to the skull and three over the ankles. A pig's foot had been placed adjacent to the human thigh. EP3 graves were almost all of adults and no mounds were raised over them. Although the sample is not large – only four complete adult burials were recovered from the entire Early Period – there were fewer burial goods when compared with earlier interments.

Metal finds became slightly more common during the Middle Period not only in the form of finished socketed axes but also the stone moulds in which they had been cast. Ceramic styles changed too, the potter adding such novel features as pedestalled bases and sharply-carinated shoulders. One burial urn contained fish vertebrae, suggesting that they were designed to carry food for the dead.

As the Middle Period proceeded, so the preferred styles of pottery continued to change, but always following the same basic traditions of manufacture, by means of both moulding and shaping by the paddle and anvil technique. Animal bones continued to be interred, and some burial urns smashed. MP4 yielded more burials than any other. Most are oriented to the southwest and have a standard assemblage of four vessels placed beyond the head, associated with several bivalve shellfish, a grave offering which recurs widely in other sites. Burial 32 had five such shells near the skull and three, pierced animal canine teeth in the vicinity of the neck, indicating the presence of a pendant at the time of burial. The fragmentary remains of an ox skull were found in the vicinity of his right arm and a chicken had been placed over the chest area. Burial 85 included a bronze socketed axe and abundant remains of a large bovid. Two crucibles containing fragments of casting spillage attest to local metallurgy during MP4, while MP6 revealed a configuration of post holes which Bayard has reconstructed as a structure measuring 12 x 6 m. The 12 burials belonging to this phase were oriented in a north or northwesterly direction. By this juncture, orienting burials to the southwest returned. Ceramic styles changed, red-slipped vessels with flat bases becoming popular. A bronze halberd-like instrument and a bracelet demonstrate the continuing availability of bronze. No burials belonging to MP7-8 were found during the 1968 excavation season. Thirteen inhumations belonging to this period were recovered during 1966. None contained animal bone.

Non Nong Chik

Smaller excavations at other sites in the western margins of the Khorat Plateau have provided further useful information. In the year following the completion of excavations at Non Nok Tha, a site survey was undertaken within the confines of Phu Wiang. This monadnock looks like a large volcanic crater. Easy access is possible only through a narrow defile in the mountain wall cut by a river. Within the ring of uplands, flat land covers about 14 square kilometres. It is now densely settled by rice cultivators who take advantage of the encircling hills, with their forest cover, for dry season hunting. The interior has the advantage of receiving water which runs off from the hills, and there are perennial streams which link with a series of swamps and ultimately flow into one major river. Non Nok Tha lies on the northeastern outer edge of the Phu Wiang upland. The survey in the interior discovered a series of prehistoric and early historic sites and small test squares were excavated in two of them. One, known as Non Nong Chik, looked particularly promising because its surface was covered with fragments of cord-impressed pottery, resembling that from Non Nok Tha. It lies at the confluence of two streams in an enclave of soils suitable for rice

Below and below left: Non Nong Chik is a Bronze Age cemetery in the shadow of the Phu Wiang upland.

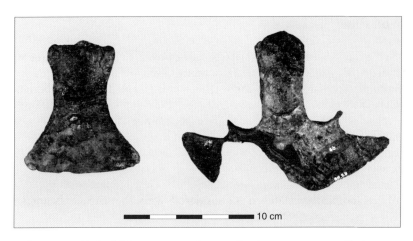

cultivation. Only 150 metres to the north, the mountain wall rises sharply, providing a series of horizontally-stratified resource zones.

Excavations, which covered 12 square metres, encountered complete pottery vessels in association with inhumation burials. Eight stratigraphic layers were recognised within which five burials were located. Animal bone was included in the burials but the small sample did not yield any stone bracelets or shell beads. Perhaps the most important aspect of Non Nok Chik, apart from its location, was its funerary pottery, presence of bronze and iron, and its radiocarbon dates. The pottery sherds have been analysed on the basis of their surface finish and type of tempering agent used (Buchan 1973). It would have been desirable to compare the two assemblages on the basis of complete vessels, but there were too few from Non Nong Chik. In terms of surface finish, the material matches that from the Non Nok Tha MP5-6. Whereas there was a period of abandonment after the Middle Period at Non Nok Tha, Non Nok Chik was used as a cemetery throughout.

Non Pa Kluay

During 1984-5, Wilen (1989) expanded our knowledge of the prehistory of the Upper Nam Phong valley area by undertaking a site survey and excavation programme in the area to the west of Non Nok Tha. He identified 25 prehistoric village and cemetery sites most of which, as in the Ban Chiang region, were located so as to have easy access to soils suited to modern rice cultivation. At Non Pa Kluay, he excavated an area of 15 square metres down to a depth of 2 m, and in the lower of two cultural horizons, he recovered Bronze Age material. He found a close similarity, in terms of pottery forms and decoration, with the material beginning with the Middle Period at Non Nok Tha. Similar bivalve sandstone axe moulds were recovered. His four radiocarbon determinations when pooled, indicate settlement within the period 1300-975 BC.

Non Praw

Non Praw is located 30 km northeast of Non Nok Tha, and is similar
in its small size and shallow stratigraphy. Two mortuary phases have
been proposed for the 25 burials (Buranrak 1994). The earlier burials
were interred with ceramic vessels, shell beads and bracelets, but no
bronze grave goods were found. Burials of the second phase
incorporated bronzes, including axes and bracelets, but they were
probably cut from a layer which included iron slag. However, no iron
grave goods were found. One axe in a distinctive crescentic form is
very similar to an example from Non Nok Tha, and in the absence
of any radiocarbon dates, it is considered likely that the site belongs
within the period 1000-500 BC.

Above and top: Chester Gorman
in 1975, clambered down the
excavation square left with all
skeletons in place by an early
Thai excavation at Ban Chiang.
At the base, he found the burial
of a man wearing bronze bangles.

Ban Chiang

The 1974 excavation of Ban Chiang revealed Bronze Age graves over
a Neolithic cemetery, while Bronze Age graves were at the base of
the sequence in the area opened a year later. The earliest Bronze
Age graves belong to the third phase of the Early Period (EP), and
continue into the Middle Period (MP). They were laid out in clusters
or possibly rows, each containing the remains of men, women,
children and infants. Dating this Bronze Age cemetery has been
fraught with problems. As at Non Nok Tha, there was no clear
association between charcoal samples and the event being dated,
such as the interment of a particularly individual. The results fuelled
speculative claims for bronzes that would have ranked among the
earliest in the world (White 1982a). There are, however, three
conventional radiocarbon determinations that come from *in situ*
Bronze Age contexts. The first involves a large sample of charcoal
from a hearth found just 45 cm above the natural substrate, and the
result is 1115-875 BC. A second determination is 1675-1430 BC,
and the third (930-805 BC) lies just above the surface from which
later Bronze Age graves were cut. As at Non Nok Tha, the application
of AMS dates to rice chaff found in mortuary ceramics might be
expected to resolve the chronology of the Bronze Age, but this is not
yet the case. Burial 63 comprises an infant jar burial found in the
southern cluster, at a depth of about 3.30 metres below datum. It
has been ascribed to EP III, and the resulting determination is 4800-
4510 BC. Burial 47 also belongs to EP III, a male grave lying in the
central cluster that appears to have been dug into the natural
substrate from an early point in the sequence. It dates to 3770-3370
BC. These unacceptable results do not give one confidence when
reviewing the remaining three that are available from this layer. One
of these comes from burial 72, also a deep early grave cut into the
natural substrate, and the result is 1950-1600 BC. This burial belongs
to EP II/III according to White, and the base of the grave contained
a nodule of bronze. The remaining two dates come from burials 59
(EP Va) and 56 (EP Vb). These lie on the same line and orientation,

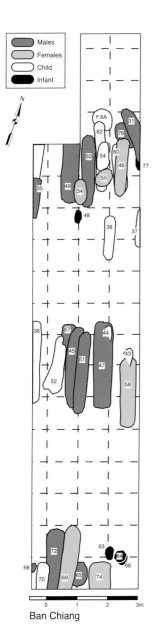

Males
Females
Child
Infant

N

F.6A

Ban Chiang

0   1   2   3m

at depths of 3.50 and 3.10 metres respectively. The dates are 1740-1450 and 1320-1000 BC. At least the latter should post date the determination of 1115-875 BC from the charcoal-rich hearth which lies nearby at a depth of 3 metres.

These results do not facilitate a clear and logical conclusion. One could argue for a date in the vicinity of 2000 BC for bronze at Ban Chiang, but this would contradict two determinations from Neolithic graves in the 1974 excavation, which date the preceding phase to 2050-1500 and 2190-1880 BC. Equally, one could propose that bronze casting was established within the period 1500-1000 BC. The former would indeed require us to invest in this site, an independent origin to metallurgy. The latter would harmonise with virtually all other dates now available for the Southeast Asian Bronze Age, and is currently preferred.

The earlier Bronze Age graves in the 1975 area underlay the remains of a clay furnace, surrounded by ceramic crucible fragments still retaining bronze from the casting procedure. A casting mould and crucible fragments were also found in the 1974 excavation. Copper and tin ingots must have been obtained by exchange, heated and then locally cast. However, bronze grave goods were rare. A socketed spear was found with the young man in burial 76. Burial 38, that of a five-year old, included bronze anklets, and a mid-aged male from the 1974 season was interred with a socketed bronze axe lying next to his head, and several bronze bangles on his left wrist. Most Bronze Age graves, however, were devoid of bronzes, but contained up to three pottery vessels.

The 1975 excavation at Ban Chiang was too small and narrow to sustain meaningful social interpretations. However, the distribution of Bronze Age graves suggests disposition in rows.

Above right: A row of early Bronze Age infant burial jars at Ban Chiang.

Ban Na Di

Ban Na Di is located only 23 km southwest of Ban Chiang. It was one of the sites identified during the 1980 site survey in the vicinity of Lake Kumphawapi, and excavations commenced in November 1980 (Higham and Kijngam 1984). It was located near the confluence of small tributary streams which command a tract of low terrace soils now under wet-rice cultivation. White (1982) has suggested that such a position would have favoured prehistoric settlement because of the relatively gentle flood regime associated with the middle courses of such tributary streams. That flooding was a problem during the early occupation of Ban Na Di, however, is indicated by the numerous sand lenses found there which had been deposited by floodwater.

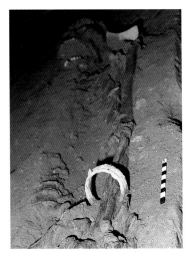
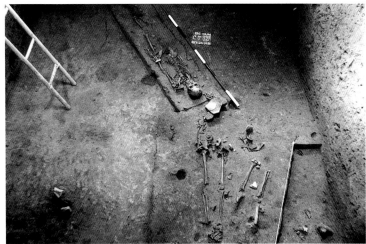

Above and above right: A Bronze Age grave at Ban Chiang contained the remains of a man with a bronze axe, bronze bangles and a complete incised and painted pottery vessel.

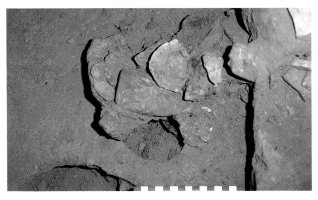

A mould and pieces of crucible demonstrated that bronze casting had been undertaken at Ban Chiang.

Left: The pottery vessels from Ban Chiang came in a variety of shapes and sizes.

The site revealed a stratigraphic sequence including five prehistoric levels to a depth of 4 metres below the present ground surface. The basal level comprised occupation material which included the remains of freshwater molluscs and a wide range of mammalian and fish bone. Some of the bones derived from domestic cattle, dogs and probably pigs. An innovation at Ban Na Di was the screening of a sample of all excavated soils through a 1 mm mesh, resulting in a large sample of very small bones and carbonised rice grains. The analysis of this microfauna revealed much emphasis on fishing. Indeed, the faunal spectra derived from sites where mesh sizes were larger or not used must be regarded cautiously. This lowest level also yielded much pottery, pits containing occupation refuse, and hearths. There were several broken fragments of crucible to which metal scoria still adhered, fragments of bronze and bronze artefacts.

Layers 6 and 7 were associated with a change in the use to which part at least, of the excavated area was put. Two areas 30 metres apart were excavated, and both yielded burials laid out in rows, and superimposed over a depth of almost 2 metres. The mortuary rite matches that at Ban Chiang and Non Nok Tha except for local variations. Thus, the food remains found comprise the left fore limbs

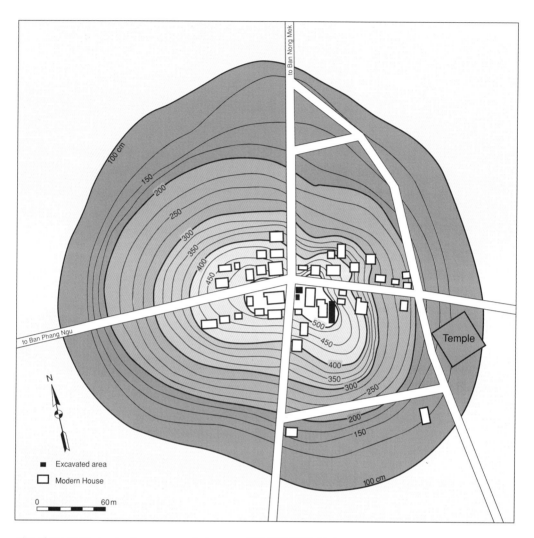

Plan of Ban Na Di, showing the area excavated.

These moulds and bronzes come from looted contexts in the region of Ban Chiang. They demonstrate local casting in sandstone bivalve moulds.

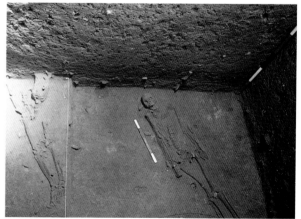

Bronze Age graves at Ban Chiang included a variety of grave goods. The man on the right hand side wore a bone pin in his hair and tigers' teeth beads round his neck. He also held a bone spearhead pointing directly to the antler of a small deer.

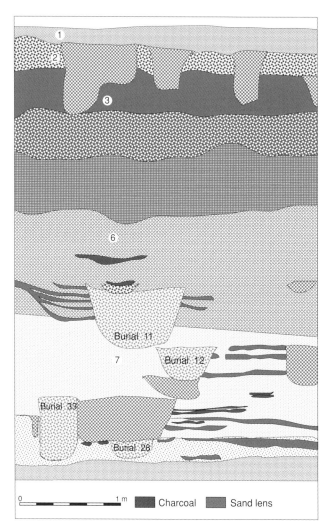

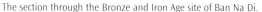

The Bronze Age burials of Ban Na Di were laid out in orderly rows.

The section through the Bronze and Iron Age site of Ban Na Di.

A cross section through a ceramic crucible at Ban Na Di contains bronze scoria. Actual size.

of pigs and less frequently of cattle. The orientation is invariably on a north-south axis and bodies were interred with a variable assemblage of artefacts, which includes pottery vessels, clay figurines and items of personal jewellery made from shell, stone, bronze and in the latest graves, of iron. Grave goods were associated with the remains of children, adolescents and adults of both sexes, but not with very young infants. The pottery vessels were often found to be complete, and they contained food remains, such as fish bone and, in one case, the fore limb of a pig.

During the buildup of layers 7-6, the area excavated was not restricted solely to use as a cemetery. There were also pits and hearths outside the burial area, and as in level 8, crucibles and bronze were found. One particularly interesting feature comprised the remains of a clay-lined furnace ringed by bronze detritus and the remnants of crucibles. It had been used to heat copper and tin to melting point prior to casting. That this occurred on the spot is

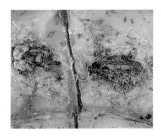

The earliest bronze in Ban Na Di graves was for casting wire-like ties to repair stone bangles. (Scale 2:1).

further documented by the recovery of stone mould fragments. Two of the latest graves in this mortuary phase included a few iron offerings.

Much charcoal at Ban Na Di was found in hearths, furnaces and sealed pits. The deposition of thin but discrete sand lenses made it possible to conclude that material beneath them was not disturbed by later activity, such as grave digging. The dated charcoal comes from *in situ* contexts, and the determinations suggest that the basal layer was deposited within the period 1300-900 BC. The Bronze Age cemetery, which reveals three successive phases, probably falls somewhere within the span 900-400 BC, although the radiocarbon determinations are not precise due to the complex calibration curve at this period.

Although by no means a large excavation, this Bronze Age exposure is notable for two reasons. The opening of two areas permitted a comparison between the mortuary treatment of two groups over time. Moreover, a furnace was recovered as at Ban Chiang, ringed by complete and fragmentary crucibles, bronze-casting spillage and a sandstone axe mould fragment. The examination of the metal still adhering to the crucibles indicated a mixture of copper and tin.

The mortuary clusters contained the remains of men, women, infants and children. Men were interred with the head pointing to the south, women in the opposite direction. Graves were specifically placed over the ancestors, in such a way that it is possible to divide the sequence into phases. The earliest, phase 1A, matches the earlier Bronze Age graves at Non Nok Tha and Ban Chiang in yielding very little bronze. Indeed, the only bronze found was in the form of a cast wire to repair broken stone bangles. Pottery vessels dominated the mortuary offerings, but one also finds the limb bones of domestic cattle, exotic stone bracelets, shell beads and clay figurines of cattle, deer, humans and elephants. Phase 1c saw more grave goods within essentially the same death ritual. The first bronzes were found in mortuary contexts, including 19 bracelets with one woman. A child wore one bronze bracelet, and a further three accompanied a young woman. We also find cowrie shells, shell disc beads, which may well have a coastal origin and shell bracelets. Cattle and pig fore limbs and even the skeleton of a chicken had been placed with the dead, perhaps as part of mortuary feasting. Even during the final phase of this cemetery, bronzes were rare. Three graves contained a total of four bronze bangles, a child wore two bronze anklets and a man was interred with a bronze coil. Rather more graves contained the fore limb bones of domestic cattle and pig, while one man wore 13 exotic shell bracelets. Almost 1,400 shell disc beads were recovered, divided between four graves out of a sample of 24. Two of the pottery vessels are virtually identical with examples from Ban Chiang during phase MP VII, confirming that in fact, this final phase properly belongs to the early Iron Age.

A comparison between the graves in each area excavated has shown that one is consistently richer than the other. A statistical test known as multidimensional scaling has pinpointed a child, two men

All the elements of bronze casting at Ban Na Di are to be found in a modern iron forging workshop, from the bellows to the charcoal-fired furnace and wind break.

Left: The site of Ban Na Di has provided evidence for all the stages of bronze casting: A, crucibles; B-C, sandstone moulds; D, clay mould.

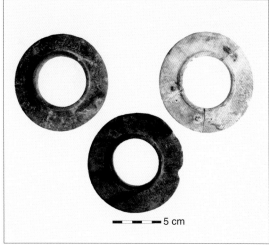

and a woman as being unusually well endowed with grave goods when compared with the group as a whole. Close inspection reveals that most of the exotic ornaments, all the clay figurines and most of the bronzes come from one cluster. This disparity in wealth is found in all three phases. Yet the differences are not sufficient to mask an underlying similarity. It is as if one group, while richer, still belonged to the same social stratum.

Identifying such continuities and distinctions can only be made on the basis of large burial samples. That at Ban Na Di was barely large enough to warrant social inferences. Two other sites, however, have been opened sufficiently to permit a review of the social dimensions. Ban Lum Khao is located in the upper Mun Valley, and Nong Nor lies just behind the eastern shore of the Gulf of Siam.

Slate and marble bangles from rich burials at Ban Na Di came to the site by exchange.

Left: All clay figurines of cattle, elephant and deer were found in the rich Ban Na Di graves.

An early burial of a woman, from the poorer group of graves at Ban Na Di. She was accompanied by pottery vessels and the limb bones of a domesic bovid.

A row of Bronze Age burials at Ban Na Di.

In this grave, an adult man and woman were buried together but lying in opposite directions.

Amphan Kijngam, co-director of the Ban Na Di excavation, uncovers burial 26.

One of the rich male burials at Ban Na Di was found wearing exotic marine shell bangles.

The remains of an infant in the rich enclave of graves at Ban Na Di were associated with clay figurines of cattle, and an exotic stone bangle.

This man from Ban Na Di wore an exotic marble bangle which had been repaired in antiquity with bronze ties.

Above: The burials at Ban Lum Khao were extensively recorded before being lifted.

Above left: At Ban Lum Khao, a sample of all the cultural material recovered was passed through a flotation chamber to extract micro-organic remains, such as rice grains and fish bones.

Left: The excavation of Ban Lum Khao took place towards the edge of the mound. Contour in metres.

BAN LUM KHAO
AMPHOE NON SUNG

■ Excavation 1995-6

0   100m

N

101

99

98

100

97

95

Prasat Stream

This child at Ban Na Di was found interred under a crocodile skin shroud.

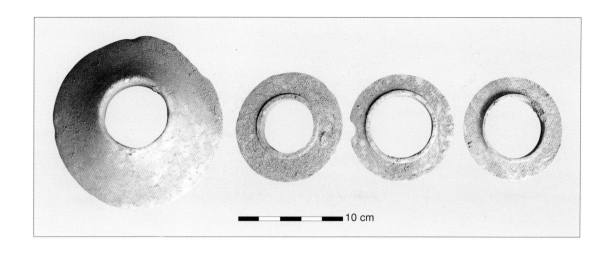

10 cm

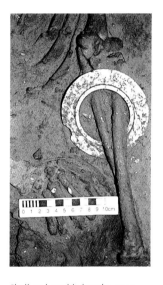

Shell and marble bangles were worn by the dead at Ban Lum Khao, but no bronzes were recovered from a site in which bronze was undoubtedly being cast.

Ban Lum Khao

We have seen that this site was settled during the late Neolithic period. The area excavated, which measured 14 by 10 metres, was then used as a Bronze Age cemetery of which 111 graves were uncovered. This cemetery falls within the period 1400-500 BC, but no greater precision is possible at present due to a lack of datable material. There are four phases. In the earliest, nine burials were found, all but one oriented to the east. Phase 2 is essentially transitional to the main bulk of the burials, which were set out in five apparent rows, with the head directed to the south or southwest. Except where one row is only partially within the excavated area, all contain the remains of men, women, infants and children. During the final phase, four burials and possibly five were again oriented with the head to the east. The pottery vessels from phase 4 are very close in form to those of the earliest Iron Age in this area, and thus probably date in the 7th to 6th centuries BC.

Although a wide range of grave goods was recovered, no bronzes were present. Yet the recovery of crucible and mould fragments indicate local bronze casting. Ceramic vessels were the dominant mortuary offering, the prevailing forms varying with time. During phase 3, excavators found many examples of a local form of red slipped vessel with a trumpet-shaped rim. These fell out of favour by mortuary phase 4. Shell was preferred for personal jewellery. The ubiquitous Neolithic and Bronze Age shell disc beads dominated the assemblage. The majority of the 62 bangles found in burials were fashioned from shell, most being worn on the wrist, but some may have been used as anklets. Three ceramic anvils were recovered, two from male graves and one from that of a woman. Seven adzes were found, most in the graves of infants or children. Women's graves furnished one bone and one stone adze. Six burials contained ceramic spindle whorls, but these artefacts were common in the cultural matrix of the cemetery, 88 being recovered. Four of the burials with spindle whorls belong to phase 4, including the graves of two infants and two women. Earlier whorls were associated with a young man,

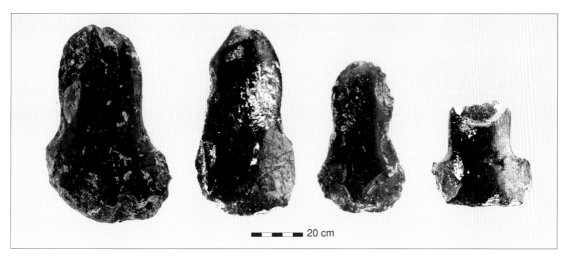

Stone adze heads were widely used during the Bronze Age at Ban Lum Khao, and some were placed with the dead as mortuary offerings.

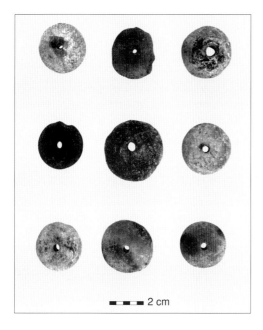

and an infant interred in a mortuary jar. Apart from a small number of stone abraders and red ochre in seven graves, animal remains were the most common offering beside ceramic vessels. Sub-adult pigs dominated the assemblage, but one grave contained a dog's skull, and another the antlers of a sambar deer.

O'Reilly (1999) has undertaken a detailed analysis of the spatial and social dimensions of this cemetery. He has identified five rows of graves representing all burials orientated with the head to the south or southeast. Even with a relatively large exposure such as that at Ban Lum Khao, one encounters the problem of boundaries, and we do not know where the rows terminate, and how many graves there are in each. However, it is possible to visualise five partial rows of

Like many other Bronze Age sites, the prehistoric inhabitants of Ban Lum Khao made cattle figurines of clay.

Left: Spindle whorls from Ban Lum Khao indicate the preparation of yarn for a weaving industry.

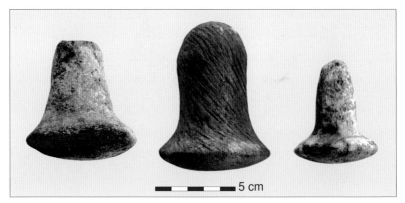

These anvils were used to shape pottery vessels at Ban Lum Khao.

Although no bronze grave goods were found at Ban Lum Khao, there is no doubt that casting took place there, as is seen by clay moulds for a projectile point and an axe.

graves, each including the remains of men, women, infants and children. There appears to be some patterning in the placement of infant graves at the feet of women rather than men, while men and women do not cluster, but are distributed within each row.

Ceramic vessels are the most common mortuary offering. O'Reilly recognized 15 forms, and considered their distribution in terms of time, space and the sex and age of the deceased. He found that there was a development of distinct forms over time, with cord-marked pots being preferred in early graves, red-slipped, trumpet-rimmed vessels in the third phase burials, and globular vessels with parallel-sided rims in the latest graves. Apart from a distinct form of lidded infant mortuary jar, however, there was no discernable relationship between ceramic form and the other variables reviewed.

When turning to the other grave goods, O'Reilly gave a point for each item, and estimated wealth by the total number of offerings with each person. Poor individuals were defined as having fewer than 10 points, rich as having over 20, with intermediate people lying between the extremes. The vast majority, 95 of the 111, were poor. Only three were found to be rich, all belonging to the final mortuary phase. An assessment of each type of mortuary offering against gender, age and location failed to reveal any significant pattern. Pig bones, for example, were found in 13 burials but apart from a regular occurrence in the latest phase, there was no recurring relationship with any other specified group. Shell beads were found in all mortuary phases and rows. Shell bangles were associated with all age groups and sexes, while five women and two men wore bangles made of exotic marble. One particular style of bangle, however, was found to be restricted to older individuals. While one might expect stone adzes to be interred with men, in fact they were commonly found with infants, children and women. Spindle whorls would be expected to occur with women, but they were found with people of all age groups and both sexes. Ceramic anvils for fashioning pottery vessels were confined to three graves, all of mortuary phase 3, two being male and one, female. Bivalve shellfish appear to have been imbued with considerable symbolic meaning not only at Ban Lum Khao, but also at many other Bronze Age sites. We find shells from

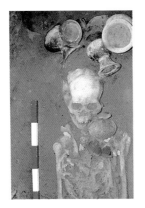

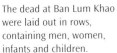
The dead at Ban Lum Khao were laid out in rows, containing men, women, infants and children.

Above, left and far left: Pottery vessels were very common as grave goods at Ban Lum Khao.

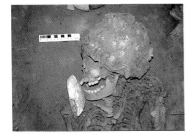
Many people, young and old, were interred at Ban Lum Khao with large freshwater bivalve shells.

Above and right: Infants at Ban Lum Khao were interred in large, lidded pottery vessels. Most were found at the feet of female graves.

eight species associated with the dead, either near an adult body, or outside infant mortuary vessels. Half the occurrences were with infants or children. Bronze offerings were extremely rare, and none can be classified as a specific artefact form. Thus a ball of copper alloy only 6 mm across was found in the grave of burial 39 from the final mortuary phase. A fragment of copper alloy was found in the mortuary vessel of the infant burial 16. A second ball of copper or bronze occurred in the grave of burial 56, a seven-year old, while a fragment of bronze near the skull of burial 88, a 13-year old, might possibly have been an earring. Fragments also occurred with burials 12, an infant, and burial 103, a foetal infant.

Above: The final mortuary phase at Ban Lum Khao saw a marked increase in the quantity of grave offerings placed with the dead.

The inclusion of grave goods with infants has in the past been used as a means of identifying ascribed rather than earned status in a community on the premise that the dead did not live long enough to achieve personal standing. On the other hand, infants might well have

These large ceramic vessels were made of standardised form for infant burials at Ban Lum Khao.

20 cm

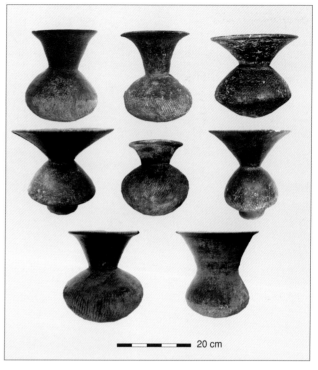

20 cm

Middle period graves at Ban Lum Khao had distinctive red-slipped vessels as grave goods.

10 cm

Early graves at Ban Lum Khao had small, circular cord-marked bowls as grave goods.

been accorded a relatively wealthy burial in order to project the personal status of family members. In the case of the infants from Ban Lum Khao, it was noted that those in the second row were interred with an average of almost six items per individual, whereas those in the first row had an average of only 1.5. A statistical analysis suggested that the row 2 infants were in fact more wealthy than others. No such differences were noted for the 16 child burials, nor between the grave goods of infants and children. Even when the well-endowed phase 4 burials are included, no row stood out as being richer than any other. Nor were there any differences between the mortuary treatment of men and women, or between wealth and men of differing stature. In terms of age, however, it was found that people who died between the ages of 30-39 were rather richer than any other age category with an average of almost nine items, whereas those aged over 40 had a mean of half this figure. It is evident that there is a sharp distinction in terms of wealth, over time. Phase 1 burials had an average of 4.26 items, phase 3 had 4.61, but with phase 4, the figure rises threefold to 15.

The dominant impression of this assemblage is uniformity of treatment rather than lack of differentiation on the basis of sex, age or location. Only with the final few burials, which were found grouped at the western edge of the excavated area and on a new orientation, was there a sharp rise in the quantity and range of grave goods.

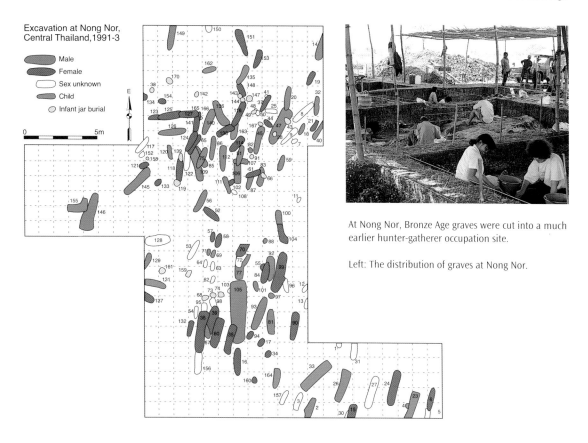

Excavation at Nong Nor, Central Thailand,1991-3

- Male
- Female
- Sex unknown
- Child
- Infant jar burial

0   5m

At Nong Nor, Bronze Age graves were cut into a much earlier hunter-gatherer occupation site.

Left: The distribution of graves at Nong Nor.

Nong Nor

The Bronze Age graves at Nong Nor were cut into a third millennium BC coastal occupation site (Higham and Thosarat 1998a). Some graves were excavated through the shell midden into the natural substrate, others were situated over the earlier settlement layers. The exposure of over 400 square metres of this site revealed 166 graves, divided into eastern and a western groups. The latter lay in rows, as at Ban Lum Khao, while those in the eastern group, although showing some row formation, were more diffusely distributed. The thinning out of burial density at the margins suggests that most of the cemetery has been uncovered. Unusually, no evidence for occupation remains were encountered. It is as if the Bronze Age cemetery lay apart from the settlement. Nevertheless, there are numerous similarities between Nong Nor and the other cemeteries of this period. Apart from burial in rows, we find consistency in orientation in which the head was usually oriented to the east. Some individuals, as at Ban Lum Khao, were found on a north to south axis. Pottery vessels dominated mortuary offerings, although the range of forms differed from those of Ban Lum Khao. Similar marble bangles were found, pigs' foot bones accompanied the dead, and shell disc beads were worn. Infant skeletons, contained in ceramic vessels, often lay at the feet of women. Yet there were also distinctive differences, involving a greater range of grave goods.

Small socketed copper implements from Nong Nor were probably imported from the Khao Wong Prachan Valley. Maximum height, 5 cm.

This child was interred in a grave at Nong Nor far larger than was necessary.

The horns of a large bull enclose the skull of this male adult at Nong Nor.

Uncovering a Bronze Age burial at Nong Nor. Note the upturned bowl over the chest.

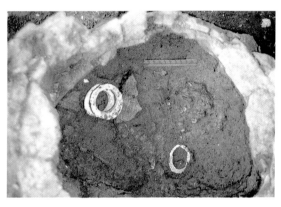

There was a rich enclave of graves at Nong Nor, incorporating the burials of a man and four women. They wore many exotic bangles.

Infants at Nong Nor were interred in pottery vessels, often with their own shell jewellery.

The eastern part of the cemetery of Nong Nor appears to have been later: virtually all the exotic stone jewellery was found in this sector.

Burial 105 at Nong Nor occupied a grave about 4 metres long. The man wore a large bronze bangle and range of other prestigious offerings.

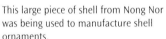

Above and left: These bangles from Nong Nor were made from shell, marble and bronze. The bangles vary between 10-14 cm in diameter.

Pierced tigers' tooth pendants from Nong Nor were worn round the neck.

This large piece of shell from Nong Nor was being used to manufacture shell ornaments.

Shell was used to manufacture shell ear ornaments at Nong Nor. (Width 4.5 cm).

At Nong Nor, we find more bronzes, usually in the form of bangles. Of 50 complete graves, seven included bronze jewellery. Two people were buried with clusters of copper-socketed implements resembling those cast at Nil Kham Haeng, and their form and lack of any evidence for alloying with tin, point to exchange with the production centres in the Khao Wong Prachan Valley. Tin ornaments were also found: one man wore earrings, while a woman was found wearing spiraliform bangles. There was also a unique range of exotic stone jewellery, including rare items of carnelian, talc, jade and serpentine. Some serpentine bangles were repaired, as at Ban Na Di, with tie wires of cast bronze. The people of Nong Nor fashioned shell neck pendants not yet recovered from any other site, and chose to inter dogs' crania regularly with the dead. Shell bangles were often found, some of which were made locally as evidenced by unfinished examples. One person was interred with tigers' canine pendants. Sandstone whetstones were a further mortuary offering found with some regularity.

The sample of graves is large enough to encourage a quest for patterning on the basis of statistical analyses. This involves relationships between the disposition of the dead on the basis of age,

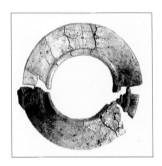

This serpentine bangle from Nong Nor was repaired with bronze ties, and was severely burnt.

This jade pendant from Nong Nor was converted from a broken bangle. Width 4.6 cm.

Serpentine was found at Nong Nor in the form of bangles and this ear pendant. Width 3.3 cm.

These carnelian beads from Nong Nor are the earliest known from prehistoric Thailand. The largest is 6 mm wide.

The blanks cut from shell preforms are convincing evidence for the local manufacture of shell bangles. These were placed near the skull of one of the burials at Nong Nor.

sex and location within the cemetery. The degree to which different categories of grave offering contributed to variability was first computed by means of a principal component analysis. It was found that the remains of dogs, pigs, marble bracelets, shell pendants, shell bead necklaces and belts, grinding stones, bronze bangles and certain forms of pot predominated. Potentially significant items, such as jade and carnelian ornaments, were so rare, however, as to contribute only negligible variability to the overall picture. When applying the principal component analysis to the 49 intact graves on the basis of the presence or absence of a particular artefact, we find that the majority cluster in one group. These have few mortuary offerings. Five males, three females and a child on the other, hand, are separated by their complement of marble bangles, shell pendants, and dog crania. Another group is distinguished by the presence of pottery vessel form 10, and all lie in the eastern sector of the cemetery. This statistic sets five men and three women apart as being relatively wealthy. A second distribution plot on the basis of the fourth and fifth most significant contributors to variability shows that some men are separated by the presence of a grinding stone, the only artefact which seems to set men apart from women.

One can also apply this statistic on the basis of the quantity of artefacts found. In this case, shell pendants, marble bangles, grinding stones, conus shells and pottery forms 13 and 14 distinguish five relatively wealthy graves. Four stand out for their multiple exotic bangles; there is one man and three women, and they are grouped in close proximity in the western sector. A man in the eastern group is also set apart by his four conus shells and multiple pottery vessels. These same graves were also separated from the majority when a second statistic, multi-dimensional scaling, was applied.

There was no clear separation of adult graves on the basis of the age of the deceased. The rich enclave of female burials identified above, for example, comprises one young, a mid-aged and an older woman. Advancing age did not attract more grave goods. On the other hand, graves in the eastern and western sectors were distinguished one from the other, largely on the basis of one form of vessel. Qualitatively, it is also noted that virtually all the talc, carnelian, jade and serpentine ornaments were found in the eastern sector. Ten burials contained serpentine ornaments, but there was no relationship between its presence and age or sex. It was found with three older, one mid-aged and four young men and with three women, one of each age group.

Two spatial groups have been isolated, their distinctiveness being most easily explained by a horizontal stratigraphy in which the easterly group is later. The exotic stone ornaments concentrate in this group almost exclusively. Within the earlier group, five graves in close proximity have been set apart on the basis of the quantity of their ornaments. The single male is also distinguished by an outstandingly long grave, a uniquely large and heavy bronze bangle and a tin earring. Caution must also be applied in considering this set, because many graves in the same row are incomplete for one reason or another. There is no evidence, other than the placement of grinding stones with men, for a bias in terms of wealth with gender, while children were accorded the same mortuary ritual and range of grave goods as adults. There is no evidence for a correlation between bronze and wealthy graves, or graves of a particular age group or sex. Bronze and tin were preferred for ornaments, with bangles predominating, while copper was found in the form of small, socketed chisel-like implements. There are 60 bronze or copper artefacts from all graves combined, represented by 38 bangles, four earrings, 15 socketed implements and three coils.

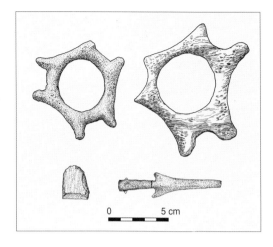

No other sites in Southeast Asia have been opened on a sufficient scale to permit a consideration of social variables. However, smaller exposures have still furnished useful information. Excavations at Khok Phlap, for a example have revealed a further coastal Bronze Age site behind the shore of the Gulf of Siam. It is a low mound covering an area of about 1.5 ha (Daeng-iet 1978). No radiocarbon dates have yet been published, but the parallels with the other sites described above are clear. Several burials were accompanied by whole pottery vessels containing sea shells. Ornaments included bracelets made of turtle carapace, stone, shell and bone as well as of bronze. One grave contained three anvils used in making pots in addition to four complete vessels. The inhabitants of the site showed a predilection for coloured stone beads and ear pendants, while their interest in bronze extended to barbed metal tips for their arrows. The presence of Bronze Age occupation in northern Thailand has been demonstrated at Ob Luang, where a single excavated grave included bronze and shell bangles, shell and carnelian beads and pottery vessels (Prishanchit *et al.* 1988).

Khok Phlap has provided evidence for Bronze Age occupation near the coast of the Gulf of Siam. The bangle at the top left is of bronze, the other was made from turtle shell. There is also a stone adze head and a bronze spearhead.

The Bronze Age in Bac Bo

No site in Bac Bo has furnished mortuary samples comparable with those from the Khorat Plateau and Central Thailand. Nevertheless, all evidence points to a closely similar Bronze Age culture. Dong Dau is the most important site not least because of the unusually deep stratigraphic record (Ha Van Phung 1979). It is located to the east of most Phung Nguyen sites, within sight of the Red River. It was recognised in 1961, and excavations undertaken in 1965 and 1967-8 uncovered 550 square metres to a depth of between 5 and 6 metres. A fourth season in 1981 added further to our understanding of the material culture of this phase (Ngo Si Hong 1987). The mound itself covers about 3 ha. Its basal cultural material has been ascribed to the final Phung Nguyen sub-phase, and while the pottery of the Dong Dau site reveals Phung Nguyen origins at least in style and mode of decoration,

Dong Dau is the site which gives its name to the Early Bronze Age in Bac Bo, northern Viet Nam.

we also find compelling evidence for a local and vigorous bronze industry. Ngo Si Hong (1987) has published half a bivalve mould for casting a socketed, bronze axe, while Trinh Sinh (1977) has stressed that many of the Phung Nguyen phase stone artefacts were copied in bronze. There are also intriguing parallels with material from the Northeastern Thai sites, not only in the small furnaces for casting bronze items, but in the ceramic cattle figurines.

The bivalve moulds recovered by Ha Van Tan from a small (50 square metre) excavation in a Dong Dau context at Thanh Den are virtually identical with those from the Khorat plateau. The 30 or so fragments of stone and clay moulds were designed for casting axes and fishhooks. The site has a cultural stratigraphy of only 1 m, and the three radiocarbon dates match very closely the dates obtained for the Bronze Age in Northeast Thailand. Bronze was also employed to make socketed spearheads, arrowheads and chisels. The Dong Dau axe began to take on the initial pediform shape so indicative of later decorated examples from the Dong Son Iron Age. This site has also yielded nephrite bangles and rings which recall Phung Nguyen prototypes, some of which appear to have been manufactured at the site (Nguyen Kim Dung 1998).

Towards the end of the second millennium BC, the Dong Dau developed into the Go Mun phase. Go Mun is located only 3 km northeast of Phung Nguyen, and indeed the 30 or so known Go Mun sites are located within the same general area as those of Phung Nguyen and Dong Dau. There have been four campaigns of excavations at Go Mun, commencing in 1961 and finishing a decade later. In all, 1,500 square metres have been excavated, the cultural stratigraphy being only 1 metre deep. As at Phung Nguyen, stone adzes were in the main quadrangular. Of the 87 recovered, 80 were quadrangular, and only one, shouldered. Similar stone chisels to those from Phung Nguyen were also encountered. The inventory of bronze artefacts reveals that many forms in stone were copied in metal. There are also bivalve moulds for casting axes and arrowheads. Thirteen axes have been found, and seven chisels. The spearheads, arrowheads and bracelets were likewise rendered in bronze. Fishhooks were the most abundant bronze artefact, followed by narrow projectile points. One sickle was recovered, and the figure of a seated individual which was presumably cast by means of the lost wax technique. The Dong Dau pottery bears curvilinear and rectangular patterns which look like developed Phung Nguyen motifs, and it is in these that Ha Van Tan (1980) sees models for the decoration later found on the well-known Dong Son drums. It is apparent from the excavations carried out at Go Mun and related sites that bronze working was increasing in intensity and range of artifacts.

There was also a coastal aspect to settlement in the Bac Bo area. We have already considered the site of Cai Beo and the Da But grouping of sites. Vietnamese archaeologists see these as ancestral to various so-called middle and late Neolithic cultures which occupied the coastal tract north and south of the Red River delta. Thus the Ha Long culture of the islands in the northern sector of the Gulf of Bac Bo is seen as derivative from a Cai Beo context. They base this

Left and far left:
The sandstone moulds and bronze axes from Thanh Den are typical of the Bronze Age from Thailand to Hong Kong. These examples come from, Viet Nam.

opinion on the similarities in the rectangular and shouldered adzes recovered. Sites of this group also yield polished stone bracelets, beads and pendants not dissimilar to Phung Nguyen examples. Moving south of the delta, we encounter sites of another coastal group, called after the site of Hoa Loc. This group is known for a most unusual form of decorated pottery with a quadrangular shaped rim. They also used clay seals with deeply excised patterns resembling those found much later in Iron Age contexts in Northeast Thailand. Stone adzes and grinding stones are common and large stone hoes recur. The faunal associations from Hoa Loc are dominated by marine species, but Vu The Long has also noted the remains of domesticated dog, pig and probably cattle. Le Van Thieu (1979) has indicated that some of the pigs' teeth display a bimodal size distribution, probably reflecting the presence of wild and domesticated animals. Hoa Loc itself is located on a raised sand bar now about 4 km behind the shoreline. It is evident that as the sea level fell back from its post-Pleistocene high, so coastal settlement followed. A few pieces of bronze were found at Hoa Loc when it was excavated in 1976. It seems to equate, in terms of its metallurgy, with the latest Phung Nguyen sub-phase in the inland area.

The Lower Mekong Valley and its Hinterland

The analysis of the Bronze Age in this nodal region has advanced to the point that Pham Duc Manh (2000) now distinguishes an Early and a Late Bronze phase. The former belongs to the second phase of his Dong Nai culture, the latter to the third phase. Local bronze casting was definitely attested at Hang Gon (Saurin 1963), although this site has never been systematically excavated. Indeed, the material collected by Saurin was revealed by a bulldozer when clearing woodland. Surface sherds there cover an area of 350 by 150 m, the site lying on a ridge which commands the junction of two streams. Its particular interest lies in the discovery of three sandstone moulds, two for casting axes and the third for casting three ring-headed pins. Saurin stressed the typological similarities between the shape of the

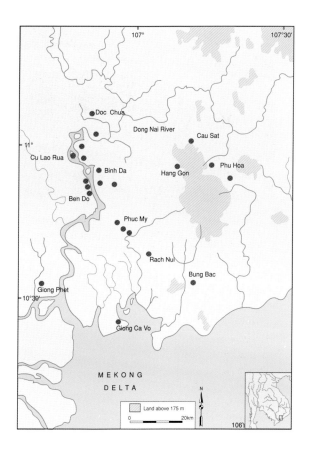

The distribution of prehistoric sites in the Dong Nai Valley.

axes and specimens known from the Red River valley, Luang Prabang in Northern Laos and from the Mlu Prei region in North Central Cambodia. The site had a cultural stratigraphy of only 0.5-1.0 metres and neither iron nor glass beads were found among the material turned up by the bulldozer. A radiocarbon date of about 2000 BC has been obtained from an organic crust adhering to a potsherd, but little if any value attaches to such a sample. The cultural sequence in this area, and in particular the date of metallurgy there has, however, been clarified by recent Vietnamese investigations.

These have concentrated in the riverine flats which comprise the northern margins of the Dong Nai delta. This delta area is a maze of channels which flow through dense mangroves, but access to the sea, and therefore to major exchange networks, was always possible. The low-lying and swampy nature of this landscape has preserved wooden remains in a series of sites, foremost being Cai Van, Cai Lang and Rach La. Wooden posts up to 2.2 metres long, still bearing planks, indicate river-side villages comprising houses raised on stilts above the flood level. The material culture from these sites includes abundant numbers of stone adzes, pottery and the ceramic anvils used to shape the clay vessels. Shell bangles were manufactured on the site, for the circular cores have been recovered. Unusually, wooden bobbins for making nets have also survived. These sites were also centres for bronze casting. One clay mould still contained the axe within, while sandstone and clay moulds for casting barbed points, fishhooks and a spear were also recovered. Resin survived, and may well have been used to caulk boats or waterproof pottery vessels, while there are reports of parts of a crossbow. Dating these sites is not easy. There are four available radiocarbon dates, two from Cai Van and one from Cai Lang and Rach La. Three derive from the wooden posts, with one from a dagger. Those from Cai Van range between 1900-1275 BC, while Cai Lang dates to 1770-1370 BC and Rach Ga, 1650-1110 BC. It should be recalled that these sites reveal up to four phases of occupation, and the samples dated, large wooden posts, may well have inbuilt age, having come from old trees. Sites with crossbows and halberds cannot date within the second millennium BC.

By phase four, bronze was abundant and locally cast. In 1976, the important site of Doc Chua on the bank of the Be River was discovered, and excavations ensued then and during the following year. The finds documented a mature tradition of casting bronze. No fewer than 50 mould fragments of clay or sandstone were found, and implements locally cast included tanged arrowheads, axes, small bells, socketed spearheads, harpoons and chisels. Examination of the sandstone moulds has revealed several which were incomplete before being discarded due to imperfections. The process of cutting and polishing the interior surfaces of the sandstone was most demanding. The shape of the axes, chisels, arrowheads and spearheads is remarkably similar to the examples from Northeast Thailand (Le Xuan Diem 1977). There are also general resemblances in some stone artefacts, such as the bracelets and adzes. The radiocarbon date of 1195-130 BC derives from charcoal from a depth of 1.0 metres at the site.

The village of Samrong Sen in 1970. This site is the birthplace of prehistoric archaeology in Southeast Asia.
(Courtesy Dr. Roland Mourer)

In 1994, excavations covering 405 square metres at the equally significant site of Bung Bac uncovered many stone bivalve moulds for casting axes, as well as partially-completed stone bangles, and the roundels taken from the centre of bangles once completed (Pham Duc Manh and Nguyen Giang Hai 1996). The ten radiocarbon dates from Bung Bac fall between 1200-400 BC, indicating the likelihood of settlement from the late second millennium BC. A further important site of Phuc My was excavated in 1998. It lies adjacent to the Dong Nai River, and Trinh Sinh (2001) has described a wide range of moulds for casting bronze axes. Some of these axes would, on completion, have been embellished with animal figures adjacent to the sockets. There are also spindle whorls and clay stamps similar to those found in Khorat Plateau sites, demonstrating a relatedness between sites all along the Mekong River and its tributaries. One of the most intriguing results, as research has extended into the interior plateaux, is the recovery of 26 sites in the vicinity of Pleiku. Ascribed to the Bien Ho culture by Nguyen Khac Su (1995), these sites have yielded high quality ceramics and shouldered stone adzes, and their economy involved rice cultivation as well as hunting and fishing. This new chapter in our understanding of the Bronze Age is only now beginning to be appreciated.

There was thus a network of bronze-using communities from the mouths of the Mekong up to the Khorat Plateau, and extending into the surrounding uplands. A major link in this proposed chain is Samrong Sen, an occupation and burial site already alluded to, with a stratigraphy almost 6 metres deep, situated on the banks of the Chinit River. The site was first investigated by Noulet (1879), but excavations adopting any semblance of stratigraphical control were undertaken only in 1902 and 1923. Mansuy (1902, 1923) recognised three layers, one of which attained a depth of 4.5 metres and was said to incorporate numerous shell lenses.

Given the almost complete absence of stratigraphical control in a site having a lengthy period of occupation, only the most general conclusions are possible. Among these is the clear relationships which exist between the shouldered and rectangular adzes of Samrong Sen and those from the lower Mekong sites. Armbands and beads of stone also link this site with others in the Mekong catchment. Pottery is less easily paralleled elsewhere. Much of the ware is plain, and

Several spearheads were placed with the dead in the Nyaunggan cemetery.

decoration is, in general, confined to impressed or incised geometric motifs. The complete vessels probably come from inhumation graves, though flooding is said to have redeposited the human bone in antiquity. A characteristic form has a broad pedestalled base supporting an open bowl. Some were decorated all over, others left plain. Painting is absent. While there are no precise parallels between these vessels and those from Northeast Thai sites, Loofs-Wissowa has pointed out a remarkable similarity between two complete vessels from Samrong Sen and the earliest style recovered at Ban Chiang.

Mansuy recovered a fragment of bronze mould from Samrong Sen, while unprovenanced bronze artefacts fall within the range of types documented in the Lower Mekong, Northeast Thailand and coastal Viet Nam. The stratigraphical associations of the tanged arrowheads, socketed axeheads, bells, armrings, fishhooks and chisels are unknown. During a visit to the site just before the second world war, Janse collected various artefacts and these have been examined by Murowchik (1986). They include a crucible still containing scoria, erroneously described by Janse as a spoon (Janse 1951), and several bronzes, including bracelets, socketed spearheads, axes and a bell. The analyses of the alloy composition of five of these artefacts has revealed that three specimens have a high (11.74-26.47%) lead content. Murowchik's examination of these bronzes further indicates a technological tradition of casting and annealing which precisely matches that represented in the other sites of the Mekong catchment. Indeed, this tradition extends up into the very headwaters of the Mekong, where a bivalve axe-mould has been recovered (Wang Dadao pers. comm.). Shellfish from two locations have been combined to provide one radiocarbon sample, which yielded a date of 1280±120 BC. The material dated comes respectively from 1.0 metres and 1.5 metres below the surface, so at best dates only the later part of the cultural sequence. However, a date in the late 2nd millennium BC would fit the typology of the bronze artefacts.

Samrong Sen must surely represent many similar sites in Central Cambodia. Indeed, Mansuy was aware of a very similar site, to judge from surface finds, at nearby Long Prao. It has never been excavated, but Lévy (1943) has examined three prehistoric sites located near the headwaters of the Sen and Chinit rivers. Surface remains from O Pie Can covered an area of about 1 ha. The site is located at the confluence of two streams, and the culture layer was 40 cm in depth. Lévy has reported finding pieces of sandstone moulds on the surface, as well as crucible fragments containing bronze, and pieces of iron slag. The excavations also revealed sandstone moulds for casting a sickle and an axe. The shape of the former is very similar to those from Go Mun contexts in Viet Nam. The site also yielded many fragments of stone and clay bangles and clay stamps bearing deeply incised curvilinear designs. Reports from looters at nearby O Yak referred to human inhumation burials incorporating bronze bracelets, animal bone offerings and brown-red glass beads. Burials were also noted in eroded material at O Pie Can. The surface of the third mound, O Nari, included much pottery as well as fragments of polished stone adzes and some bronze. As at Samrong Sen, the adzes were both shouldered and rectangular in shape. Stone beads and bracelets as well as round clay pellet-bow pellets were also recovered there.

Central and Coastal Viet Nam

The coastal plain which abuts the Truong Son Cordillera between the Ca and Dong Noi valleys is generally narrow. Only where the Thu Bon, Con and Ba rivers reach

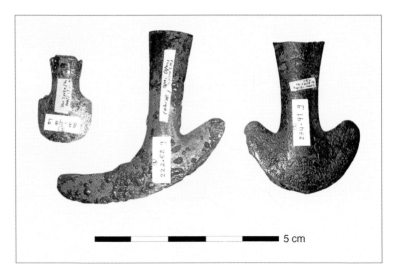

Bronze socketed axes from Nyaunggan burials belong within the Southeast Asian Bronze Age tradition.

the sea, are there enclaves of good agricultural soils. Archaeological research in these areas is in its infancy, but already it is clear that the Thu Bon valley was occupied in prehistory by a society proficient in metallurgy. At Binh Chau, Ngo Sy Hong (1980) has investigated occupation and burial remains. Three mounds have been excavated, each covering between 0.5 and 1.0 ha. Today, all command tracts of flat rice fields. Preliminary findings have revealed that the occupants inhumed the dead, in association with several pottery vessels, some of which were decorated with red, black and white designs. The widespread form of split earring was rendered in fired clay at Binh Chau. Of particular note were the fragments of crucibles and moulds found, in addition to bronze socketed axes and tanged arrowheads. Two radiocarbon dates (1185±130 and 794±40 BC) indicate contemporaneity with Dong Dau-Go Mun assemblages to the north, and Doc Chua to the south.

Explorations in the coastal plain centred on Hue and extending north to Dong Hoi have revealed further evidence of Bronze Age settlement, but, as yet, it seems confined to the first millennium BC (Reinecke *et al.* 1999). This region commands a pass across the Truong Son Cordillera to the Mekong and beyond to the Khorat Plateau, and this may well have been employed by the Bronze Age for the transmission of goods and ideas. Two jar burials at Ban Vang incorporated decorated bronze bangles reminiscent of those found in Northeast Thailand. Other Bronze Age sites have been identified at Ba Long, Huyen Cu and Nhu Le.

It is also evident that Bronze Age settlement extended into the interior. Excavations in an area of 106 square metres at Lung Leng, 15 km west of Kontum, have revealed a major Bronze Age occupation. There are numerous shouldered stone adzes and pottery vessels, as well as hoes and pestles. Bronze-casting moulds reveal local expertise in metal working, and the production of socketed axes. (Nguyen Khac Su and Tranh Quy Thinh 2000).

The Chindwin River near Monywa: this area is rich in copper ore.

Above right: The excavated area of Nyaunggan lies on the flank of a large extinct volcano.

Right: Nyaunggan commands an extensive view over the surrounding area, the dry interior of Myanmar.

The Chindwin Valley

Until recently, no Bronze Age sites were known in Burma. Given its wealth of copper ore deposits, this gap in our knowledge was all the more surprising. The discovery of the site of Nyaunggan in the Chindwin River valley has now dramatically altered our understanding of the extent of the Southeast Asian Bronze Age. Nyaunggan is a cemetery which lies on the edge of an extinct volcano overlooking a broad flood plain. Excavations have uncovered many inhumation graves associated with pottery vessels, exotic stone ornaments and bronzes. The bronzes incorporated socketed axes and spearheads displaying a considerable variety of forms and sizes. Unfortunately, none of the skeletons has been lifted for detailed analysis, and pottery vessels still lie where they were uncovered. Some of the latter are very large and one can discern animal bones within. The contents remain in place, and it is not known whether or not they contain infant remains. No datable charcoal has been recovered, and insufficient collagen remains to obtain radiocarbon dates from the human bone. However, to judge from the form and size of the bronzes, and the absence of iron, the cemetery most probably belongs in the first half of the first millennium BC.

The stratigraphic sequence at this site does not reveal any evidence for occupation: the burials lie within culturally sterile

These exotic stone bangles of unusual shapes were characteristic of Bronze Age Nyaunggan. (Maximum width 12 cm).

material. It may well be that more Bronze Age cemeteries have not been found because they lie on elevated terrain covered by naturally-deposited soil. Finding more sites like Nyaunggan, and the settlements where the people responsible lived, are exciting challenges in the future of Burmese archaeology.

The Bronze Age: Subsistence

The subsistence base which underwrote the expansion of human settlement during the Bronze Age remains little known, but some general variables are beginning to respond to laboratory analysis. There are several sources of information. These are initially, the location of settlements relative to available resources. The resources themselves are documented on the basis of food remains from excavated sites, though some survive more readily than others, and we must guard against bias due to differential preservation. The same reservation applies to the recovery of artefacts associated with subsistence activities.

Having ascertained what people ate, we may take our appreciation of subsistence a stage further by considering the size of settlements, their likely population and the capacity of the territory in the vicinity of the site to provide for the number of people. The acid test for the success of subsistence is of course, the health of the people. This can be considered on the basis of their skeletal remains.

We usually find settlements on slightly elevated ground, adjacent to tracts of low-terrace soil in the middle courses of tributary streams. Mudar, however, has also shown in the Lam Maleng Valley that some Bronze Age sites were located on the upper terrace, perhaps as specialised foci for the manufacture of stone artefacts. White (1982) may have identified one major element when she stressed that the slightly elevated locations were optimal for access to land under regular but not deep flooding. Wild rice still grows along the margins of such small streams, and its growth during the wet season is dependent on the regular but not excessive presence of surface water. It is, therefore, possible that the expansion of natural swampland by judicious clearance of natural vegetation expanded the habitat suited to rice. Proximity to water is equally important for people as well as domestic stock, while flooded terrain today is a rich source of aquatic species including fish, shellfish, amphibians and reptiles.

Whereas the siting of individual settlements can be readily considered, it is far more difficult and at present nearly impossible to reconstruct and assess the changing pattern of settlements across the landscape. All attempts at identifying prehistoric sites within a circumscribed area on the Khorat plateau faced the same problem. The recognition of a surviving prehistoric site is not difficult. What is next to impossible short of excavation, is knowing on the basis of surface features, at what periods in the past the site was occupied. Thus, at Ban Chiang Hian, the prehistoric deposits attained a depth of over 6 metres, and none of the early pottery styles discovered at that depth through excavation was represented on the site's surface. How then, are we to know if other sites in the area have early occupation horizons? The distribution of prehistoric sites in the Kumphawapi area appears to show a light network of settlement over the low-lying terrain, with the uplands being avoided. This would be a false conclusion. Excavation at Ban Muang Phruk, which is located close to the shore of Lake Kumphawapi has shown that settlement there commenced only in the Iron Age. Indeed, few sites are known to have been occupied during the Neolithic and Bronze Ages. All such early sites are set back from the zone of maximum flooding, and it seems a reasonable supposition that this reflects conditions compatible with the exploitation of rice and both forest fringe and aquatic fauna.

Biological remains from all the sites under review are abundant and well preserved. This allows insight into the economic basis, as well as aspects of burial ritual and behaviour. This latter situation reflects the placement of animal bone in human graves. It is, however, necessary to stress that the assessment of a given site's subsistence base is heavily dependent on the degree to which screening of the prehistoric deposits is undertaken. The absence of sieves results only in the retrieval of large bones, but at the other end of the scale, the application of flotation through screens of under 1 mm mesh size, as applied at Ban Lum Khao and Nong Nor, results in a large sample of very small items, which range from tiny land snails to a myriad of fish bones.

Few species were represented in human graves at Non Nok Tha. Pig and cattle bones predominate with a total of 45 and 36 individuals respectively from graves of all periods. Others lag far behind. There are only two dogs and one water buffalo specimen. Perhaps due to the absence of screening, fish are found rarely and are confined to the contents of funerary vessels. There are also the

Fishing remains as vital today as it was during the Bronze Age. Here, rice farmers are fishing with bamboo traps during the height of the dry season in Surin Province, Thailand.

remains of two chickens, three deer and three fragments of turtle. The prehistoric occupants of Non Nok Tha placed pig remains, sometimes complete animals, in human graves. This has led to the survival of relatively complete skulls. Adult wild pigs have long and narrow crania. The three intact adult skulls from the Non Nok Tha burials are short and relatively broad, indicating a domesticated breed. The cattle bones from burial contexts at Non Nok Tha were significantly smaller than modern wild ones, suggesting that cattle too, were domesticated.

One of the surprising features of the animal bones is the rarity of water buffalo. This animal is of critical importance to the modern inhabitants because its strength allows it to draw a plough through rice fields. Dog bones too, are relatively rare but there is no doubting the presence of a domestic breed from the earliest occupation, because a complete skeleton was recovered from an Early Period burial for diagnosis. Both cattle and pigs are common in the non-burial contexts. Other animals present are the sambar deer, pig deer, muntjak and tiger. A small number of fish and turtle bones were found, suggesting the exploitation of water resources. Four species were domesticated from the site's earliest contexts – cattle, pig, dog and chicken. They were raised for ritual use and judging from butchering marks and charring on non-funerary specimens, for consumption. There was also an element of hunting, with a concentration on the larger game, particularly the deer.

Given that the site lies adjacent to modern rice fields, and the inhabitants not only maintained domestic stock but were familiar with bronze, the investigators were interested in the possibility that rice was cultivated there. During the late 1960s, hardly anything was known of the prehistoric environment, but the presence of fish and water turtle bones did suggest exploitation of aquatic resources, and wild rice still grows in low-lying swampy habitats on the Khorat plateau. In the absence of any rice grains, Bayard turned to an analysis of the material used to temper clay when making pottery. Although an admixture of sand was the predominant technique used during Early Period 1, about 1.5% of the 680 sherds examined were tempered with sand and rice chaff. This proportion rose to 5.7% in

Early Period 2 and 13.5% in Early Period 3. The Middle Period funerary vessels contained small fragments of rice chaff. Botanists are divided on the status of the rice remains. Chang (1976) has suggested that it lies between a wild and a weed rice. Vishnu-Mittre (1975) could not be sure whether it was cultivated or wild. Yen (1982) has likewise been unable to determine whether the rice chaff used to temper the clay used at Ban Chiang comes from a wild or domestic species.

At Ban Na Di, flotation was employed to recover rice grains and Chang and Loresto (1984) have concluded that they were cultivated. Faunal remains from many sites indicate intensive fishing, and the collection of shellfish and turtles in a low-lying and swampy habitat. Many wild mammals were hunted, and domestic cattle, pigs and dogs were raised. This is shown at Ban Lum Khao, where the late Neolithic occupants encountered a low-lying, marshy environment, which, to judge from the great size of the fish and water buffalo bones, had encountered little if any previous predation. In terms of the larger mammalian fauna, the pig is relatively common throughout the sequence. Cattle are rare, while the water buffalo appears regularly only in the lower layers. The dog is present throughout the sequence but in low frequencies. Eld's deer is the commonest cervid, appearing with abundance in layers 3 and early layer 2, but later becoming rare. The small and large deer, probably muntjak and sambar, were found consistently, but never in large numbers. It is clear that domestic cattle and pigs were maintained, but that hunting continued consistently throughout the Bronze Age.

By passing a sample of all cultural contexts through the flotation chamber, a very large sample of small faunal remains was assessmbled. While frogs and turtles were well represented, fish dominated the sample (Thosarat 2000). No artefacts which one might associate with fishing were recovered, but a similar situation would be encountered today, where nets and traps are widely employed but would not survive archaeologically. Indeed, the sample in terms of species frequency closely matches the relative abundance of fish consumed in the same area today. *Ophicephalus* (the snake head) is the most abundant, followed by *Mystus*, *Anabas* (the doctor fish), *Clarias* (the wriggling catfish) and *Fluta* (the swamp eel). All are adapted to a wide range of freshwater habitats, including swamps, streams and wet season rice fields. *Wallagonia attu*, the great white sheetfish, is also relatively abundant, preferring large rivers and lakes. Only two species reveal changes in relative frequency over time. The swamp eel was rare in early layers, but became more common in layer 2. By contrast the great white sheetfish became increasingly rare.

The swamp eel is widely consumed today, and many of its bones have been found in the Neolithic to Bronze Age site of Ban Lum Khao. It can grow to a length of 75 cm.

It is also noted that the series of Neolithic pits contain fish species in similar proportions to the later layers, except that they include a respectable number of bones from the swamp eel. Consequently, it is concluded that there were no major changes in species frequency during the prehistoric occupation of Ban Lum Khao. Fish comprised a vital and important part of the prehistoric diet, and were taken from an environment which incorporated freshwater swamps, streams, rivers and by inference, rice fields. The ritual as well as subsistence role of fish is also demonstrated by the finding of the snake head as a mortuary offering in two late burials, a practice which continued into the Iron Age at Noen U-Loke.

Subsistence: Summary

Subsistence activities included harvesting rice, maintaining domestic stock, hunting, trapping, fishing and collecting shellfish. There is little doubt too, that this represents only a partial picture. Even today, when the casual observer would conclude that subsistence is dominated by rice and fish, much gathering and foraging is also undertaken. Women will return to the village with a basket containing dung beetles, bamboo shoots, wild yams, mushrooms and frogs. Many vegetables are grown and wild plants collected. Termites and ants are considered delicacies. It is unfortunate that so many possible sources of food leave no trace in the archaeological record. Nor would hunting or trapping implements made of wood survive. Indeed, bamboo remains to this day the medium for a wide range of fish and animal traps. The principal implement which has survived is the stone axe or adze. These are relatively small, due no doubt to the local rarity of finely grained stone and constant sharpening. They could, however, have been critical in clearing natural vegetation, creating conditions suited to feeding cattle and encouraging rice.

The initial settlers lived in a monsoon environment which incorporated lakes, clear perennial streams and deciduous woodland. They selected slightly elevated terrain and cleared the vegetation in low-lying wetlands to encourage the proliferation of rice. It is highly likely that this rice was of a domesticated strain. They also maintained domestic cattle and pigs, and introduced domestic

Burial 20 from Ban Non Wat. Partially revealed in 2002, it included the remains of a young teenager and over 30 pots.

chickens and dogs. The local wild fauna was hunted or trapped, and both fishing and the collection of shellfish were prominent activities. This subsistence base was multi-facetted. No reliance was placed on any single activity. At the same time, the investment in permanent facilities such as wooden houses and the maintenance of cemeteries over many centuries suggests a commitment to permanent, sedentary occupation.

The People of the Bronze Age

During the past two decades, several samples of Bronze Age human skeletal remains have been recovered through excavation. These are large enough to allow some insight into the health of individuals and groups during the Bronze Age. The sites in question are Non Nok Tha (Douglas 1996), Ban Lum Khao, Nong Nor and Ban Na Di (Domett 1999). The human remains from Ban Chiang have also been considered in detail, but the sample has been divided into early and late groups. The former includes Neolithic with Bronze Age remains, while the latter spans the Bronze and Iron Ages (Douglas 1996). This rules out specific consideration of the Bronze Age people. With the possible exception of Ban Lum Khao, the inhabitants of Bronze Age settlements enjoyed a long local ancestry, and were therefore likely to have adapted to the potential health problems of their environment. As Domett has shown, this would have harboured many pathogens, few of which leave traces in the skeleton. Diarrhoea is the most common immediate cause of infant mortality in the area today, and can result from several infections with the rotavirus the most common, but *Shigella* and *Salmonella* are also potent. Respiratory problems, particularly in long periods of dry heat, also cause infant deaths. Parasites of the intestinal tract, such as the hookworm, can cause very poor health, since it feeds on the host's blood. Roundworm, liver and intestinal flukes are widely encountered today. The anopheles mosquito is one of the most widespread health risks, since it spreads the *Plasmodium protozoa*. The latter feeds on haemoglobin in the red blood cells, thus leading to anaemia and commonly, death. Severe anaemia can be traced in the skeleton through a thickening of the cranial vault (porotic hyperostosis), and the upper part of the eye sockets (cribra orbitalia).

The age structure is one of the basic indicators of health. We have seen, for example, that infant mortality was very high at the coastal hunter-gatherer site of Khok Phanom Di, with a figure in excess of 50% of all individuals being recorded for the earlier mortuary phases. The age profiles for the Bronze Age reveal far fewer infant deaths, the figure for infants under a year of age ranging from 11% at Nong Nor to 19% at Ban Na Di and Ban Lum Khao. The figure for Non Nok Tha may not be strictly comparable, because it was obtained by a different specialist. Moreover, the soils at this site were very hard, and infants may be under represented, with only 5.5% of the sample comprising infants under a year of age at death. There was a fairly high incidence of death among those aged under 10 years, followed by a sharp fall until the age of about 20. At this point, mortality rose again, particularly among females. This may well reflect the problems afflicting women in pregnancy and childbirth. More men are found in the older age groups, with barely one person in ten living beyond about 40 years of age. Non Nok Tha stands out for its very high number of older individuals, but this might reflect a combination of sampling problems and analysis by a different authority. Most women from Ban Na Di showed evidence for pregnancy, but this figure fell markedly at Ban Lum Khao to about half the pelves examined.

The average stature was very similar at each site. Douglas has divided the Non Nok Tha sample into early and late groups, and the men and women of the former were the shortest encountered. Later individuals were as tall as those at the other Bronze Age sites. There are conditions which originate in generalised poor health in childhood. One of these, dental enamel hypoplasia, was found in about a quarter of all adults at Khok Phanom Di, but this figure fell to between 11-12.6% for the females of Ban Na Di, Ban Lum Khao and Nong Nor, and between 11-15.6% for the men. Bone mass may be used as an indicator of the adequacy of the diet. The measure known as Nordin's score shows that the men and women of Ban Na Di, Nong Nor and Ban Lum Khao had similar values compatible with a good level of nutrition. Moreover, the diet was not cariogenic. Only 2.8% of the adult teeth at Non Nok Tha had caries, a figure which varied between 5.2 and 6.5% at the other three sites.

Men and women at all four Bronze Age sites suffered from joint degeneration, but the incidence suggests different work patterns between the sexes, and no individual appears to have suffered from acute conditions. The men seem to have been more involved, as one might expect, in heavy manual labour, but there is no recurrence of degeneration in the right shoulder joints which at Khok Phanom Di, might have resulted from manning water craft. The number of bone fractures was not great, but broken forearm bones and clavicles among men might be due to parrying blows as one might expect in interpersonal conflict.

The mean stature of men and women of the Bronze Age (cm) compared with Khok Phanom Di.

	female	male
Khok Phanom Di	154.3	162.2
Non Nor	156.1	167.2
Ban Lum Khao	154.7	164.7
Ban Na Di	155.9	168
Ban Chiang	154.7-153.7	166-165.4
Non Nok Tha early	1.52	1.64
Non Nok Tha late	1.55	1.66

Comparatively, the Bronze Age samples provide a generally similar picture of health, stature and life expectancy. The people of Ban Lum Khao appear to have suffered more than those of the other sites, in terms of a higher death rate among younger women, while the men had the lowest stature of any of the Bronze Age sites. Non Nok Tha was probably occupied over a longer period than the other sites, and here the trends over time reveal a reduction in the number of young people dying, linked with an increase in mean stature. These almost certainly reflect better health, for, again, the indicators changed for the better over time. There was progressively less evidence for anaemia, while the frequency of teeth with enamel hypoplasia fell during the later phase. However, osteoarthritis increased over time, with particular stress being seen to the male shoulders, hands, elbows and feet.

The Bronze Age: Summary

The Bronze Age of Southeast Asia can be traced from Lingnan to the Chindwin Valley, and from Yunnan to the Mekong Delta. We can pursue the technical basis of this Bronze Age from the mines to the ore processing and smelting facilities and thence to the casting of ingots and their arrival in agricultural village communities. There, smiths used small, clay-lined furnaces to bring their copper and tin ingots to melting point before casting socketed axes and spears in bivalve moulds. Arrowheads were also cast, while clay moulds were used for casting bangles by the lost-wax technique.

The growing corpus of well-provenanced radiocarbon dates indicates that this distinctive bronze-working tradition became established within the period 1500-1000 BC. However, very few sites have been scientifically examined, and it is possible that the initial date will ultimately fall in the first half of the second millennium BC. There is no way of isolating origins. On the one hand, it is noted that Lingnan, a component region of this tradition, lies open to the exchange of goods and ideas flowing south from the early Bronze Age civilizations of China. The former assuredly took place, for we have the jades and bronzes which arrived. The latter might have involved the introduction of the properties of copper and tin ore when smelted. If the Southeast Asian Bronze Age did not originate in such a context of exchange, then it would represent one of the two or three known discoveries of ore reduction and the use of metal.

There is no evidence for a new population entering the area during the initial Bronze Age. On the contrary, such data as are available suggest continuity from the Neolithic. We do not know how much bronze was in daily use, but it was decidedly rare in mortuary contexts. Indeed at Ban Lum Khao, it was hardly represented in any of the 111 burials examined. Nevertheless, there were long-established exchange networks that would have sped the transmission of ideas as well as ingots.

The larger excavations have provided sufficient information for us to appreciate some aspects of social organisation, although again, we need much larger samples. There is virtually no evidence for domestic structures or the population size of different settlements, but the opening of cemeteries has revealed little evidence for distinctions in social rank or wealth. It seems that settlements were generally smaller than 5 ha in extent. They were located to provide access to gently flooded lowlands suited to the cultivation of rice. Fish comprised a vital part of what would have been a well-balanced diet, while domestic cattle and pigs were raised, and the local game was trapped and hunted. Evidence for the social organisation associated with the mining and exchange of copper suggests a long tradition of community participation without the formation of controlling elites. In the Khao Wong Prachan Valley, there were changes in the means of smelting and casting. Burials tended to become more richly endowed with grave goods, but again, there is no associated evidence for a social hierarchy (White and Pigott 1996).

By the middle of the first millennium BC, however, major technological changes spread rapidly across Southeast Asia, bringing the knowledge of iron working, and introducing new problems and opportunities.

The snake head is the most widely consumed of all freshwater fish in Thailand. It can grow to a length of a metre. During the dry season, they sink into muddy hollows, and can be prised out by hand.

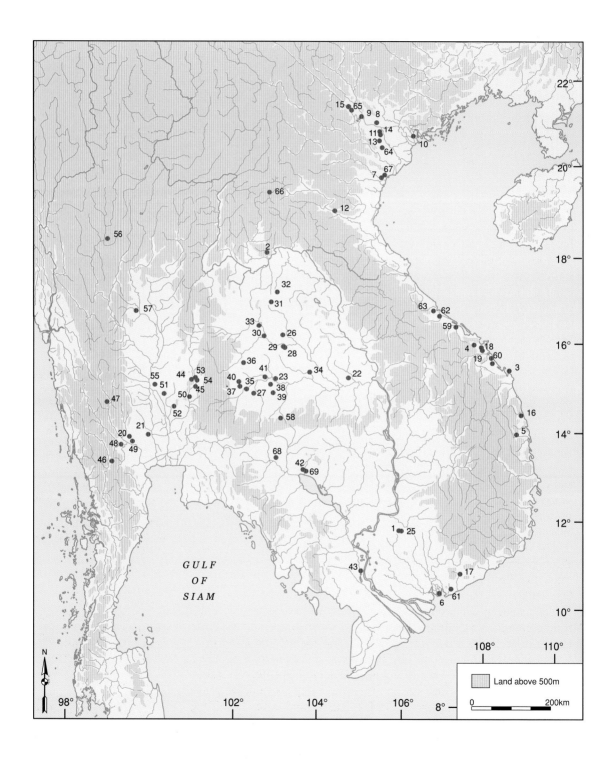

Chapter Five

The Iron Age

Iron has the potential to stimulate far-reaching changes in society. Iron ore is much more widespread in Southeast Asia than the sources of copper or tin, and iron can be converted into ornaments or heavy and effective tools or weapons. Current dating evidence suggests that iron was being used in Southeast Asia by between 300-500 BC. As with bronze, we do not know whether a knowledge of iron working was introduced, or originated locally. The haematite in the Khao Wong Prachan Valley was employed as a flux to aid copper smelting, and this would be an avenue to the development of a local iron industry. On the other hand, two exotic sources cannot be set aside. Iron was first appearing in Xinjiang in the 9th century BC, and in Mongolia by 650 BC. As was the case with the earliest bronze, Di Cosmo (1999) has suggested that iron was introduced from the west by contact across the steppes. The date of the earliest iron east of Xinjiang, however, is by no means finalised. It may well have become established during the late Spring and Autumn period (770-481 BC) and certainly enjoyed a rapid development during the period of Warring States (480-221 BC). An iron cauldron from the state of Jin was cast in 536 BC. Casting iron requires considerable control over heat, and the application of many centuries of acquired skill in the art of casting large bronzes was early applied to this new metal. Wrought iron items were also manufactured. Early weapons would often combine an iron blade with a bronze hilt or guard (Cho-Yun Hsu 1999).

The state of Chu dominated the middle Yangzi Valley, and tombs from cemeteries including Yiyang, Changsha, Shaoshan and Baihewan have yielded the vast majority of iron in China which dates to the Spring and Autumn or early Warring States periods (Bronson 1999). Cast-iron objects have been found in the Changsha cemetery, and items of Chu origin or inspiration found their way south in Lingnan. Excavations in the cemetery of Yinshanling, located in the Guizhiang Valley of Guangxi Province, have uncovered 108 graves which include, as grave goods, Chu imports and iron axes, chisels and scrapers (GZAR 1978). Iron was thus in regular use in Lingnan towards the end of the Warring States period. Knowledge of iron might then have penetrated the Red River area.

Opposite:
The distribution of the principal Iron Age sites mentioned in the text. 1. Banteay Meas, 2 Lao Pako, 3. Xom Oc, 4. Go Mun (Sa Huynh culture), 5. Con River, 6. Giong Ca Vo, Giong Phet, 7. Dong Son, 8. Co Loa, 9. Lang Ca, 10. Viet Khe, 11. Chau Can, Xuan La, 12. Lang Vac, 13. Minh Duc, 14. Phu Luong, 15. Hop Minh, 16. Sa Huynh, Long Thanh, 17. Phu Hoa, 18. Tam My, 19 Pa Xua, 20. Ban Don Ta Phet, 21. U-Thong, 22. Ban Kan Luang, 23. Ban Sawan, 24. Phon Savan, 25. Krek 52/62, 26. Muang Fa Daet, 27. Thamen Chai, 28. Muang Phet, 29. Ban Chiang Hian, 30. Non Chai, 31. Ban Muang Phruk, 32. Ban Chiang, 33. Don Khlang, 34. Non Dua, 35. Phimai, Ban Suai, 36. Non Tung Pie Pone, 37. Non Muang Kao, 38. Ban Don Phlong, 39. Ban Takhong, 40. Noen U-Loke, 41. Ban Krabuang Nok, 42. Lovea, 43. Angkor Borei, 44. Ban Chaibadan, 45. Ban Pukree, 46. Khao Jamook, 47. Tham Ongbah, 48. Ban Kao, 49. Dermbang Nang Buat, 50. Sab Champa, 51. Chansen, 52. Ban Tha Kae, 53. Si Thep, 54. Ban Nong Daeng, 55. U-Taphao, 56. Ban Wang Hi, 57. Ban Wang Hat, 58. Ban Bung Noi, 59. Con Rang, 60. Go Ma Voi, Long Thanh, Sa Huynh 61. Giong Ca Vo, 62. Tra Loc, 63. Gio Son, 64. Ngoc Lu, 65. Dao Thinh, 66. Phon Savanh, 67. Quy Chu, 68. Phum Snay, 69. Baksei Chamkrong.

During this same period, prehistoric communities in Southeast Asia were becoming increasingly involved in long-distance maritime trade. It has often been assumed that they were supine partners in this new development, as Indian entrepreneurs took the initiative. This is not necessarily so, given the widespread evidence for maritime contact between the mainland and islands of Southeast Asia, and the progress, over many preceding millennia, of expansive human settlement by sea. Such exchange might have introduced Southeast Asian people to the properties of iron, as well as the attractions of Indian glass and etched carnelian jewellery. On the other hand, it is equally possible that the properties of iron ore were recognised in the Chao Phraya and Mekong Valleys independently, for there is a thread of evidence in favour of the forging of iron artefacts by about 500 BC.

With the end of the Period of Warring States, Bac Bo, Yunnan and Lingnan were exposed to the predatory ambitions of China under the Qin and Han. A series of warrior chiefdoms rapidly developed to withstand this colonial threat, and just as rapidly succumbed to superior force. For those shielded by the Truong Son Cordillera and uplands of Laos from direct attack, the Iron Age took a different course which involved increased social and technological sophistication that was to generate the development of indigenous states.

The Dong Son Chiefdoms

The Red River delta and the valleys of the Ma and Ca rivers have a less extreme climate than most of low-lying mainland Southeast Asia, largely because the dry season is tempered by moist winds which move across the gulf of Bac Bo. On reaching land, they form a low cloud cover often associated with drizzle. As Gourou (1955) has shown, this moist climate permits two crops of rice per annum on favourable soil. The Red River is given to sudden rises in level, a characteristic compensated for in the last few centuries by the construction of embankments. Such is the load of silt brought down by the Red River, that the delta is advancing rapidly. During the prehistoric period, the delta area would have been subjected to widespread flooding and indeed, the Phung Nguyen sites are located in the more elevated middle country above the delta proper. Thereafter, there was a continuing process of expansion involving occupation of the upper and middle delta itself.

The sequence of Phung Nguyen, Dong Dau and Go Mun phases described above witnessed a major transformation with the development of the culture of Dong Son. Paradoxically, the site of Dong Son is peripheral to the main concentration of activity on the delta, being

Dong Son lies beside the Ma River, and commands a river crossing.

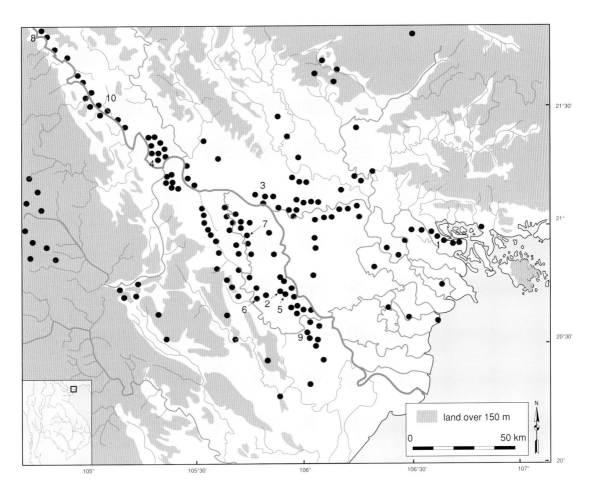

The distribution of Dong Son sites in Bac Bo. 1. Viet Khe, 2. Chau Can, 3. Co Loa, 4. Lang Ca, 5. Xuan La, 6. Minh Duc, 7. Phu Luong, 8. Hop Minh, 9. Ngoc Lu, 10. Dao Thinh.

located on the southern bank of the Ma River. It was here that first Pajot and then Janse undertook excavations which revealed a rich prehistoric cemetery containing objects of bronze, iron, pottery and semi-precious stones in addition to Chinese exports (Janse 1958). This was the first exposure to Europeans of a rich bronze-using society in mainland Southeast Asia, and its origins were sought in the context of prehistoric societies in Eastern Europe which exhibited similar proficiency in working metals. More recently, Vietnamese scholars have sought less exotic origins in stressing the continuity, in terms of decorative motifs, between the Phung Nguyen pottery and the Dong Son bronzes. This has encouraged them to stress cultural continuity throughout the prehistoric occupation of the Red River valley.

Our appreciation of the Dong Son people is coloured by literary allusions to the area which have survived in Chinese documents. The Dong Son phase was, in fact, contemporaneous with a major imperial Chinese expansion under the Han. Viewed from the Han capital, the Dong Son people were the most distant of several groups known as the southern barbarians. The images of Dong Son aristocrats depicted on their daggers, however, belies this description. We see individuals dressed in elegant clothes wearing impressive headdresses and

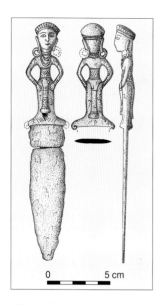

This bronze dagger from the Dong Son culture shows the dress and appearance of an aristocrat. Note the elaborate hat, earrings and necklace.

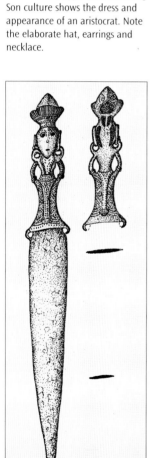

Left: A second Dong Son aristocrat reveals an elaborate headdress, large earrings, bangles and an elegant costume.

Above and top: The ramparts of Co Loa are still most impressive.

ornaments. Although most of our information on Dong Son comes from burial sites, one major settlement probably dates, at least in part, to the period under review. This is Co Loa, located 15 km northwest of Ha Noi on the flood plain of the Red River. There are three sets of ramparts at Co Loa, the two outer ones being moated and of an oval plan, the innermost being rectangular. There is some literary evidence that Co Loa was established as a centre during the 3rd century BC. This has been confirmed by the recent recovery of Dong Son style pottery under the middle rampart. In 1982, a complete Dong Son bronze drum was located near the central part of the site, containing over one hundred socketed bronze ploughshares. One of the most critical points about Co Loa is its size. The outermost ramparts cover about 600 ha, two hundred times the area of Phung Nguyen.

No concentrated survey of settlement sites has been undertaken for the Dong Son phase, and most of our information is drawn from cemeteries and the contents of graves. This information is also restricted in the sense that many cemeteries are found in acidic soils and human bone has not survived. The site of Quy Chu is located 2 km north of the Ma River near Dong Son itself. Nguyen Viet's excavations in 1976-8 encountered burials belonging both to the Dong Son Iron Age and its local predecessor, the Quy Chu phase. Radiocarbon dates for the Quy Chu material fall between 875 and

Left: A cache of crossbow bolts was found at Co Loa.

Far left: Many socketed bronze ploughshares were found inside a drum at Co Loa.

Below left: Early Dong Son burials from the cemetery of Quy Chu, excavated by Nguyen Viet in 1976. (Courtesy Dr. Nguyen Viet)

Below: The Dong Son cemetery of Quy Chu being excavated by Nguyen Viet in 1976. (Courtesy Dr. Nguyen Viet)

600 BC. No such complete human remains were found at Dong Son, where burials were recognised more from the disposition of artefacts than from the presence of human remains. 314 burials were found at Lang Ca, but hardly any human bone. Even so, the excavators noted that a small group of graves were differentially rich, containing axes, daggers, situlae and spearheads. Further evidence for rich burials has been found at Viet Khe and Chau Can (Luu Tran Tieu 1977). Both have yielded opulent boat burials. The richest at Viet Khe was interred in a hollowed tree trunk about 4.5 metres in length, and containing over 100 artefacts. No human remains were found, but there is little doubt that the bronze weapons, receptacles and utensils were grave goods. This particular coffin also contained bronze bells, relatively small drums and even a painted wooden box. The bronze sword, paring knife, spear and arrowheads are virtually identical with those from Yinshanling in Lingnan, although no iron items were found. This, together with the three radiocarbon dates available, suggest a third century BC date for this cemetery.

Wooden artefacts, as well as human remains, were found inside some of the eight boat burials found at Chau Can. These are smaller than the Viet Khe example, and contain fewer grave goods: bronze axes and spearheads, ceramic vessels and earrings made of a tin-lead alloy. The favourable conditions within the wooden coffins also made it possible to recover organic material, including a gourd ladle, the

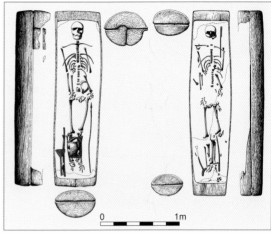

wooden hafts of spears and axes, fragments of woven fabric and
wooden trays. A single radiocarbon date from the original excavation
in 1975 suggests that this cemetery dates to within the period
500-200 BC. This has been confirmed in the excavation of December,
2000, when two further wooden coffins were unearthed at a depth of
two metres below the present ground surface. Further organic
remains were found, in the form of fabric and cordage, as well as
spears and ceramic vessels (Nguyen Viet, pers. comm.).

Xuan La, located only 10 km from Chau Can, is a third boat
coffin cemetery but in this instance, the dating is made much easier
by the recovery of Chinese coins minted between AD 9-23. Burial 3
was found with the skull resting on six iron spades that recall Chinese
forms. A further set of spades lay beside the left elbow. There are
ceramic vessels, but also a wooden bowl and a flat disk. A gourd
ladle lay beside the ankles. Bronze weaponry continued in favour, an
arrowhead and a spearhead being found in the grasp of the left hand.
Other graves from this cemetery reveal a wide range of wooden
mortuary offerings, including further trays, boxes and carved human
figures. However, compared with Viet Khe, Xuan La yielded few
bronze vessels, and no drums or other large sumptuary bronzes
(Pham Quoc Can and Trinh Can 1982). Seven wooden coffins from
Minh Duc have yielded wooden trays, lacquered wooden vessels, and
an iron hoe or spade. A further boat coffin has been found just south
of Hanoi at Phu Luong (Ha Van Tan 1994). Woven fabric clothing
or shrouds also give an impression of the energy expended on the
Dong Son mortuary rituals.

Ha Van Phung (1995) has reported a major mortuary find from
Hop Minh. A large bronze vessel, was recovered, containing the
remains of a four-year-old child. It was splendidly decorated with
war canoes, containing armed warriors. Each has a raised fighting
platform, with warriors aloft holding spears and bows. A frieze above
incorporates widely-employed depictions of houses, rice processing,
plumed warriors and people playing drums. On this occasion, some
drums appear to lie on their sides under the eaves of a house. Upper
and lower friezes involve rows of deer and birds. The assemblage also

included a disc ring broken in antiquity and repaired with cast bronze in the form of wire, just as was the case at Ban Na Di, a bronze dagger, an axe and pottery vessels.

The suggested local origin of the Dong Son bronze industry has been supported by recent research at Dong Son itself. The first use of the cemetery involved burials accompanied by pottery vessels but only a few bronze axes, spearheads and knives. These are said to equate with the Go Mun phase in the Red River valley, dating to 1000-500 BC. The second phase saw a proliferation of bronze artefacts and extension of types to include daggers, swords, situlae and drums. It is dated to the period 500-0 BC. The third and last prehistoric phase comprises burials containing objects of Chinese origin such as seals, coins, mirrors and halberds. Ha Van Tan (1980) has suggested a date within the first century AD for these burials. Indeed, the site was later used for interments in the Han style following the incorporation of the delta region into the Han Empire during the first century AD.

We can learn much about the people of Dong Son from these surviving bronzes. As has been demonstrated at the Dong Son cemetery, both the quantity and range of bronze artefacts increased greatly from about 500 BC. This intensification of production can be illustrated in two ways. The Co Loa drum for example, weighs 72 kg, and would have entailed the smelting of between 1-7 tonnes of copper ore (Nguyen Duy Hinh 1983). One burial from the Lang Ca cemetery contained the remains of a crucible and four clay moulds for casting an axe, spearhead, dagger handle and a bell. The mould for the dagger handle suggests that it may have been intended as a bi-metallic weapon, with the blade itself of iron. Bi-metallic spears are known from Dong Son. The crucible, while retaining the shape of the earlier ones found in Dong Dau contexts, is much larger. Indeed, it could have held 12 kg of molten bronze (Vu Thi Ngoc Thu and Nguyen Duy Ty 1978). Many novel, decorated artefact forms were cast. The drums, situlae, and rectangular ornamental plaques suggest an interest in ritual and ceremony, while the daggers, swords and halberds reflect concern with personal weaponry. Nor was agriculture overlooked: the socketed bronze plough shares represent a profoundly important innovation in the field of agriculture. One of the most impressive categories of bronze, however, comprises the ritual vessels.

A bronze spear found within a wooden coffin of the Dong Son culture at Chau Can during the 2000 excavation. Note the remains of fabric and twine.
(Courtesy Dr. Nguyen Viet)

A complete ceramic vessel found in a wooden coffin at Chau Can in December, 2000.
(Courtesy Dr. Nguyen Viet)

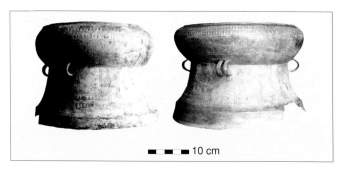

Dong Son drums found in 1997-8 at Gio Son and Tra Loc, Quang Tri province, Viet Nam province. (Courtesy Dr. Andreas Reinecke)

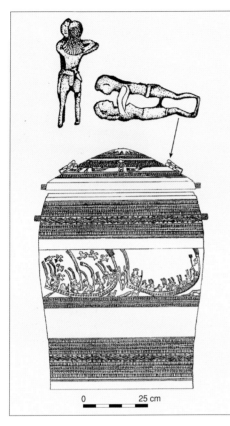

Decoration on the surface of the Co Loa drum shows houses, people pounding rice, four drums being played, a musical group and feathered warriors. Width 65 cm.

Left: This magnificent bronze vessel from Dao Thinh has handles in the form of copulating couples.

0   25 cm

is the ritual vessels. The huge *thap* from Dao Thinh stands 81 cm high, and was decorated with boats and geometric designs. The lid had four handles of cast copulating figures. These not only hint at a reproductive symbolism for these vessels, but also show the male to have an elegant and singular headdress. He is also seen wearing a dagger at his belt.

Lang Vac is a particularly important Dong Son cemetery, located in the valley of the Ca River. Excavations have revealed a rich assemblage of bronze offerings, including daggers, axes, socketed spearheads and a bracelet with attached bells. Two daggers had hilts in the form of human figures (Ngo Si Hong 1983). A crossbow trigger mechanism indicates knowledge of Chinese weaponry, while miniature and large bronze drums were present. The wealth of the graves, and indeed the location of the site some distance upstream, are most easily explained by the proximity of a source of tin, while the one acceptable radiocarbon date indicates settlement by 100 BC, and ending in the early first millennium AD.

The Dong Son metal worker was a master in the difficult field of bronze casting, but the status of local iron working is not clear. During the Dong Son phase, Chinese iron technology reached a high level of proficiency. Their methods involved the demanding system of iron casting rather than forging. It is known from documentary sources that iron objects were exported from China to the south during this period, and the presence of some bi-metallic spears, comprising iron blades with cast on bronze hilts, shows that iron, if by now locally worked, remained rare. It is also instructive to note the lack of iron in the rich burials of Viet Khe and Chau Can. The status of iron during the Dong Son phase requires detailed analyses to determine whether the objects were cast or forged. Evidence for local iron smelting is also basic to an appreciation of iron and its importance to the local people. At present, the direct Chinese contact with Dong Son people is the most likely means whereby knowledge of iron casting reached Bac Bo. The specialised bronze workers there would doubtless have been interested in its properties. Iron did not threaten the central role of bronze in agriculture, war or ceremonial. The casting of bronze plough shares is a direct application of metallurgical skills to the intensification of agriculture, and the social implications of this need to be explored.

There are numerous methods for cultivating rice, some being more efficient and productive than others. In the previous chapter, it was concluded that early rice cultivation involved the clearance of competitors to rice in naturally-flooded river or stream margins. This could have been effected during the dry season by means of fire, the axe and the hoe. It essentially involves interference with the natural vegetation in favour of rice, a plant which grows wild in such marshy habitats to this day. The amount of land which can be brought under cultivation by this means however, is limited both by natural factors such as soil slope and extent of flooding, and human factors, such as the amount of land which can be cleared and cultivated by manual labour. Ploughing represents a radical change. Equipped with a buffalo-drawn plough, a man can cultivate far more soil than if restricted to a hoe, and can also produce surpluses over and above subsistence requirements. Ploughing itself aerates the soil and turns over and kills weeds before the rice is planted. Under the anaerobic conditions of the water-logged rice field, such weeds actually encourage rice by decomposing and releasing nutrients into the water.

The rice plant is further sustained by oxygen in the water, and nitrogen fixed by the indigenous blue-green algae. Indeed, rice can be grown year in, year out even on the poorest soils if there is a sufficient supply of gently percolating water. Today, the dominant form of lowland rice farming in Southeast Asia involves the creation of nearly level rice fields demarcated where necessary by low bunds or walls of soil. Where the terrain is flat, fields are large. Where there is more slope, they tend to be terraced and smaller in size. The bunds retain rainwater, which is allowed to flow slowly through the fields to the natural stream or lake shore. Water is not introduced to the fields, but its natural flow through them is controlled. With the onset of the monsoon, the farmer ploughs and harrows his fields with an iron plough share drawn by a solitary water buffalo. He then transplants rice manually from a seed bed into the awaiting paddy field. Weeding and tending is much easier when the rice is planted in rows rather than broadcast, and returns are predictably higher than under broadcasting (Hanks 1972). This system entails high labour input initially, in the creation of fields, during the early part of the rainy season, when it is necessary to prepare the soil and transplant seedlings, and at the end of the wet season, the time to harvest,

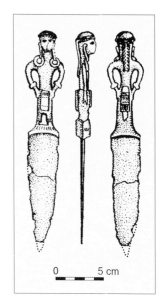

A dagger from Lang Vac with a human form as the hilt, shows the sophistication of Dong Son dress.

thresh and transport the crop for storage. The surpluses generated by this system have underwritten the modern states of Southeast Asia. A major issue then, is the antiquity of this intensive plough-based agricultural system.

There are two sources which help resolve this issue, one archaeological and the other literary. The Chinese under the Han Dynasty interred the dead and depending on their status, buried with them objects used or required by the living. Where such items were too large for inclusion in a grave, they rendered clay models. Among these models are agricultural scenes (Bray 1984). It is stressed that these are Chinese, but they are contemporary with later Dong Son, and indeed, the Han impact was direct with the incorporation of Bac Bo into their empire in the first century AD. One such model depicts the agricultural system described above. Moreover, the bronze ploughshares which are so common in Dong Son contexts are very similar to those found in China at the same date.

The second source of information is literary. Wheatley (1983) has reviewed the relevant Chinese sources, and stressed that in the later part of the second century BC, the area was designated a Chinese protectorate which decreed that "the Lac chieftains, in whose persons were institutionalised customary rights to land, be confirmed in their traditional authority".

Nguyen Viet (1983) has built on these two sources of information by considering the botanical and technological evidence for rice farming. He has concluded that the first millennium BC witnessed the adoption of plough agriculture requiring water control, and double cropping of rice on favourable terrain.

It is fortunate that the Dong Son bronzesmiths decorated their drums with scenes drawn from the world around them. These allow a glimpse into the activities of the very lords described in Chinese documents. We can, for example, recognise the importance attached to elegant boats equipped with cabins, and fighting platforms. They were crewed by paddlers and carried plumed warriors. The very spears, halberds and arrows found in aristocratic graves are seen in action, either being fired or in one case, chastising a captive. The Dong Son drums themselves are represented, mounted in sets of two or four, on a platform, while the houses were raised above ground level on piles, and had supported gable ends decorated with bird-head carvings identical with those seen on the canoe prows.

The new excavations at Dong Son confirm a rapid change from the Go Mun to the Dong Son phase proper, with a major intensification in the quantity and range of bronze artefacts. These include, for the first time, swords and daggers as well as objects of ritual and ceremonial importance such as drums, situlae and decorative body plaques. The skill required to cast a massive drum surely entailed specialised workshops. As Trinh Sinh (1996) has shown, the alloys comprised copper, tin, lead and arsenic, and literally hundreds of copper pins were employed to separate the two clay moulds during the pouring of molten bronze. Intensification is also identifiable in subsistence and exchange, particularly with Han China. This is again seen in the third and last brief period at Dong Son, when

An archer stands on a fighting platform from the Ngoc Lu drum.

0   5 cm

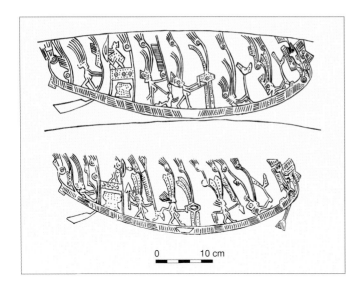

Two war vessels from the Ngoc Lu drum.
Note the warriors and captives.

0   10 cm

Chinese imports peaked. In AD 43, the warrior-aristocrats of Dong Son, who had survived many centuries of Chinese expansion, invasion and periods of subjugation, finally succumbed and were incorporated as a province of the Han Empire.

Although the culture of Dong Son is the best-known expression of the transition to the centralised chiefdom in mainland Southeast Asia, it was not alone. The trend to centralisaton was widespread. The foremost symbol of the new aristocracy, the Dong Son drum, is by no means confined to the valleys of the Red and Ma rivers. The distribution of such drums covers much of southern China where rich chiefdoms contemporaneous with the Dong Son phase are well known. Beyond the reach of the Han Empire, however, Iron Age societies developed without the threat of colonialism.

Coastal Viet Nam

As one moves south of the Ca River and beyond the Hai Van Pass, one encounters a series of sites which contrast markedly with the Dong Son culture, although the two groups were exchanging prestige items one with the other. Nine Dong Son drums, for example, have been unearthed in the Con River valley of Binh Dinh Province since 1997 (Dinh Ba Hoa 1998). Two have been identified by metal detection in Quang Tri province at Tra Loc and Gio Son. The discovery of the relevant sites, which extend for 700 km along the littoral of central and southern Viet Nam began in 1909, when a French customs official, M. Vinet, encountered a collection of urns containing cremated human remains at Thanh Duc, near the village of Sa Huynh. Parmentier (1918) later visited the site and reported in some detail. By then 120 jars had been unearthed over an area measuring 80 by 50 m, and they were found to be grouped, and to contain cremated human remains in association with a range of grave goods. This Sa Huynh burial practice stands out in Southeast Asia.

A cranium with a bicephalous ear ornament still in place, from Giong Ca Vo.
(Courtesy Dr. Andreas Reinecke)

While jar burial occurred in Northeast Thailand from the Neolithic, it was normally reserved for infants, and the body was not cremated. Yet the Sa Huynh jar burials have been found along the coastal tract almost from the mouth of the Mekong to the southern boundaries of Bac Bo. Moreover, the charcoal associated with the cremated human remains and concentrations in the vicinity of the vessels are unusually good sources of radiocarbon samples.

Saurin (1963) has described such an urnfield at Hang Gon. The cemetery covered an area of about 100 by 50 m, the lips of the burial urns being between 0.2 and 1.0 metres below the present ground surface. The urns were provided with covers, but contained no bone, perhaps due to local acidic soil conditions. There was, however, much charcoal and burnt soil. Many burial offerings were ritually broken. Smashed pottery vessels were placed inside the large urns. Polished stone adzes were damaged, bowls deformed and even the sockets of iron axes, broken. Small and durable items of jewellery, such as ear pendants and beads, however, remained intact. Some beads of imported carnelian, agate, olivine and zircon were found at Hang Gon as well as blue and red glass beads and a solitary bead of gold. There was also a distinctive nephrite ear pendant representing a double-headed animal. Iron working is documented in the form of slag as well as axes and the swords. Three radiocarbon dates confirm the contemporaneity of the Hang Gon urnfield with the Dong Son sites further to the north. One sample from within a jar was dated to 240±150 BC, and a second from around the same vessel was 350±150 BC. The third sample comes from an organic residue in a vessel, and is dated to 150±150 BC. Marginally earlier dates, as well as the same type of double-headed animal ornament, came from the nearby site of Phu Hoa (Fontaine 1972). The dates in question are 350±140 and 540±290 BC.

More recently, a major excavation covering 200 square metres at Giong Co Va, near Ho Chi Minh City, has uncovered 339 jar burials and 10 inhumation graves (Dang Van Thang and Vu Quoc Hien 1995). This is one of several Sa Huynh sites which lie just behind the present shore, in a situation commanding the northern branches of the Mekong River. The dead were interred within vertically-placed jars often in a seated position and of those sufficiently well preserved for further analysis, 14 were male and 12, female. Several infants were also recovered (Nguyen Lan Cuong 1995, Nguyen Thi Hau 1995). The burials were accompanied by a wide variety of grave goods, foremost being 21 double animal-headed ear ornaments in glass and jade. There were also beads and bangles of shell, exotic stone and glass, while some ornaments were fashioned of gold. Nguyen Kim Dung *et al.* (1995) have described, in detail, the jewellery from this site and a second cemetery at Giong Phet. The quantity and quality of the stone jewellery reflect a rich society which participated in widespread exchange. There are, for example, 883 carnelian beads fashioned in a wide variety of shapes. There are 242 jade beads, 125 in agate and lesser numbers fashioned from garnet and rock crystal. Three split earrings with decorative projections were recovered, one being fashioned from carnelian. The pottery vessels display many forms, and bear panels of intricately incised designs. One pottery vessel was ornamented with four animals' heads similar to those on the ear pendants. A single radiocarbon determination of about 400 BC has been obtained. The strategic location of these sites near the Mekong Delta, and wealth of exotic ornaments, represents a critical late prehistoric stage in the subsequent formation of the Funan state.

Vietnamese prehistorians have further concentrated their efforts on enlarging our understanding of Sa Huynh in the area where it was discovered, as well as slightly to the north in the Thu Bon valley. Ha Van Tan (1980) has concluded that the richest and most informative of the recently examined sites is Tam My. Trinh Can and Pham Van Kinh (1977) have recovered large funerary urns there. The burial goods included iron spearheads, knives and sickles as well as bronze spearheads and bells. A double animal-headed ornament found there matches those from Hang Gon and Phu Hoa. There is also a stone ear pendant which looks like an evolved form of those found in Go Mun contexts, and at Khok Phlap in Thailand. The Sa Huynh occupation also extended to offshore islands. At Xom Oc on Ly Son island, Pham Thi Ninh (2000) has reported a coastal occupation and mortuary site in which the inhabitants collected considerable quantities of shellfish and also extensively fished. Artefacts include bronze arrowheads and iron knives, but a particular feature of this site is the number of artefacts fashioned from tridacna and turbo shells (Pham Thi Ninh and Doan Ngoc Khoi 1999).

The Sa Huynh sites confirm that by the end of the 1st millennium BC, a string of communities occupied favourable coastal tracts along the shores of Central Viet Nam. By that juncture, there was a widespread use of iron, and an exchange system incorporating exotic glass and stone jewellery. Reinecke's (1996) review of the distribution of the distinctive nephrite ear pendants in the form of two animal heads has stressed their wide distribution, the 70 known specimens coming from 15 sites. In the Sa Huynh area, they concentrate in two groups, one in Da Nang-Quang Nam, the other to the south in the vicinity of Saigon. In 1994, a major new site was encountered by villagers at Go Mun, west of Da Nang. Over the

Below left: Excavations in progress at the Sa Huynh settlement and cemetery of Long Thanh, Quang Ngai Province, Viet Nam. (Courtesy Dr. Andreas Reinecke)

Excavations at Con Rang, the most northerly Sa Huynh site known. Note the jar burial being uncovered. (Courtesy Dr. Andreas Reinecke)

Right: Excavations in March 1999 at Go Ma Voi, Quang Nam Province, revealed jar burials with bronze, iron and glass grave goods. (Courtesy Dr. Andreas Reinecke)

Bicephalous ear ornaments and split rings are characteristic of the Sa Huynh culture. 1-7, nephrite, 8, glass. (Courtesy Dr. Andreas Reinecke)

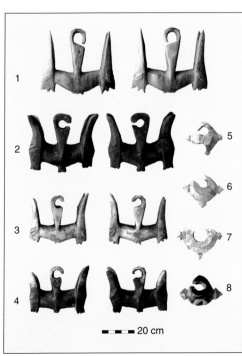

ensuing years, the cemetery was destroyed by looting, but Reinecke was able to assemble some of the looted items, and excavate in the only intact part of the site (Reinecke and Lu Duy Son 2000). They reveal the wealth of the mortuary rituals. There were double animal-headed ear ornaments and split earrings of jade. Beads were made of carnelian, agate, gold and rock crystal, and there were bronze bowls, and iron axes and spearheads. Some burials also contained ceramic spindle whorls. It seems that the jade ear ornaments at better-preserved sites are found in relatively rich burials that probably contained high status men, given their association, for example at Pa Xua, with an iron axe and socketed spear (Vu Quoc Hien 1991). Their concentration in Sa Huynh contexts strongly indicates local manufacture, further supported by the discovery of unfinished examples. However, their distribution reveals wide, maritime exchange links. One has been found on Botel Tobago island, southwest of Taiwan, and another from Palawan in the Philippines. Two examples come from Central Thailand, at Ban Don Ta Phet and U-Thong. Although most were fashioned from nephrite (a variety of jade), seven specimens are made of glass, which raised the likelihood that considerable skill in local Southeast Asian glass making was in place by AD 100 at the latest. The people of Sa Huynh were also engaged in exchange with the Western Han of China, for two sites have recently furnished Chinese mirrors of Han form. One of these came from within a Sa Huynh mortuary vessel from the site of Binh Yen. The second came from inside a Dong Son drum from Phu Chanh (Yamagata et al. 2001).

The Sa Huynh homeland is precisely the region that, five centuries later, entered history with a Cham-speaking state heavily under the influence of Hinduism. Is it not likely, that the singularity of the urn burial rite and the Cham language reflect the same Austronesian population? There is some supporting evidence for this supposition. When the Chinese described the Cham burial rite, we find that the dead were placed in urns the quality of which varied with the status of the deceased. The remains were then consigned to the sea. The present Cham language, according to Blust (1996) has its closest parallels in the Acehnese and Malayic languages of Southwest Borneo. At present, the consensus of all evidence points to a relatively late intrusive settlement of this region by sea from Borneo, a move which resulted first in the culture of Sa Huynh, and then the development of the Cham states.

If one employs mortuary ritual as evidence, there are some hints that Sa Huynh settlement reached further into the interior of Southeast Asia than has hitherto been realised. The urn burial rite has been identified at Ban Kan Luang, in the lower valley of the Mun River. Here, burials goods included bronze bracelets, axes, spears and arrowheads. The site has also yielded iron slag. Much further up the Mun Valley at Ban Sawan, very large ceramic vessels placed mouth to mouth have been found, although no grave goods were recovered. It may be possible that some Cham-speaking people crossed the Truong Son passes to infiltrate the Mun Valley during the Iron Age.

The Plain of Jars

The origin of the cremation cemeteries on the Plain of Jars in upland Laos might also relate to Sa Huynh expansion. Seventy years ago Madeleine Colani (1935) undertook fieldwork in the uplands comprising the northern Truong Son cordillera, specifically to enlarge our knowledge of a series of sites there characterised by large stone burial jars and free-standing stone slabs or 'menhirs'. Only with the recovery of glass and metal artefacts in the Khorat basin sites during the last few years, has it been possible to appreciate the date and cultural affiliations of the upland groups

Phon Savanh (formerly Ban Ang) is the most impressive and complete site. It is located at an altitude of just over 1000 m, and dominates an extensive area known as the Plain of Jars. This site clusters round a central hill within which Colani identified and excavated a prehistoric crematorium. There were two groups of huge stone burial jars in its vicinity, one on a raised area which Colani ascribed to a ruling group. The largest jars, which were hewn from

The excavations at Phon Savanh, Laos, on the Plain of Jars.

Top: Dr. Thongsa Sayavongkhamdy excavating the area surrounding one of the stone jars at Phon Savanh, Laos.

Below left: On the Plain of Jars, Phon Savanh is one of the most important sites, with over 250 stone burial jars.

This view of the site of Phon Savanh was taken in front of the crematorium cave. (Courtesy Dr. Thongsa Sayavongkhamdy)

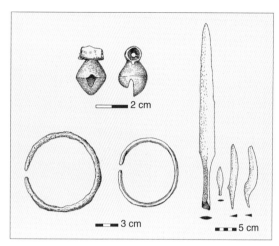

The material culture from Phon Savanh includes bronze bells and bangles, and iron knives, spear and arrowheads.

The enigmatic circular sites of eastern Cambodia incorporate impressive banks and ditches..

discs found in the vicinity suggest that they were formerly lidded. She found a richer set of grave goods there than in the other rather larger assemblage of jars. The burial offerings found at Phon Savanh and, indeed, in the other related sites, include glass and carnelian beads, cowrie shells of coastal origin, bronze helices, bells and bracelets and knives, arrowheads and spearheads of iron. The presence of clay-mould fragments reveals local bronze casting, while iron slag points to local iron working. Of course, some of the metal artefacts could also have been imported.

More recent research at this site has involved a series of excavations, and the recognition of a quarry at Pu Keng, nine kilometres distant, in which complete and incomplete jars were recognised (Sayavongkhamdy and Bellwood 2000). The excavations revealed the presence of a complete pottery vessel, and graves containing comminuted human bone. One was covered with a stone slab decorated with schematised human figures.

The parallels with the material culture lie in the Iron Age of the Khorat Plateau, although one bronze figurine recalls Dong Son traditions. A date in the region of 300 BC- AD 300 is consistent with the material found in and around the stone mortuary jars. Explaining the origins of the people in question and how they disposed of the manpower to move and shape such impressive stone funerary monuments is not so easy. Colani may well be correct in suggesting that these people were placed to control exchange routes between southern China, Bac Bo and the burgeoning chiefdoms of the Khorat area. She also noted that the uplands in question are to this day a major source for salt and, indeed, control of the salt trade may well have provided the resources for the importation of exotic goods from some considerable distance.

The Basalt Plateau of Eastern Cambodia

At least 31 circular occupation sites cluster on the elevated basaltic plateau of eastern Cambodia and adjoining parts of Viet Nam. The red soils are so acidic that organic material does not survive, and even the ceramics and stone artefacts are heavily pitted or patinated. These have been known for many years. Groslier (1966) concluded, on the basis of his excavations at the site of Banteay Meas, that these sites dated between 3000-1000 BC, and represented the most important exposure of Neolithic sites in Southeast Asia. While this claim is now seriously dated, the enigmatic nature of these sites remains. Essentially, they comprise a circular raised bank, still standing as much as 4 metres above the surrounding terrain. These enclose an inner channel or moat, which rises to an interior platform up to 200 metres in diameter. Each is equipped with an entrance which often incorporates quite complex auxiliary banks.

Recent excavations in several of these sites have scarcely clarified the cultural affiliations (Dega 1999). Material remains concentrate on the outer perimeter, with a slight rise in frequency towards the centre. They comprise many pitted pottery sherds bearing cord-marked, incised and dentate-stamped decoration, and a varied industry in basalt and sandstone, which incorporates shouldered adzes, chisels and whetstones. The latter were made and modified at the site, and bear much evidence for usage. There is no surviving evidence for bronze or iron, nor associated evidence, such as clay or stone casting moulds. Dega (1999) also noted an absence of any exotic items which could illuminate both exchange patterns and by inference, chronology. On all these grounds, it would seem that Groslier was correct in assigning these sites to the Neolithic. This would appear to gain support from two radiocarbon dates, each obtained from rice-chaff temper recovered from potsherds (1920-1690 and 2620-2350 BC). However, Carbonnel (1979) has published a further determination which suggests that the sites may only be 1000-2000 years old. The situation has become further confused by the recovery, in a firm cultural context at the site of Krek 52/62, of part of a glass bracelet (Haidle 1999). This can only belong to the Iron Age or later.

At present, it is noted that these occupation sites might represent Iron Age adaptation to a relatively remote part of the Southeast Asia, where it was possible to cultivate rice in the low-lying stream margins which lie in striking distance of these embanked settlements. The extreme acidity of the soil has extinguished the organic fraction of the archaeological record, making it very difficult to determine more than the basic repertoire of stone and ceramic artefacts.

The excavation of Krek site 52/62.

A view looking south from the outer wall of site Krek 52/62, showing the edge of the inner platform and the circular ditch round the site.

The Mekong Valley

Towards the end of the Bronze Age, the occupants of the Khorat plateau lived in autonomous villages in which certain descent groups might have achieved relatively high status. Population expansion, involving the foundation of new settlements, was not constrained so long as there was sufficient favourable agricultural land along stream or river margins where flooding was not severe. Such enclaves were not limitless. The Khorat plateau includes substantial elevated terraces and hilly areas quite unsuited to the cultivation of rice. Bronze Age settlements are known in the favourable valleys which feed the Songkhram, Chi and Mun rivers. While pottery styles suggest tight regionality even to the village level, under appropriate analytical techniques, settlements may be linked by the recognition of exchange in valuables that reached out into the surrounding hills for copper, tin and stone, and to the coast for trochus and cowrie shell ornaments.

5 cm

A complete vessel from a possible burial at Krek 52/62.
(Courtesy Dr. Gerd Albrecht)

A shouldered adze and grinding stone from Krek 52/62. Scale 2 cm. (Courtesy Dr. Gerd Albrecht)

Just after the second world war, Williams-Hunt (1950) analysed a series of aerial photographs covering the Khorat Plateau. He identified many large mounds enclosed by moats and banks, which clustered in the Mun-Chi drainage basin. Most sites are oval in plan, and some look as if they have been added to. Thus, Muang Fa Daet comprises three moated enclosures with a fourth feature thought to have been a reservoir nearby. Williams-Hunt also concluded that three sites were considerably larger than the rest, indicating a hierarchy of sites. Similar oval moated sites are now known on the margins of the Bangkok plain, and in northeastern Cambodia. They are intriguing not only for their distribution pattern, size and date, but also for their origins. It is this last point which we will consider first.

Quaritch-Wales (1957) was attracted to these sites in the Mun valley, excavating small squares at Thamen Chai and Muang Phet. The sites yielded a cultural stratigraphy of between 2-3 metres. He recovered iron down to the basal layers of Muang Phet, and concluded on the basis of ceramic typology that the first settlement reflected at least influence from, if not occupation by, people from the Chao Phraya valley. Quaritch Wales regarded the presence of iron as a result of contact with India, and concluded on the basis of a radiocarbon date that the sites were first occupied during the first millennium AD.

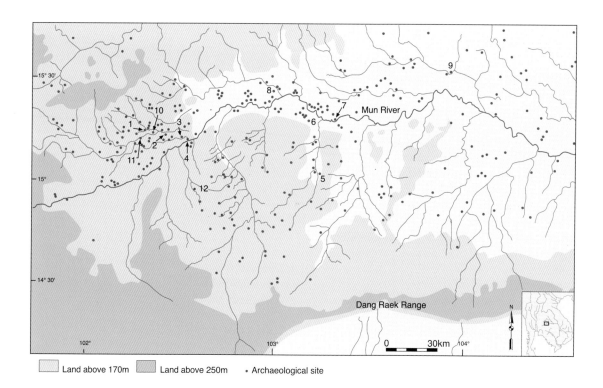

1. Noen U-Loke, Ban Non Wat, 2. Ban Prasat, 3. Ban Tamyae, 4. Phimai/Ban Suai, 5. Ban Takhong, 6. Ban Don Phlong, 7. Non Yang, 8. Non Krabuang, 9. Non Dua, 10. Ban Lum Khao, 11. Non Muang Kao, 12. Muang Phet.

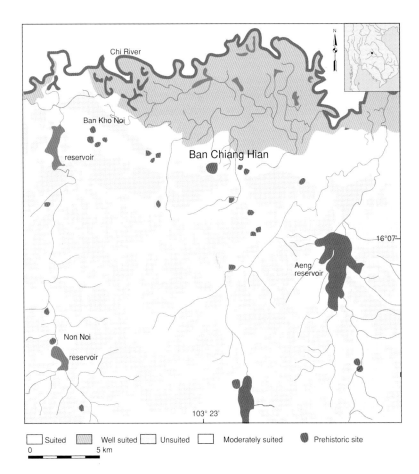

The distribution of sites in the Middle Chi survey area, showing the central location of Ban Chiang Hian, the large moated site.

The Chi Valley

The best documented settlement pattern analysis incorporating a moated site took place on the southern margins of the Chi River. The chosen study area incorporates the Chi flood plain, which reaches a maximum breadth of 7 km. Three tributary streams flow north across the flood plain and into the main river. They have smaller flood-plains surrounded by low terrace terrain of varying width that gives way to the slightly more elevated land of the middle terrace.

The prehistoric sites concentrate near the low terraces of the tributary streams and fringe the extensive tract comprising the Chi flood plain. One site in the latter area, Ban Chiang Hian, incorporates a double set of moats, intervening banks and a reservoir. Three sites have been excavated, including Ban Chiang Hian itself. All yielded a distinctive red-on-buff painted ware in the lowest occupation layers. At Ban Kho Noi and Ban Chiang Hian, this was superceded in the mid first millennium BC by a plainer ware. At that juncture, the excavators found the first evidence for iron and the water buffalo. The mound of Ban Chiang Hian covers about 38 ha. It exceeds by far the size of all other prehistoric settlements in the surveyed area and was in all probability a special, central site.

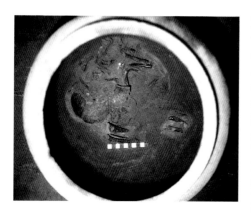

Excavation of the whole pots at Ban Na Di revealed the remains of tiny infants within.

Non Chai is a most important Iron Age site, situated in the upper reaches of the Chi catchment. It was located on a small surviving tract of the old middle terrace, so as to command low-lying alluvial soils which are today classified as moderately suited to rice cultivation. The size of the site cannot be stated with precision because it has been removed for road fill. According to plans made after removal had commenced, it covered at least 18 ha. Pisit Charoenwongsa's excavations took place in 1978, and they suggested that it had formerly covered about the same area as Ban Chiang Hian (Bayard *et al.* 1986). It was, therefore, considerably larger than any known Bronze Age site. Kijngam's review of the faunal remains has emphasised the many shellfish, fish, crabs, frogs and water turtle from early layers, and indicated access to a low-lying easily flooded terrain. The early settlers also maintained domestic water buffalo, cattle, dog and pig, and hunted deer, crocodile, rhinoceros and many small mammals (Kijngam 1979). The pottery from Non Chai is dominated by red-slipped and painted wares which echo later Ban Chiang styles (Rutnin 1979). In this context, the radiocarbon dates confirm a relatively late prehistoric settlement, and a rapid buildup of cultural material. Apart from one date of about 2300 BC for the lowest layer, the rest vary little throughout the cultural layers. While the excavator has yet to comment on the context and status of the earliest date, an eroded section near the excavated area revealed a thin band of occupation followed by a sterile soil build up, then in turn evidence for the continual occupation of the site. Thus some occupation may have occurred during the second millennium BC, but the weight of evidence points to continuous occupation from towards the end of the first millennium BC. The excavators have suggested that phase 1 dates from about 400 BC, phases II-III between 300-200 BC, phase IV to 1-200 BC and phase V into the second century AD. The material culture includes small amounts of iron slag from this phase, but iron slag only became common in phase IV. There are also four glass beads from contexts earlier than phase III at the site, and over 200 belong to phases IV and V. The surge in the number of beads probably dates to about 200-0 BC. Clay moulds for casting bronze bracelets and bells are likewise found in phase III-V contexts, though fragments of bronze and crucible fragments were identified in layers attributed to phases II-V.

The critical point about this well-dated site is that it covered at least 18 ha at some point during the period from 300 BC until about AD 250, when it was abandoned. At present, we do not know at what point in its sequence, if any, the site actually attained that area under continuous occupation. If it did, and a population figure of 50 people per ha is adopted, then the site would have harboured, at its maximum extent, about 1,000 people. If estimates of nearly 40 ha for the site's area are adopted then the population could have been twice that figure. The pottery is very distinctive in form, surface finish and fabric, differing from that from Ban Chiang Hian. A few sherds, however, are probably exotic imports from the Middle Chi Valley sites.

Uncovering an Iron Age grave during the 1975 excavation at Ban Chiang.

The settlement pattern survey in the region round Ban Chiang Hian has shown that the smaller village communities so typical of the Bronze Age continued in occupation. Excavations undertaken in several such sites in the Chi and Songkhram valleys allows us to trace the transition into the Iron Age in the smaller sites away from the newly-emerging main centres. The excavations at Ban Chiang and Ban Na Di, for example, have revealed evidence for a cultural dislocation at about 300 BC. It will be recalled that levels 6 and 7 at the latter contained a cemetery, the latest two burials incorporating iron artefacts. Layer 5 represents a radical change in activity. It yielded the remains of a bronze-casting workshop complete with crucibles, furnaces and clay moulds for casting bells and bracelets. The crucibles, while similar in shape and size to those in preceding layers, were now tempered with rice chaff rather than grog. The bronze alloy from layers 6 to 8 comprised a 10-12% tin bronze. That found in level 5 was much more variable. Lead became a common additive and a few pieces were made from the very high (over 20%) tin bronze which was used in the manufacture of decorated bowls recovered from Ban Don Ta Phet in Central Thailand. The bronze industry during layers 4 to 5 produced bracelets, bells and bowls. Axes and spears, which characterised the Bronze Age repertoire, were no longer manufactured in bronze. It is considered highly likely that the metal working during the period, as at Non Chai, represents an increased degree of specialisation.

During the Iron Age at Ban Na Di, it seems that an area was set aside for infant burials in lidded jars.

Layer 4 saw a return to use as a burial ground, but on this occasion exclusively for infants. Their remains were found in lidded urns, associated with artefacts of bronze and iron and in one case, with five blue-glass beads. The bronzes comprise miniature bracelets and the iron artefacts, knives and a socketed tip for a digging stick very similar to those found at Ban Don Ta Phet. These were coated with the remains of rice, which survived through impregnation with iron oxide. The grave ritual now distinguished between the area used for burying infants as opposed to adults, a distinct departure from the earlier level 6-7 cemetery phase.

The range of artefacts found in levels 4-5 also differs. There were no more clay figurines. Shell disc beads and shell bracelets were no longer exchanged, and most of the beads were now made of orange or blue glass. Although a few iron artefacts were found in two level 6 graves, levels 4-5 yielded iron slag, which indicates local smelting of iron ore. One of the most impressive indices of change is Vincent's finding that the pottery was now made from a new clay source, and the tempering material was quite different from the earlier tradition (Vincent 1984). This new temper was prepared by mixing together rice and clay balls and lightly firing them. The material was then crushed and mixed with the raw clay. Wichakana (1984) has analysed the range of rim forms in all layers, and has identified a major change with the transition from levels 6-7 to 5. The body decoration also changed, from a preference for plain or cord marked and incised and painted finish to red-slipped or red-on-buff painted designs.

Burial 11 at Ban Chiang was associated with a collection of pigs' jawbones as mortuary offerings.

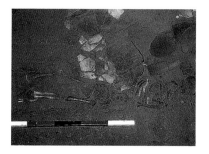

The skeleton of an infant from Ban Chiang lies alongside a series of pottery vessels. A dog's skeleton had been placed over the body.

Few Iron Age red-on-buff painted vessels were recovered during the 1975 excavation at Ban Chiang. This one came from burial 11.

Early Iron Age spears at Ban Chiang had an iron head and a bronze haft. This was a widespread technique in southern China and Vietnam at this period. (Length 28.5 cm)

The replacement of a cemetery by a bronze-working atelier and the clarity of associated changes in material culture pose the question of whether we are dealing with the replacement of one group of people by another. Before considering this issue, it is necessary to enquire whether a similar change occurred at other sites in the area. Three have provided some useful information. One is Ban Muang Phruk, which is located 10 km southwest of Ban Na Di, and only 2.5 km from the present, dry-season bank of Lake Kumphawapi. A small excavation in 1980 revealed stratigraphy to a depth of 3.6 metres. The basal cultural layer contained pottery, the rims, temper and surface decoration of which match closely that from levels 4-5 at Ban Na Di (Wichakana 1984). There is no hint of any pottery reminiscent of the Bronze Age assemblage from Ban Na Di. Only 1 km east of Ban Muang Phruk, there is a cluster of small mounds. One has been investigated, and was found to have built up as a result of salt extraction. The basal layer contains some red-slipped pottery, and has been dated to the first couple of centuries AD.

At Ban Chiang, White (1982a) has identified a major change in the cultural sequence which she dates to *c* 300 BC. One grave assigned to the Middle Period was associated with two bimetallic spearheads, the blades being made of iron and the socketed hafts of bronze. Virtually identical artefacts have been found in Dong Son contexts. Iron became more abundant in the Late Period, which was also defined on the basis of a new ceramic ware. Pots were now painted with red designs on a buff background. This much publicised 'Ban Chiang Painted Pottery', which has now been dated between 300 BC- AD 200, bears decorative patterns of great beauty. Motifs include curvilinear and spiral designs, and representations of humans, animals and insects. The excavated sample of Iron Age graves at Ban Chiang is too small to provide useful comment on social organisation, but on the margins of the site, Bannanurag and Khemnark (1992) have traced the plan of Iron Age graves that have been uncovered, but not further excavated. These reveal rows of graves, in which the dead were often covered in the notable painted pottery vessels.

No detailed petrographic analyses have yet been undertaken on a reasonable sample of Ban Chiang Late Period pottery, although two pots have been looked at in detail, and seem to fall into the same

These clay rollers from Ban Chiang of unknown function are often found as grave goods.

Left: These looted pots would have come from Iron Age graves at Ban Chiang or related sites. Very few such painted pots were found during the 1974-5 excavations.

technological tradition as the Iron Age layers at Ban Na Di (McGovern, Vernon and White 1985). The Late Period graves are also associated with grave goods which find close parallels at Ban Na Di. We find the same clay rollers or seals. These have a hole running down the centre, and the exterior surfaces have been excised to form coupled geometric and curvilinear designs. They have been variously interpreted as being rollers to impart patterns onto cloth, and as cylinder seals to impress an ownership mark on a plastic medium, such as clay. Since they have a convex outer surface, and would require fresh inking with every revolution, the latter interpretation is preferred. It is also supported by the discovery at Ban Na Di of what must surely be a handled rather than a cylinder seal. The Late Period graves also include glass beads, paralleled at Ban Na Di, and the same high tin bronze identified at Ban Don Ta Phet and Ban Na Di was used in the manufacture of a Late Period necklace.

Similar changes have been identified in other excavations. At Don Khlang, Schauffler noted that an early horizon of burials was

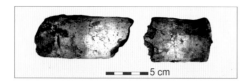

A ceramic tuyere from Lao Pako provides evidence for local iron working.

A pottery vessel from a probable Lao Pako burial.

A probable mortuary assemblage at Lao Pako.

Screening all excavated material from the Lao Pako excavation.

Right: Lao Pako seen across the adjacent river. (Courtesy Dr. Anna Källén)

The excavation of Lao Pako, Laos.

superceded by a layer containing painted pottery, glass beads and iron artefacts. One later pit was filled with several water buffalo skulls. More recent excavations have revealed a further 17 burials, the lowest incorporating an iron bracelet. Many mortuary rituals long established at the nearby Bronze Age site of Non Nok Tha, however, continued at this small, two hectare site. We find the same interment of pig and cattle limbs, while the ceramic vessels and bronze axes are also of the same tradition (Buranrak 1994a).

Lao Pako in Laos

Excavations at Lao Pako, a settlement site on the Laotian side of the Mekong River, have recently uncovered evidence for domestic and ritual activities (Källén 2000, Karlström 2000). One area involved iron forging, in the form of slag and tuyeres, while spindle whorls attest a textile industry. Two clay rollers match those found at Ban Na Di and Ban Chiang, except that the central perforation does not extend right through the centre. These, together with aspects of the pottery forms and the available radiocarbon dates, suggest occupation within the period AD 1-500. No burials were encountered, but a concentration of complete vessels may represent infant jar burials, the bone within having succumbed to the acidic soils of the area. The excavators describe this site as peripheral to the major changes documented in the Iron Age communities to the east and south. Indeed, this interpretation could equally apply to Ban Chiang and Ban Na Di when they are compared with the sites in the Chi and Mun Valleys.

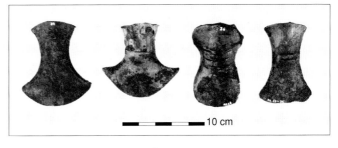

10 cm

These four bronze axes came from burial 7 at Don Khlang.

The Mun Valley

Large moated settlements are thickly distributed in the Mun River valley. Up to 1995, a number had been investigated through relatively small exposures. Some revealed initial occupation during the Iron Age, others, such as Ban Prasat, contained Iron Age layers over a Bronze Age cemetery (Phommanodch 1991).

Moore (1986) has undertaken an innovative and important study of these Mun Valley sites by reviewing them on the basis of their size, architecture and distribution. She began by calculating the area of each. The resulting data are not directly comparable with the areas of Ban Chiang Hian and Non Chai because she included the moats and ramparts in her figures, whereas the area of 38.5 ha for Ban Chiang Hian was taken within the outer earthworks. Nevertheless, the figures are of considerable interest. In her small group, the area varies up to 20 ha. Sites of the intermediate group have areas of between 21 and 40 ha, while the large sites extend up to 68 ha. These areas are far greater than those estimated for Bronze Age villages.

The distribution of these large enclosed sites includes the flood plain of the Mun River, the lower terrace, middle terrace and, on three occasions, the high terrace. Compared with the Bronze Age sites, there seems to have been a significant expansion of settlement to include the elevated middle and high terraces. When Moore turned to the architecture and degree to which sites encompassed moats, she found that these elevated sites incorporated more water control systems, and commonly exhibited more stages in their expansion. This is hardly surprising where water supply was likely to be a particular problem in the drier middle and high terrace areas.

Until 1995, excavations in the Mun Valley sites were on a small scale. One of the earliest took place in the valley of the Lam Siao Yai, which is found about 60 km southeast of Ban Chiang Hian. Non Dua, a large moated site, is located so as to command an extensive deposit of rock salt as well as low terrace soils suited to rice cultivation (Higham 1977). The salt exposure, known as Bo Phan Khan, is surrounded by evidence of industrial activity in the form of mounds and quantities of thick-walled pottery. Production involves passing water through salty soil. The resulting brine is then boiled in flat metal trays. Excavations in one of the mounds round the deposit exposed evidence for salt extraction to a depth of six metres and commencing, according to the radiocarbon date, in the first century or two AD. Some examples of the crudely-fashioned industrial wares were found during excavations within the moated site itself, which suggests that its occupants were concerned with the extraction of the salt. The extent of the activity, measured in terms of the huge mounds which have accumulated all round Bo Phan Khan, points to the production on a scale far greater than would have been necessary to satisfy local demand. Non Dua, the moated site, also yielded a deep stratigraphic sequence and the initial phase of occupation has been assigned to the period 500-1 BC. Some of the distinctively decorated rims and body sherds have been noted in phase two at Ban Chiang Hian, but, otherwise, the pottery there was not matched in the Middle Chi valley.

Welch and McNeill (1991) have concentrated on the distribution of prehistoric sites in an extensive area centred upon the modern town of Phimai. Ban Suai, a prehistoric site, lies on the outskirts of Phimai itself, and excavations there in 1966 revealed a substantial Iron Age presence. Further excavations in 1998 confirmed the presence of Iron Age material under the central shrine of the Angkorian period temple enclosure (Talbot 2000). Welch and McNeill have divided the prehistoric sequence into four major phases, named Tamyae (1000-600 BC), Ban Prasat (600-200 BC), Phimai (200 BC-AD 300) and late Phimai (AD 300-600). There are few Tamyae phase sites, and they are confined to the alluvial lowlands flanking the Mun River. The number of sites belonging to their Prasat phase increased by a factor of four, and some were now extending into the low and middle terrace areas, while 53 sites were ascribed to the Phimai phase with further expansion away from the low-lying alluvium.

Higham and Thosarat began a second field programme in 1994, in the area west of Phimai. This involved both site surveys and excavations, that at Ban Lum Khao requiring a revision of Welch and McNeill's proposed dates, for we have seen that the equivalent to their Tamyae phase is as early as 1450 BC. The Prasat phase burials there, in the absence of any iron, probably date between 1000-500 BC. Many large Iron Age sites were visited during the survey, and smaller mounds dedicated, it is thought, to the production of salt on a major scale, were identified. The clustering of such mounds in the vicinity of the large settlement sites probably reflects the establishment of intensive exploitation of the salt for exchange as well as local consumption. Moreover, Nitta's excavations at a complex of salt-making mounds at Non Tung Pie Pone, located northeast of the survey area, revealed evidence for processing during the Iron Age.

Two Iron Age sites were chosen for excavations designed to answer a series of key questions. The first was to examine through mortuary evidence, the nature of social organisation during the Iron Age. Achieving this goal required the opening of a considerable area to obtain a large enough sample. The second was to isolate changes in the mortuary rituals through time, in order to appreciate, if possible, how social organisation was developing. Was there, for example, an increase in social ranking as one group within the community assumed status and authority over others? Such changes occur within the context of broad social, technological and economic behaviour. It was therefore important to assess how technology developed, whether the subsistence base was enlarged or made more efficient, and whether there was any evidence for increased inter-community friction and strife. Warfare is a considerable stimulus to the vesting of authority in leadership. It also, as we have seen in Bac Bo, places demands on iron production and the forging of weaponry. Iron smelting and salt processing place great demands on timber for fuel. Forest clearance, which also provides for the expansion of rice fields, involves major environmental changes, and it is always vital to weigh cultural change in conjunction with the sustaining habitat. This poses one the major issues which has demanded consideration ever since the first air photographs of the Iron Age sites were taken: what is the nature of the surrounding banks and moats? What were they for, and when were they in use? Contributing to this issue entails excavations on a huge scale, for they may extend over a distance of well over 100 metres from the edge of the settlement mounds.

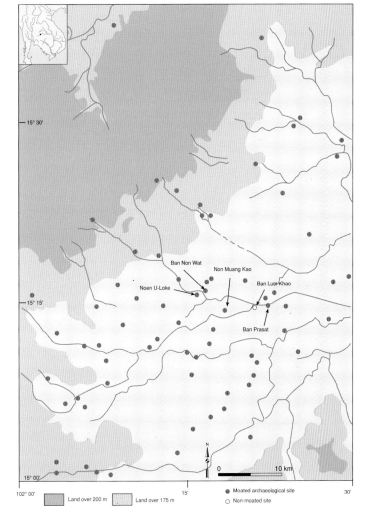

The location of prehistoric sites in the Mun River valley study area.

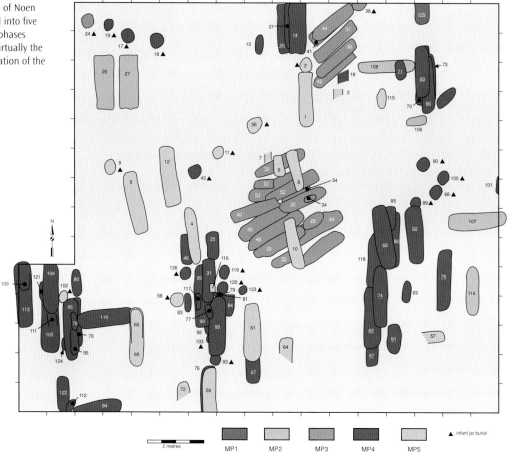

The graves of Noen U-Loke fall into five mortuary phases covering virtually the entire duration of the Iron Age.

MP1 MP2 MP3 MP4 MP5 ▲ infant jar burial

2 metres

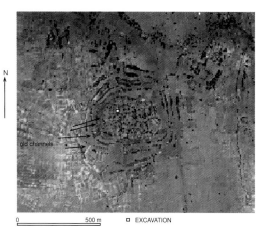

0   500 m   □ EXCAVATION

The moats of Noen U-Loke are clearly visible in the aerial photograph.

Noen U-Loke

Noen U-Loke was chosen for a major excavation programme, because it had previously been opened by the Fine Arts Department under Wichakana (1991), and his excavation encountered Iron Age burials. Moreover, this site seemed to be ringed by as many as five moats. It covers 12 hectares, far larger than Bronze Age sites, but considerably smaller than a second excavated site, Non Muang Kao. This double-peaked mound covers 50 hectares and is also ringed by multiple channels. Over two seasons, 220 square metres at Noen U-Loke were excavated to a depth of five metres. A total of 126 inhumation graves were divided into five mortuary phases (MP) on the basis of their depth, and stratigraphic relationships. MP1 was represented by part of only one grave, the pottery vessel from which recalls latest Bronze Age vessels from Ban Lum Khao. The second phase incorporates six burials, representing three men, two women and an infant. Some of the pottery vessels are quite distinct from the Bronze Age repertoire, but others are almost identical with those

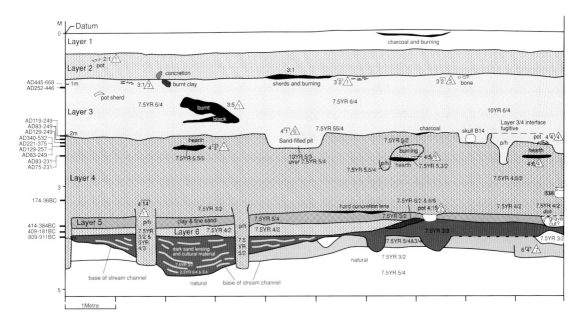

from late Ban Lum Khao. The time interval between the two cannot be great, but in phase 2, we find the first iron grave offerings. These graves lie between two sets of radiocarbon dates. Preceding determinations fall between 400-200 BC, while a determination later than these graves is 200-1 BC. It would, therefore, be reasonable to suggest that these earliest Iron Age interments belong within the period 300-200 BC, with a preference being earlier rather than later within that span.

The skill of the iron workers is already evident in the range and quality of the items interred with the dead during MP2. The earliest grave contained a woman who wore iron bangles and an iron neck ring or torc. It seems that iron was initially preferred for ornaments, but a slightly later grave, that of a man, contained a socketed iron hoe or axe, and a large, socketed spearhead. He probably commanded some standing in his community, for his other grave goods were impressive in variety and quantity. Pottery vessels filled with fish skeletons lay beyond his ankles, together with two bronze spearheads, shell disks and a modified bovid bone pierced at one end and polished all over. He wore bronze bangles and torcs, together with a necklace of tigers' canine teeth. The pottery vessels from these early burials are very similar in form and decoration to those from the latest Bronze Age graves of Ban Lum Khao.

No iron grave goods were found in the MP3 burials, which probably date within the first two centuries AD. Burials were now found in two tight clusters, each containing the remains of men, women, children and infants. The earlier incorporated very few ceramic vessels as grave goods, and few bronzes. However, it did include the earliest agate pendant and glass beads, indicating the opening of exchange relationships in a new range of exotic ornaments. Complete skeletons of young pigs also accompanied the dead. Pig remains, and an absence or rarity of pottery vessels were also features of the later cluster, but a major innovation in mortuary

This woman from Noen U-Loke mortuary phase 2 was found with iron jewellery, including torcs and bangles.

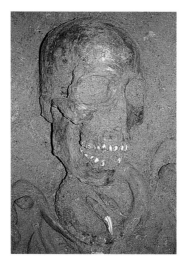

Burial 27 at Noen U-Loke contained the remains of a man richly endowed with grave goods, including shell ear discs, bronze spears, an iron spear or dagger, tigers' canines, bronze torcs, pottery vessels filled with fish, an iron hoe and a large bronze bangle.

This extraordinary ornament was found on a mortuary phase 3 skull from Noen U-Loke.

1 cm

2 cm

The man in burial 27 at Noen U-Loke wore a necklace of tigers' teeth.

Above right: Burial 26 at Noen U-Loke wore these matching boar's tusks, modified to a pointed end.

Right: Burials 26 and 27 at Noen U-Loke.

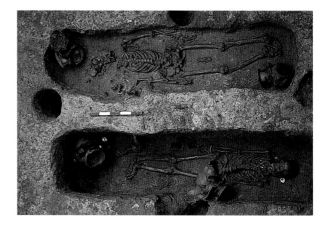

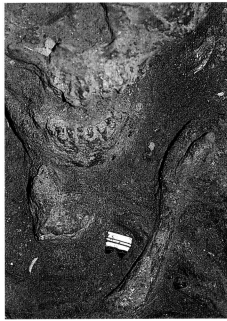

Agate pendants were commonly found in the neck area of Noen U-Loke burials.

Left: Pottery vessels from Noen U-Loke mortuary phase 2 are almost mirror images of those found in the latest phase of the Bronze Age at Ban Lum Khao. The pot at top right contained fish skeletons.

10 cm

behaviour involved filling the grave with white, silicified rice, large quantities of which had to be removed before revealing the human remains. Inhabitants of villages in the area north of the Great Lake in Cambodia today prepare unhusked rice over heat and offer it to the spirits on special occasions. The rice prepared in this manner looks quite similar to that encountered in the graves, and a spiritual reason for this practice seems highly likely. Exchange for exotic stone ornaments expanded, agate pendants now being regularly worn round the neck, while all but one of the carnelian beads recovered came from this phase and cluster. It was formerly thought that agate and carnelian ornaments found in Southeast Asia originated in India, but recent geochemical analyses now indicate a potential source in Central Thailand (Theunissen *et al.* 2000). Glass beads were also more abundant. One of the later graves appears to have been cut through a burnt clay floor overlying the cluster. The floor was littered with pottery vessels and the burnt bones of a dog. We do not know if this structure was used for occupation, with ancestors perhaps buried below, or represents a mortuary building of some sort.

MP4 comprises a further four clusters of interments, the orientation of the graves now being on a north-south axis. Three

Agate ornaments were found with many of the dead at Noen U-Loke during mortuary phases 3, 4 and 5. Carnelian beads, probably from a source in Central Thailand, were found in mortuary phase 3B.

1 cm

Noen U-Loke incorporated a number of clay floors.

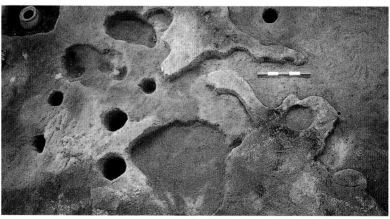

Work under way in the area of burial cluster 4A at Noen U-Loke.

The woman in burial 113 at Noen U-Loke wore a necklace of gold and agate beads.

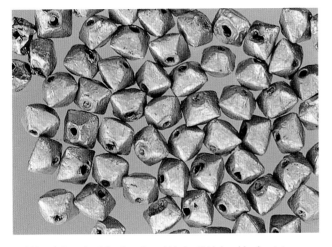

Gold beads from burial 113 at Noen U-Loke. Each bead is about 4 mm wide.

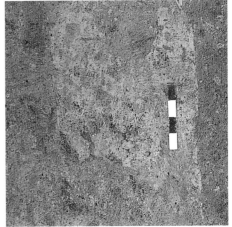

Some mortuary phase 4 graves at Noen U-Loke were found within clay coffins.

clusters form a line from east to west, with an intervening space of about four metres between each. There were further elaborations in the mortuary rituals. Some of the graves were lined and sealed in clay. The bodies were then placed in a deep bed of white, silicified rice, accompanied by rich offerings. A 25-30 year-old woman in MP4 cluster A wore a necklace of agate and gold beads, and two agate neck pendants. The increase in the quantity of bronze ornaments was particularly notable: she wore two ear spirals, 38 bangles, 64 finger rings and seven toe rings. Interspersed with these bronzes lay a silver toe ring and a silver finger ring. Like many of her contemporaries, she was accompanied by an iron knife, this particular one being covered in the remains of woven fabric that might represent her clothing, or a shroud. It is also most notable, that pottery vessels now accompanied the dead. They fall within the style widely known in the upper Mun Valley as 'Phimai Black', characterised by a thin fabric, burnished with various designs and fired to a deep and lustrous black finish. These vessels might well come from a specialised manufacturing

Infant burial jars at Noen U-Loke were large, and of a distinctive form.

Iron Age pottery in the upper Mun Valley is characterised by a lustrous black finish with burnished patterns. It is very thin, and probably made by specialists.

centre, because the tools for fashioning and decorating pottery vessels are very rare. Spindle whorls for producing yarn were relatively common as grave goods, however, indicating a local weaving industry. Other burials in the cluster confirm the importance attached to bronze ornaments. An adult male wore 42 toe rings and a belt, as well as a silver bangle. Another adult wore a bronze torc, and a second man was found with the remains of one or perhaps two bronze belts. Nor were bronzes restricted to adults. An infant was found with 17 bangles, at least 12 anklets, and a necklace of agate and glass beads.

Cluster 4B is probably contemporary with 4A, but there are no clay cappings to the graves and it is therefore impossible to identify the depth from which they were cut. This cluster includes up to 14 infants or children, and only six adults. There were fewer bronze ornaments, but more spindle whorls than in cluster A. A woman who died when over 40 years of age was found with her head placed within a large black pottery vessel, whereas cluster A graves often had a bowl placed over the head. Such slight differences in ritual might reflect different preferences between families over a few generations.

Cluster 4C burials lay to the east, again with an intervening space. The clay capping of some graves suggests contemporaneity with cluster 4A. We find the rice-filled graves, and many bronze ornaments. The richest man, who died when aged between 25-30 years, wore four bronze belts of circular cross section with a sophisticated device to secure each in place. He wore two large bronze discs, probably inserted within distended ear lobes, over 20 bangles, more then 125 finger rings, and in excess of 35 toe rings. Pottery vessels encircled the head, and an iron knife lay beyond the shoulder. Bimetallic rings, made of bronze and iron, were found regularly with phase 4 burials. One man was buried with a pottery vessel that contained a large, socketed spade. A late grave within this

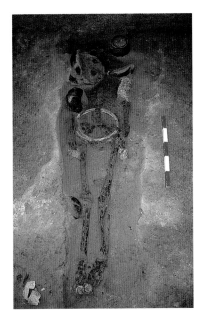

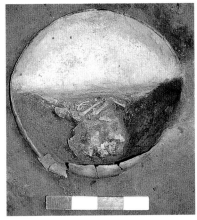

Noen U-Loke Burial 14 was the richest to be discovered at this site. The man wore three bronze belts, 150 bronze bangles, bronze toe and finger rings and ear coils of silver covered in gold.

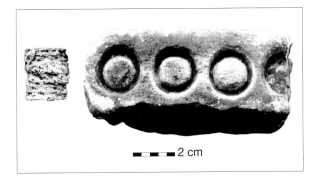

cluster, that of a woman who died when in her late thirties, revealed again a proliferation of bronzes. In this instance, she wore seven earrings and a spiral, 26 bangles, 64 finger rings, 10 anklets and three bimetallic rings. There is also a standard form of tanged iron knife, and many pottery vessels and glass beads. Infants were not overlooked. A 3-9 month-old was found with bronze anklets, bangles, finger and earrings, a glass bead necklace, and complement of fine pottery vessels. A group of infant jar burials integral with this cluster included one in which the infant skeleton was covered in white rice. The latest MP4 cluster contained the richest burial. This man, aged between 35-40 years at death, wore 75 bronze bangles on each arm, and three bronze belts. Other bronzes included over 60 finger rings, four large toe rings and four finger spirals. He wore silver ear spirals covered in gold and many glass beads. A tanged iron knife lay over the left wrist, and many pottery vessels were in place round the cranium. Unfortunately, other burials in this cluster were badly disturbed, but at least one infant was buried with an impressive array of bronzes, glass beads, bimetallic rings and an agate pendant.

The fifth mortuary phase is dated later than AD 300, and might have covered a century or more, because burials were found only half

The finger rings found in such profusion at Noen U-Loke were cast in open clay moulds like this example from Ban Prasat.

Left: Excavating burial 14 at Noen U-Loke.

Top: Even infants were interred under a bed of protective rice at Noen U-Loke.

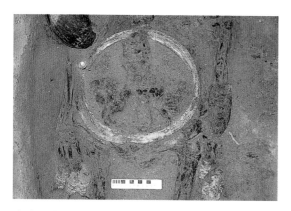

The belts finally exposed on burial 14 at Noen U-Loke.

The skill of the Noen U-Loke bronze worker is seen in this expertly made catch for the belt found with burial 14. Width 5 cm.

1 cm

Silver earrings covered in gold foil were found with burial 14 at Noen U-Loke.

a metre below the present mound surface down to a depth of 1.77 metres. The basic ritual of death remained the same: inhumation on the back, with the head orientated to the north. But there were also a number of developments. Rice was no longer placed in the graves, and clustering ceased. The range and quantity of bronzes fell markedly, while iron offerings now included sickles and a tanged spearhead. One young man was found with an iron arrowhead embedded in his spine.

Technology

The importance of Noen U-Loke derives not only from an unparalleled succession of Iron Age graves, but also from the abundant evidence for the technological skills of the inhabitants. Iron smelting and forging, presumably of the local laterite ore, were undertaken at the settlement, and the output was employed for ornamentation, in agriculture, forest clearance and in conflict. The availability of spades, hoes and sickles must have provided for more extensive and efficient rice cultivation and part of the surplus was used ritually. Bronzes were also locally cast, and the quantity and range reflects not only a surge in the availability of ingots through exchange, but also high skill in casting spirals, belts and torcs. There is some evidence too, that glass beads were manufactured locally. The two salt-making sites to the west of the main site were accumulating during the Iron Age. Ceramics of high quality were used in mortuary rituals, while many pits of unknown purpose were also filled with complete pottery vessels. Yet even during the Iron Age, stone adzes were still used. The many spindle whorls and remains of fabric reflect a weaving industry. There are also a few ceramic anvils for shaping pottery vessels, but their scarcity hints at the presence of specialised manufacturing centres within the exchange orbit of the inhabitants.

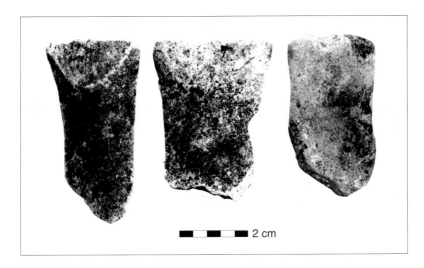

These ceramic moulds from Noen U-Loke were probably used to create the sockets in conjunction with the casting of socketed axes. One was found covered in a thin film of lead, as if the final bronze axes was cast by a 'lost lead' technique.

Even during the Iron Age, stone adzes were used at Noen U-Loke.

Above and left: A clay mould for casting an axe from Noen U-Loke.

One of the bronze spearheads from burial 27, Noen U-Loke.

Ceramic anvils for shaping pottery vessels are very rare at Noen U-Loke. This might be a result of specialist manufacturing centres elsewhere being responsible for the superb vessels found at the site.

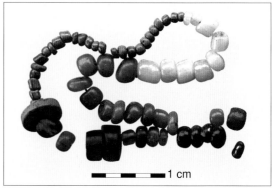

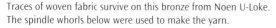

Traces of woven fabric survive on this bronze from Noen U-Loke. The spindle whorls below were used to make the yarn.

Right: Glass beads were commonly found as grave goods at Noen U-Loke and Non Muang Kao.

The iron masters of Noen U-Loke forged a wide variety of artefacts, and the numbers recovered indicate standardised production. Their output included massive spears, that on the left still retaining part of its wooden haft, points and tanged knives, ridged knives and hoes. One of the ridged knives is covered with rice grains from the rice that filled the grave from which it was recovered.

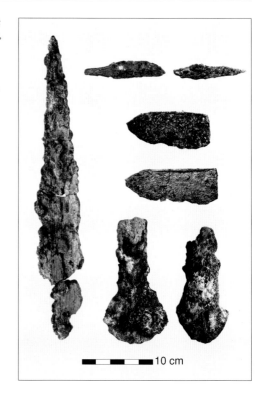

Iron sickles from Noen U-Loke provide evidence for the application of iron technology in agriculture.

Intercutting furnaces at Noen U-Loke probably represent an industrial area.

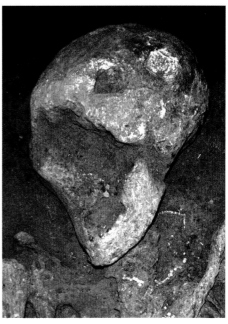

A glass bead necklace from mortuary phase 3B, Noen U-Loke

The Environment and Economy

An analysis of the deposits at the base of the excavation revealed an old stream channel and layers that accumulated under swampy conditions. When deep sections were cut across the moats round the settlement to define their form, date and use, they were found to have been laid down by slow-moving water. Taken in conjunction with old river beds visible from air photographs, Boyd *et al.* (1999) have been able to reconstruct a low lying, swampy habitat round the site. The encircling banks and water-laid deposits within the moats have been examined at six sites, and the radiocarbon dates all fall in the period AD 1-500 (McGrath and Boyd in press). Thus, the later Iron Age occupants were able to invest much energy in constructing earthworks to control water flows, although their precise purpose remains elusive. They may have been defensive, or to provide water during the dry season. They would have supplied a steady supply of fish. Further investigations are necessary before this issue can be clarified. However, there is   a hint in a 7th century inscription of Jayavarman I, who ruled a kingdom south of the Dang Raek Range, which noted that he went to war in the autumn, when his enemy's moats were dry.

The cultivation of rice was a mainstay of the subsistence economy. We find carbonised rice in profusion, the use of burnt rice in mortuary rituals, and attention being given to the provision of iron agricultural implements. This is hardly surprising, given the surge in the number and size of settlements during the Iron Age.

Above and below: This young man, buried face down at Noen U-Loke, had been killed by an arrow, six centimetres long, lodged in his spine.

Some lidded pots were found at Noen U-Loke and Non Muang Kao, complete but unassociated with burials.

Noen U-Loke is one of the smaller settlements with an area of 12 hectares. Non Muang Kao was at least four times larger. Domestic cattle, pig and water buffalo dominate the faunal remains. There are suprisingly few fish bones, although they were placed in mortuary vessels during the earlier occupation. Shellfish were collected from the surrounding swamps, rice fields and streams.

Warfare

Friction between different groups is a stimulus to the rise of leaders. Even in the second mortuary phase, we find evidence for iron and bronze weaponry, but the most compelling evidence for fighting is to be found in the distribution of iron projectile points. These do not find their way into mortuary offerings, save for one found embedded in a young man's spine that was probably the immediate cause of death. Such arrowheads dramatically increased in frequency in the later contexts, a potential indication of conflict.

Non Muang Kao

This site lies 10 km to the southeast of Noen U-Loke and was excavated as part of the same research programme. Non Muang Kao, or Mound of the Ancient City, is a very large Iron Age site within a series of moats and banks. Boyd (2000) has noted that the original settlement took advantage of a low natural mound adjacent to a major river. It is particularly unfortunate that the cultural layers are so hard

The plan of Non Muang Kao, showing the area excavated.

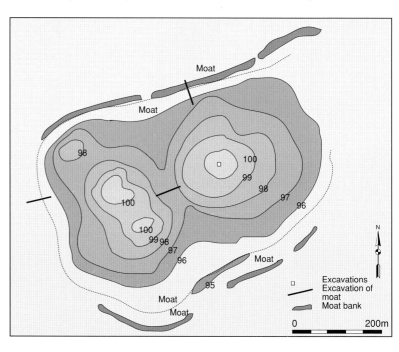

Lidded pottery vessels were often found at Non Muang Kao and Noen U-Loke. They had no relationship to a burial, but may have been some form of votive deposit.

Right: The excavation of Non Muang Kao furnished a series of superimposed clay floors. This example had an upturned lip along one edge

Burial 2 at Non Muang Kao had many bronze bangles.

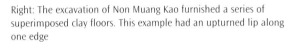

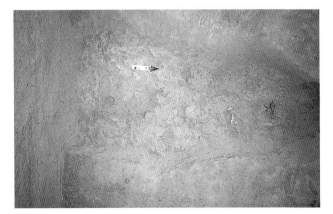

Above, above left and left: Clay buildings, represented by floors and walls at Non Muang Kao, were found superimposed one over the other. (Courtesy Dr. D. O'Reilly)

The pottery vessels from the Non Muang Kao graves could well come from the same workshops as those from Noen U-Loke.

as almost to defy excavation, while the preservation of bone is very poor. However, the concrete consistency has preserved a series of superimposed clay floors, associated with postholes that still contain the form of the wood, and wall foundations. Ten successive floors were revealed, the upper eight being superimposed. Foundation trenches for the walls were up to half a metre deep. On three occasions, a lidded Phimai Black bowl was found, placed within a hole just large enough to accommodate the vessels. These were also encountered at Noen U-Loke, and do not seem to have been associated with burials. O'Reilly (2000) has suggested that these floors represent a domestic structure subjected to periodic reconstruction. They were also associated with graves lined with the same clay as was employed in the floor covering. Despite the great difficulties encountered by O'Reilly when excavating this site, it still holds the key to understanding the nature of domestic structures and their relationship with the interment of the dead.

Grave goods are very similar to those found at Noen U-Loke during MP4. Moreover, burials were laid out on the same north-south orientation. Burial 6, for example, wore 14 bronze bangles. There were banded agate and glass beads, bimetallic rings and virtually identical Phimai Black pottery vessels. The fine stratigraphic sequence allowed the 11 burials to be placed in sequential order, and again like Noen U-Loke, earlier graves were filled with rice, while later ones were also lined and capped with clay.

Although only a tiny fraction of the site has been excavated, the square, placed in the middle of one of the twin peaks, revealed initial occupation about half way through the sequence at Noen U-Loke, at about 50 BC. If this represents the actual situation, then it hints at a growing population in this region, and the foundation and rapid expansion of new settlements.

Other Excavated Sites in the Mun Valley

Excavations at several other large Iron Age sites in the Mun Valley have added further to our understanding of this period. Ban Suai lies within the present town of Phimai, and was excavated in 1966 by Parker. Only preliminary results are available, but they mention a most unusual structure comprising a low platform made of burnt clay, covering an area of about three by two metres. It was raised 10-15 cm above the surrounding area, and had been subjected to several episodes of burning. Pottery vessels had been placed in three corners of the structure, all containing human bone. This evidence for an Iron Age ritual structure near to the site of first an early historic period brick temple, and then the main shrine of Angkorian Phimai, might indicate an element of continuity from the Iron Age into the period of early and mature states.

Agate pendants at Non Muang Kao are identical to those from Noen U-Loke.

At Non Yang, downstream from Phimai, Nitta (1991) found similar clay floors in the upper, excavated layers of this deep mound. These were laid down over a raft of split logs, and were associated with clay walls bearing mat impressions. Lidded ceramic vessels were found, without reference to human burials, under the floors as if they represent a form of foundation offering. Further structural features included a ditch 70 cm deep, with a row of post holes at the base. The mortuary ritual involved jar burials disposed in groups of five or six vessels one of which contained three skulls.

More evidence for clay structures was also found during the excavation of Ban Don Phlong. Here, Nitta (1991) found 17 furnaces for smelting iron ore associated with the foundations of a clay building. These overlay a cemetery in which some graves were lined with clay. Grave goods included glass and agate beads, and bronze bangles and rings.

Ban Takhong lies on a tributary stream flowing north to the Mun River. Small test squares excavated by Elizabeth Moore (1992) encountered a stratigraphic sequence six metres deep that incorporated clay floors and wall foundations. Most burials were found within ceramic vessels, but there was also an unusual flexed inhumation. The lowest mortuary jar was found resting on a turtle carapace. Further south, villagers have unearthed many iron weapons at the site of Ban Bung Noi. Analysis of a bronze bracelet obtained through excavations by the Fine Arts Department has revealed a 23% tin bronze alloy (Niyomka and Adsvamas 2000).

At Ban Krabuang Nok, Indrawooth excavated a further Iron Age site where cultural remains had accumulated to the unparalleled depth of 8.5 metres (Indrawooth *et al.* 1990). The lowest layers belong to the early Iron Age and, again, the preferred burial practice involved interment within a large ceramic vessel.

Muang Phet was the first large Iron Age site on the Khorat Plateau to be examined archaeologically (Quaritch-Wales 1957). A further excavation undertaken by McNeill (1997) has refined our knowledge of the sequence. This is a relatively small mound, covering six hectares and is ringed by two moats and three earth ramparts. It is located in the upland zone of the survey area chosen to cover all the

Excavations at Baksei Chamkrong, Angkor, revealed Iron Age furnaces under a historic period brick wall.

principal landforms in the Phimai area. The initial occupation phase belongs to the period when Phimai Black pottery was in vogue, and has provided a radiocarbon determination of AD 260-320. For the first time, the excavators emphasised the ramparts and moats in their strategy. At Muang Phet, McNeill has obtained two radiocarbon dates within the period AD 200-550 for the layers under the rampart. The layers comprising the rampart itself contain Phimai Black Iron Age sherds, but no historic wares. The dates for these embankments thus match those for the Upper Mun sites.

The faunal remains are also interesting in their contrasting pattern when compared with the sites on the flood plain below. No turtle remains were found at Muang Phet, and shellfish adapted to flowing streams are far less frequent. This important new information suggests that the uplands, with their less favourable habitat for rice cultivation, were settled later than the river flood plains, and were generally smaller. The excavators are confident that the moats and ramparts were set in place during the Iron Age, probably between AD 200-500.

These discoveries at individual sites all contribute to a pattern, which cannot be ignored. Some sites in the Middle-Lower Chi and the Mun valleys grew differentially large. They were ringed by earthern embankments which retained water as moats. The reservoir at Ban Chiang Hian suggests that it was necessary to assure a water supply for a large populace. Iron weapons and tools are found, and glass beads were favoured. There is a consistent thread of evidence in favour of population growth and movement. The same conclusions have resulted from Moore's (1986) consideration of the sites in the Mun Valley. She has suggested on typological grounds rather than on the basis of excavated material, that the sites there reflect an expansion of settlement into the surrounding middle terrace areas. Water conservation measures became more intensive in this new environment, but the benefits included access to iron ore and the necessary reserves of timber for the smelting process.

Like a lunar landscape, looting has destroyed virtually all the Iron Age site of Phum Snay in Cambodia.

Dougald O'Reilly in the foreground, directed a rescue and training programme at Phum Snay in February 2001. At last, an Iron Age site in Cambodia is responding to careful excavation.

Burial 5 at Phum Snay involved an infant, buried with ivory bangles, and several pottery vessels beyond the feet.

Cambodia

The Iron Age of the plains bordering the Mekong as it traverses Cambodia to the sea is barely known. However, Moore's review of air photographs has singled out a series of sites north of the Great Lake which closely resemble the Iron Age moated sites of the adjacent Mun Valley. Malleret (1959) has investigated the mound of Lovea, one such site, and has reported the recovery of human remains and bronze artefacts. The nature of late prehistoric settlement in this, the heartland of the later state of Angkor, is only now responding to field

Above: Burial 22 from the Angkor Borei Iron Age cemetery.

Above left: This Iron Age burial was found at the base of the cultural sequence at Angkor Borei.

Middle: Excavating the Iron Age cemetery at Angkor Borei. (Courtesy Dr. Miriam Stark)

Koum Sourith mapping the Angkor Borei Iron Age cemetery.

Above right: Burial 20 from the Angkor Borei Iron Age cemetery.

Above far right: A bird's eye view of the excavations at the Angkor Borei Iron Age cemetery.

Right: Burial 27 from the Iron Age cemetery of Angkor Borei. (Courtesy Dr. Miriam Stark)

research. At Angkor, for example, the remains of an Iron Age occupation were found in front of the Baksei Chamkrong temple in February 2001. These confirmed earlier reports of a prehistoric occupation in the shadow of the Bakheng, the hill at the centre of Yashodharapura, the city foundation of King Yashovarman (AD 889- *c.* 910).

Phum Snay is a very large Iron Age settlement strategically located on the route from the Great Lake to the Chao Phraya Valley. It came to prominence in 1999 on account of severe looting by the villagers in order to sell beads. The site today resembles a battlefield, dimpled with looters pits and liberally strewn with human remains, discarded iron and bronze artefacts, and unwanted broken pottery vessels. The villagers have described some remarkable finds: a skeleton wearing a bronze helmet inlaid with gold, and much evidence for bronze and iron weaponry and exotic carnelian, agate and gold jewellery. One discarded skull was found stained with bronze from such a helmet. Excavations in February 2001, under the direction of Dougald O'Reilly, took place in one of the few enclaves which remained intact. In an area of 5 by 15 metres, the excavators encountered a relatively shallow stratigraphic sequence yielding much evidence for the subsistence economy and ceramic tradition, and several complete burials. One involved an infant interred with the head to the west, with several pottery vessels beyond the feet and six ivory bangles on each arm. Further excavation seasons are planned, but the prospects for a proper understanding of the Iron Age in this vital area are bleak, for as soon as a prehistoric site is recognized by the local villagers, it is immediately plundered for beads.

Similar problems have faced research in southern Cambodia, where Miriam Stark is investigating the early city of Angkor Borei. She has recently identified an Iron Age inhumation cemetery below the historic layers, a finding of the greatest significance in any investigation of early state origins.

The Pasak Valley

The Pasak River flows from north to south on the western edge of the Phetchabun Range. It lies in an intermediate position between the Khorat Plateau and the broad plains of the Chao Phraya River system, and archaeological research in advance of the dam construction on the Pasak River has led to the discovery of a series of Iron Age sites (Daeng-iet and Youkongdee 1998). At Ban Chaibadan, 104 square

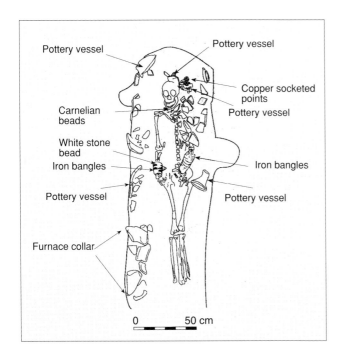

Burial 1 from operation 4 at Nil Kham Haeng includes, as grave goods, a furnace chimney for facilitating the smelting of copper ore. (Courtesy Dr. Vincent Pigott)

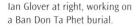

Ian Glover at right, working on a Ban Don Ta Phet burial.

Top: Excavations in progress at Ban Don Ta Phet.

Top right: A burial from Ban Don Ta Phet, showing a set of bronze bowls. (Courtesy Dr. Ian Glover)

metres were exposed in 1996-7, resulting in the recovery of 30 inhumation graves, of which five have been identified as male, nine as female, and 10 contained infants or children. The sex of the remaining six could not be identified (Choosiri 1998). Grave goods provide a series of close parallels with Noen U-Loke. There are similar glass beads and bronze bangles, iron axes, knives and spears and in one case, the same style of gold beads. Gold earrings were also found with one of the interments, while pottery vessels regularly accompanied the dead. Spindle whorls and moulds point to local weaving and bronze casting. A like range of grave goods was also found during the excavation of Ban Pukree. The five inhumation burials uncovered were associated with glass and jade beads, jade bangles, iron tools, bronze bangles, ivory earrings and spindle whorls. These sites reveal that the Pasak Valley was occupied by communities similar to those of the upper Mun area.

The Chao Phraya Valley

The Chao Phraya Valley occupies a central position in the prehistory of Southeast Asia. Not only is it rich in mineral wealth and well aspected land for the cultivation of rice, but it is also nodal in exchange routes. Copper production continued in the Khao Wong Prachan Valley at Nil Kham Haeng, and the burials of the copper workers as with the preceding Bronze Age, shows a close link with their activities. Burial 1, for example, incorporates several pottery vessels, 18 copper-socketed points, iron bracelets on each arm, five carnelian beads strung as a necklace, and most significantly, a complete furnace chimney for facilitating the smelting of copper ore.

To the west, the Three Pagodas Pass leads to the Gulf of Martaban and India, and to the east, the Bang Pakong Valley gives access to the extensive lowlands of northern Cambodia and the Great Lake. The Gulf of Siam permitted movement of people and exchange of goods and ideas by sea. Excavations and site surveys have confirmed the strategic importance of this area. We find strong

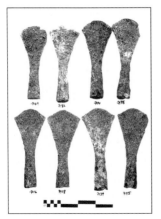

This bronze situla or bucket from Ban Don Ta Phet almost certainly originated in the Dong Son culture of northern Viet Nam.

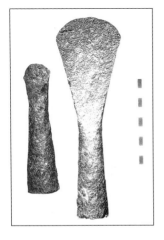

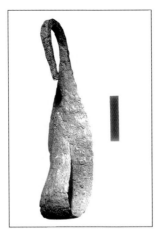

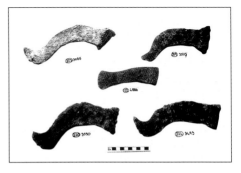

Top left, top far left, above left and above: Iron tools and weapons from Ban Don Ta Phet.

evidence not only for a new plane of social wealth in the cemeteries, but also the development of craft specialisation and the inception of maritime exchange involving India, island Southeast Asia and Viet Nam. As was the case in the Mun and Pa Sak Valleys, we also encounter large settlements ringed by banks and moats.

Ban Don Ta Phet

Ban Don Ta Phet provides the clearest evidence for these developments. This cemetery site has been the object of several excavation seasons since its discovery in 1975 (You-Di 1978, Glover 1980, 1983, 1998, Glover *et al.* 1984) and it already plays a central role in our understanding of the late prehistoric period in Central Thailand. It is located on the western margins of the Chao Phraya lowlands, not far from the Three Pagodas Pass. As Glover's excavations have shown, it provides compelling evidence for exchange contact with India and Viet Nam, the development of specialist bronze working, and investment of much energy in mortuary rituals. The available radiocarbon dates suggest occupation during the first half of the fourth century BC.

Iron tools are often found as grave offerings at Ban Don Ta Phet. (Courtesy Dr. Ian Glover)

The bronze bowls from Ban Don Ta Phet show intriguing scenes: they probably derive from India through a distant exchange network.

Above and top: Bronze bowls, probably made in India, are a particular feature of the mortuary offerings at Ban Don Ta Phet. (Courtesy Dr. Ian Glover)

5 cm

Below: This superb carnelian lion found at Ban Don Ta Phet must come from India.

Unfortunately, bone does not survive in the acidic soils there, but excavations have revealed dispositions of artefacts with the occasional scrap of bone which are clearly the remains of human interments. One of the largest exposures of an Iron Age cemetery in Southeast Asia has revealed rows of burials orientated on an east-west axis. The establishment of a specified, possibly elite burial enclave is suggested by the provision of an encircling moat and ditch. When compared with Bronze Age burials, the grave goods are considerably more abundant and the range of materials is greater. Thus Glover *et al.* (1984) have described four burials from the 1980-1 season in which the number of complete or fragmentary pots averaged twenty per burial, a far higher figure than in Bronze Age assemblages. The burials were also associated with tools and weapons made of iron, ornaments and bowls made from bronze, and both stone and glass beads. One bronze bucket is closely paralleled in the Dong Son culture of Viet Nam, and is almost certainly an exotic import.

The blades of socketed iron spearheads were often bent back to break or ritually kill them prior to burial. One iron implement looks very like a modern sickle blade, while the application of iron technology is revealed by the socketed tips for either digging sticks or hoes, harpoons and knives. The beads were manufactured from agate, carnelian and glass. Some of the etched beads follow Indian techniques of decoration, while the manufacture of glass is highly likely to be of Indian inspiration.

The burials at Ban Don Ta Phet have also furnished a series of thin-walled bronze bowls which exhibit interesting features (Rajpitak and Seeley 1979). They are decorated with incised motifs and, occasionally, representations of people. The alloy employed is a high (19-21%) tin bronze, which is very brittle and hard to work, yet imparts a golden colour. The bowls were turned on a lathe to a remarkably thin finish, and then incised with decorative scenes. Nor are they restricted to Ban Don Ta Phet. Bennett and Glover (1992) have reported similar specimens, including images of women with elaborate hairstyles, from Khao Jamook to the southwest. This technique, in addition to the brittle nature of the high tin alloy, would have demanded a long apprenticeship. Bowls with a generally similar composition and form have been found widely distributed in India. One comes from Coimbatore in southern India, and two from the Bhir Mound at Taxila, dating to the late first millennium BC.

This nephrite ear ornament was almost certainly imported from a Sa Huynh manufacturing site along the coast of Viet Nam. (Courtesy Dr. Ian Glover)

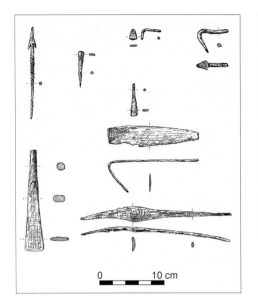

A bronze cockerell on top of its cage, an unusual bronze from Ban Don Ta Phet.
(Courtesy Dr. Ian Glover)

Far left: Iron implements from Ongbah burial 8 include iron projectile points, an axe and hooks.

A further example was found at Adichanallur in Tamil Nadu (Glover 1998). Although local manufacture cannot be ruled out, the many high tin bronze bowls known from India makes an exotic source more likely. The inferences are clear: that exchange linked Indian and Southeast Asian societies towards the end of the first millennium BC, and that some individuals at Ban Don Ta Phet were interred with exotic ornaments.

A superb carnelian lion must take pride of place among such imported items. A second but broken specimen was found in the same burial context, and further examples are known from Khuan Lukpad and Khao Sam Kaeo in Peninsular Thailand. The lion was often used to symbolise the Buddha, and it is not unlikely that some inkling of Buddhism was already reaching Southeast Asia by this period. Several lions rendered in semi precious stone or bronze have been recovered from the Bhir mound at Taxila, dated from 100 BC-AD 200 (Indrawooth 1999). There is also a double-headed animal ear ornament of the type which is characteristic of the Sa Huynh sites of coastal Viet Nam. All the bronzes were for decoration: no weapons were encountered. The most unusual items were four bird figurines, including one of a fighting cock standing on top of its cage, a scene re-enacted in villages across Southeast Asia to this day.

Burial 8 from Ongbah shows the prevalance at the site of iron implements as grave goods.

Tham Ongbah

The rise of a social echelon distinguished by high rank is further confirmed at Tham Ongbah. This massive cavern is located in the upper reaches of the Khwae Yai River. Sørensen (1973, 1979) has recovered some information from the site, following its near destruction by looters. He found that the burial technique comprised extended inhumation in wooden boat-shaped coffins. A radiocarbon

A general view of the Iron Age cemetery of Tha Kae.

determination of one such coffin gave an estimate in the last three centuries BC. There were also several intact burials within the cave, of which ten were excavated. These lacked the wooden boat coffins, but both groups contained a similar assemblage of iron implements. Sørensen has suggested inferior social status rather than chronological change to account for such a disparity in wealth. The ten poorer burials have yielded several well-preserved iron implements, thereby affording insight into the uses this metal was put to, presumably during the last century or two of the first millennium BC. Burial 5 incorporated an iron hoe on the chest. Burial 6 included a tanged knife, possibly a spear head, and five beads. Other burials yielded chisels and arrowheads. One contained seven iron objects, all placed near the ankles. Similar arrowheads, socketed axes, chisels and knives were found in burial and late occupation contexts at the Bang site, Ban Kao.

It is particularly unfortunate that we are unable to present a list of associations between funerary artefacts and the boat coffins left by the teams of looters who destroyed Tham Ongbah. Sørensen, however, has recovered fragments of artefacts which hint at the wealth they once contained, and has interviewed the looters' labourers to establish certain relationships between stray finds and the original contents of the coffins. On the basis of this admittedly unsatisfactory but necessary procedure, it is possible to point out that the coffin burials included strings of beads round the waist and neck. They had also included bronze and iron artefacts including ear rings, bracelets and at least one bronze vessel. A set of drums was found nearby and were probably associated with the coffins. These elaborate objects were decorated with zones of different motifs, including flying birds, human beings and geometric designs.

Contact of one sort or another between the occupants of the Chao Phraya and the Red River valleys is also indicated by a more recent find at Dermbang Nang Buat. Suchitta (1985) has reported a series of artefacts of Dong Son affinities, including a fragment of cast iron, and the remains of ornamented drums and bowls. The casting of

A burial from the Iron Age cemetery of Tha Kae. Note the dog skeleton at the left shoulder, and an iron point by the left elbow. (Courtesy Dr Roberto Ciarla and Dr Fiorella Rispoli)

iron is a technique developed in China and alien to any Indian-derived method of iron-working. Whether this find reflects exchange or an actual movement of people from Bac Bo remains to be seen.

The presence of moated settlements in the Chao Phraya lowlands has long been known, and some were major centres of the Dvaravati civilization. Excavations at Sab Champa and Chansen have provided evidence for initial occupation during the late prehistoric period. At Chansen, Bronson and Dales (1973) found a basal cultural layer containing an inhumation burial associated with a socketed iron hoe or plough share. This same context has yielded the remains of water buffalo bones. Veerapan (1979) has discovered inhumation graves at the moated site of Sab Champa, associated on this occasion with pottery vessels and moulds used in bronze casting. Ban Tha Kae has yielded, in its middle phase, glass, carnelian and nephrite ornaments belonging to the Iron Age (Hanwong 1985). Ciarla and Rispoli have also reported the presence of large ceramic vessels, a socketed iron axe or hoe and bronze and shell jewellery from Iron Age graves at this site. It is also evident, as at Sri Thep, that the large centres of the Dvaravati civilization were raised over Iron Age settlements. There, Tankittikorn (1991) found evidence for late Iron Age occupation, together with five burials one of which, on the same north to south orientation as at Noen U-Loke, was interred with iron and carnelian grave offerings. Iron tools and ornaments were also found with the burials unearthed at Ban Nong Daeng, just 12 kilometres to the southwest. Wilaikeo (1991a, b) has added further to the list of finds, with the recovery of Iron Age burials from the huge moated site of U-Taphao.

Adult burials at Ban Wang Hi were set out in a group with pottery vessels, iron and exotic stone grave goods. (Courtesy Dr. Jean-Pierre Pautreau).

Top: The mortuary offerings from an Iron Age grave at Tha Kae included pottery vessels, an iron axe and bronze and shell jewellery. (Courtesy Dr Roberto Ciarla and Dr Fiorella Rispoli)

The iron implement with this burial at Ban Wang Hi was probably for harvesting rice.

Right: There was an impressive quantity of iron artefacts with this inhumation burial at Ban Wang Hi. (Courtesy Dr Jean-Pierre Pautreau)

Ban Wang Hi

Recent fieldwork has also filled a void in our understanding of the Iron Age of the Chao Phraya catchment, by investigating sites in the northern tributary valleys. Ban Wang Hi lies on the bank of the Kwang Stream, three kilometres southeast of Lamphun. Early trial excavations undertaken first by the Fine Arts Department and then by Jean-Pierre Pautreau (Pautreau *et al.* 1997, Pautreau and Mornais 1998) revealed inhumation graves associated with glass, agate and iron grave goods. It was during the 1998 season that 17 burials were uncovered, and a full appreciation of the range of offerings, and the energy expended in the mortuary ritual became apparent. Adults of both sexes, children and the newly born were found grouped and overlying earlier interments with the head usually orientated to the southeast. Mortuary rituals included the provision of clay coffins, and probably a flexible shroud or covering for the body. One adult was found actually holding a sword in his left hand, with socketed spears lying beside his head. He also wore attractive glass earrings and glass beads. Infants were interred in lidded ceramic vessels, with their own set of grave goods which could include miniature iron artefacts, glass and agate beads and cowrie shells. Bronze bracelets, one covered in small bronze bells, were also found. Unfortunately very few organic items have survived in this Iron Age cemetery, which seems to present one phase of use during prehistory. The material culture, however, indicated a date within the period 200 BC to AD 200. The excavations at Ban Wang Hat, just west of the later capital of Sukhothai, have likewise revealed Iron Age burials in association with exotic ornaments of carnelian, agate and glass (Saraya 1997). The proliferation of Iron Age sites in this area has been confirmed by the recognition of many settlements also yielding exotic stone and glass beads, and evidence for extensive iron smelting, in the valley of the Lamphan River (Songsiri 1997).

An important step towards a fuller understanding of this period has been taken by Ho (1984). Within the context of her analysis of the material from the excavations of Khok Charoen, she undertook a series of site surveys. These suggested strongly that after an initial occupation during what she calls the early metal age (equivalent to the Bronze Age), there was a move toward centralisation wherein one site grew differentially large, and it is assumed, exercised political dominance over others in its area. Indeed, Ho was able to identify three distinct areas each dominated by its large, ultimately moated site. The centres are about 30 km distant from each other. She has ascribed these sites to a 'high metal age', which saw a marked increase in bronze working and the initial use of iron. It is important to note how her results from the Chao Phraya valley match those proposed by Moore and Welch in the Mun, and Higham and Kijngam in the Chi valleys.

There are then, strong grounds for suggesting that there was a trend towards centralisation during the mid to late first millennium BC, but the chronological relationship between it and initial direct or indirect contact with exotic coastal traders remains to be determined. Contact with the Red River valley is also apparent, as evidenced in the drums from Tham Ongbah, the few bronzes in the Dong Son tradition at Ban Don Ta Phet and the recently discovered cast iron object in association with objects of Dong Son type found at Dermbang Nang Buat (Suchitta 1985).

This man at Ban Wang Hi was interred with two iron swords beside his head.

Far left: Even children at Ban Wang Hi were buried with iron tools.
(Courtesy Dr Jean-Pierre Pautreau)

The Origins of Iron Age Chiefdoms

Two contrasting areas in Southeast Asia witnessed the development of centralised authority and ranked social structures. The first centres on Bac Bo, and is distinguished by the military threat of the expanding Han Empire. The second incorporated the Mekong and Chao Phraya valleys, the restricted coastal plains of Viet Nam south of the Hai Van Pass and the upland Plain of Jars. Earlier Bronze Age settlements were relatively small and, it is argued, autonomous. During the Iron Age, some settlements became much larger, and were foci of craft specialisation and intensified production.

There is a recurrent thread of evidence that from the mid second millennium BC, bronze casting was adopted within small village communities. These were already linked by exchange in exotic stone and shell ornaments and ceramics. Such durable items may well have accompanied perishable products, such as cloth and feathers, and they have been described under the heading of primitive valuables. It is argued that they underwrote the maintenance of economic, social and political relationships between the participating communities. Thus the exchange of valuables and the establishment of affinal ties promoted alliance. Imbalance or fluctuations in access to valuables involved oscillations in rank. Within such a system, much devolves upon the leaders of dominant lineages. They had superior access to prestige valuables, could foster affinal relationships and play an entrepreneurial role in the transfer of goods.

The distribution of stone, marine shell and metals, the principal surviving materials documenting such exchange, reflect goods crossing the landscape using a variety of routes and in different directions. Further research will surely illuminate the former existence of interlinked exchange networks with major concentrations, in for example the Chao Phraya catchment, the Mekong valley and the maritime tracts of Viet Nam. The early knowledge of bronze, and later traffic in ingots, would have travelled along these networks. The system was also internally flexible with regard to permanence of rank. It is worth pausing to review such flexibility, as it will sharpen our perception of changes which took place with the Iron Age.

Most Bronze Age settlements were located in small stream valleys and along the margins of main river flood plains. Rice cultivation probably involved land subjected to only a limited degree of monsoon flooding. Climatic unpredictability involving drought in some years and major flooding in others, however, would doubtless have prejudiced predictable success in the rice harvest. The broad-ranging subsistence activities would have buffered communities against climatic extremes. At the same time, however, intensifying production to permit participation in a prestige goods exchange system would have come more readily to those commanding the most extensive tracts of cultivable land or valued resources, such as copper ore, marine shell, high-grade stone or good potting clay. Under these conditions, certain communities might prosper unduly.

The Iron Age in Bac Bo saw the growth to prominence of one settlement and its occupants over others within its orbit. This took place in conjunction with intensification in several areas of social engagement. In terms of agriculture, there was the advent of ploughing and double cropping. As Goody has cogently shown, the application of animal traction to soil preparation greatly magnifies production and thereby makes it more feasible to concentrate a strategic surplus (Goody 1976). A rice surplus can be employed to attract and maintain followers, thereby concentrating people. It may also be converted into visible status objects, not least the great ceremonial drums, situlae, body plaques and, in terms of prowess, daggers, swords and axe-halberds. There was a great proliferation of skill on the part of the Dong Son smith, and much more metal was mined, moved and shaped. It is self evident that the organisation and purpose of all this activity, involving as it did the maintenance of permanent ateliers and control over often remote ore sources, involved intensification. In this manner, permanent ranking of an elite, craft specialisation and intensified agriculture form a triad of linked variables. Nor must it be forgotten that the Dong Son aristocrats controlled the maritime and riverine routes which exposed Bac Bo first to the importation of Chinese goods, and then the admission of Chinese armies. Under a similar set of circumstances, Haselgrove (1982) has applied a prestige good control model to the initial contact between the expanding Roman Empire and the inhabitants of Southern Britain. He noted that, where a particular lineage or group is able to monopolise raw materials or new supplies of prestige goods, it should achieve a position of dominance over its former peers.

The iron knife with this burial at Ban Wang Hi is very similar to those still used in the area. (Courtesy Dr Jean-Pierre Pautreau)

While most of Southeast Asia lay beyond the reach of Chinese imperialism, it nevertheless participated in an expanding world of international exchange. It has often been assumed that coastal communities played a supine role, to be awakened from a long sleep by the arrival of Indian entrepreneurs. This is most unlikely. The settlement of Malagasy from Southeast Asia is proof enough of a long tradition of indigenous seafaring. Two sites in particular, form the basis for an appreciation of cultural changes during the Iron Age. Ban Don Ta Phet provides evidence for trade between the Central Thailand, India and coastal Viet Nam. Exotic imports include carnelian, glass and decorated bronze bowls, although there is growing evidence for the early exploitation of local carnelian and the manufacture of glass ornaments within Southeast Asia. Bronzes reflect a new level of technical expertise, compatible with specialisation, while iron was used for weapons and agricultural implements. The cemetery itself, ringed by a ditch and bank, looks very like a special area reserved for particularly rich individuals.

Noen U-Loke is important because the sequence covers the entire millennium of the Iron Age. We can trace the initial use of iron from a source for ornaments, to the local forging of weapons and agricultural implements. Iron preceded the first availability of glass, agate and carnelian, sources for jewellery which replaced marble, slate and marine shell used during the Bronze Age. The successive mortuary phases at this site reveal significant changes, albeit within the same general tradition. Phase 3 graves were tightly clustered, and saw the innovative practice of interring the dead within a bed of burnt rice. Bronze was employed for a range of novel ornaments, including bells and spirals. Virtually all the carnelian jewellery, traced to Southeast Asian sources, was confined to this phase.

The fourth mortuary phase saw further significant changes in terms of mortuary ritual and wealth. Some individuals were interred with multiple bronze ornaments including ear discs and belts. There were also gold and silver ornaments, superb eggshell-thin ceramic vessels, iron knives, and glass and agate jewellery. In one unique instance, an egg had been placed beside the body. The clustered graves were also embellished with clay linings filled with burnt rice. It is difficult to avoid the impression that the community deployed considerable wealth, and that leading individuals were interred with intense ritual behaviour. However, this wealth declined with the final mortuary phase, although further new items were introduced, including iron sickles and at least one spear. This same phase saw a general increase in iron projectile points.

Noen U-Loke is one of many sites ringed by banks thought to have contained water in the form of moats. Their function is not yet known, although a growing population would have required a steady supply of water during the dry season. They may have had multiple uses, including defence and the provision of food, but their significance lies in the organisation of labour to provide a useful facility, together with the development of hydraulic engineering skills which were to become so prominent with the rise of civilization.

It is also important to note that Noen U-Loke is but one of a dense distribution of banked and moated sites in the Mun Valley, some of which grew to a considerable size. Non Muang Kao, for example, was four times larger than Noen U-Loke, and revealed the same elaborate mortuary rituals, as well as the remains of domestic structures. These sites are associated with clusters of small mounds which accumulated through the production of salt. Whenever such salt mounds are excavated, they reveal an Iron Age date.

It is thus possible to identify a series of cultural changes which, when considered in conjunction, direct us to possible reasons for increased political centralisation and social ranking. Iron, for example, is much more abundant in nature than copper or tin, and its ready availability for conversion into useful agricultural tools, such as spades, hoes, billhooks and sickles, provides evidence for more efficient rice cultivation albeit without the application of the plough. These tools would have encouraged and enabled the construction of banks round the growing settlements in order to control water, banks which have been dated in the upper Mun Valley to the late Iron Age

(McGrath and Boyd 2000). At Noen U-Loke, there is further evidence for the proliferation of iron projectile points, and of their use in conflict. Ban Wang Hi, Ongbah and Ban Don Ta Phet are further sites which indicate the importance attached to iron weaponry at this juncture. Bronze production took on a new impetus during the Iron Age, and the quality and quantity of the bronzes points directly to the presence of full time specialists. The bowls   of Ban Don Ta Phet and the belts and spirals of Noen U-Loke represent unprecedented levels of craft skill. The range of raw materials now used for exotic jewellery changed completely from that seen during the Bronze Age. Agate, carnelian, jade and glass replaced marble, slate and marine shell. Working carnelian and jade, or making glass beads, necessitate a new plane of expertise compatible with specialisation. The ceramic industry, particularly to be seen in the burnished black vessels of eggshell thin finish in the Mun Valley, looks very much like the product of specialised workshops.

These changes are consistent with the breakdown of the long-standing affinal alliance and exchange system between independent communities. Occupants of such sites as Ban Don Ta Phet and Noen U-Loke had easy access to iron ore and commanded nodal positions for exchange. The Sa Huynh sites likewise were able to control coastal traffic. Any movement up the Chao Phraya River would involve passage through the territory of such growing centres as Ban Tha Kae. Several interacting variables then, can be identified. Population growth and agricultural intensification are noted, and were doubtless contributory factors. But the social change was critical in that it involved much larger settlements as foci of population. There is some archaeological evidence that these centres controlled the production of salt, exchange of exotic artefacts and iron production. It is proposed that these seminal variables and their interaction reflect the flexibility and opportunism inherent in the system characterising the Bronze Age, wherein those controlling the best tracts of agricultural land and access to a new range of exotic prestige goods enjoyed considerable advantages. Intertwined in this model, is the participation in a growing maritime exchange network. The sequel is considered in the chapter below, during which late Iron Age societies will be linked in not only with what went before but also with the subsequent development of civilization.

An egg had been placed in a grave during the fourth mortuary phase at Noen U-Loke.

2 cm

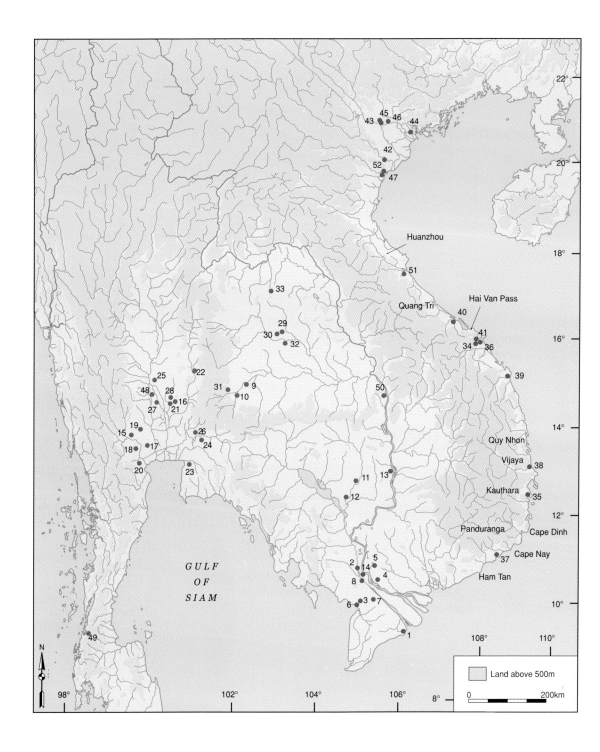

Huanzhou

Hai Van Pass

Quang Tri

Quy Nhon

Vijaya

Kauthara

Panduranga

Cape Dinh

Cape Nay

Ham Tan

GULF
OF
SIAM

N

Land above 500m

0   200km

22°

20°

18°

16°

14°

12°

10°

8°

98°   102°   104°   106°   108°   110°

Chapter Six

The Development of States

Archaeological research in Bac Bo, Northeast Thailand and the Chao Phraya valley has disclosed a pattern of settlement, a series of mortuary assemblages and a number of artefacts which suggest the former existence there of chiefdoms. Their origins have been ascribed to increased long-distance exchange, access to productive rice lands, control of strategic resources such as salt and iron ore, and the expansion of population in restricted river flood plains. By the 9th century AD, at least four states existed in Southeast Asia. Bac Bo had for centuries been a province of the Chinese Empire. The remaining three are known respectively as Dvaravati, Champa and Angkorian. Dvaravati controlled Central Thailand, Champa the coastal valleys of Central Viet Nam, and Angkor was centred on the northern shore of the Tonle Sap in Cambodia.

In terms of territorial scale, economic and social complexity, segmentation into specialised activities and centralisation of wealth and power, these states reflect the restructuring of society. Our task is to understand how the chiefdoms of the late Iron Age were transformed over a period of perhaps no more than a century, into early states. The growing body of literature on ethnographically-documented chiefdoms reveals that most chiefs and their immediate entourages played a central role in the redistribution of goods, and effected policy more by charisma than coercion. The mechanics of chiefly authority are not adapted to political control over dependents nor the extraction of regular tribute. The lack of a central exchequer of disposable wealth, therefore, precludes the maintenance of a bureaucracy to implement chiefly decisions. It is true that goods may be gifted to the chief, but this reflects the obligation of a lesser ranked kinsman rather than a legally-binding payment. While a chief might attract armed followers to his banner in times of stress, those same followers are quite liable to melt away when the crisis is over. Essentially, a chiefdom is structured along the bonds of kinship and mutual obligations. Traditional ties work against the establishment of a permanent ruling body with coercive authority.

Although many of the features of states hearken back to the Iron Age chiefdoms, there were deep-seated differences in scale. The sovereign of the state of Angkor, for example, could marshal sufficient wealth to construct such temple-mausolea as Angkor Wat,

Opposite:
1. Bai Xao, 2. Angkor Borei, 3. Oc Eo, 4. Go Thap, 5. Go Hang, 6. Nen Chua, 7. Go Xoai, 8. Nak Ta Dambang Dek, 9. Phimai, 10. Phanom Wan, 11. Ishanapura, 12. Ampil Rolum, 13. Thala Borivat, 14. Wat Po, 15. Ban Don Ta Phet, 16. Ban Tha Kae, 17. Nakhon Pathom, 18. Pong Tuk, 19. U-Thong, 20. Ku Bua, 21. Lopburi, 22. Sri Thep, 23. Muang Phra Rot, 24. Dong Si Mahosod, Sa Morakod, 25. U-Taphao, 26. Dong Lakon, 27. Ban Khu Muang, 28. Ban Di Lung, 29. Muang Fa Daet, 30. Kantarawichai, 31. Muang Sema, 32. Ban Chiang Hian, 33. Nong Han, 34. My Son, 35. Po Nagar, 36. Dong Duong, 37. Song Luy, 38. Thanh Ho, 39. Chau Xa, 40. Hue, 41. Tra Kieu, 42. Ninh Binh, 43. Co Loa, 44. Viet Khe, 45. Ke Noi, Phau Thau, 46. Quang Yen, 47. Lach Truong, 48. Muang Dongkorn 49. Khong Thom, 50. Wat Phu, 51. Qusu, 52. Bim-Son.

This bas relief from Angkor Wat shows a princess carried aloft on a splendidly-ornamented palanquin. It illustrates clearly the high status of royal women at Angkor.

which ranks among the largest religious edifices known. He ordered the diversion of rivers, the construction of canals and the excavation of the enormous *barays* or reservoirs, which were part of the urban landscape. The king could call upon an army of construction workers to raise and embellish the numerous temples and palaces, the roads and hospitals. The court centre was peopled by high officers of state with hereditary ceremonial and administrative responsibilities. State temples linked by river and road to the capital not only promulgated the royal cult, but also served as repositories for the surpluses of rice, oil, medicines and all the other products necessary to sustain the social system. Above all, in theory if not always in practice, the sovereign controlled the means of destruction, manifested in armies dominated by war elephants.

The mechanics whereby chiefdoms became states can be considered on the basis of the contemporary inscriptions, a series of Chinese documents, vague allusions to Southeast Asia in Indian epics and increasingly, in the archaeological record. A superficial glance at these sources, however, linked with western preconceptions, could easily lead the unwary student along a false trail. Before recent excavations revealed the full scale of Iron Age social ranking, the contrast between the states of Southeast Asia and the assumed poverty of prehistoric societies underwrote the idea that it was Indian influence which was crucial in the advent of states. The pendulum of opinion swung strongly towards this view in the writings of Cœdès. The same pendulum has now begun to swing back towards the view that prehistoric contexts within which complexity developed are of seminal importance.

Explaining state origins is one of the key issues in the study of our species, and there have been numerous approaches to identifying key variables. Wittfogel (1957) for example, stressed the importance of large-scale irrigation works and the control of the water supply in the establishment of a centralised despotism. Many authors have sought the establishment of long-distance trade and warfare within circumscribed areas as mechanisms for the means whereby wealth could be accumulated by a centralising bureaucracy (Webb 1975). Friedman and Rowlands (1977) have suggested that the elevation of a given lineage to a permanent position of power, while reliant ultimately on the productive capacity of the environment, can be effected by a concentration of first prestige and then wealth in the hands of the senior line. This group would have been closely related to the ancestral spirits and most able to underwrite the costs of competitive feasting.

There is then, no generally-accepted model which can be employed to explain the origins of the state in a particular place. Even if there were, it is doubtful if there are sufficient data for a conclusive review of the origins of the state in the lowlands of Southeast Asia. Nevertheless, some tentative feelers can be put out if only to illuminate the problems and issues to hand. Thus, many generations of workers have stressed the differences which exist between primary and secondary state formation. In the former case, the transformation occurred in isolation. In the latter, contact with another state played a part in the generation of statehood. Within this framework, all Southeast Asian states are secondary. A further issue concerns one's approach. Do we seek 'prime movers', the particular factor which explains the dislocations involved in state formation, or is it preferable to isolate as many variables as might be relevant and seek their interactions? The latter course, which was followed by Renfrew (1972) under the term 'the multiplier effect', will be adopted because it seems most likely that the development of Southeast Asian states reflects several interacting factors. Individual prowess of potential leaders is one, but we cannot divorce our deliberations from the more mundane variables, such as strategic location, soils, capacity for intensified production, and the availability of iron, all of which respond more readily to archaeological enquiry. Consequently, it is proposed later in this survey, to consider the interactions between different variables in order to establish a model incorporating several aspects of behaviour.

Viewed from the private garden of the King of Angkor, Phimeanakas rises from within the walled royal palace. The contemporary inscriptions describe this, the chapel royal, as being covered in gold.

India and China

Between approximately 300 BC and AD 300, the coastal Southeast Asian chiefdoms increasingly participated in the Southern Silk Route, a series of maritime exchange routes linking the empires of Rome and China. It is impossible to consider fully the resulting cultural changes without first exploring the objectives of the Indian and Chinese and their ideas and motives. In India, this period witnessed the rise of empires and their subsequent fragmentation into competing kingdoms. The principal participants were descended from the Indo-Aryans whose origins are obscure: some hold that they were the people of the Indus civilizations, others that they invaded India during the mid-second millennium BC, bringing with them the Sanskrit language and a body of oral traditions known collectively as the Vedic Hymns. During the ensuing millennium, small polities centred on royal dynasties developed, within which ritual and ceremony lay in the hands of the senior of four social groups or castes. These priests were known as brahmans after the word *brahma* meaning divine knowledge. The remaining three castes were known as *ksatrayas* (nobles), *vaisyas* (peasants) and *sudras* (serfs). Brahmans held the prerogative over the rites of royal consecration, but they also fulfilled advisory functions and acted as

Above and top: The Funan state witnessed the first monumental stuctures, built in brick. These buildings was uncovered at Go Thap on the Mekong Delta. (Courtesy Dr. Le Lien Thai)

ministers. Their privileged status was marked by exemption from taxes and by gifts or donations from those seeking merit. Sanskrit evolved into local languages, but was retained by the brahmans as the language of ritual and the sacred texts. There are several major and many lesser Hindu gods. During the first millennium AD, Shiva and Vishnu were the principal deities and according to the *Vogasutra*, which was the dominant form of religious expression at the time, adherents may achieve harmony with the god through supreme control of their physical and mental conditions. In a sense, such asceticism endowed the worshipper with actual control over divine forces.

Hindu worship centres on the notion that, through the provision of gifts to the god, the donor gains merit to ensure a harmonious reincarnation. The temple thus plays a key role in Hindu rituals. The image of the deity incorporates a divine essence which is nurtured by daily awakening, feeding, clothing and worship. Pilgrimages to major temples and worship through donations are major avenues to merit making, and at death, offerings are made such that the body can proceed from the realm of ghosts to join the ancestors.

Hinduism was not alone in attracting devotees. Buddhism arose from the teachings of Gautama, the Buddha or enlightened one, who lived from approximately 563-483 BC. He taught in the vernacular Pali language in order to reach the masses to whom Sanskrit was the esoteric language of the brahman elite. Neither religion was mutually exclusive and their co-existence was accepted. It would be wrong to view the brahmans as concerned only with the court and religious ritual. As ministers, they played a central role and the political theories they espoused and practiced were part of the intellectual heritage taken by Indian merchants and, indeed, the brahmans themselves, to Southeast Asia. One of the most comprehensive tracts in political theory was set down by Kautilya, chief minister to Chandragupta Maurya who established the Mauryan Empire in about 325 BC. This so called *Arthasastra* defined the state under seven heads: the king, his ministers, a territory, a fort, the treasury, an army and allies. The royal office entailed divine sanctions and the king, he argued, was possessed of a divine nature. His duties were largely paternal: to control crime through the legal system, to protect the people and to foster agriculture, industry and trade. Kautilya neatly summarised the very essence of statehood which is often reiterated to this day by anthropologists, namely the central authority, sustained by taxation and backed by coercion.

The encouragement of agriculture and trade was not an empty precept, since the collection of state revenues turned on their success. Kautilya himself advocated central participation in opening up new land to settlement, while both local and international trade were encouraged. The Mauryan Empire however, was in decline by 150 BC and fragmented into regional kingdoms, a situation which prevailed until a further period of hegemony under the Guptas (about AD 320-540). The fall of the Mauryan Empire did not inhibit trade, and it is important that the mechanics of this exchange be appreciated. Indian merchants employed the prevailing winds to travel in both easterly and westerly directions. The latter was concerned with the Iranian and Graeco-Roman worlds, and was stimulated by increasing demands for oriental goods originating with the establishment of peace within the Roman Empire. The conduct of trade was facilitated by a currency based on silver and copper coinage, the use of the Brahmi script by specialised merchant guilds in both eastern and western ports, and by the encouragement from merchant bankers who underwrote trading voyages and received interest on their investments. Roman involvement in Indian trade is marked by several writings, not least *The Periplus of the Erythraean Sea*. This compendium of useful information includes a map and a list of goods which made up the bulk of the traffic. We find that the Romans were interested in silks, pepper, pearls, ivory and textiles, while for their part, the Indians took glass, copper, tin, lead, orpiment, wine, antimony and gold coins. The physical embodiment of this exchange system has been revealed by Wheeler's excavations at Arikamedu (Wheeler 1954). This Indian site, which was probably the port of Poduca cited in *The Periplus*, yielded Roman coins, pottery, beads, intaglios, lamps and glass.

The earliest evidence for writing in Southeast Asia comes in the form of small seals from sites such as Oc Eo. These examples are in gold.

If the Indian merchant guilds prospered on the western trade route, why not also in an easterly direction? The seasonal wind pattern across the Bay of Bengal reflects the regular rise and ebb of the monsoon and maritime technology was well equipped to cope with the necessary distances. Moreover, their boats were large enough to handle at least 200 tons of cargo. The fact is that Indian merchant venturers did sail eastward in growing numbers, and their exploits were incorporated into Hindu epic literature. The *Ramayana*, for example, is a classical mythological saga about the exploits of the hero-king, Rama. The fabled land beyond the sunrise is referred to in the Indian literature as *Suvannabhumi*, or *Suvarnadvipa*, the 'land of gold'. Gold there was to be found, but the voyages were perilous.

While Indian and Southeast Asian vessels were crossing the Andaman Sea well before the end of the first millennium BC, it is probable that interest in the area intensified after the emperor Vespasian, who succeeded in AD 61, prohibited the export of gold coinage from the Roman Empire. This edict indicates the drain on the empire's resources to make up for an imbalance of trade, and, indeed, it is significant that the majority of Roman coins found in Indian contexts belong to the preceding Julio-Claudian dynasty. The first Indian merchants who traded with Southeast Asia came from a country with a sophisticated and mature tradition of statehood. They were familiar with the notion of a supreme monarch and inherited the established role of the brahman in both ritual and state administration. They visited Southeast Asia to sell, and to fill their holds with trade goods. The seasonal pattern of the prevailing wind, in which nor'easters dominated between November and May, and south west winds from May to November, meant that landfall in Southeast Asia lasted for some months. Among their passengers were Hindu brahmans and Buddhist monks.

Votive deposits from the Funan site of Da Noi include Buddhist and Visnuite symbols, and the conch shell, indicating prosperity. The goldsmiths also fashioned outstanding ornaments.

China also brought to Southeast Asia a mature tradition of statehood, but under quite different circumstances. As in India,

Vishnu was a popular Hindu god among the people of Funan in the Mekong Delts. This statue comes from Go Thap. (Courtesy Dr. Le Lien Thi)

Right: The outline of a rectangular, moated city on the Mekong Delta was first recognized from aerial photographs. This plan is based on the vestiges of the cities, canals and buildings seen from the air. The city was occupied during the first half of the first millennium AD.

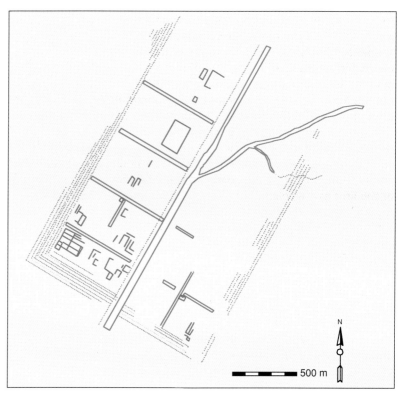

China saw a series of centralised dynastic polities, with intervening periods of regional fragmentation and conflict. Between the end of the Western Zhou and the unification under the Qin in 221 BC, China witnessed the period of the Warring States. It was during this time of strife that iron became the predominant metal, with applications in both agriculture and warfare. The brief period of Qin rule, which saw the initial work on the Great Wall, was followed by over four centuries of relative internal peace under the Western and Eastern Han. The central authority set in train wars of territorial conquest in both the northwestern and southern border areas, which involved the incorporation within the empire of formerly independent or quasi-independent territories. This process impinged into Southeast Asia when the Red River delta was seized, and incorporated as provinces or 'commanderies'. The end of the Han dynasty saw the formation of the southeast Chinese state of Wu in AD 222. This state was cut off from the northern Silk Route to the west by intervening states, a situation which fostered interest in a southern, maritime trade route on the part of the Wu and their successors, and the first actual descriptions of mainland Southeast Asia to have survived originate in a mission despatched by the Wu emperor. According to Wolters (1982), this visit was designed to gather intelligence on the proposed southern maritime route to India and ultimately, Rome. Such visits, and reports by embassies to the Chinese court from Southeast Asian states, were incorporated into official histories of the succeeding Chinese dynasties. Whereas the Indian accounts of *Suvannabhumi* are couched in vague allusions and romantic fables, the Chinese dynastic annals and geographic tracts belong to a tradition of scrupulous historic scholarship, and provide an invaluable corpus of source material. It must be noted however, that many texts passed through more than one hand before being set down in their present form, and the chances of errors are high.

Thus, at about the same juncture, the maritime chiefdoms of Southeast Asia came into contact with two expanding states. We must now consider the impact of this contact on the cultures of the area as a whole.

Funan: a Delta Trading State

The lower reaches of the Mekong are flat, low-lying and prone to flooding. Without human modification, the land behind the fringing mangrove belt would probably have been dominated by an open marshland flora. Geographically however, the area has at least two strategic advantages. In terms of east-west exchange, it is a nodal point for transporting goods between the routes over the Malayo-Siamese isthmus and the coastal ports of Viet Nam and Southern China. The marshlands of the delta lack many of the raw materials which were in demand locally and for exchange, not least metal ores and forest products. The area was, however, able to control the flow of goods which were available via the Mekong valley, from a rich hinterland which extended across the plains of Central Cambodia and up to and beyond the Dang Raek range onto the Khorat plateau. This hinterland was both rich in mineral wealth and according to recent archaeological research, had been studded with agricultural villages which had used the Mekong valley as an exchange route for millennia. It is important to appreciate that the impact of flooding from the Mekong is greatly alleviated by the peculiar drainage pattern into the Tonle Sap and, to a lesser extent, the Mun River. Such is the weight of water carried by the Mekong, that a proportion flows back into the Tonle Sap. The Mun River also backs up when the Mekong is in spate. Consequently the flat deltaic land to the south is, once drained, able to support the cultivation of rice.

The archaeological record for the Delta and its margins reveals the presence of Iron Age communities already in a position to take advantage of maritime exchange. At Angkor Borei, Stark *et al.* (1999) have encountered an Iron Age cemetery deeply stratified below the later walled and moated city. The dead were interred with a range of grave goods, including complete pottery vessels. At Go Hang, a series of glass, agate and carnelian beads have been recovered, forms which resemble those from Noen U-Loke, in association with a radiocarbon

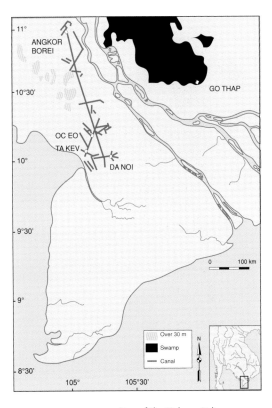

Map of the Mekong Delta, showing the distribution of canals and major sites of the Funan civilization.

This gold coin of the Roman Emperor Antoninus Pius was found at Oc Eo, and illustrates the widespread trading network that linked Funan east and west. Actual size.

A general view of the Oc Eo plain, with Mount Ba The in the background. The mound of Go Cây Thi lies in the centre of the picture, under excavation in 1999. (Courtesy Dr. Pierre-Yves Manguin)

date of 54 BC-AD 130. Further evidence for late prehistoric settlement of the delta region has been identified at Bai Xau, a site which must have been virtually on the coast when occupied two millennia ago. The following four centuries witnessed a transformation in the archaeological record which is only now under close scrutiny through excavations at Oc Eo and Angkor Borei. Essentially, the period between AD 100-550 witnessed the foundation of cities linked by a network of canals. Oc Eo is the best known city because it has been examined and extensively published by Malleret (1959-63).

This extraordinary site comprises a rectangular enceinte measuring 3 by 1.5 km. It lies behind five ramparts and four moats, and covers an area of 450 ha. Viewed from the air, Oc Eo is seen to be bisected by a large canal, from which tributary channels subdivide the site into segments. Further enquiries undertaken before the second world war by French archaeologists have revealed that the canals of Oc Eo are part of an extensive series which linked further settlements in this flat terrain into a network (Paris 1929, 1931, 1941a). Some canals reach seaward of Oc Eo, intimating that the site was set back from the shoreline but was still linked with the sea.

Malleret's excavations in 1944 revealed the presence of foundations in stone and brick for impressively large structures. Malleret has suggested that the building, which was constructed of large granite slabs set on brick foundations and supporting a brick superstructure, was a temple. The excavator, who was subjected to extraordinary difficulties in the field as a result of the activities of looters, was able to assemble a very large sample of the site's material culture, as well as evidence for the local manufacture of pottery and jewellery (Cœdès 1947). We have already seen that two millennia ago, the Indian sub-continent participated in a trading network which incorporated the Roman Empire to the west and the Han to the east. Many of the small artefacts found at Oc Eo confirm the presence of a delta-trading state. Thus, Malleret recovered two Roman medallions, one minted during the reign of Antoninus Pius (AD 138-161) and the other in that of his successor, Marcus Aurelius (AD 161-180). There is also a corpus of jewellery of Mediterranean origin or inspiration. This linkage of the Roman and Chinese empires is demonstrated by the discovery of a Chinese mirror which belongs to the same period as the Roman coins. Along this same route, there came Iranian coinage, Indian-inspired jewellery and the Indian script. As de Casparis (1979) has shown, the earliest Indian script at Oc Eo belongs to the late first and early second centuries AD, and is found on small portable objects such as rings and seals. Later Indian writing there takes us down to the fifth century, indicating a period of occupation and trade lasting several centuries.

The local manufacturing industries attested at Oc Eo are a blend of introduced articles and local production techniques. The manufacture of glass beads for example, was introduced from India but employed clay crucibles with a long local ancestry. The clay anvils used to shape pots were virtually identical with those used locally for millennia. The bivalve stone moulds for casting tin pendants match those found in the Mekong valley, but used in bronze casting, for the previous 1500 years. The range of raw materials which were converted into jewellery covers practically the whole gamut of the available metals, precious and semi-precious stones. As if to confirm the name of *Suvannabhumi*, Oc Eo yielded so much gold that looters attracted from far and wide panned the whole site. The list of raw materials used, principally for the manufacture of jewellery, includes diamond, amethyst, jet, amber, malachite, orpiment, sapphires, rubies, serpentine, feldspar, antigonite, topaz, beryl, zircon, jadeite, garnet, opal, jasper, onyx, agate, carnelian and quartz.

Buddhism reached Funan by at least the 4th to the 6th centuries AD, as seen in these stunning wooden images from Go Thap on the Mekong Delta.
(Courtesy Dr. Le Lien Thi)

Although alluvial gold can be found in the environs of Oc Eo, most of the precious stones as well as supplies of tin, copper and iron would have been imported from some distance. The quantity and range of goods which exchanged hands at Oc Eo exceeds by far that evidenced at any other site in Southeast Asia. It was not only a port, but also a major manufacturing centre which could dispose of sufficient labour to dig out the moats and erect the girdling walls, as well as manufacture the bricks for imposing religious monuments. Oc Eo was but one node in an extensive settlement network. The canals which radiate from Oc Eo include a link to Ta Kev, which was probably the actual port. The system links Ta Kev and Oc Eo with Da Noi, whence an arterial canal covers nearly 90 km to Angkor Borei, probably the pre-eminent centre. Indeed, one Chinese report noted that the capital was situated 500 *li* (200 km) from the sea, making it an inland settlement. The canals have not been dated, but the nodal position of Oc Eo leaves little doubt that they belong within the period when the site was occupied (2nd-7th centuries). Their function has not been subjected to intensive scrutiny, but it is surely likely that they fulfilled more than one purpose. One was probably to facilitate drainage of the marshy delta terrain, and thereby improve agricultural prospects. Water volume in the Mekong is markedly seasonal, for between May and November, the monsoon brings heavy rains just as the headwaters are

Below left: A scene from the 1998 excavation of the 5th-10th century site 1 at Linh Son, on the lower slopes of Mount Ba near Oc Eo. Remains of a 5-7th century brick structures can be seen in the foreground. In the centre and background lie the 8th-10th century stone buildings probably belonging to an Angkorian period reoccupation.

Below: The 1999 excavation of the 5th-6th century temple site at Go Cay Thi, on the Oc Eo plain.
(Courtesy Dr. Pierre-Yves Manguin)

An example of the Oc Eo style orange ware from Angkor Borei. (Width 24 cm).

Fine orange ware vessels, of unprovenanced origin, from the Angkor Borei Museum. (Height, 7 cm). (Courtesy Dr. Miriam Stark)

A fine buff ware kendi vessel from Angkor Borei. (Width 26 cm).

filled with the melting Himalayan snows. The canals may have been built to expedite drainage just as their modern counterparts do. One canal which proceeds in a southeasterly direction from Angkor Borei terminates in a tributary of the Mekong. The way in which the canals link settlements also makes it likely that they were used to convey goods between the centres of population. Modern analogy also discloses that the construction of canals in deltaic terrain encourages the foundation of new settlements in what was formerly a marshy wasteland (Hanks 1972).

Pierre-Yves Manguin and Vo Si Khai have recently returned to Oc Eo after an interval of half a century in order to investigate the nature of the brick structures, obtain an accurate chronological framework and, if possible, date the walls and moats. Their fieldwork at Linh Son has already clarified aspects of the sequence. Linh Son is located on the slope of Ba The Hill, overlooking Oc Eo and the delta. The earliest layer, dated to about 100 BC-AD 100 incorporated a large, lidded vessel which contained possibly scraps of bone, some gold and a carnelian bead (Manguin and Vo Si Khai 2000). This early phase was followed by the construction of a substantial brick building in turn covered by a layer representing abandonment of the site. Radiocarbon dates place this structure within the period AD 200-850, while the associated pottery indicates that it belongs to the period of Funan. The modern temple of Linh Son lies adjacent to the excavations. It was built on a mound which in all probability, covers a large brick temple of the Funan Period. That the temple was in use after the decline of the Funan state in the mid 6th century, however, is seen in the Ba The inscription, which dates on stylistic grounds to the late 6th-early 8th centuries, records the building of a brick temple for a King Nrpadityadeva.

Oc Eo was linked by a canal with Angkor Borei, a second city whose brick walls enclosed 300 ha. Miriam Stark has set in train a major research programme designed first to realise a city plan incorporating all the surface monuments and water tanks, then to investigate its history through excavation (Stark *et al.* 1999). The squares already opened reveal a five-metre accumulation of cultural deposits which commenced by the third or fourth centuries BC. The historic occupation, which is characterised by thin orange ceramic vessels, belonged at least within the 1st to the 6th centuries AD, while, to judge from the style of a statue of Vishnu, brick temples were in place by the 7th century. Dating the walls and the *barays*, one of which covers an area of 20,000 square metres, will add much to our understanding of the history of this delta state.

The delta is prone to extensive deep flooding, and understanding how the occupants of the cities and smaller settlements adapted their rice agriculture to this problem is a key issue. Fox and Ledgerwood (1999) have recently made an important contribution in identifying the likely practice of flood-recession farming. This technique is followed where deep flooding rules out wet-season cultivation. The flood water is trapped behind bunds, or in reservoirs, and released into the rice fields as the annual flood retreats at the start of the dry season. It traditionally involved the use of human power in moving such irrigation

Excavations at Angkor Borei in 1996 uncovered the foundations of brick temples.

Part of the Phnom Da temple, south of Angkor Borei. Phnom Da was a sacred hill.
Left: The excavation of Angkor Borei uncovered a deep sequence which began in the late prehistoric Iron Age. (Courtesy Dr. Miriam Stark)

water into the channels and, ultimately, the rice fields. Yields are high, because the fields are covered annually with a fresh layer of silt laid down by the floods. Ploughing is not necessary due to the soft nature of the newly-laid silt. The low-lying basin surrounding Angkor Borei would have been well adapted to flood-recession farming, as would much of the delta terrain to the south, and indeed in the low-lying riverine and lacustrine flood plains to the north. Today, farmers sow rice in their seedbeds in December, and plant out the rice into the previously-flooded fields in January. Since this rice is growing during the dry season, it is necessary to irrigate the fields from either natural or man-made reservoirs. Although now accomplished with pumps, it was achieved with a variety of techniques involving human labour, such as the water shovel, within living memory. The harvest usually begins in March. Fox and Ledgerwood (1999) have not only identified an agricultural system well capable of sustaining large concentrations of population, but have also stressed how Delvert (1961) mapped its potential in the inland areas which were to form the heartland of later states.

Vietnamese archaeologists have also been active on the Delta. At Nen Chua, excavations have uncovered a brick and stone foundation for a temple which contained a *linga*, that is a phallic object of veneration, and gold ornaments (Le Xuan Diem *et al.* 1995). This monument incorporated small brick-lined cells which contained cremated human remains associated with gold leaves. These were decorated with human forms, one of which probably represents Shiva and Vishnu. Radiocarbon dates indicate use between AD 450-650. At Go Thap, a large burial

A stone *linga*, found at a village near Angkor Borei in Cambodia. (Courtesy Dr. Miriam Stark)

mound covers a late prehistoric settlement. Brick-lined pits revealed cremated human remains accompanied by glass and semi-precious stone beads, and gold foil. The gold leaves were decorated with images of Hindu deities, including Vishnu represented as a turtle. The radiocarbon dates place this cemetery within the period AD 400-600. Further gold leaves have been recovered from the brick temple foundation at Go Xoai, in association with a fifth century Sanskrit text.

Archaeologically, these finds represent the transition to statehood. Fortunately, we can derive further insight into this vital period from Chinese Dynastic histories and the early indigenous inscriptions. A most important reference to the occupation of this area was contained in the reports of the emissaries Kang Dai and Zhu Ying, who visited the country in about AD 250. It was they who were sent by the Wu emperor to gather information about a southern trade route to India. Their account is long since lost, but later writers quoted it at length. We are told that the traditional history of the area, named Funan, refers to the founding father of the dynasty as Kaundinya, an Indian, who married a local princess. He governed the country, and was succeeded by his male descendants. According to Pelliot (1903), this union must have taken place towards the end of the first century AD. *The History of the Liang Dynasty*, which was compiled in the seventh century, noted that the founder of the line of rulers gave his son authority over seven dependant settlements. This statement suggests a developing centralised authority structure. It was also put into practice by Hun P'an-huang, one of the successive rulers of this early dynasty. Having attacked and conquered chiefs on the periphery of his domain, he installed his sons and grandsons in their place.

His son, P'an P'an, had only a brief reign and was succeeded by a leader of military prowess known to the Chinese as Fan Shih-man. Once enthroned, this leader undertook wars of conquest against his neighbours, and then mounted a maritime expedition which subdued over ten coastal kingdoms. During the 25 years or so prior to the visit of Kang Dai, there was a series of dynastic assassinations by claimants to the throne, one of which was perpetrated on a son of Fan Shih-man by another successful soldier, Fan Hsun. This same period saw the first embassy from Funan to China, a visit which may have precipitated the decision to send a mission south. Whatever the case, the Chinese went beyond allusions to dynastic friction and wars of conquest, and described the people as living in walled settlements which contained a palace. They stressed the importance of agriculture, and noted the local taste for engraving stones with chisels. There was a system of taxation, paid for in gold, silver, perfumes and pearls. The local people also used a script of Indian origin. Indeed, the Chinese encountered a representative of the Indian Murunda king.

This inscription from Go Xoai on the Mekong Delta probably dates to the 7th or 8th centuries AD. It sets out a sacred Buddhist text. (Length 21 cm).

According to *The History of the Liang Dynasty*, the next major stage in the Chinese perception of local history came when a second Indian, who also took the name of Kaundinya, was accepted as ruler. This event allegedly took place in the early years of the fifth century AD. This brahman, it is said, "changed the rules according to the customs of India". We find for example, the adoption of the Sanskrit honorific title 'Varman'. The literal meaning of this word is armour, and it may be translated as 'protected by', or 'protégé of'. The preceding part of the name may refer to a particular Hindu god, or to a notable attribute. Thus the name Mahendravarman means 'protected by or the protégé of the great Indra' and Jayavarman, 'protégé of victory'.

We should not take the Chinese accounts literally. They viewed the maritime state within their own perceptions of what a state should be. In addition, the surviving accounts are later copies and we do not know the degree to which they were modified or embellished. Inscriptions are more immediate documentary sources, although they too must be treated judiciously.

Gold plaques bearing religious motifs were found in the foundations of the brick temples at Go Thap.
(Courtesy Dr. Le Lien Thi)

The wall and moat at the southeast corner of Angkor Borei. Dating the period of construction is a most important objective in unravelling the history of this site. (Courtesy Dr. Miriam Stark)

The research team at Angkor Borei, led by Miriam Stark, sampled lake sediments for pollen to reconstruct the ancient environment. Here, Paul Bishop (left) takes a core from the Eastern Baray at Angkor Borei, with assistance from Um Moninita and a workman. (Courtesy Dr. Miriam Stark)

Members of the excavation team screening materials from the 1999 excavations at Wat Komnou, Angkor Borei. (Courtesy Dr. Miriam Stark)

The distribution of prehistoric settlements and the principal sites of Funan and Chenla, showing the location by king of the inscriptions.
1. Samrong Sen, 2. Ban Na Di, 3. Non Pa Wai, 4. Nil Kham Haeng, 5. Nong Nor, 6. Ban Lum Khao, 7. Non Nok Tha, 8. Non Muang Kao, 9. Noen U-Loke, 10. Ban Don Phlong, 11. Non Yang, 12. Ban Takhong, 13. Ban Krabuang Nok, 14. Non Dua, 15. Lovea, 16. Nen Chua, 17. Go Thap, 18. Oc Eo, 19. Da Noi 20. Angkor Borei, Phnom Da, 21. Go Hang, 22. Nak Ta Dambang Dek, 23. Wat Luang Kao, 24. Ishanapura, 25. Wat Kdei Ang, Wat Chakret, 26. Aranyaprathet, 27. Roban Robas 28. Kuk Prah Kot, 29. Wat Po, 30. Tuol Kok Prah, 31. Wat Po Va, 32. Wat Prei Val, 33. Tuol Prah That, 34. Prah Kuha Luon, 35. Tan Kran, 36. Wat Baray, 37. Tuol Nak Ta Bak Ka, 38. Wat Tasar Moroy, 39. Ayutthaya, 40. Wat En Khna, 41. Lovek, 42. Wat Khnat, 43. Ampil Rolum.

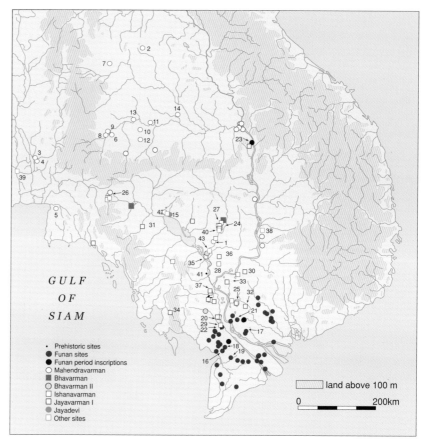

The practice of raising inscribed stelae began during the latter half of the history of this maritime state. The few inscriptions which have survived from the state of Funan provide invaluable information. The principal text was set out in Sanskrit, the language of Hinduism. A damaged example from Go Thap, for example, records a king whose name began with Ja-, which was almost certainly the ruler known as Jayavarman. It commemorates the consecration of a footprint of Vishnu by Gunavarman. As is often the case with the inscriptions, the incidental information is most interesting. In this case, we are informed that the prince was sent to reclaim land from the marsh. This was probably achieved by the excavation of drainage canals, which to this day have survived as a dominant feature of the archaeological landscape. The inscription ends with a warning that "whoever subverts these gifts to their own use, will suffer with those guilty of the five great crimes". In the Hindu canon, these included the murder of a brahman, intoxication, adultery with the master's wife, and complicity in the above. A second Sanskrit inscription, from Nak Ta Dambang Dek describes Rudravarman as a son of Jayavarman, who appointed the son of a brahman as inspector of the royal property. Neither inscription carries a date, but on stylistic grounds, Cœdès (1931) has assigned them to the early sixth century. A third inscription alludes to a military victory by Jayavarman, and then proceeds to record a religious foundation by his queen, Kulaprabhavati

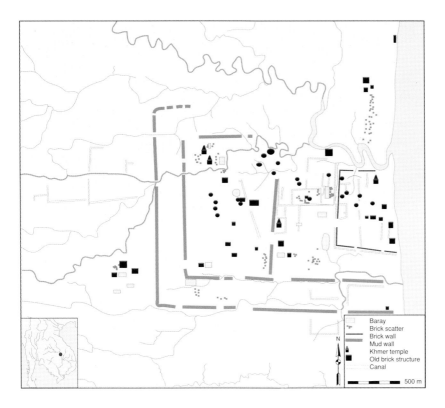

The site of Wat Phu on the bank of the Mekong River in Laos, was of transcendent importance to the people of Angkor. It lies in the shadow of the Lingaparvata, a mountain with a summit in the form of a *linga* or phallus. The first of a series of cities there was founded by King Devanika, who 'came from afar' to found a kingdom in the late 5th century AD.

	Baray
	Brick scatter
	Brick wall
	Mud wall
	Khmer temple
	Old brick structure
	Canal

500 m

Summary

The transition to the state in the Mekong Delta took place swiftly during the early centuries AD. Archaeologically, this is manifested in walled cities, brick temples, extensive canals, a writing system and monumental statuary. The traditional Iron Age mortuary ritual of extended inhumation was replaced by cremation, and the adoption of exotic cults is seen in images of Indian deities, together with the taking of Sanskrit royal names. These developments took place in the Mekong Delta, an area strategically placed for participation in the southern, maritime silk route. Control of this jugular node also involved the interior, the most likely origin for the wood, plumage and beasts which were sent as tribute to the Chinese court. The elements of a social overlay to the archaeological record are found in the written record: we read of kings, a legal system, taxation, warfare and subjugation of rivals. Yet important issues remain unresolved. Was there, for example, a unitary state which straddled the delta, or were there a series of competing polities? What is the date for the inception of monumental architecture, and what factors might explain the decline of the delta as a centre of political power in the 6th and 7th centuries? The last question is perhaps the most readily answered. A state which rose on the foundation of international trade also withered as the Chinese increasingly by-passed the mouths of the Mekong in favour of transit through the islands of Southeast Asia. But as the Delta state declined, so interior, agrarian states began to develop, and to these we will now turn.

State Formation in the Mekong Valley: Chenla

This view over the city of Wat Phu, beside the Mekong River, was taken from the summit of Mount Lingaparvata, the holy mountain of the people of Angkor.
(Courtesy Dr. Patrizia Zolese)

This region incorporates the Mekong valley between Phnom Penh and the Dang Raek mountains, with lateral branches to include the drainage basin of the Tonle Sap and the Mun River valley. The formation of a maritime state athwart the Mekong Delta was bound to have an impact on interior communities, if only for the demands placed on production to satisfy new trading relationships and the supply of exotic goods. We can obtain a first glimpse of the impact of these events at Noen U-Loke, the later stages of which were contemporary with the establishment of Oc Eo as a coastal emporium. It was during this period that burials became markedly richer. The dead were now interred with gold, silver, glass, agate and carnelian ornaments in clay-lined coffins filled with burnt rice. We find evidence for friction in the form of iron weaponry, for marked agricultural intensification, the large-scale production of salt, and provision of banks to retain and control water. There was also a sharp increase in the demand for bronzes, which were now cast at such a level of technical sophistication that specialised workshops are highly likely. Between AD 300-400 in these interior valleys, such settlements remained in the late Iron Age. The ensuing two centuries witnessed a social transformation with the foundation of states.

The rapidity of this change is seen by comparing the late Iron Age settlement of Noen U-Loke with the construction of a city at Wat Phu, on the bank of the Mekong River. Here, a huge natural *linga* crowns a local mountain, turning it into a place of great sanctity during the later Ankorian period. An inscription from this area, dated to the second half of the 5th century, names a King Devanika, meaning celestial protection or divine inspiration. He came to rule there from afar as supreme king of kings, having obtained victory over innumerable enemies. His celebratory rituals involved, he said, the donation of thousands of cattle. Although mute, the archaeological record bears witness to this change at Phimai in the Mun Valley. Here, excavations have revealed late Iron Age occupation under a layer containing the remains of a brick temple structure which in turn, underlay the foundations for a major Angkorian stone temple (Talbot 2000). At Phnom Wan, higher up the Mun Valley, a further stone temple covered an Iron Age cemetery in which the burials shared the same orientation. Single-chambered brick temples are thickly distributed in the lowlands under review. The oldest is found at Phum Phon in Surin Province, a temple built in the 7th century Prei Kmeng style, one sanctuary of which is still relatively intact.

The layout of temples and precincts in the centre of Ishanapura.

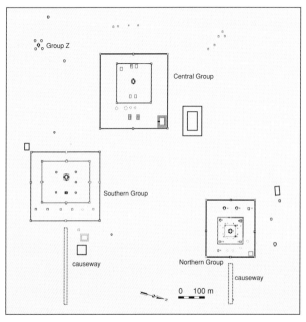

Group Z

Central Group

Southern Group

Northern Group

causeway

causeway

0   100 m

Little remains of the lintel and exterior decoration of the main shrine at Phum Phon.

Above left: Excavations adjacent to the main shrine at Phimai uncovered brick foundations of a Chenla-period temple.

Left: Phum Phon is one of the oldest surviving brick shrines of the Chenla Period in Thailand.

Fieldwork initiated over a century ago by Aymonier (1900-1903) and continued by Parmentier (1927) has laid the foundations for an appreciation of the nature of the major settlements of this period, but the concentration on brick sanctuaries at the expense of the total configurations of the settlements means that to this day, we have no city plans available. All we know is that like Oc Eo, the surrounding moats were square or rectangular. The largest and most important site has been identified, on the basis of epigraphic evidence, at Ishanapura, now known as Sambor Prei Kuk. This great site is located in the valley of the Stung Sen, which flows on a parallel course with the Mekong and empties into the Tonle Sap River. The design of the buildings there follows a broad tradition: they are usually raised on a platform, and comprise a single-chambered shrine room surrounded

A brick temple from the Northern Group, Ishanapura.

The brick-lined *baray* in the Central Group, Ishanapura.

Stone lintels at Ishanapura contain distinctive floral decoration. This lintel is from structure 1 in the Central Group.

Right: The decoration on the brick temples at Ishanapura incorporated images of palaces and members of the court. This example comes from temple 16 in the Northern Group. (Courtesy Dr. Yasushi Kojo)

by thick walls which rise to a considerable height. The central sanctuary of the southern group at Ishanapura for example, measured 17 by 13 metres at the base, and rose to a height of at least 16 metres.

The object of the sanctuary was to house the statue of the deity, or the sacred *linga*, for which purpose a pedestal was set up in the sanctuary chamber. Since the rituals involved the use of lustral water, a small drain and exterior gargoyle were often provided. There was usually just one door into the shrine room, but the remaining three walls were provided with false doors. These temples were decorated: the lintel over the doorway, which was made of carved stone in contrast to the brick structure itself, was embellished with carvings. The sanctuary walls likewise bore ornamental carvings and mouldings, but only in a limited area. Many surfaces were left plain. The architects were not familiar with the structure of the true arch and they used the corbelled roof to vault ceilings. This imposed a restriction on enclosed space which persisted throughout the Angkor period, and which involved the continued use of wood for secular buildings. Perhaps because of the necessarily small area within the central sanctuary, this structure was surrounded by one or two walled precincts which housed subsidiary sanctuaries. Both the walls and

This temple, found to the south of the South Group at Ishanapura, incorporates excellent images of the Chenla-period palaces.

gateways into the sacred enclosure were vehicles for decoration, which includes images of elite palace buildings, complete with their occupants.

These are general features. Let us now look in more detail at the religious monuments of Ishanapura. The layout of the central area reveals the presence of three walled precincts, each dominated by a large sanctuary. These were designated the central, southern and northern groups by Parmentier (1927), whose initial plans have recently been augmented by a Japanese research programme (Kojo, pers. comm.). The southern group comprises one principal and five lesser sanctuaries, set within an inner wall which was in turn enclosed by an outer enceinte, measuring 300 by 270 metres. A further row of six sanctuaries lie within this second enclosure which in turn gives access through a *gopura*, or gateway, to a causeway. The four inscriptions reveal that this was a foundation of King Ishanavarman. An inscription found on the eastern door of the exterior wall, refers to the power and majesty of the king and records his military success in expanding the territory of his parents. An inscription found in tower F records the installation of a *linga* by a brahman in the service of the king. The northern group is also surrounded by a double wall, with a central shrine and numerous subsidiary sanctuaries. Outside

A so-called 'flying palace', seen on the temple S13 of the Southern Group at Ishanapura.

Left: The temple precincts of Ishanapura were surrounded by impressive brick walls. (Courtesy Dr. Yasushi Kojo)

The walls sourrounding the temple precincts were often decorated, as in this scene from a Hindu epic on the wall round the Southern Group.

The wall round the inner precinct of the Southern Group at Ishanapura is particularly well preserved. (Courtesy Dr. Yasushi Kojo)

the eastern gate on the outer wall, an avenue leads to a large reservoir demarcated by earthern banks.

No inscriptions have been found with the central group. Like the other two, it has a central sanctuary which was raised on a platform reached by a flight of steps. Carved lions guard access to the immediate surrounds of the temple terrace, the sanctuary of which measures 14 by 14 m, with walls 2.8 metres thick. An aerial reconnaissance of Ishanapura has revealed that the sanctuaries are set within a double-walled enclosure measuring 2 by 2 km. The reservoir was found outside the city walls.

Van Liere (1980) has considered the hydraulic system of Ishanapura. One of the problems, is that the site was occupied for many centuries following the end of Ishanavarman's reign. Indeed, it was a centre of culture and learning during the period of the classic Angkorian state (Osborne 1966), when it was linked to the great road system laid down under Jayavarman VII. It is, however, quite feasible that some of the reservoirs and the moated enceinte of Ishanapura were constructed during the 7th century. These were probably designed more for supplying the moats, religious foundations and urban populace than for irrigating rice fields.

Ishanapura contains the largest and most impressive religious monuments from this period, but several other sites have also revealed a nucleus of impressive brick sanctuaries. Ampil Rolum, 35 km southwest of Ishanapura, for example, incorporates three largely ruined sanctuaries some of which have yielded inscriptions. The archaeological remains of Thala Borivat are large and impressive. This site commands a major trade route, where the valleys of the Se San and Sre Pok give access to the territory of the Chams. Bénisti's (1968) analysis of the decoration of the Thala Borivat lintels has led her to date them earlier than those of Ishanapura, and it is on such chronological evidence that Lévy (1970) has suggested the site as a major centre.

The architectural style and particularly the decoration on wall surfaces and door lintels are rich sources of information on the religious practices of the period, and their inspiration. Dowling (1999) has recently reviewed the five successive art styles of Chenla, and has suggested that monumental sculpture in stone originated during the reign of Ishanavarman. Benisti (1970) has considered the range of motifs and figures, and reviewed their parallels in Indian temple contexts. Take for example, the *makara*, a fantastic marine monster commonly depicted on the lintels. Similar depictions are represented in India by 300 BC. A frieze of geese is another popular motif in the middle Mekong valley which has an Indian origin. The decorative motif incorporating foliage, employed at Ishanapura has its parallels in India at Ajanta and Ellora Cave XIV (about AD 550). Even such simple geometric motifs as the chequer-board are represented in both areas. At Ishanapura, embellishment to the outer walls of temples involved the depiction of a storied building revealing personages within. A similar building adorns the wall of Ajanta Cave XIX in India. The *kudu* motif, which comprises a niche or circlet often containing a human head, is common in Chenla art and there is even a ceramic representation at Oc Eo. This motif had a long currency in India from Amaravati to Pallava art. Bénisti's detailed review has established that the closest parallels with the art of this period lie in the Indian styles seen at Ajanta, Ellora and Mamallapuram, and dated to the period AD 500-650.

Chinese accounts and a large corpus of inscriptions provide a social overlay to this archaeological framework. Both must be treated with caution, for if the Chinese texts were our only source of information, we would assume that a state called Chenla existed in this area. Originally a vassal to the kingdom of Funan, its King Chitrasena seized Funan and subdued it. The principal city of Chenla housed over 20,000 families. In the middle there was a great hall, wherein the king, probably Ishanavarman, gave an audience every third day. At these audiences, the king wore a cap covered in gold and precious stones, and reclined on a couch made of different kinds of aromatic wood. He was accompanied by five great officials and many lesser functionaries, and his person and palace were protected by armed guards. His kingdom incorporated thirty other cities, each ruled by a governor.

This simple pattern of a stable, centralised monarchy is not borne out by the analysis of inscriptions. These were carved in stone, with texts often in both Sanskrit and Khmer, and were usually erected to commemorate the construction and benefaction of a temple. The Sanskrit text began with a eulogy of the king, if it was a royal foundation, followed by a list of donations, such as workers and land, which was written in Khmer. These inscriptions, many of which are dated, have provided much important information. Thus, the location of a particular stela, allied to its message, may allow an archaeological site to be identified as the seat of a named sovereign. Others recall military campaigns and territorial claims which allow us to establish the areas which were under the sway of individual kings. The corpus of inscriptions has, in like vein, allowed the bare essentials of regional dynastic sequences to be unraveled and the achievements of particular rulers, catalogued. Where a foundation was sponsored by an official, then his name and duties may be obtained, as well as those of his ancestors. Vickery (1998) has exhaustively analysed the archaic Khmer texts, and revealed how they provide insight into the social status of those in the service of temples, their duties, and aspects of the landscape, such as the boundaries of rice fields, water tanks, paths and orchards (Jacob 1978, 1979).

Most attention, however, has been directed to those inscriptions which mention the names of rulers, in order to reconstruct regional, dynastic sequences. One particular royal lineage, which was based for at least part of its history at Ishanapura, is the best known. A most informative inscription dated to AD 667 informs us that the rulers of this dynasty were served by members of an elite family which traced its origins back to the the rule of Rudravarman, thought to be one of the last kings of Funan in the early 6th century. Thus there appears to have been a smooth transition from one state to another.

We know little of Bhavarman, the first king of this dynasty, save that he was descended from a King Viravarman, and that his court centre was probably near Ishanapura. One text describes him as the overlord of one Narasimhagupta, ruler of a place called Indrapura. He died in about AD 600 and was succeeded by his brother Mahendravarman. The latter set up a series of inscriptions in the Mun Valley claiming military victories, although, in reality, these were probably no more than seasonal raiding expeditions. His son Ishanavarman, from his centre at Ishanapura, appears to have established his rule over an impressive area. Far to the west at Jyesthapura, he placed his son in control. In 627, the ruler of a place called Tamrapura acknowledged his vassal status under Ishanavarman, but also described how he was in charge of three dependencies, named Cakrankapura, Amoghapura, and Bhimapura. Identifying these sites is not possible, unless further relevant inscriptions are found. From Wat Po, 250 km south of Ishanapura, we find a reference to the illustrious and heroic Ishanavarman, a ruler who in a text from his capital, is said to have extended the territory of his parents. These fragments of information unanimously imply that he established a growing central control over dependent settlements, an important way station in the establishment of a state.

Bhavavarman II is also a fleeting figure, but the inscriptions of his great grandson, Jayavarman I (*circa* AD 635-680), reflect significant consolidation of central authority. Their distribution centres on the lowlands on either side of the Mekong, with extensions into the rich rice lands of Battambang and on to the coast of Chantaburi. Their contents inform us on two vital issues. The first is the use of official titles, such as President of the Royal Court, which was located at a centre called Purandarapura. Another prescribed punishment for those who disobey a royal order. Two brothers of high social standing were appointed to a variety of posts: officer of the royal guard, chief of rowers, military chief, and governor of Dhruvapura. Another highly-ranked courtier became chief of the elephants, reminding us of the traditional role of elephants in warfare. A further text mentions a chief of the royal grain store. These high officials were rewarded with honorific symbols, such as a parasol embellished with gold. The trends already evident under Ishanavarman were greatly strengthened under his great grandson: with Jayavarman I, we can identify the establishment of a state. It was, however, ephemeral. Only one inscription of his daughter Jayadevi survives. Thereafter, the dynasty disappears from the historic record.

Although the dynasty centred at Ishanapura and Purandarapura is the best known, it was not the only such line of rulers. Control of the Mekong exchange route would have conferred considerable power and in the vicinity of Stung Treng, the inscriptions describe a line of four rulers which began with King Indraloka, followed by at least three generations of queens. At Bhavapura, we read of a line of three 8th century kings whose names all ended in -aditya, meaning the rising sun. We lack the historic details present in the longer and more informative Ishanapura inscriptions, but the presence of local sovereigns suggests that the development of states took place within multiple centres. Towards the end of the period of Chenla, one such centre was established east of the Mekong at Banteay Prei Nokor. This huge site, the moats and ramparts of which still dominate the flat landscape, was probably the capital from which Jayavarman II began his odyssey westward to found the Kingdom of Angkor.

The transition to states requires not only a sovereign, but also a court and regional administration responsible to the centre. In Vickery's analysis of the inscriptions, he has identified the titles of highly-ranked individuals and traced their social responsibilities over time. When the Chinese visitors first described Funan, they employed the title *Fan* for the rulers. This term is probably cognate

The moat of Banteay Prei Nokor still retains water.

Above left: Banteay Prei Nokor is a huge moated site east of the Mekong River. This view, taken from the surrounding wall, shows the wall continuing on the horizon. The rice fields in the foreground are the interior of the city.

Left: Brick temples of the late Chenla period dominate the centre of Banteay Prei Nokor.

with the Khmer title *Pon*, which is often encountered in the inscriptions until AD 719. The title was attached to individuals of very high status, including the sons of a king, as well as to regional leaders. It was inherited through the female line, such that the title passed from the *pon* to his sister's son. Such inheritance may well have been rooted in the prehistoric past, where we encounter rich female burials occupying central positions in the Noen U-Loke mortuary clusters. The epigraphic evidence reveals that *pon* founded or administered temples and provided ideological and economic leadership. They initiated or maintained ponds or reservoirs, and stored or deployed through exchange, rice, cloth, silver, domestic stock and other agricultural surpluses. Although the temples and gods might give the impression that Hinduism was generally adopted, the Khmer texts reveal that local and ancestral deities were also venerated under the title of *kpon* or *vrah kamraten an*. Many local gods or spirits were females and indeed, highly-ranked women were prominent in temple rituals.

Pon was an inherited title, and its use indicates the elaboration of rank within 7th century society. The title *mratan*, on the other hand, was evidently in the gift of the sovereign, and was accompanied by tangible emblems denoting high status. As the title *pon* became rare, so appointees to high office under Jayavarman I are more frequently encountered. This trend provides an intimate glimpse into the subtle changes which were occurring as central authority increasingly replaced a plethora of local, hereditary leaders.

The Khmer language texts also provide insight into the lower-ranked members of society. Whereas the elite had Sanskrit names, the majority of the population retained their Khmer names, and their duties towards the temple reflect an agrarian society tied to the seasonal round of rice cultivation. Since agricultural surpluses underwrote the maintenance of court centres, it is to be expected that labour was tightly controlled. The term *knum* was employed to describe such workers. This is currently translated as slave, but as Vickery has pointed out, it is more likely to have implied membership of a junior lineage. We are informed on many of their duties: the majority worked in the rice fields, but there were also leaf sewers, iron workers, cooks, herdsmen, spinners, weavers and perfume grinders. Their names and duties are known to us through the inscriptions set up in the brick temples which dominate the archaeological landscape.

Temples have survived because they were constructed of brick and stone, but the palaces and rural settlements, being made of less durable materials, are hardly known to us. The temple held a key position not only in terms of religious worship, but also in the economy. Under the administration of the *pon* and his elite circle, the temple was the centre for the accumulation of assets. Agricultural surpluses, domestic stock and craft products such as cloth or silver were stored and deployed through the medium of the temple. Thus the workers could gain merit and provide for the propitiation of ancestral spirits through their labour, while the *pon*, themselves sustained through such surpluses, commanded the accumulation and exchange of the assets. In this manner, further land and its surplus could be purchased, and the rank and power of a particular lineage, increased. The detailed recording of land boundaries, reservoirs and the labour force are all part of this system based on agrarian wealth. It is also hardly surprising to find that the sovereign took a close interest in land ownership and temple transactions, because undue wealth in the hands of a provincial grandee posed a real or potential threat to the central court.

This trend to the concentration of wealth and power in the person of a charismatic leader ran counter to a deeply entrenched social norm of inheritance through the female line. This social mould appears to have fractured under the line of Jayavarman I. His ancestors were referred to posthumously under the divine title *vrah kamraten an*. Jayavarman himself was accorded this title during his lifetime. This aura of divinity may have been sufficient to develop a new route of direct inheritance in the male line, as well as to ensure his authority over regional affairs previously under the control of *pon*.

Chenla: Summary

With the decline in maritime trade in the 6th century, the focus of developing political centrality moved from the Delta to inland, agrarian societies. The archaeological record comprises numerous brick and stone temples which concentrate in the valley of the Mekong River and its tributaries. Several regional dynasties with royal titles are recorded in the inscriptions, the best documented being centred at Ishanapura and its environs. During the course of the 7th century, there was a palpable tightening of central authority over outlying regions. Local leaders, styled *pon*, controlled production and deployment of wealth, but traditional routes of inheritance through to the sister's son weakened the maintenance of power between generations. There was, however, a progressive increase in central authority in the dynasty which included Jayavarman I, whose inscriptions reveal the replacement of *pon* by royal appointees with the title *mratan*. The control of productive land and labour, or strategic assets such as the course of the Mekong River, as well as the acknowledgement of divine status, underwrote the rise of several regional states over this period of increasing social complexity. Although superficially, the Sanskritisation of elite names and adoption of Hindu divinities has traditionally stressed the strength of Indian influence, a detailed review of the Khmer language texts reveals these to have been an Indic veneer over the continuation of powerful local deities and a cult of the ancestors.

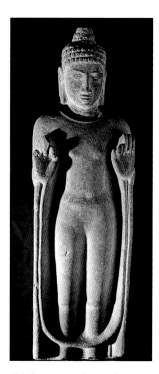

This fine statue of a standing Buddha reveals the popularity of Buddhism in the state of Dvaravati.
(Courtesy Anat Bamrungwongse)

The Chao Phraya Valley

The Chao Phraya is the principal river which debouches into the Gulf of Siam. There are three other main rivers: to the west, there are the Mae Khlong and Ta Chin and to the east, the Bang Pakong. The Chao Phraya has numerous tributaries, that which concerns us most being the Pa Sak, which originates in the Phetchabun mountains. This area is one of the major rice-producing regions of Southeast Asia, a situation which largely results from the construction of flood and water control systems during the past century (Judd 1973). The flood plains of these five rivers and their numerous smaller tributaries however, would have provided in their 'back swamps' a suitable milieu for the extensive cultivation of rice. During the late prehistoric and early historic periods (500 BC-AD 900), the sea level was probably rather higher than at present, and the extensive buildup of the Chao Phraya delta was at an earlier stage. Archaeological sites now set back from the coast, therefore, were likely to have had direct access to the sea.

While the low-lying riverine flood plains provided a suitable terrain for rice cultivation, they were lacking in tin, copper, iron and lead ores. This deficiency, however, was compensated for by routes of communication to both the Cambodian plain and the headwaters of the Mun River and so on to the Khorat plateau. Like the Lower Mekong area, it was positioned so as to control a major communication route to India by means of the Three Pagodas Pass, and commanded a rich hinterland. Involvement with maritime exchange is seen not only in the Indian historic records, but also the presence of exotic artefacts in the area. Thus, a coin of the Western Roman emperor Victorinus AD 268-70 minted in Cologne, was found at U-Thong. We can also read of Buddhist missionaries being sent, to Southeast Asia. A text named the *Sasanvamsappadika* describes how the Emperor Asoka ordered a mission east by Gavampti, Sona and Uttara in the mid third century BC (Glover 1998).

The Archaeology of Dvaravati

Excavations at many Iron Age settlements have identified a rich and vigorous series of late prehistoric trading communities in the margins of the Chao Phraya flood plain. Several sites are now known which reveal the presence of late prehistoric communities long adapted to the environments on the margins of the Gulf of Siam. We have already seen that the cemeteries at Ban Don Ta Phet included glass, agate and carnelian beads of Indian origin or inspiration. Excavations at Ban Tha Kae have revealed three occupation phases in a stratigraphic sequence 2.5 metres thick. This site was a centre for the manufacture of shell jewellery and pottery vessels, as well as bronze casting. Iron working was added in the middle layers and some of the beads were made of blue and orange glass and agate. By the late prehistoric period, the local population used several artefacts with parallels at Oc Eo. There is a gold bead, querns and stamp seals.

Occupation reveals continuity from the late prehistoric period, through a middle period which incorporates Indian trade objects to a late period with a clear relationship in terms of material culture, with Oc Eo. The archaeological remains from Ban Tha Kae covered a roughly oval area 1 km long and 700 metres wide, giving an area of over 40 ha. As in the Mekong Delta, and at about the same time, there was then a rapid period of state formation. Two silver medallions from beneath a sanctuary at Nakhon Pathom, the largest known site, proclaim that it was 'the meritorious work of the King of Sri Dvaravati'. The script is in south Indian characters of the seventh century. If it were necessary to rely on documentary and epigraphic evidence alone, we would know that the Chao Phraya Valley was one of several strategic points in the development of exchange relationships with India, and that by the seventh century, a state existed, whose kings were familiar with Sanskrit. Mon was the indigenous language, but Sanskrit names were accorded the sovereigns. Religion incorporated Buddhism and the worship of Vishnu.

The worship of Vishnu was practiced at Dong Si Mahosod in Central Thailand.
(Courtesy Anat Bamrungwongse)

This process is best documented at Chansen (Bronson and Dales 1973, Bronson 1979), a site now surrounded by a moat and ramparts. The cultural sequence comprises six phases. The first two are prehistoric and date between 800 BC-AD 200/250. Unfortunately, no burials were identified so no range of grave goods including possible Indian imports is available. The period 2 level has, however, yielded an ivory comb decorated with a goose, two horses and Buddhist symbols, in association with two radiocarbon dates suggesting a first to second century AD context, or possibly a little later. Phases 3-4 are dated between AD 200/250-600/650. They have yielded tin amulets, pottery stamps, decorative bronze bells and stone bivalve moulds for casting jewellery. All are paralleled at Oc Eo. Bronson has also described eight bowls in a metallic black ware with parallels in Sri Lanka. He has suggested that they may be actual imports of exotic pottery.

Thus far, the sequence of events is very similar to that outlined at Ban Tha Kae, but from period 5, the situation differed, in that a roughly circular moat was formed, with an internal diameter of about 640 m, associated with an external, rectangular reservoir. Judging from the increased quantities of pottery recovered from this settlement area, there was a sharp increase in population at least during the last two phases. The pottery now belonged to a style found in the Dvaravati sites of the Chao Phraya Valley rather than the earlier local forms. The excavation of Chansen reveals continuity of occupation from the late prehistoric through to the seventh century establishment of sites which have many features in common, and which have been ascribed to the Dvaravati state.

Most commentators have concentrated on the major moated sites and certainly, it is these which have provided the clearest evidence for the acceptance of the Buddhist religion and centralised political authority. They have in common, a moat and bank, the outline of which differs markedly from the rectangular geometry seen in the Mekong Valley sites. Usually they are of an irregular plan, being oval

The Dvaravati civilization of central Thailand provides much evidence for the adoption of Buddhism. This fine statue comes from Dong Si Mahosod. (Courtesy Anat Bamrungwongse)

or sub-rectangular. They were commonly situated so that a stream fed the encircling moats. Where excavation has taken place, the foundations and remains of the superstructure of religious buildings have been recovered, laterite and brick being the dominant building materials. The buildings include *stupas* and *caityas*. A *stupa* is a circular structure, built to house relics of the Buddha or his disciples, or to commemorate a place or event in his life. Often the focus of pilgrimages, the *stupa* has the form of a cupola on a raised platform. A *caitya* is a building or temple which houses a sacred object, such as an image of the Buddha. Such Buddhist monuments have been found both within and outside the moated perimeters of the major Dvaravati centres. The brick superstructure was covered in stucco decoration, and the wall niches provided space for images of the Buddha and animal figures. Quaritch Wales (1969) has divided the major Dvaravati centres of the Chao Phraya Valley into three regional groups which he has labelled Western, Central and Eastern. There is no reason to suppose that these were political units.

The major sites in the Western group are strategically located on the flood plains of the Mae Khlong and Chao Phraya rivers. Pong Tuk, the first to be identified and excavated, has yielded the remains of Buddhist structures, but is not moated. When Cœdès (1928) visited it, he was shown a bronze Byzantine lamp of a style current during the 5th to the 6th centuries AD, together with a Buddha image of similar date. Excavations revealed the laterite foundations of a series of Buddhist religious structures. A circular building is thought to have been a *stupa*, and a square building may have been a *caitya*, or shrine. A third comprises a rectangular structure to which access was gained by a flight of steps. Bases for columns were noted, and it is probable that it represents the remains of a *vihara* or meeting hall. The discoveries at Pong Tuk were the first archaeological evidence in the Chao Phraya area for a society which had adopted Buddhism and had the capacity to raise large religious structures of stone and brick.

U-Thong was occupied for many centuries prior to the development of the Dvaravati state, and the impressive artefactual remains have provided many parallels with Oc Eo. The site is ringed by an oval moat which encloses an area of 1,690 x 840 metres. This moat links with a small stream. It was here that the copper inscription was recovered, recording the accession of Harshavarman to the lion throne. Although there was room for Shivaism in the religious practices at U-Thong, the great majority of the recorded structures are of Buddhist inspiration. As is often the case, the *stupa* foundations are distributed inside and beyond the moats. Excavations by Boisselier (1968) revealed the foundation for a Buddhist assembly hall about 200 metres east of the moats as well as the foundations for three octagonal brick *stupas*. These excavations also furnished the fragmented remains of the stucco which covered the brick superstructure. Motifs include plant ornaments, mythical *garudas*, *makaras* and *nagas* as well as lions. To judge from the description of the lion throne in the U-Thong copper tablet, and the number of terracotta models of the lion discovered, this animal may have had some special significance to the occupants of this site. Indeed, most writers have referred to it as being a Dvaravati royal capital at one stage (Quaritch Wales 1969, Diskul 1979).

Nakhon Pathom is the largest Dvaravati settlement, having an approximately rectangular plan measuring 3,700 by 2,000 metres. The two silver medallions bearing the inscription 'meritorious deeds of the King of Dvaravati' were found beneath a sanctuary within the moated area. Cœdès has dated the foundation on the basis of the script to the seventh century AD, and the sanctuary in question may have been associated with the Pra Paton *caitya*, a large and impressive structure in the centre of Nakhon Pathom. This building was of considerable importance: it was altered on three occasions during the Dvaravati occupation of the city (Dupont 1959). It was designed as a rectangular building, access being by flights of steps at each end. The basement pediment has exterior panels decorated with alternating *garudas* and elephants. Each flight of steps is flanked by carved lions. The exterior walls of the *caitya* itself bore five inset niches each containing a stucco statue of the Buddha. Several artefacts were found under the central tower. They included a bronze chandelier, bells, cymbals and a representation of the Buddha which Quaritch-Wales ascribes to an early phase in the art of Dvaravati. Excavations away from the monuments in what may have been an occupation area by Indrawooth (1984) have revealed a relatively thin occupation layer. Artefacts include several which recall prehistoric forms, including spindle whorls, bronze ornaments and iron spears. There are many smaller artefacts from Nakhon Pathom which date from the Dvaravati period, including statues of the Buddha, and stucco or mouldings used in the decoration of the religious buildings. Perhaps the most important for those concerned with identifying the presence of social stratification are two terracotta trays (Boelès 1964). The complete specimen measures 125 x 150 mm, the surface being decorated with the symbols of royalty. There are fly-whisks, parasols, conch shells, two turtles, thunderbolts and elephant goads from which Quaritch Wales (1969) has noted survivals in the Thai royal regalia to this day. Lyons (1979) has suggested that this artifact may have been used in the investiture of a ruler.

Ku Bua reflects all the essential characteristics of Dvaravati centres: a roughly rectangular moated enclosure with a stream feeding the moat, and Buddhist foundations within and outside the perimeter (Indrawooth 1999). Excavated by Rattanakun (1992), the site incorporates at least 11 religious structures within the moats and 33 beyond. This site is smaller than Nakhon Pathom, measuring 2,000 by 800 metres. Just as at Nakhon Pathom, however, there is a raised and rectangular central *caitya*, measuring 45 by 22.5 metres and abundant evidence for the application of stucco decoration to the religious monuments. Some of those found at Ku Bua are particularly interesting in that they probably illuminate the activities of classes of individuals who lived or visited the settlement. One depicts a seated royal personage, and another, a group of musicians playing stringed instruments and cymbals. There is a graphic portrayal of prisoners with their hands bound, the last in line being kicked by their guard. A delightful scene shows a high status female, perhaps a princess, and

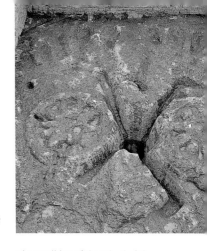

The rendition of the Wheel of the Law at the Dvaravati ceremonial site of Sa Morakod.
(Courtesy Anat Bamrungwongse)

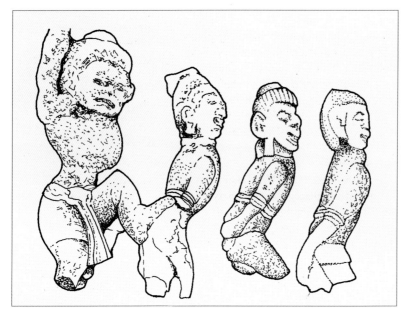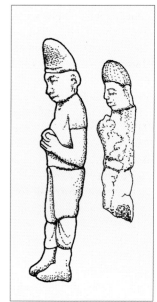

The stucco figures of Ku Bua reveal many aspects of life in a Dvaravati centre. Here we see prisoners and Semitic traders.

her attendants. Then too, there are servants carrying goods, soldiers, and perhaps most intriguing of all, a group of individuals whom Lyons (1965) has described as possibly foreign, Semitic traders, although Quaritch Wales has warned that these figures may represent fictitious characters from Buddhist *jataka* stories. Whoever they are, their personal jewellery, such as the disc earrings, are characteristically Dvaravati. It is hard not to associate these lively figures with the realities of social structure characteristic of Ku Bua and the other centres of the Mae Khlong Valley.

The Lopburi region was rich in late prehistoric settlement. The presence there of a major Dvaravati centre is known from the discovery of Buddhist images, one bearing two lines of Sanskrit text dated to the 8th century. A stone 'wheel of the law' has been found at Lopburi, inscribed in Pali. The wheel of the law was set in motion by the Buddha during a sermon delivered in a Benares deer park and several such wheels have been found in Dvaravati contexts. Pali is the vernacular language which was used by the Buddha, in contrast to the sacred brahman language of Sanskrit. A mid 8th century Mon inscription recorded the gift of slaves and cattle to a monastery (Cœdès 1958). Lopburi was subsequently occupied by the Khmer and remains a thriving regional centre to this day. Hence, nothing is known of the layout and size of the settlement during the Dvaravati period, although excavations in 1987 uncovered a *stupa* base with stucco decoration, and four votive tablets depicting the Buddha (Jermsawatdi and Charuphananon 1989).

Lopburi is located so as to command the junction of the Chao Phraya and Pa Sak rivers. About 100 km up the valley of the latter river, one finds the large moated site of Sri Thep. An extension to the moats more than doubled its size to 4.7 square km. Tankittikorn (1991) has shown that the site has prehistoric origins, while historic occupation began in the 6th century, and lasted at least into the 13th century AD. There are several major monuments within the moats. The 6th to 7th century Khao Klang Nai structure is centrally placed, and was richly ornamented in stucco. One frieze depicts crouching dwarves, some with the head of a lion, or a cow. Further finds include part of a wheel of the law and bronze images of the Buddha. Later monuments reveal continuing occupation, under influence from Angkor. Prang Song Phi Nong and Prang Sri Thep, for example, were built in the 11th to the 12th centuries. Images of Shiva, Vishnu, Surya and Krishna have been found at or near Sri Thep as has the expected evidence for Theravada Buddhism. The presence of so much evidence for Hinduism should not occasion surprise for the site is strategically located so as to control communications between the Chao Phraya Valley and the Mun Valley, an area which comprised part of the growing states of Chenla. Sri Thep would thus have been much more exposed than the western margins of the Chao Phraya Valley to Khmer contact.

The Bang Pakong Valley is also directly exposed to Cambodia. There are three large moated settlements there, which control the passage from the Gulf of Siam up the river valley and so towards the Tonle Sap. The site closest to the sea is known as Muang Phra Rot. It is sub-rectangular, and its moats enclose an area of 1,350 by 700 metres. Quaritch-Wales has suggested that the feet of a statue there belong to an image of Vishnu, and he has also reported a stone relief of the Buddha together with Brahma and Indra. Quaritch Wales went further, and expanded the edge of an area dug as an irrigation tank into a test square which revealed a thin layer of Dvaravati-style sherds. Further excavations by Sulaksananont (1987) also uncovered a layer containing Dvaravati ceramics dated from the 6th to the 11th centuries. This site was included in an area subjected to intensive survey for archaeological remains in 1984. The pottery found on the surface was matched at several small, unmoated settlements within the surveyed area. This suggests that the moated city was contemporary with dependant agricultural villages in its hinterland. Furthermore, the presence of marine shells at Muang Phra Rot suggests that it was located much closer to the sea than it is at present (c. 26 km). It is also interesting to note that a stone mould for casting tin amulets, identical to those from Oc Eo has been found there, indicating an earlier occupation of the site than has been accepted hitherto.

Dong Si Mahosod is very similar in size and shape to Muang Phra Rot. It measures 1,500 by 800 metres and has a rectangular reservoir which covers 2 ha at the northeast corner. Pisnupong (1992) has directed major excavations here, and identified four phases of occupation. The first covers the late prehistoric Iron Age to the 6th century AD, and includes ceramics which recall those typical of the sequence in the upper Mun Valley. Just towards the end of this early phase, a water tank was excavated and ringed by a laterite wall. The latter was decorated with *makaras*, lions and elephants in the style of the 6th century (Pisnupong 1993). The second phase saw the construction of a series of monuments, and belongs to the 6th to the 8th centuries. Occupation continued into the third phase, which is

The popularity of Buddhism in Central Thailand is seen in the numerous images of the Wheel of Law, originally set in motion by the Buddha himself. (Nakhon Pathom National Musuem)

characterised by exchange in Chinese ceramics dating to the 9th and 10th centuries, while during phase 4, the site came under strong influence, if not control, from Angkor. A large ceremonial complex, which incorporates two Buddha footprints, lies at Sa Morakod, just three kilometres to the southeast.

Sukawasana (1996) has excavated a further large moated Dvaravati settlement at Dong Lakhon in Nakhon Nayok Province, where, again, prehistoric occupation preceded the establishment of an historic centre. At U-Taphao, excavations by Wilaikaeo (1991a, b) following earlier investigations by Manit Vallibhotama have furnished an impressive collection of Dvaravati coins, and evidence for a local iron-smelting industry based on the high quality local ore deposits. Ban Khu Muang occupies a strategic location just west of the Chao Phraya River, and has been the focus of training excavations undertaken by Silpakon University. The basal contexts in a cultural context up to four metres deep indicates initial settlement in the period AD 300-550, and material items recall ceramic vessels and tin ornaments found at Oc Eo. The second and third phases include religious structures characteristic of Dvaravati (Silpakon University 1980).

Past studies of the Dvaravati material have concentrated heavily on art history. This situation has been redressed by an important analysis of the evidence for iron working undertaken by Suchitta (1985). His excavations at Ban Di Lung, about 40 km northeast of Lopburi, have revealed evidence for local specialisation in iron smelting and forging. He recovered much slag, as well as surviving fragments of tuyères, nozzles, iron ore and clay furnaces. His radiocarbon determinations fall within the 6th and 7th centuries AD, and reflect the presence of a specialised iron-working village. The interior of many of the moated sites in the Chao Phraya Valley likewise reveal concentrations of iron slag, which indicate a widespread practice of iron working by the direct method of smelting and forging.

Inscriptions are a vital documentary source for Funan and the states of Chenla. This newly discovered stela is being stamped to preserve a copy of the text.

The Inscriptions

The large corpus of inscriptions associated with the religious monuments in the Mekong Valley have, as we have seen, formed the basis for a detailed examination of social change (Vickery 1998). There are far fewer inscriptions from the Chao Phraya sites, but their texts nevertheless provide glimpses of social life. The name of the polity centred at Nakhon Pathom comes from two coins inscribed with the Sanskrit text *Sridvaravatisvarapunya*, or 'meritorious deeds of the King of Dvaravati' (Diffloth 1981). Six surface finds of coins from Muang Dongkorn also refer to the King of Dvaravati (Bhumadhon 1987). The word Dvaravati itself means 'which has gates', perhaps referring to the gates giving access to the city through the encircling walls. The same text but in the Kharosthi script is also known (Kaewglai 1991). A further instance of a royal leader comes from a copper inscription, dated to the mid 7th century, from U-Thong. It reads "Sri Harshavarman, grandson of Ishanavarman, having expanded his sphere of glory, obtained the lion throne through regular succession". The king then recorded meritorious gifts to a *linga*. We do not know if the Ishanavarman named in the inscription was the same sovereign who ruled at Ishanapura in Cambodia, although the date would not rule him out. As in Cambodia, Harshavarman of U-Thong stressed his exalted ancestry and hinted at territorial conquests. There are two brief inscriptions from Lopburi written in Mon, a language closely related to Khmer. A further text from this site, inscribed on the base of a statue of the Buddha, names a person called Arshva, son of the King of Sambuka. Perhaps the most informative text within this corpus of inscriptions, however, comes from Sri Thep (Weeraprajak 1986). Dating stylistically to the 7th century, it records "In the year... a king who is nephew of the great King, who is the son of Pruthiveenadravarman, and who is as great as Bhavavarman, who has renowned moral principles, who is powerful and the terror of his enemies, erects this inscription on ascending the throne". Once again, we find that royal ancestry, religious zeal and military success attended accession to kingship.

Documentary Sources

The documentary sources for protohistoric and early historic societies in this area are also poorer than are those for the lower Mekong Valley and Cambodian plain. Earlier Chinese sources are all based on hearsay rather than direct observation, while Indian references are of a general and illusory character. The earliest possible reference to the Chao Phraya Valley area is contained in the History of the Early Han. It records a journey which originated on the south Chinese coast, and ended at a place called Huangji. It was a very long journey which lasted about one year, and, most interestingly, involved a ten day sector which was undertaken on foot. Wheatley (1961: 9) has suggested that the ultimate destination was the eastern shores of India, and that the overland sector involved perhaps, the Three Pagodas pass.

The itinerary will only ever be generally known, but two points particularly stand out. First, the events described took place about 100 BC. Secondly, as the historian Ban Gu states: "From the barriers of Rinan (southern Bac Bo) it is about nine and a half months journey to Shenli (possibly the Chao Phraya Valley). It is rather more than ten days' journey on foot to the country of Fugandulu, whence it is something over two months' voyage to the country of Huangzhi (probably India)....(officials and volunteers) put out to sea to buy lustrous pearls, glass, rare stones and strange products in exchange for gold and various silks.....It is a profitable business for the barbarians, who also loot and kill." (tr. Wheatley 1961). The possible route of this most important passage may well, according to Wheatley, have included the Three Pagodas pass. If this is correct, then here is documentary confirmation of the early exchange of Indian objects, the glass and rare stones, at least, being archaeologically recoverable.

The next relevant text is *The History of the Liang Dynasty*, which was written in the early seventh century and drew on earlier documentary sources. We read of a maritime expedition by Fan-man, ruler of Funan in the early third century AD. Apparently he "used troops to attack and subdue the neighbouring kingdoms, which all acknowledged themselves his vassals. He himself adopted the style of Great King of Funan. Then he ordered the construction of great ships and crossing right over the Gulf of Siam, attacked more than ten states" (tr. Wheatley 1961). The location of these entities is not easily resolved, but it is clear that they were situated on the shores of the Gulf of Siam. Tun-sun is the best known, because it receives further mention in *The History of the Liang Dynasty*. It was a centre of intensive long distance exchange in exotic goods. The author states: "More than 3,000 *li* from the southern frontier of Funan is the kingdom of Dunsun, which is situated on an ocean stepping stone. The land is 1,000 *li* in extent; the city is 10 *li* from the sea. There are five kings who all acknowledge themselves vassals of Funan. The eastern frontier of Dunsun is in communication with (Bac Bo), the western with India. All the countries beyond the frontier come and go in pursuit of trade... At this mart East and West meet together so that daily there are innumerable people there. Precious goods and rare merchandise, there is nothing which is not there." (tr. Wheatley 1961). The location of Dunsun is not known. Recent excavations conducted at Khlong Thom in Krabi province, revealed the sort of site which corresponds to the written record. Veeraprasert in describing the material found there in 1983, has drawn our attention to a range of artefacts matching many found by Malleret at Oc Eo. These include glass and carnelian beads in various stages of manufacture, inscribed stone seals and stone moulds for casting jewellery (Veeraprasert 1985). Such exotic materials stress the role of a strategic location in the exchange of goods between India and both Southeast Asia and China. The point was not lost on Fan-man, who resolved to bring it and other maritime entities under his hegemony.

Dvaravati: Summary

In most syntheses of the Dvaravati sites, it is assumed that they comprise constituent parts of a kingdom, with a capital first at U-Thong and later at Nakhon Pathom. Quaritch Wales has gone further, and considered that this Dvaravati state expanded into the Mun and Chi valleys in Northeast Thailand. But the existence of a state encompassing the entire region of the Chao Phraya, Bang Pakong and Mae Khlong valleys, while feasible, is not yet based on any firm evidence. Indeed, our knowledge of Dvaravati is still at a preliminary stage. We know that the area is strategically placed to take advantage of long-distance trade originating in India, and that there were long-established prehistoric communities there when such trading links were forged. There are some finds from Chansen, Ban Tha Kae and Muang Phra Rot which indicate links with the material culture of Oc Eo. From the mid 7th century, a series of large moated settlements were foci for the construction of monumental Buddhist structures in laterite and brick. Buddhism was not exclusive by any means, and the sites in the Pa Sak and Bang Pakong valleys indicate adherence to Hinduism as well. There is evidence from U-Thong, Nakhon Pathom and Ku Bua for the presence of a ruling class, of conflict, an army and the taking of prisoners. Indeed the very presence of moats and ramparts at the main sites hint at a need for defence. At present, there is no evidence in favour of a unified state as against a series of small ones each vying for ascendancy. Some evidence in support of the latter comes from the period just prior to their incorporation within the expanding Angkorian kingdom. It is recorded in the Pali chronicles from Chiang Mai, that the king of Haripunjaya (a Mon kingdom based in Northern Thailand at Lamphun) attacked Lavo (Lopburi), then under the rule of king Ucchittachakkavatti. The latter is described as the king of Lopburi rather than of Dvaravati. *The History of the Song Dynasty* refers to Lavo rather than Dvaravati in AD 1001 (Pelliot 1904: 233). The truth may fall between the two extremes and, as in the Mekong Valley, periods of unity under rulers of vigour were punctuated by episodes of fragmentation and regional autonomy.

The Mun and Chi Valleys in Northeast Thailand

Northeast Thailand has two major rivers, the Mun and the Chi, which meet at Ubon and flow into the Mekong. It was shielded from early and direct contact from either Indian traders or the expansion of Funan. Indeed, the Phetchabun range lies between these two river valleys and the Chao Phraya system, and the Dang Raek Range lies between them and the lowlands bordering the Tonle Sap and the

Muang Sema has an impressive series of brick structures in the centre of the city.

Monsoon rains have revealed an Iron Age cemetery under the ramparts of Muang Sema.

The outer moat of Muang Fa Daet remains recognizable on the ground.

Brick structures dominate the central area of Muang Fa Daet.

middle Mekong. There is, however, an artery of communication via the Mekong Valley, and access to the Chao Phraya system is effected down the Pa Sak Valley or further to the south, west from Nakhon Ratchasima. The lower and middle reaches of the Mun Valley were integral with Chenla, and reveal a similar pattern of early brick temple shrines. However, the upper Mun and the Chi valleys incorporate monuments closely paralleled in the Dvaravati sites of Central Thailand. It is possible that this distinction has prehistoric roots, involving Khmer speakers in the middle and lower Mun and Mon speakers in the upper Mun and Chi valleys.

There are two sites which stand out on account of their area and richness of religious structures, Muang Sema in the Mun Valley and Muang Fa Daet in the region of the middle Chi. To judge from their plans, these sites were progressively enlarged. Muang Fa Daet ultimately covered an area of 171 ha, and Muang Sema grew to rival it in size. Both have revealed prehistoric occupation under the historic layers (Indrawooth *et al.* 1991).

Muang Fa Daet is strategically situated near the confluence of the Pao and Chi rivers, in an area favourable to the extensive cultivation of rice on backswamps. Its position provides control of the route north via the Pao Valley to the Sakon Nakhon basin, and it is likewise axially situated to take advantage of traffic up and down the Chi Valley. It was initially reported by a local revenue official who disclosed to Seidenfaden (1954) that there were over two thousand *sema* stones there. That figure might have been an exaggeration, but there is no doubting that the site was the focus of an intensive use of these sacred boundary markers. The location of the actual precincts is now lost due to the relocation of the stones to the principal modern village within the ancient site. They still provide much information because they are carved to depict Buddhist scenes. One shows the Buddha together with Indra and Brahma. A second shows him with his wife and son following his enlightenment. It is particularly interesting because it shows him seated in front of a wooden hall or *sala* which provides a glimpse of the nature of secular architecture at that period. A town wall and gateway defended by soldiers at the base of this *sema* stone give an idea of what once lay above the barely

An image of the walls, gates and defenders of Muang Fa Daet, taken from a *sema* stone.

perceptible ramparts which still demarcate this ancient settlement. Muang Fa Daet was also provided with a substantial rectangular reservoir which covered an area of 15 ha, and recalls similar structures at Chansen and Dong Si Mahosod in the Bang Pakong Valley, and Ishanapura in the valley of the Stung Sen. Further parallels with the former area are seen in the number of brick bases to support *stupas*, characteristically ringed by the remains of stucco ornamentation.

Kantarawichai is a smaller moated site situated 20 km west of Muang Fa Daet. Excavations there in 1972 revealed the foundations of a Buddhist ordination hall, built of brick over a laterite base measuring 37 by 10.5 metres. A foundation deposit comprised a bowl containing 66 silver plaques (Diskul 1979). These are of exceptional interest, because they parallel in many respects the motifs and characteristics of the Buddhist buildings of which only the foundations remain. Diskul has identified one figure as a deity-attendant of the Buddha. He has a halo and wears a crown, earrings and an elaborate necklace. A second figure is a royal personage who likewise, wears ear ornaments and a necklace. The parallels with these plaques lie in Muang Fa Daet and to the southwest, in the Dvaravati sites of the Chao Phraya Valley.

The region of Nakhon Ratchasima is nodal in any regular contact between the Mun and the Chao Phraya valleys. Indeed, the name means the royal frontier city. Its predecessor was the moated site of Muang Sema. It was probably enlarged on two occasions, and the presence there of brick structures and stone representations paralleling those from Dvaravati indicate a large centre similar in date to Muang Fa Daet. Iron Age occupation is seen in the presence of Phimai Black pottery and later prehistoric burials. Hanwong's excavations have also revealed a higher layer containing artefacts characteristic of the Central Plains Dvaravati sites, including bronze Buddha images and part of a wheel of the law. A seventh century inscription from this site records in Sanskrit and Khmer the donation of buffaloes, cattle and slaves of both sexes to a Buddhist community

0   5 cm

The excavations at Kantarawichai recovered a number of silver plaques which add to our knowledge of the early adoption of Buddhism in Northeast Thailand.

by the king of Sri Canasapura. Another Sanskrit inscription found at Phu Kiao Kao, 50 km northwest of Chaiyaphum, is dated stylistically to the 7th-8th centuries and mentions a king Jayasingha-varman. At Hin Khon 35 km south of Nakhon Ratchasima, King Nrpendradhipativarman erected four sema stones and founded a Buddhist temple during the 8th century. He gifted rice fields, ten pairs of cattle, gold and silver utensils, an elephant and a plantation of 20 betel nut trees. Finally, an inscription, doubtless relocated, found in Ayutthaya and erected in AD 937 by a ruler called Mangalavarman, records that his ancestral line of kings ruled over Sri Canasapura. This inscription is also in Sanskrit and Khmer rather than the Mon language, which was used in most inscriptions of the Chao Phraya Valley, and supports the finding that a Buddhist state held sway in the Mun Valley over several generations.

As was the case for Dvaravati, we remain largely unaware of the relationships between sites and the presence, or otherwise, of states on the Khorat plateau. In purely geographic terms, hegemony from such outstandingly large centres as Muang Fa Daet and Muang Sema over their surrounding territory would seem likely. It should not be forgotten, however, that contemporary events in the middle Mekong, where inscriptions are much more numerous, reveal a fluid political situation where centrality reflected the prowess and vigour of individual rulers and was constantly prone to fragmentation.

There are some intriguing hints that such a situation also existed on the Khorat plateau. These come from the consideration of local folklore, and have been commented on by Seidenfaden (1954) and Keyes (1974). The former recorded a mythical story of the founding of Muang Fa Daet in AD 621. It was evidently founded by Chao Fa Ra-ngum, the younger brother of the ruler of Nong Han. Evidently, the older brother was jealous of Ra-ngum and sent him into exile. The younger prince travelled south, following the course of the Pao River until he reached the site of Muang Fa Daet and established his own principality. Apart from some outposts, his power did not extend beyond his city walls. His daughter was subsequently wooed by a neighbouring ruler, and war ensued, leading to the death of Ra-ngum and his neighbour.

Keyes has described two further myths which relate to the same area, and record actual place names. One accounts for the origins of Bang Fai, an annual festival which takes place just before the arrival of monsoon rains. It owes nothing to Hinduism or Buddhism, but has very ancient roots. At present, several villages participate in a competition for the biggest and most powerful rocket, which is represented as a phallus. The idea is that the rocket should reach the clouds, fertilize them and induce rain. It is an occasion for uninhibited jollity, which brings together several communities to a central location. The local legend of Bang Fai and its origins recounts a genealogy beginning with Phaya Khom, the ruler of Nong Han, whose marriage with Nang Pathumath resulted in two sons and a daughter called Nang Ai. The oldest son ruled over Ban Chiang Hian and Ban Iat, the younger son over Muang Si Saeo and Phak Waen. One grandson controlled Muang Hong and Muang Thong, and the second, Muang Phang. Keyes has noted that some of the personal names have a Sanskrit origin and that some place names are paired, for example Ban Chiang Hian with Ban Iat, and Muang Hong with Muang Thong. Apart from Nong Han, all these sites are situated in the middle and lower valley of the Chi River. It is interesting to note that the sons of a given noble or royal line boasting Sanskrit names ruled over individual centres with at least one named subsidiary settlement. This structure recalls that described for the initial stages in the formation of Funan, where the king placed his sons in charge of settlements within his domain and is a small thread of evidence for the existence of a polity with dependent vassals. If the folklore reflects some sort of proto-historic reality, these princelings engaged in rivalries expressed not only in a rocket tournament, but also in genuine warfare.

The *sema* stones at Muang Fa Daet have been relocated along a village track, but their number remains most impressive.

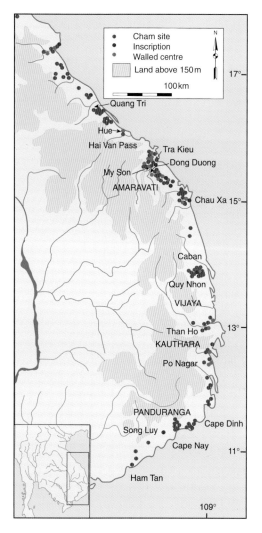

Champa

We have seen that the proto-historic settlement in the coastal tracts of central coastal Viet Nam involved cremation. The ritual involved the interment of the human ashes in a large pottery urn, often in association with grave goods made of iron, and exotic stone jewellery. The aforementioned group is called after the site of Sa Huynh. Cremation is an unusual burial practice in mainland Southeast Asia during the prehistoric period, but became widespread with increased Indian influence. The Sa Huynh culture was located in an area where later inscriptions reveal Cham as the vernacular language. This is an Austronesian language, and speakers occupied a narrow coastal strip, where flat land was at a premium. The rivers are short and prone to sharp flooding when rains are heavy on the Truong Son cordillera to the west. The enclaves of flat land are cut where mountain spurs reach out to the coast. These divide the coastal strip into distinct valley systems, and blur any semblance of territorial continuity. In this respect, the area lacks the unifying characteristics of the major river valleys. An inscription by King Sambhuvarman dated to about AD 600 mentions the country of Champa, which was clearly centred upon Amaravati, but remains of unknown extent. It is highly likely that it covered more than the immediate sustaining area of the sacred centre of My Son.

Given such geographic fragmentation and the constrained nature of the coastal plain, exchange and communication along this coast was most easily undertaken by sea. To the west lay the Truong Son range, which provided a major obstacle to communication with the Mekong Valley, save for three passes. This long coastline was nevertheless strategically placed, particularly as the pace of maritime commerce accelerated with Chinese interest in a southern route to India and the Roman Empire. Not only were the Cham speakers who controlled this inhospitable coast able to supply goods sought for the China trade, they also collected dues from ships which passed by or through their harbours. Parmentier (1909, 1918) has recognised five major sub-divisions in this long coastline which were recognised politically by the Chams themselves. It must be stressed, however, that the political organisation of Champa was fluid, and changed with time. Reference to polities by name must be reviewed in the overall context of the inscription, as well as its location. As Southworth (2000) has argued, what seemed to early scholars as a series of provinces within a homogeneous state might not be the case. The designation 'province' to the names accorded parts of Champa originated in Finot's analysis of an inscription from Po Nagar, installed

The massive central shrine at Po Nagar is a monument to the power of Cham rulers.

by King Jaya Harivarmadeva in AD 1160 (Finot 1903). This king claimed to have defeated Kambuja (the Khmer), Yavana (the Viet), Vijaya, Amaravati and Panduranga. This is the earliest record of the location Amaravati, while the first reference to Vijaya is of about the same date. Kauthara was first mentioned in an inscription of King Satyavarman from Po Nagar in AD 784. A kingdom known as Panduranga was recorded in an inscription from Po Nagar, dated to AD 817, which describes the *senapati* or commander-in-chief of this kingdom.

The first geographic region of Champa lies between Ham Tan and Cape Dinh, an inhospitable stretch of coastline with thin, sandy soils. It was a refugium for the Chams when on the point of annihilation by the expanding Viets, and is the only part of the coastal tract which retains significant numbers of Cham speakers. There are very few Cham monuments there. Between Cape Dinh and Cape Nay, however, there are three well-watered valleys separated by low passes. There are some surviving vestiges of evidence for irrigation systems and several Cham sites. The area was known to the Chams as Panduranga.

North of Cape Dinh, the coastal strip broadens into a plain about 70 by 70 km in extent. There are many sites here in a region known to the Chams as Vijaya. The region of Amaravati, however, which lies between the Hai Van pass and Quy Nhon, was the dominant area of

A view from Da Nang north torwards the Hai Van Pass. This area was the major centre of Cham civilization.

Cham political centrality. It has a reasonable area of land available for agriculture, and several well-sheltered harbours. The last area lies north of the Hai Van pass, with most archaeological sites being concentrated in the vicinity of Quang Tri. The relative importance and political reach of these polities named in the inscriptions almost certainly changed markedly over time. There may never have been a period when Champa was unified into one state.

Being located on the doorstep of China's most southern commandery, it is hardly surprising to find that most of the documentary evidence for the Chams is found in Chinese sources. There is a consistency in these descriptions, from which several important points emerge. The first is that there were episodes of warfare and raiding on the southern frontier of Rinan which were repulsed either by punitive expeditions or resolved through diplomacy. At times of a relatively weak administration, when central authorities were engaged in internal friction, the 'barbarians' beyond the frontier had less to fear from reprisals, and were able to make territorial gains. The second point is that such periods of open conflict were punctuated by the restoration of tribute missions to the Chinese court. The Chinese histories recorded such missions as coming from the state of Linyi (after AD 757, known as Huanwang). It is from such Chinese histories, too, that we are informed of the civil centres of Linyi, while the names of their overlords up to the early 6th century are known almost exclusively from Chinese sources.

The most important Chinese sources are the itineraries of Jia Dan (AD 730-805). One described the route from southern China to India via the coast of Viet Nam (Pelliot 1904). As Southworth (2000) has noted, this brought the traveller to the most southerly commandary of the Tang Kingdom, known as Huanzhou. Beyond lay Champa, described by Jia Dan as a series of kingdoms, rather than a unified state.

The Archaeological Remains of Early Champa

My Son was one of the major ceremonial centres of the Cham civilization.

Archaeological research into the states of Champa has barely begun, but we must turn to it for primary sources of Cham history. The principal centres concentrate in riverine plains, though it must be stressed that the distribution map includes all sites known, and is not confined only to those dating up to the death of Rudravarman II in AD 758. Indeed, the majority of sites probably date to the later dynasties. Nevertheless, the trends of religious architecture were established by the 7th century, when Vikrantavarman initiated a major building programme at My Son. According to Parmentier (1904, 1918a), he was responsible for sanctuary F1. This has in common with later temples there, and, indeed with those ascribed to the Chenla period, the provision of an exterior enclosing wall within which was set a single-chambered sanctuary. The temples were built of brick, and the exterior surfaces bore strip pilasters, false doors and window niches. The complete plan of My Son represents an extraordinary concentration of effort and continuity of construction over a period which began with Bhadravarman and continued at least to the reign of Jaya Indravarman towards the end of the 11th century. This ceremonial centre was one of several which have been identified in Champa.

In the southernmost polity of Kauthara, there is the centre of Po Nagar. The six sanctuaries there also cover a lengthy time span, beginning before the 7th century AD with a wooden structure burnt down in AD 774. The northwest tower dates to AD 813 and further sanctuaries were added at intervals to AD 1256. At the end of the 4th dynasty in AD 757, the political centre of Linyi moved briefly to the southern provinces, and the early inscriptions of Po Nagar reveal

The main sites of the Chams are located where there is a large coastal plain. They are invariably backed by the eastern foothills of the Truong Son Cordillera.

that the onset of sanctuary construction there commenced in earnest under Satyavarman, second king of the 5th or southern dynasty.

A third major religious centre is located at Dong Duong, but like Po Nagar, the sanctuaries all belong to later stages of Cham history. Indeed the earliest inscription from Dong Duong is as late as AD 875. Less is known of the dating of the major Cham defended centres although it is known from Chinese documents that defences at Qusu for example, were in place by the 4th century AD. The archaeological traces of Cham centres of occupation reveal a number of features in common with those of Chenla, and Dvaravati, but also some local variations. They share the same provision of walls with a single moat, but both documentary and archaeological evidence indicate that the earthen ramparts were clad with brick or stone. They are located back from the coast, and as a rule on or near a river which supplied moats with water. While usually oriented according to the cardinal points, they lacked the severe geometric layout of Chenla and later Angkorian plans. They often have a bailey, or perhaps a later city annexe, built on. The citadel of Song Luy is the most southerly, being located on the coast south of Cape Dinh. It has a rampart which still stood 6-8 metres high a century ago and the river Luy flows past the site, beyond which is a small annexe.

Thanh Ho is located on the northern bank of the Da Rang River, and is particularly well preserved. The main enceinte is square, and encloses an area of 49 ha. There is a smaller annexe on the western side. The brick-built walls still stood 3-5 metres high when Parmentier visited the site in the early years of this century, and the foundations of towers were seen at regular intervals along the walls and at the corners. A 30-metre wide moat lay in front of the walls. The citadel at Caban is much bigger, the walls measuring 1,400 by 1,100 metres and enclosing an area of 155 ha. It, too, was oriented to the cardinal points, and two streams have their confluence within the centre before they enter the river which flows parallel with the eastern rampart. The foundations of perimeter towers and gateways survive, as does a large central sanctuary. This site was probably the capital of the province of Vijaya.

A smaller defended site has been identified at Chau Xa, enclosing 25 ha. It has brick or brick-revetted walls, a berm and moat. It follows the preceding two sites in having a rectangular plan, and traces of an extension are visible extending south from the west wall. Further remains of defended sites are known near Hue and at Tra Kieu. The former was located between two streams which flowed into a bend of the Hue River. Its brick walls enclose an area of about 25 ha.

Tra Kieu, known as Simhapura to the Chams, was first excavated by Claeys in 1927-8. He uncovered the foundations of a sanctuary structure, and recovered much statuary, and some inscriptions (Claeys 1927, 1931, Glover (1997). He identified evidence for settlement in the 5th and 6th centuries, but most of it, including Chinese coins, belongs to the 11th century. Two lengths of wall have been traced, but it is not possible to assess the enclosed area. Typically, the centre was located at a junction of two rivers. Further excavations on the flank of Buu Chau Hill within the city walls have been undertaken by Nguyen Chieu in 1990, and by Glover and Yamagata from 1993 to 2000. The stratigraphic sequence extended to a depth of over 3 metres below the surface in some locations, and 18 radiocarbon dates indicate initial occupation in the last two or three centuries BC until at least the 6th or 7th centuries AD. One fragment of pottery from the lowest layer has been identified as rouletted ware closely paralleled at Arikamedu in India. As at Ban Don Ta Phet, this suggests that extensive maritime exchange was in place during the late first millennium BC. Later layers included a considerable quantity of locally-made ceramics strongly influenced by Chinese wares, as well as tiles and bricks. The disposition of the latter, in association with much evidence for burning, suggests that there were several phases of rebuilding after conflagrations (Glover and Yamagata 1995, 1998, Glover *et al.* 1998).

The Dynastic History of Linyi

The Cham-speaking states which developed in coastal Viet Nam have received very little attention either by epigraphers or archaeologists, and for even the barest framework, one must turn to early French reviews of Chinese historical sources. According to Maspero (1928) it would be premature to regard Linyi as a state when it was initially alluded to in the Chinese histories. Rather, he saw it as a series of regional chiefdoms linked no doubt by a common language and further bonded by the presence of a common adversary in the form of the Han Chinese. This suggestion is supported by the *History of the Jin*, which towards the end of the 3rd century AD, noted that Linyi comprised numerous tribes which provided mutual assistance and refused submission to China. Given this situation, it is not surprising that the initial references in documentary sources recorded a raid into southern Rinan commandery, during which the local sub-prefect was killed. In this *History of the later Han*, the thousand or so belligerents were referred to as the Zhulian, and this frontier event is dated to AD 137. In AD 192, there was further border unrest and on this occasion, the Chinese refer to the leader of the uprising as

The Cham sanctuary of Po Nagar.

Zhulian, who seized part of southern Rinan and proclaimed himself king. This event set in train the first dynasty of Linyi. Between AD 220-230, the Linyi sent the first of many tribute missions northward, this one being directed to the governor of the southern commanderies. We do not know the name of Zhulian's successor, only that the middle years of the 3rd century saw continued raiding. During one such campaign, the dominant border fortress of Qusu was taken by Linyi. This centre was strategically placed on a mountain spur adjacent to the river Giang. It controlled the southern defences to Rinan and one of the few routes over the Truong Son mountains to the Mekong Valley.

In *c.* AD 270, we are informed of the first king of Linyi after the initial reference to the founder of the dynasty, Zhulian. He was evidently the grandson of the founder, and was recorded under the name Fan-Hsiung. His son was called Fan-Yi, who in 284, despatched the first official embassy to the Chinese court rather than to the governor of Jiaozhi. An interesting insight into the impact of China on the Linyi at this juncture is provided by the activities of Fan-Yi's principal adviser, a man known as Wen. The latter was of Chinese origin who through his travels, was well informed on Chinese military architecture and tactics. He brought his experience to bear by advising the ruler on the construction of walled and moated defences, and the design and manufacture of up-to-date weapons. His experience was also influential in civil architecture, for apparently he advised the king on the construction of a colonnaded hall. Only a decade after entering the king's service, Fan-Yi died and his legitimate descendants were apparently poisoned. Wen, now titled Fan-Wen, accordingly took power upon himself and in AD 336, founded the 2nd dynasty of Linyi. Fan-Wen was clearly concerned with the expansion of his territory. He evidently imposed his authority on previously independent tribes, and, while sending a tribute mission to China, continued a policy of border conflict. His embassy took a letter from him written in 'barbarian', presumably Indian, script. It should not be overlooked that the expansion of trade to southern China from Funan occurred at this time, and that Indian merchants and religious functionaries were regular callers at the ports which Fan-Wen controlled.

Fan-Wen was succeeded by his descendants Fan-Fo (349-) and Fan-Hua (AD 399-413). It was during the reign of the latter that the Sanskritisation of names and adoption of the Hindu religion were established. The evidence comes from inscriptions instigated by the ruler Bhadravarman. Christie (1970) has considered the derivation of this name, noting that according to the 6th century Shui-ching, the east gate of the capital of Linyi led to a winding road beside which was placed a stela bearing the name of Hu-ta. He has suggested that this is the Chinese rendition of the Cham word *hudah*, meaning brilliant. Sanskritisation could provide the known epigraphic name of Bhadra. We know more about Bhadravarman from surviving inscriptions (Finot 1902). That from Cho-Dinh was inscribed on a natural rockface and describes a sacrifice to Shiva by Bhadravarman or one of his descendants. The Hon-Cuc inscription is a short recital to

A fine carved pedestal supporting a *linga* from Tra Kieu. Height, 43 cm. (Courtesy Paisarn Piemmattawat)

Shiva, and an inscription from My Son records the gift of land to sustain a temple dedicated to Shiva founded by Bhadravarman. My Son is a small valley screened by hills. It houses several groups of outstanding Cham temple complexes. The data available indicate that the earliest temple there was a foundation of Bhadravarman. The establishment in his temple of a *linga* called Bhadresvara confirms the development of the state cult of the named *linga* which, as has been seen, provided a unifying force in the emergent states of the middle Mekong Valley. Among the most important of Bhadravarman's inscriptions is that from Dong-yen-chau, which contains a text written in Cham. This confirms that the Linyi were Cham speakers by the end of the 4th century AD. The Indian religion was becoming effectively established at least in court circles, because Bhadravarman's successor, Gangaraja, abdicated in order to undertake a pilgrimage to India, a remarkable if not unique event in the dynastic history of any Southeast Asian state. His departure occasioned civil war over a disputed succession.

With the third dynasty, established in AD 421, we return to king lists available only through Chinese sources. The founder was Fan Yang-mai, a name which Christie (1970) sees as a Chinese transcription of the Cham *yang-mah* or 'golden prince'. We know little of him, but his son of the same name followed in a long tradition of Linyi rulers by supporting sea-borne raiding along the coast of Rinan. This troublesome and persistent piracy goaded the Chinese to act, and the punitive expedition in 446 led to first the sack of Qusu and then the pillaging of the Linyi capital. The vengeance was terrible in terms of loss of life and booty seized. At Qusu, all inhabitants over the age of 15 were put to the sword, and gold, silver and other valuables, taken. The seizure of the Cham capital following a major military defeat at the hands of the Chinese armies led to the destruction of temples and conversion of gold statues into ingots. The recorded removal of as much as 48,000 kg of gold is some indication of the wealth which the rulers of Linyi had amassed. Apart from the resumption of tribute missions following this catastrophe, we know little of the remaining rulers of the dynasty founded by Fan Yang-mai.

An early view of My Son.
(J. Boisselier Collection, P. Dupont Fund).

A wall niche from My Son showing a devotee below a *makara*, a sea monster.

The succeeding dynasty was founded in about 529 and lasted until AD 757. The first ruler took the name of Rudravarman, and claimed descent from Gangaraja, the king of the previous line who had abdicated. This new king continued the policy of border raiding interspersed with the dispatch of tribute missions to China, but his successor, Sambhuvarman (meaning the protégé of Shiva) was the unfortunate victim of a further Chinese punitive expedition under the general Liu-fang. In the spring of AD 605, having marched past the copper columns set up to mark his southern frontier by Ma Yuan, the Chinese arrived once more at the Cham capital. There, the general seized enormous booty, including golden tablets on which were recorded the names of the preceding eighteen kings of Linyi. Liu-fang went further, and divided the conquered Cham territory into four new commanderies. Illness among his men, however, as well as difficulties in surveying the new lands and transport problems, ruled out a permanent arrangement and Sambhuvarman was able to re-occupy the capital and commence reconstruction. Wisely, he sent regular tribute missions thereafter. It was this same Cham king to whom Mahendravarman of Chenla sent his ambassador, Simhadeva. Doubtless, Simhadeva would have found himself at home at a court practicing the same Hindu religion and adhering to the same system of government as his own. Indeed, Sambhuvarman is recorded as having set in train the reconstruction of Bhadravarman's burnt temple at My Son. An inscription from My Son tells us that "Sambhuvarman's glory rose like the autumn moon".

The next two reigns followed peaceful courses, but the second ruler, Bhasadarma, was murdered by one of his ministers and the crown passed to his nephew, Bhadresvaravarman. A dynastic struggle ensued, which resulted in the coronation of Vikrantavarman I. This ruler was descended on the paternal side from Rudravarman and on his maternal side, from Ishanavarman. The union of his parents thus

Ganesha, god of wisdom.
8th-9th centuries.
(Courtesy EFEO)

Left: Cham head of Shiva.
(Courtesy EFEO)

linked the leading families of Chenla and Champa. It was, therefore, reasonable for Vikrantavarman on one of his stelae at My Son, to stress the purity of his royal blood. Indeed, his reign appears to have been relatively peaceful and was marked by the construction of brick sanctuaries at My Son together with a munificent series of donations. These, as in contemporary Chenla, included rice fields, labourers, dancers and singers, musicians, and domestic animals including elephants, cattle and water buffalo. The foundation grants, the inscriptions stress, were to provide for perpetual sacrifices and those who failed to honour this edict would suffer the same infinite punishment as those who murder a brahman. The same importance of asceticism in obtaining divine power which characterised Chenla at this juncture was observed in a further inscription which Finot has ascribed to Vikrantavarman I. The same concern with issuing regular tribute-missions and founding religious establishments continued under his successors Vikrantavarman II and Rudravarman II, with whom the dynasty ended in AD 758.

Champa: Summary

The present description of the Linyi or Cham states covers the formative period, up to the mid 8th century. Glover and Yamagata (1995) have found little evidence in the ceramics from Tra Kieu to indicate a progression from the Sa Huynh Iron Age into the period of early states, and suggest that the transition must have been very rapid. We are still ignorant of the extent to which the coastal enclaves

This sculpture of a *dvarapala*, or door guardian, is a rare example of Cham monumentality. It was found in pieces in 1934. Height, 1.07 metres.
(Courtesy Paisarn Piemmattawat)

sustained one or several states, and the possibility of a fluid situation is high. There are brief allusions in the surviving inscriptions to the construction of temples devoted to the worship of Shiva, but sanctuary construction in more durable materials was begun only towards the end of this early period. The documentary sources describe large walled centres, and archaeological research has identified such sites. Dating their development, however, is for the future. During the formative period, the Cham overlords entered into diplomatic relations with China and Chenla, and in the case of the latter, engaged in at least one royal marriage alliance. To judge from the records of Chinese wars and booty taken, the rulers not only disposed of substantial, well-equipped armies which included war elephants and a fleet, but also amassed much wealth in the form of embellished religious statues and *linga*.

The Han: Three Southern Commanderies

The lower Red River Valley and delta not only comprise one of the most extensive tracts of flat agricultural land in Southeast Asia, but also occupy a nodal position for exchange between the coasts of the Gulf of Bac Bo and the hinterland of Yunnan. It sustained a long term occupation of agriculturalists beginning with the Phung Nguyen phase and culminating with the culture of Dong Son. South of Ninh Binh, the flat agriculturally rich coastal belt narrows markedly from the broad expanse of the delta proper and gives way to the valleys of the Ma and Ca rivers. The lower valley, therefore, stands out as an oasis of flat terrain ringed by uplands and facing the South China sea. The archaeological and Chinese documentary sources, as well as surviving fragments of indigenous folklore, are unanimous in confirming the local development of one or more chiefdoms in the area during the period 500-1 BC

As the Dong Son chiefdoms were developing, major events were occurring in China which were to have a profound impact on not only the occupants of Bac Bo, but also the people who lived along the coastal fringes of central Viet Nam. Warring States, (453-221 BC), a political power struggle ensued and precipitated profound social, technological and bureaucratic changes. It must be recalled that these events occurred in the heartland of China, the basin of the Yellow River not less than 1,800 km north of Bac Bo. The interior valleys and coastal areas south of China were, at that juncture, occupied by numerous regional chiefdoms uniformly regarded by the Chinese as southern barbarians, the Nan Yue.

Three trends can be detected during the period of Warring States which ultimately affected the southern barbarians, including the Dong Son chiefs of the Red River delta. Military techniques and weapons underwent a transformation. The Warring States maintained large armies, and they were equipped with technologically radical weapons. Not least, was the development of the crossbow, together with the increasing application of iron to armaments and the tactical skills in the construction, defence and investment of walled cities. At the beginning of the Warring States period, Chinese polities were still organised along lines recalling the European feudal system. New lands were given to noble families, who were accorded limited sovereignty. Regional loyalty under these circumstances was directed to the great landed families rather than the central ruler, and the result was instability and insurrection. Shen Buhai, who died in about 337 BC, was the author of an influential text which had a lasting influence (Creel 1964). He recognised the impermanent nature of the system and advocated the appointment of bureaucrats from the central authority. No one minister, he said, should be too powerful but, rather, ministers should move in harmony, like spokes of a wheel. The end of the period of Warring States came with the supremacy of the state of Qin in 221 BC. The victories of Qin Shihuangdi, the first emperor of China, were facilitated not only by economic efficiency and army discipline, but also by a system of choosing bureaucrats on the basis of merit. The Qin dynasty hardly outlived the life of its founder, and the struggle for power which took place between 209-202 BC resulted in victory for Liu Bang, the first emperor of the Han dynasty under the regal name Han Gaodi (High Emperor). It was under the Han (202 BC-AD 220) that the Chinese exercised an increasingly direct influence over the course of events in Bac Bo.

An appreciation of this impact turns on understanding the new organisational structure imposed in conquered territories. Han rulers maintained the Qin system of a centralised bureaucracy in which the empire was divided into commanderies, each of which was sub-divided into *xian*. At the centre of each and synonymous with the *xian* was a walled settlement. Indeed, the Chinese symbol for a wall and a city are identical. Under Qin Shihuangdi, all 36 of his commanderies had a centrally-appointed civilian and military governor, and a superintendant. The Han formalised this system by appointing officials through an entrance examination, and training them from 124 BC in a university centre for administration. By AD 1, there were 130,285 centrally appointed officials in charge of the day-to-day functions of the state.

The weight of the Han military machine and the imposition of the commandery and *xian* structure were powerful tools for centralisation. With the Han, expansion into what was described as barbarian territory became state policy. The territorial extent of the Han empire can be measured by the establishment of *xian* walled centres (Creel 1964). These were essentially foci for Chinese administrative control and the collection and deployment of taxation.

According to documentary and legendary sources, the earliest impact of Chinese expansion in Bac Bo was an indirect result of the conflict between the Warring States, and the occupants of Nan Yue. In 333 BC, the Chu state subjugated Yue, and slightly later, Qin conquered Shu. Taylor (1983) has proposed that the bulk of the conquered population remained in their native villages but the rulers with armed retainers moved away from the source of attack in a southerly direction. The establishment of new principalities led to the Chinese referring to the area as 'the hundred Yue'. It is quite possible that a Yue aristocrat known in historic sources as An Duong, was one such displaced leader. He is said to have moved into Bac Bo and replaced the indigenous Hung kings in 258 BC by the kingdom of Au Lac. His capital was located at Co Loa. This date marks the inception of a period when the Red, Ma and Ca river valleys came progressively within the orbit of China. During the brief period of Qin rule, the first emperor despatched several armies to Yue to expand the imperial frontier. Among other things, the emperor was interested in the ivory, rhinoceros horn, kingfisher feathers and pearls supplied by the southern barbarians.

The step to incorporation within the Chinese empire came closer following the downfall of Qin. During the ensuing struggle for power, which resulted in the establishment of the former Han dynasty, Jiao Tuo, a Chinese administrator in the Guangdong region, seized power and proclaimed himself king of Nan Yue. The power in his southern kingdom was acknowledged by the Han emperor in 196 BC, while eleven years later, the Han empress issued an edict which forbade the export of strategic goods to Nan Yue. The list is interesting: it includes gold, iron, weapons, cattle and horses. Jiao tuo was also interested in expanding his new kingdom and his attention turned south to the Red River polity of Van Lang. By 208 BC, Van Lang had been conquered and replaced by two new commanderies: Jiaozhi in the Red River valley and Jiujen in the Ma Valley. These owed allegiance not to the Han dynasty, but to the sinicised rulers of the kingdom of Nan Yue. The relationship probably involved the extraction of tribute from chiefdoms whose structure seems to have remained intact. Indeed, a century was to elapse before the Han rulers finally resolved to replace Nan Yue with its own centrally-administered system of commanderies. They moved in 111 B.C., and in the reorganisation which followed the arrival of the successful

Chinese armies, Nan Yue was subdivided into seven commanderies of which three concern us. Jiaozhi and Jiujen remained, the former with ten districts and the latter with seven. A third, Rinan was founded, and comprised five districts. It is at this juncture, that we are again provided with a glimpse of the social organisation in the lands of the Red River delta. Evidently the local chiefdoms maintained their hold on land, and their status as regional leaders. The 'Lac' lords were familiar with the rise of the river levels during high tides, and introduced water into their rice fields, thereby intensifying production. Their leadership role in local affairs, where the Chinese presence must have been concentrated in commandery seats, was recognised by their appointment as sub-prefects within the Han administration.

There was nevertheless an inherent tension in a system where traditional leadership roles were subservient to local bureaucrats answerable to a distant court. Moreover, the pace of change accelerated. We read of the local people being "instructed in justice and ritual", required to accept Chinese marriage rituals and to wear hats and sandals (Taylor 1983). The brief interregnum between former and later Han (AD 9-23) was also an occasion when numerous Chinese sought refuge from danger in this remote southern corner of the empire.

The official biography of the governor of Jiujen from AD 25 also provides insight into Chinese aims and by inference, local conditions and changes. Jen Yen found that his commandery relied upon rice imported from its northern neighbour due to a concentration on fishing and hunting, and an insufficiency of land under agriculture. He therefore encouraged the production of iron implements and an increase in the area under cultivation. One effect of this would have been an enlarged tax revenue, and easier control over the more sedentary farmers. This increased Chinese influence on affairs in this remote corner of their empire was evidently irksome to the Lac chiefs, and in AD 40, a major rebellion broke out led by an aristocratic woman called Trung-Trac, assisted by her sister. She hailed from Me-Linh, for generations the heartland of Bac Bo, and the revolt rapidly spread to the southerly commanderies. Evidently sixty strongholds were overrun and the Chinese administration swept aside. For two years, she was recognised as paramount over the Lac lords, who briefly found themselves freed from the foreign tribute demands.

The course of events following the rebellion is well documented in the Chinese annals. In AD 42 the Chinese general Ma Yuan marched into the Red River delta area. He defeated the Trung sisters and their followers in battle, and then proceeded further south to the Ma Valley where he subjugated the rebellious chiefs and their supporters. Hitherto, the Lac lords had through several generations retained their land rights and status as local leaders. After his military successes, Ma Yuan introduced structural changes, which brought the leadership role of the surviving Lac lords to an end. Ma Yuan formalised and intensified the establishment of *xian* cities and expanded agriculture by the excavation of irrigation facilities. Taylor

Ma Yuan, in his conquest of the Dong Son chiefs, brought the southern limit of the Han Empire as far south as the Ma River.

sees the latter as implying the imposition of Chinese ownership and control over productive land and the replacement of the Lac chiefs. Ma Yuan also specified the legal obligations within the Chinese system of provincial administration. The aftermath was the establishment of the Han-Viet period. It saw the replacement of the former attempt to integrate indigenous chiefdoms with a loosely-imposed Han tribute system by the imposition of a full Chinese administration.

It is easy to be diverted by the course of historic events, from the underlying developments and changes in the economic basis of life in the Red River area. We know that the impact of Chinese contacts involved more intensive agriculture, and it is not coincidental that the Dong Son ploughshares are not only of Han type, but also restricted to the areas of Southeast Asia which fell under Han control. We know that the Qin and Han rulers were interested in exotic southern products such as ivory and rhinoceros horn, plumage and pearls. Iron was sent in the opposite direction, while salt and slaves were important in the exchange activities. It should not, however, be overlooked that the Red River delta occupied a nodal position in the developing maritime trade with the coastal communities of Southeast Asia, India and beyond even to the eastern provinces of the Roman Empire. Wang (1958) has traced the history of the so-called Nanhai (southern sea) trade. Essentially, the great expansion of the Chinese Empire brought a new order of demands for goods. Particularly during periods of relative peace, this exposed the indigenous societies of coastal Southeast Asia to a concept of extraction and trade radically distinct from that described above for the autonomous, ranked communities or even developing chiefdoms.

Even if no documentary sources had survived, the major changes described above would have been evident from the archaeological record. Any further increase in our appreciation of the period of Chinese expansion is far more likely to come from the archaeological than the documentary sources. We have seen that the expansion of the Chinese empire had a growing impact on the Dong Son chiefdoms of the Red and Ma river valleys. There is evidence for such contact in the later graves of the Dong Son cultural phase, in the form of Chinese artefacts. Janse (1958), for example, found in prehistoric grave number 2, both Chinese coins and beads made of glass and carnelian. His tomb number 1 contained a bronze vase with tripod feet and ringed handles of Chinese inspiration. The great boat coffin from Viet Khe near Haiphong was richly endowed with Chinese bronze vessels and arms, while the Red and Ma valleys have yielded numerous Han type ploughshares, crossbow bolts and trigger mechanisms and axe-halberds.

The Dong Son burial rite centred on inhumation, sometimes in a coffin, in association with pottery vessels, bronze artefacts and jewellery which was often exotic, such as glass and carnelian. Some graves were particularly rich and surely house the Lac aristocrats themselves. This ritual changed markedly, and the available chronological evidence points to a date later than the punitive campaign of Ma Yuan. The new burial rite involved the construction of a brick-chambered tomb under an earth mound. These were grouped together so as to form a necropolis. The first such chambered tomb was investigated in 1896 (Parmentier 1917) at Ke-noi, just outside Hanoi. The tomb comprised five chambers, but it had been looted in antiquity and little remained within. The scattered finds were nevertheless interesting. They included a bronze spearhead and part of a clay house model. The provision of such models is a characteristic of Han tombs in China. Further tombs were reported in the vicinity of Quang Yen, northeast of Haiphong, while another from Phau Thau was found intact. It was a far simpler structure than the example from Ke-noi, comprising but two chambers. Grave goods included Chinese coins, a Han-style bronze bowl and several pottery vessels. The example from Nghi Ve is particularly impressive, having a whole series of underground chambers and niches. The most complete survey of Han dynasty tombs was undertaken by Janse (1947) in the years preceding the second world war. In all, he identified thirteen groups, and excavated numerous individual burials. Although no structure approaches that from Ke-noi in complexity of design, the rich burial offerings in the few intact tombs reveal how the Han-Viet were prepared to invest much energy and wealth in burying the dead. The tumuli average 20 by 17.5 metres and some still stand to a height of 2-3 metres. The chambers were constructed of brick which was locally made and often decorated. No complete skeletons have survived, but fragments of wood in some graves suggest the use of wooden coffins. It may be that the acidic soil has destroyed human remains, but it is also possible that bodies were ultimately removed to China for interment.

Most of the grave structures comprised two chambers, one for the burial and the smaller one for placing the grave goods. The most impressive necropolis was found in the vicinity of Lach Truong. This site is located east of Thanh Hoa, and the river estuary there is still a haven for coastal shipping.

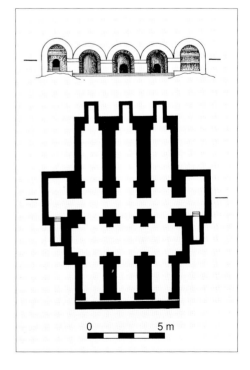

The Han Chinese introduced their own style of burial into Bac Bo, which involved subterranean brick chambers complete with objects owned by the dead. This particularly impressive example comes from Nghi Ve.

0   5 m

Bronze drums were the icon of the rich Dong Son chiefdoms of the Red River valley. With incorporation of their land into the Han Empire, their power rapidly waned.
(Rachaburi National Museum)

Janse (1947) has suggested that it was formerly a Han port, a situation which might explain the variety and richness of the grave furniture. There is a great variety of pottery vessels, some of which are glazed. Glazing was not practiced in prehistoric Southeast Asia, and the technology of closed kiln firing to sustain a high temperature over a lengthy period of time was one of the technological innovations introduced into the area by the Han. Jars, cups and tripod-based bowls were used in cooking and eating, but pottery lamps and incense burners also represent a departure from the styles and techniques employed by the Dong Son potters. One tray from Lach Truong burial 1 is particularly interesting. Its central motif is of Chinese inspiration, comprising three fishes with heads touching. Yet it also bears a design of circles linked by tangents, a traditional design of the local bronzesmiths.

The few intact burials have revealed a wealth of bronze objects, but very little iron. The bronzes are in stark contrast to those from late Dong Son burials. The manufacture of the decorated drums and situlae were replaced by a range of artefacts imported from China, or at least inspired by Chinese prototypes. The clearest evidence of Chinese inspiration lies in the strings of coins, many of which were minted during the rule of the usurper Wang Mang (AD 9-23). These coins must be earlier than the burials, but by how much is hard to ascertain. Indeed, such coins are still to be seen in Viet Nam, where they are used as good-luck charms. The bronze tripods, vases and kettles all reveal Han inspiration, but, again, there are some novel bronzes which suggest that the heirs to the Dong Son bronzesmiths remained active. The bronze lamp from tomb 3 at Lach Truong is of particular interest. It is dominated by a human figure which is not Chinese. He wears a necklace and bracelets, while there are dwarves on his knees playing musical instruments. Three branches are also embellished with small figures of musicians, each holding a lamp. Two lamps take the form of a chicken and the other, of a dragon. The provision of oil-burning lamps in Han China was a widespread practice, but this particular lamp owes as much to local and Indian inspiration as to Chinese.

Metallic decorated mirrors, bells and belt hooks are of more obvious Han origin, while the rare weapons include Han crossbow triggers and axe-halberds. The impact of the Han technology is also seen in the rare survival of lacquer work and the wrapping of some grave goods in silk cloth. Personal jewellery included beads made from glass, amber, carnelian, agate and rock crystal. Occasionally, too, Janse discovered jade or jade-like split rings which have a wide distribution in late prehistoric contexts. Indeed, some have been found in the Dong Son burials.

Clay house models are particularly interesting, because they provide some insight into domestic architecture. It is evident that security was considered necessary because the domestic quarters were ringed by a single or double wall. In the latter cases, the area between the walls provided accommodation for animals and, perhaps, slaves. The walls provided foundations for a house of one or two stories, access being gained by a removable wooden staircase. Roofs were probably constructed of thatch or split bamboo, kept in place by wooden ridge poles. The walled enclosures also contained miniature ovens with cooking pots in place, together with a well. One example from Tho-Dai contained a miniature conical granary. The design of such house compounds contrasts markedly with the pile dwellings depicted on the earlier Dong Son drums.

Lach Truong is one of the most impressive of the Han-Viet cemeteries in Jiujen commandery. It comprises approximately 30 tumuli, located on a plain of the Linh Truong Giang River, about 5 km from the present coast. Janse has excavated 27 tombs, the mounds of which varied in length between 10-35 metres. Only tombs 3 and 4 were found intact, so the information which the tomb group once contained has been largely lost. The two undisturbed examples reveal considerable grave wealth. One comprised three compartments under a 35-metre long mound. The archway leading from the 'chapel' into the mortuary chamber proper covered the bronze lamp already described. The chapel also housed several other bronze receptacles including a jar and a basin containing a bowl. One bronze bottle was still partially covered by silk material. Unfortunately the coffin and human remains have not survived, but the mortuary chamber contained an iron sword, some carnelian beads and three bronze cymbals, and the remains of red lacquer. The third chamber also housed two bronze kettles and a number of pottery containers including a steamer for cooking. The excavator suggested that these vessels had formerly been placed on wooden shelves, and fell when the wood decayed.

The mound of burial 4 measured 25 by 17 m, and was probably terraced into two tiers. The brick structure had three chambers on a brick pavement, and was found intact. The central mortuary chamber did not contain a coffin, but that from burial 8 did reveal one, made from a tree trunk and measuring 2.75 by 0.60 metres. The burial 4 mortuary chamber contained an iron cauldron, two bronze bowls, two sets of Han coins, a disc-shaped mirror and a bronze bird-headed handle to a cane. The bird in question is probably a pigeon, symbol of longevity. One antechamber contained 36 complete pots, and the other revealed an iron lamp, and more ceramic jars and vases.

Bim-Son is a second major necropolis. It comprised 15 mounds of which tomb 1A was undisturbed. In this case, two human tibiae indicated that the human remains had not been disturbed or removed in antiquity. The funerary remains were rich and Janse has suggested that they were the possessions of a military mandarin. An iron sword with a blade 1.25 metres long, in an iron scabbard, was a prominent item among the grave goods. It was associated with an iron dagger as if they made a set. The scabbard was embellished with an applied jade ornament. Bronzes included bowls, a belt hook and mirror, and a bronze tripod-bowl with handles and a decorated lid.

The distribution of these Han-Viet tumuli reveals a preference for lowland tracts of good agricultural land and waterways. It is unfortunate that so little archaeological attention has been paid to the settlements which presumably existed in the vicinity of the burial grounds. The potential of settlement archaeology is only too obviously

Inscriptions are a vital source of information on the Cham civilisation. This example comes from My Son.
(Courtesy Paisarn Piemmattawat)

shown by the recent excavations at Co Loa. These revealed, as should be expected for a third century BC foundation, Dong Son-style pottery under the middle rampart. Within this enceinte, excavations also uncovered a magnificent Dong Son-drum which contained over one hundred bronze ploughshares, while a cache of Han style triple-barbed arrowheads was found outside the ramparts. The very kilns which were used to fire the tiles, bricks, glazed pottery and house models which were used in the construction and embellishment of the tombs are of equal interest. Tam Tho Phu comprised a mound 37 by 34 metres in extent which covered the remains of a brick kiln. It was among the vast quantity of wasters from this enclosed kiln that Janse (1951) identified parts of miniature houses as well as glazed ceramics and even spindle whorls and net weights. Some of the roof tiles bore imprints of the Chinese characters for 'long life' and 'joy'.

The real turning point in the Chinese contacts with their three southern commanderies of Jiaozhi, Jiujen and Rinan came with the campaigns of Ma Yuan. The imposition of Han adminstration changed the basis of land tenure and the emasculation of the Lac aristocrats described in the surviving literature and Vietnamese folklore is confirmed by archaeological investigations. Henceforth, events in Bac Bo were greatly influenced by political events in China. The imposition of the Chinese commanderies on indigenous chiefdoms cannot have failed to have an impact on the inhabitants of adjacent territory.

The Formative Stage of Southeast Asian Civilisation: A Review

Our sources for the consideration of rising cultural complexity in Southeast Asia comprise Chinese texts, Indian tales, inscriptions and the evidence of archaeology. The Chinese documents are a vital source, but must be treated judiciously. Most references passed through several hands before being set down, since the earliest documents have perished. Moreover, they were made by travellers or, more often, Chinese scholars residing in China and imbuing their words with distinctive prejudices and expectations. Distinguishing reality from preconception is not easy under such circumstances. Indian sources are less demanding in the sense that they are not intended as historic documents, but are rather a mixture of legends and tales. Inscriptions are a major source, but, again, must be handled with circumspection not least because the rulers who had them inscribed and set in place may well have had in mind the projection of an image rather than the description of historic fact. Thus the conquest of a region by an outstandingly potent overlord may in reality have been no more than a face-saving raid. If we are ever to come close to appreciating the processes involved in state formation in Southeast Asia, the only way open is to expand greatly our knowledge gained from archaeology. Sadly, archaeological information is partial in coverage, contextual control and quality of publication. This situation has caused Wheatley (1983) to adopt the pessimistic stance that the data to hand prejudice a proper consideration of state formation. This is a valid standpoint, but it should also be stressed that archaeological information is steadily accumulating while theoretical approaches are now more sophisticated than when Cœdès (1968) assembled his comprehensive analysis of the Indianised states of Southeast Asia.

Much of our knowledge of early states in Southeast Asia comes from inscriptions, such as this Angkorian period example from Wat Enkosei at Angkor. It was placed at the entrance to the temple.

Among the most critical advances has been a clearer understanding of the cultures of Southeast Asia prior to Indian and Chinese contact. The traditional view arose in the context of a pessimistic if not patronising view of indigenous culture, associated with a paucity of information. This view held that Indian expansion encountered a stone-age society of little complexity. Within this framework, such innovations as metallurgy were late and derivative, and the acceptance of Indian religious and political ideas was passive and inevitable, just as blotting paper absorbs water. A contribution of recent archaeological research has been to establish, beyond reasonable doubt, the existence of village communities in the major river valleys whose subsistence included rice cultivation. From at least 2300 BC, these village communities participated in an exchange network which saw exotic goods change hands over many hundreds of kilometres. It has already been suggested that this exchange of exotic goods reflects flexible lineage ranking within autonomous village communities. These people had been familiar with bronze working for at least 1,000 years before the first Indian contact. The settlement data support the hypothesis that there was a trend towards centralisation during the

Iron Age (500 BC-AD 400), which involved certain centres expanding significantly in area relative to others.

These chiefdoms were, to various degrees, participants in an expanding maritime exchange network. This, the 'Southern Silk Route', involved the Roman Empire to the west, and the Chinese Empire to the east. Inhabitants of the Mekong Delta, peninsular Thailand and Malaysia, the coast of Viet Nam and the Chao Phraya Valley all had the opportunity to profit from such maritime trade. As it happens, these areas of extensive, flat and deeply-flooded deltas and river valleys were those most susceptible to agricultural intensification given adequate technology and labour. Those occupying the interior plains of the middle Mekong and Khorat plateau were also early participants but at second hand, and they, too, occupied tracts of land which favoured agricultural intensification.

It has been shown that Indian religion, architecture, scripts and the Sanskrit language were incorporated into the indigenous cultures. This occurred among Mon speakers in the Chao Phraya Valley, Khmer speakers of the middle and lower Mekong and the speakers of Cham in central coastal Viet Nam. Moreover, the earliest phases of this phenomenon have been identified in areas which controlled the coastline, with later manifestations in the plains of the middle Mekong and river valleys of the Khorat plateau. In early views of state formation, this evidence for Indian influence, allied to the notion of a passively receptive Neolithic populace, made the process so obvious as to discount the need for explanation. The Indian colonialist and Indianisation models are no longer tenable. A more sophisticated and scrupulously-documented model has recently been advanced by Wheatley (1983). He stressed the acceptance of Hinduism by the later prehistoric chiefly elite as an important factor in the intensification and reinforcement of centralisation. He sees this move to a self-identification with Shiva of the emergent ruler, Wolter's 'Man of Prowess', as an expedient which enhanced the ruler's own sanctity and thereby affirmed his grip on power (Wolters 1979). Early evidence for this comes from the inscriptions of Bhadravarman of Champa. Vyadhapura, the city of the hunter, was a major centre of Funan. The hunter in question was Shiva. Wheatley does not discount other inputs. In his own words, it is not improbable: "that the settlements of Ksatriyan adventurers and their followers and the trading factories of merchant corporations played a part in this transformation" (Wheatley 1983: 296). But he favours a primary role for Shaivism, and in stressing the term *nagara* in the very title of his book, sees the emergent city as a symbolic and ritual centre above all else.

The view adopted here differs from that advocated by Wheatley, in that it views the millennium spanning the later prehistoric to early state formation as a continuum, and the Indian presence as but one of several variables whose successive conditions reflect their mutual interplay. This approach is influenced by the results of recent examples of growing cultural complexity under conditions which resemble those inferred for Southeast Asia. Let us consider three of these. The first occurred during the 19th century in the Malagasy

Republic, and has been described by Bloch (1977). It is a particularly relevant example, because it is concerned with Austronesian speakers who grew rice. The principal points are these. The Merina occupied a terrain characterised by hills, restricted valleys and marshland. Rice cultivation in valleys entailed the diversion of water into small-scale terraced fields. Land was owned by descent groups or 'demes'. These were endogomous, and concerned to retain land tenure. Valley-wide decisions were taken by a consensus of elders. These cultivators were subjected to predatory and opportunistic bands of brigands who occupied defended hilltops and exacted tribute in the form of rice. Bloch calls these 'pre take-off states'. The ruler was not involved in agriculture other than as a predator.

In contrast, 'take off-states' were those wherein the military brigand took an active role in rice agriculture. This involved marsh drainage, a task requiring a major input of labour for the excavation of dykes. The result was greatly increased output, and a move from the fortified hilltops to the plains adjacent to the reclaimed marsh. Increased production went directly to the king, who was able to sustain his followers. Labour was supplied as corvée (four days labour per week is the quoted figure), or by taking slaves. The latter required predatory wars and therefore, a well-supplied army. Such take-off states engendered rivalry and war. They tended to be transient. That of King Andrianimpoinimerina, however, involved durability and a massive expansion of territory, because the king had preferred access to European trade goods and, not least, to firearms with which to equip his army. Therefore the cycle of slave wars leading to marsh irrigation to provide food for the maintenance of the army was secured. Growth was very rapid, but the variables were inter-dependent, and contact with an expanding but on this occasion, European state was one of several critical elements.

Ekholm (1977) has considered the effect of exotic prestige goods in a second African context. She prefaced her review by stressing that "In Central Africa, power relations are established, consolidated and maintained through the control of prestige articles". These are, she asserts "absolutely indispensable for the maintenance of social relations". This situation reflects the use of rare prestige valuables in various rites of passage, for example, in the payment of bride price and appropriate recognition of status in mortuary practices. A chief who controlled the source of prestige goods, which in Central Africa included copper, salt and shells, also controls a source of power. Such goods can be invested in people as retainers and followers at the expense of peripheral groups, thereby attracting more people and increasing demands on food production. The arrival of a new source of prestige goods can have a double effect. First, if their acquisition and disposal is restricted to the chief, then his prestige is enhanced. Moreover, the exchange of local products for the prestige goods places a further call on intensified production, be it for agricultural products, raw materials, manufactured goods or slaves. Indeed, the slave trade exercised a considerable impact on the development of complex society by emphasising the distributional role of strategically-placed chiefs. A corollary to the new supply is that peripheral chiefs may develop their own source and thereby out-flank and rival their former superiors. This possibility encourages the coercive expansion of the area ruled by the senior line.

The third instance of growing cultural complexity has been reported by Alpers (1969) for the Yao. This group occupies an inland tract of East Africa in Malawi. Traditionally, life centred on the village led by the headman. Kinship was matrilineal and the social core of each village was a set of sisters whose oldest brother was the headman. The power of each headman was determined by the size of his village, but set against his ambition to increase numbers was a tendency for fission as younger brothers or maternal nephews to the headman moved off to found their own villages. Therefore, villages rarely exceeded 10-15 huts sheltering 50 or 60 people.

This mould, however, could be broken by attracting followers other than matrilineal kinsmen. Yet how were followers lured to one leader and not another? One way was to display outstanding leadership skills as a hunter. Another was to control trade, and particularly the trading caravans to the coast. The export commodities began with ivory and soon incorporated slaves. The Swahili and Arab traders on the coast supplied in return, beads, cloth and salt. This trade was controlled by the headman-chief. He had the usufruct of one tusk from each elephant killed in his territory, and the duty to bless the departing caravan in the name of the ancestors. On the caravan's return, he had the prerogative to distribute the cloth, brass wire and beads to his followers. With the accumulated goods at his disposal, the chief was able to purchase slaves, with a preference for females whom he could marry and thus increase his followers. The point about slave wives was that the children remained his own and were not able to depart to found a new village under a younger leader. It is recorded that the great chief Mataka I Nyambi (*c.* 1800-1876 to 9) accumulated 600 slaves in this manner.

The career of this king is worth recounting. Frustrated by life in a village controlled by his grandmother, he set out to found his own. There, he and his followers wove baskets, which they exchanged for iron hoes. These were in turn exchanged for slaves. When he had sufficient warriors, he began raiding to augment the number of slaves. His prowess attracted numerous followers to his capital at Mwembe. When he died, he was buried with 30 youths and 30 girls along with their guns and large quantities of beads, cloth and salt. By that time, Mwembe had grown to incorporate at least one thousand houses. Such a concentration required increased production of food, and in the 1860s, Livingstone described spring-fed irrigation channels feeding terraced fields and cassava even being cultivated on narrow ridges on the town's thoroughfares. It had been traditional practice to level a house and move on the occupant's death. At Mwembe a new house was built nearby and the levelled ground laid down to crops.

Mataka did not maintain a standing army because all men were warriors. He did, however, appoint administrators for his trade caravans, and disposed of power by the ownership of guns obtained by coastal trade. As head of the lineage, he attracted deference through his proximity to the ancestors, but this only applied to his own relatives. Therefore, we find his successor, Mataka II Nyenje (*c.* 1876 to 1885) appointing his heirs and cousins to rule over dependent villages within his chiefdom. This ruler employed Arabs as scribes, and was converted to Islam. On his death, he was interred under the verandah of the mosque at Mwembe. Mataka I and II were not the only great territorial chiefs who rose to prominence with their growing control over coastal trade. Makanjila was another, and he followed his military and trading success by adopting Arab ways. Livingstone noted that his followers planted coconuts round a lake to imitate the vegetation of the coast, and built *dhows* after the Arab fashion. An English visitor to the capital in 1877 was able to converse with Makanjila in Swahili, and noted that lessons were being given on the Koran. The chief's residence copied the coastal architectural style. Fourteen years later a raid on his house yielded several boxes containing letters in Swahili and Arabic. Like Mataka, Makanjila was converted to Islam. A third chief, Monjesa, adopted Islam in about 1880 and changed his name to the Arab Zuraf.

The importance of these three examples drawn from the period of European and Arab expansion along the African coast, is that it allows us to grasp the interplay between several aspects of behaviour over time. The significant variables began with the tension between expansive and fissioning tendencies in autonomous village communities. Men of prowess broke the impasse by building up a group of followers. This was achieved through success in war and trade. Trade goods gave emergent chiefs added scope to attract retainers, and the larger settlements which followed required agricultural intensification. Territorial chiefs increased their standing by adopting the styles and customs of the Swahili and Arab coastal traders. They adopted writing, Islam and its religious architecture.

The African experience has been lucidly summarised by Goody (1971). Centralisation of power and authority are, in his view, related to several variables. Foremost is control of the means of destruction, which in turn provides for the maintenance of peaceful conditions necessary for long-term trade to prosper. Such trade is a source for the extraction of taxes for the central authority. Within this context, control of the source of weapons, or of iron and iron workers, or the horse, are seen as crucial. Now the control over sea-borne foreign traders operating through entrepôts is very much easier to achieve than the more diffuse continental exchange with fewer fixed nodes. Indeed, the Ashanti and Dahomey refused to countenance the passage of guns across their territory since to do so would have allowed possession of force to pass into the hands of their neighbours. These rulers were able to centralise and concentrate power, therefore, by establishing a fort with a magazine of guns and paid marksmen. Such a state of affairs bears profound implications when we turn to Southeast Asia.

In Eastern and Central Africa and in Malagasy, the incorporation of novel goods into an existing system was an important variable in the generation of new social forms. What is needed is a general model for such growing complexity as an exploratory framework for reviewing the Southeast Asian data. Such a general framework has been formulated and applied to the development of complex society in the Aegean area by Renfrew (1972). His scheme isolated the component parts of cultural and environmental systems, and mapped their interactions through time. This identified as crucial the multiplier effect, that is the way in which change in one aspect of behaviour promotes and is in turn affected by change in another.

The brief excursion into Africa no less than earlier application of the systems approach, stress the importance of weighing general aspects of behaviour and identifying interactions between them. The rise of the Merina state for example, involved intensified agriculture, exchange with Europeans, slave raids, appropriation of surpluses and personal ambition. It would be absurd to promote one as any more or less significant than another. In his application of the multiplier effect, Renfrew (1984) isolated a specific example and considered it within the general model. We shall now do the same for Southeast Asia.

The initial or starting conditions for the development of states are not clearly defined. Indeed, the period 500 BC-AD 400 is one of the most important but until recently, the least-known periods of Southeast Asian prehistory. Recent excavations at Noen U-Loke have been illuminating, and current research at Angkor Borei and Oc Eo promise to add further vital information. Noen U-Loke is unique in providing a sequence of mortuary, industrial and residential remains which cover the entire period of the Iron Age. Even during its early phases, some individuals were interred with considerable mortuary ritual, but the major changes took place during the period between AD 1-400. We find a significant increase in the energy expended in interring individuals of high status, whose grave offerings included unprecedented quantities of bronze ornaments as well as gold, silver, agate, carnelian and glass jewellery, associated with clay coffins filled with burnt rice. These interments were contemporary with an increase in iron weaponry, the production of salt on an industrial scale, the application of iron to agricultural efficiency and the construction of encircling walls round settlements which enclosed and controlled the flow of water.

These changes took place as the occupants of the Mekong Delta were developing exchange relations with exotic offshore traders. If it is the case that for at least two millennia and possibly much longer, status was signified by the ownership and disposal of exotic goods, then the impact of a new source must become an important variable in our attempt at explanation. This takes several forms. First, the source was unequal in availability and gave a major advantage to communities most able to attract and control the purveyors of new rarities. Those occupying trans-peninsula or coastal-estuarine situations would have been particularly favoured. Second, the new commercial contacts involved two-way exchange. Local products were exchanged, and through their demands, initiated intensified acquisition of goods which were often not immediately available in the coastal areas. We might, therefore, expect the impact of coastal exchange to have a ripple effect deep into the interior. Indians brought not only exotic goods made of glass and carnelian, but also exotic religions and notions of kingship. One particularly favoured area was the flood plain of the lower Mekong. The land is flat and regularly flooded but with appropriate drainage, rice cultivation is possible. It is well placed to control the flow of goods into the Mekong Valley, but is itself devoid of iron, many of the precious or semi-precious stones and spices which are strong candidates as items increasingly in demand.

No preference is given to a particular variable in accounting for the change which witnessed the development of the Funan state. Rather, different aspects of behaviour are reviewed in conjunction. With reference to socio-political change, it is argued that the advent of a new range of exotic goods provided local leaders with the means of controlling access to status. Their chance to control the concentration and export of slaves, food, spices and gold provided a gateway to attracting and sustaining followers. A further means of augmenting control over status goods was to manufacture them locally, an activity documented at Oc Eo. This entailed the sustenance of specialist craftsmen. The concentration of followers had its impact on the food supply. Intensification of production was necessary, and this was assisted by the excavation of drainage canals. To judge from Kang Dai's account of his visit to Funan, by the 3rd century the ruler Fan Shih-man was engaged in sea-borne raids to enlarge his domain. This is to be expected, and may well have been, in part at least, an attempt to secure a monopoly over the supply of novel prestige goods which were now reaching Southeast Asia in growing quantities. It is interesting to note that his ambitions were directed towards coastal areas like his own rather than inland. We owe a debt to the Chinese sources for confirming a further prediction, that the ruler's sons were despatched to rule over the new dependencies. The clearest evidence for galvanizing corvée or slave labour to the interests of the state is to be seen in the extensive network of canals which crossed Funan. These certainly linked major settlements, but were also probably excavated to facilitate drainage, thereby intensifiying rice production. Nor should one overlook the extent of the moats and defences of Oc Eo, and the large brick structure which was built in its central area. Such an investment in agricultural and defensive works recalls the concern for augmenting production which characterises the rise of the Merina state in 19th century.

It is also illuminating to find that one of the few Funanese inscriptions, albeit rather late in the period, describes how Gunavarman, the son of the king, was responsible for the reclamation of marshland. It is noted that thus far, the role played by Indians themselves is restricted to the supply of prestige valuables to the Funanese aristocrats. The immediate impact on local societies may well have been as a catalyst, but, naturally, the Indian presence would have played a more direct and positive role with time. Among the principal adoptions are numbered the writing system, political philosophy and, perhaps most significant, the Hindu religion. It is here argued that the development of complexity witnessed archaeologically in the Funanese cities and canals is most logically conceived as a process in a particularly favoured area, within a local cultural matrix to which the development of exchange relations with India contributed.

The early role played by the adoption of kingship manifested through Hindu court ritual is hard to define. Wheatley (1983) elevates it to a position of central, almost seminal importance. It is not denied that it played a positive role in the projection of elevated status and in binding aristocrats to the centre through shared devotion to Shiva. Vickery's analysis of the Khmer language inscriptions, however, reveals the robust continuation of local gods, and the prominence of revering the ancestors. These have led him to describe Indian influence as an Indic veneer.

We should not be deluded by Chinese references to a state of Chenla. Wolters (1974) and Dupont (1943-6) have both shown convincingly that hegemony over most Chenla centres was the exception rather than the rule, and may have been achieved only briefly under Ishanavarman and more firmly by his great grandson Jayavarman I. Otherwise, the inscriptions rather favour the presence of competing regional states, at times asserting their independence and, at others, prepared or required to accept a tributary relationship. We can discern glimmerings through the inscriptions, of the existence of dynasties and of shifting alliances.

The events which have survived in Chinese accounts and local inscriptions must be weighed within a geographic framework. Funan was coastal, and favourably situated for maritime exchange. The presence of complex chiefdoms in the Mekong Valley as trade increased meant that state formation was very rapid. In the Malagasy context, the process took only a generation or two. The effect on the chiefdoms which occupied the interior, that is the margins of the Mekong above Phnom Penh, must have been considerable. Increased trade meant that those strategically placed could combine the control of exotic goods with intensified agricultural and industrial production. Those occupying the Stung Treng area entered into exchange relations with coastal Viet Nam and the Delta. The early Khmer structures in Chantaburi also show expansion to the coast in a westerly direction. An inscription from Chantaburi also records the foundations of a temple by Ishanavarman (Cœdès 1924). The Mun Valley chiefs could have enriched themselves by the production of salt and iron, as well as control of the riverine exchange route.

The demise of Funan occurred as the Mekong Delta was by-passed by Chinese trade vessels. However, the chiefs of the Mekong Valley, whose wealth was agrarian, continued to prosper. At least one aristocratic line served both the last Funan ruler and a new overlord in the interior. There are reasonable grounds for supposing that Funan was, for three or four centuries, a major trading state. Archaeologically, the extensive canal system, the large defended centres of Oc Eo and Angkor Borei, and intensive production sustain such a conclusion. In terms of Chinese documents, we learn of taxation, large military expeditions and the exchange of embassies. The evidence for Chenla favours multiple centres, at least one of which saw state formation under Jayavarman I. It was a period of militarism, punctuated with bids for overlordship. Centres such as Ishanapura housed monumental religious structures and a royal palace, together with brahmans, bureaucrats, and armed retainers. The rulers wore rare, prestigious goods, and were personally identified with the cult of Shiva. But Ishanapura was not a durable capital of the state of Chenla. Ishanavarman may have achieved a brief hegemony over other centres, but the pattern perceived from inscriptions was of competition and warfare between the regions.

Within such a framework, possessing Shiva's favour and exalted ancestry were advantageous. It is significant that much energy was expended in the construction of temples in permanent materials to advertise the rulers' identification with Shiva and the ancestors, and that resources were allocated to embellish and endow the foundations with land, livestock and officiants. Being the favoured protégé of the god, as well as being the object of brahmanic consecration, doubtless enhanced a ruler's hold on loyalty. But there were other variables as well, and they have no less significance. One was the need to back spiritual authority with military prowess, men and arms. The physical projection of religious pre-eminence was the temple, which required artisans and functionaries. Both necessitated raw materials and agricultural surpluses. The regional rivalries fed on competition, and its fabric comprised many strands: there was competition for land, strategic dominance, religious sanctity, for labour and raw materials.

Naturally, the Chenla of Chinese accounts exhibits its own specific properties, not least the incorporation of the Hindu religion as an element in dominance strategies. The extensive documentary and epigraphic evidence for this adoption of Indian religious and political systems has laid a false scent: it has in some respects, made it seem necessary only to account for why the natives became 'Indianised' in order to understand the origin of Southeast Asian statehood. It is argued that the development of inland agrarian states involved the interplay of several variables, We need to trace the changing settlement patterns, extent and intensity of exchange in prestige goods between major centres and peripheries, excavation within centres to illuminate the spatial layout of structures and trace through the defensive works and buildings, the date and duration of occupation. The techniques for recovering the economic, social and technological data are available. Most of all, it is crucial to view the cultural changes in the middle-lower Mekong as part of a continuum rooted in the prehistoric past. 'Indianisation', the adoption of the Hindu religion, was not forced on the local inhabitants, it was one of several variables with adaptive potential for change in the local system. The changes which occurred, underwritten as they were by the expansion of rice cultivation, were directed towards intensificaton and competition within the polities we know of as Chenla.

One of the most interesting aspects of Southeast Asia during the first millennium AD, is that intensification akin to that considered in the middle and lower Mekong occurred in the Chao Phraya Valley and coastal plains of Viet Nam among people with different languages. We have seen that the vernacular language of Chenla was Khmer. In the Chao Phraya, it was Mon and in the coastal tract of

Viet Nam, Cham. Despite such discontinuity in language and culture, there is evidence that similar variables were involved in the pattern of growing cultural complexity. In the Chao Phraya Valley, the dominant settlements and largest monumental structures are found round the margins of the Gulf of Siam. We lack the epigraphic evidence to ascertain whether the defended sites were at any stage foci of small, separate states, but the logic of attaining regional hegemony was great, as it would have provided the paramount with control over the resources of the entire area and concentrate wealth derived from exchange. As yet, however, we lack the textual, epigraphic and archaeological information necessary to consider in more detail, how the variables interacted.

The Cham-speaking area of coastal Viet Nam presents some interesting contrasts with the lower Mekong, which warn against employing the well known Chenla and Funan experience as typical. Thus the northern Cham area was exposed to direct military threat from China and, indeed, suffered a series of major punitive campaigns. The long, narrow coastal strip meant that no lowland area was precluded from early contact with the coastal traffic in prestige goods of distant origin. We are not yet equipped to consider events there in any detailed way. It is, however, true that urban architecture and military techniques were early influenced by Chinese practices, and that the identification of local rulers with Shiva, as in the case of Bhadravarman, occurred surprisingly early. A local variation of some importance was probably speed of communication by ship. Supremacy in naval warfare, and the rapid transport of armed retainers by sea, may well have been instrumental in securing control over the long coastline. Naturally, monopoly over dues imposed on the merchants plying the route from Funan to South China would have concentrated considerable wealth in the overlord's hands. To judge from the weight of booty allegedly taken by the Chinese, a proportion of such wealth was employed, as in Chenla, to project the king as an embodiment of Shiva and at the same time, of exalted ancestry.

Vietnamese was already spoken in Bac Bo when Chinese expansion reached south. The incorporation of the Dong Son culture into the Han Empire represents a quite different course towards complexity than the more internally-generated developments to the south and south-west. The archaeological record for the last three or four centuries BC reveals an aristocratic chiefdom in which the Lac Lords held preferential land rights and may already have engaged in intensified agriculture by utilising flood waters generated by tidal flows. These aristocrats were incorporated into the Han bureaucratic machine, but tribute payments were now diverted towards the Chinese state or to local functionaries. Agricultural intensification under the Han probably involved the introduction of the plough. The Han had by then, also developed the inundation technique of wet rice cultivation, and this, together with transplanting rice from seed beds, may have been introduced as well. This most productive technique for expanding the area under agriculture and maximising returns is now employed across lowland Southeast Asia. After the campaign of

Ma Yuan in response to the Trung sisters' insurrection, Han administration became markedly more rigorous and extractive.

Early States: Summary

Relevant and available data for a consideration of rising cultural complexity reveal and patterned interaction between certain variables. The point of departure is the existence in the early 1st millennium BC of independent village communities engaged in the exchange of prestige goods, and within which there was lineage ranking. There followed the development of differentially large centres which represent chiefdoms. At this juncture, the last few centuries BC, increased maritime exchange was at its most effective in certain strategic coastal tracts which provided the opportunity for agricultural intensification and control over riverine routes to the interior plains or mountain passes. The coastal chiefs of the lower Mekong were particularly well placed to take advantage of the new trading opportunities. They were able to accumulate and distribute novel prestige goods and commence local manufacture. Three variables were soon manifest: concentration of population in large centres, agricultural intensification by draining marshland and warfare for territorial expansion and the accumulation of slaves. Conquered land was placed under the relatives of this expanding state. The overlords also adopted the Indian script, titles and the Hindu religion. Their polity was known to the Chinese as Funan. We can detect similar changes in Champa and the Chao Phraya area.

Initially, the interior chiefdoms of the middle Mekong had restricted or second-hand access to the coastal trade and associated religious and political changes. Caught up in a situation of rivalry and emulation, they developed alternative routes via Chantaburi and across the Truong Son passes to Champa. Those to whom iron was readily available, who controlled tracts of good rice land and trade routes, not least the Mekong Valley itself, were, if ambitious and energetic, able to attract followers. It is also highly likely that the formation of alliances for defence against larger predatory states was highly advantageous. The surviving inscriptions certainly indicate that friction on the northern marches of Funan ensued, and in conjunction with changing maritime trade routes, the delta state waned.

Power then passed into the hands of competing overlords in the interior, some of whom were able to establish hegemony over their rivals. Indentity with Shiva was a selective advantage in this process of domination, and temple-sanctaries were constructed in the ruler's base to emphasise his close affinity with the ancestral gods. Some kings, particularly Jayavarman I, established states with a wide reach. But there were also other politites which sought independence. It was a period of chronic warfare resolved, albeit partially, with the establishment of the great state centred at Angkor in the early 9th century.

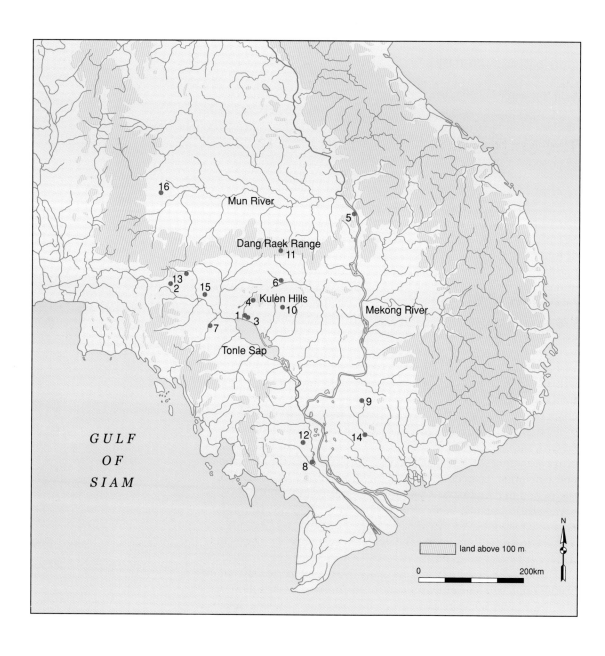

Mun River

Dang Raek Range

Kulen Hills

Mekong River

Tonle Sap

GULF

OF

SIAM

land above 100 m

0   200km

N

Chapter Seven

The State of Angkor, AD 802-1431

The establishment of a grand and long-lasting civilisation centred on the northern shore of the Tonle Sap does not represent a major dislocation with the preceding Chenla period, but rather the fulfillment of the aims of the regional rulers whose inscriptions spoke of political supremacy over wide areas (Jacques and Freeman 1998). All the characteristics of Angkor were previously represented, but they were magnified and given stability through the centralising manipulation of power exercised by a succession of rulers imbued with unusual charisma and prowess. We know of the principal historic events on the basis of the Sanskrit and Khmer inscriptions, accounts written by foreign visitors and the evidence of archaeology. Indeed, the École Française concentrated more of its research upon the epigraphy and archaeology of the monuments of Angkor than on any other topic. The name Angkor is derived from the Sanskrit word *nagara*, meaning Holy City. It is the modern name for the complex of monuments, reservoirs and walls which served as the centre of political influence over large parts of mainland Southeast Asia during the period under review. There were several other major centres but none, apart from brief episodes of civil war between claimants for power, rivalled Angkor. Its original name derives from King Yashovarman (AD 889-*c*. 910), who founded his capital there and named it Yashodharapura.

The six centuries of the Angkorian civilisation are given coherence by the establishment of this political centre. It witnessed numerous building phases instigated by successive sovereigns. These rulers were projected as divine in their inscriptions. A temple was built for the worship of the ruler, whose essence was embodied in a *linga*, a stone phallus which bore his name linked with that of Shiva. Hence, the *linga* of King Jayavarman II was called Jayesvara. It was housed in the central sanctuary which served as a temple-mausoleum for the ruler after his death. These central temples also contained shrines dedicated to the royal ancestors and thus became centres of ancestor worship.

Kingship was a hereditary and divinely-sanctioned office which in theory, devolved on the king's son, known as the *yuvaraja*. In practice, membership of the king's family down to and including the fourth generation qualified a person for the succession, the choice being made by a council of ministers which took account of the dead

Opposite:
The distribution of the principal Angkorian sites mentioned in the text. 1. Angkor, Banteay Choeu, 2. Sdok Kak Thom, 3. Hariharalaya, 4. Rong Chen, 5. Wat Phu, 6. Lingapura, 7. Battambang, 8. Ba Phnom, 9. Banteay Prei Nokor, 10. Preah Khan of Kompong Svay, 11. Preah Vihear, 12. Phnom Chisor, 13 Banteay Chmar, 14. Basak, 15. Phum Snay, 16. Noen U-Loke.

The Kulen upland was considered the sacred source of water for Angkor. It is here visible from the summit of Pre Rup, temple pyramid of Rajendravarman.

king's preference. Succession was, however, never certain and there are numerous references to conflict, not only between members of the inner court, but also involving ambitious aristocrats in the provinces.

The religious focus upon the ancestors linked with devotion to gods from the Indian pantheon represents a central unifying force. This bonding linked the temples, the sustaining communities and the functionaries not only in religious contexts, but also economically and politically. Its physical manifestation is seen not only in the great temple mausolea, but also in the symbolism of the *nagara*, or Holy City. Angkor was, in effect, the representation on earth of Mount Meru, the home of the gods. Anyone equipped with the code for this symbolism would appreciate the passage from earth into heaven.

The Dynasty of Jayavarman II

We do not know who established the first major centre in the region of Angkor. There is some evidence for prehistoric Iron Age occupation, to take advantage of the perennial streams which issue from the Kulen Hills and cross the gently sloping terrain before entering the Great Lake. The earliest rectangular city enclosure is known as Banteay Choeu, with the temple of Ak Yum within. A large part of this city was inundated with the later construction of the Western Baray (reservoir), and the temple was partially covered by the southern retaining wall of the reservoir. Stylistically, it belongs to the late 8th century, and incorporates two re-used inscriptions dated AD 674 and 704. These dates remind us that an inscription of Jayadevi, daughter of Jayavarman I, was found in the region of Angkor. Dated to AD 713, it accords her a divine title previously restricted to gods and men (Vickery 1998), and leaves us in little doubt that the land north of the Great Lake was assuming considerable political importance.

Most texts stress that Jayavarman II, who was not as far as is known a relative of Jayavarman I, was the founder of the civilisation of Angkor. In truth, we know little about this sovereign from contemporary records. Indeed, most information about him comes

from a lengthy inscription found at Sdok Kak Thom inscribed in 1052, about 250 years after the event. The few contemporary texts suggest that Jayavarman II was a leader at a centre known as Vyadhapura, probably the modern Banteay Prei Nokor. This is a very large city demarcated by a wall and exterior moat, and dominated in the centre by a group of brick temples. The Sdok Kak Thom inscription recounts that the young king came from Java, a location which has caused much speculation. Vickery (1998) has convincingly suggested that this name refers to the *Chvea*, or the Chams, who would have been close neighbours at Banteay Prei Nokor. To judge from several later inscriptions set up by a group of aristocratic families, Jayavarman departed from southeastern Cambodia with his

Transplanting rice within Banteay Choeu. The southern dyke of the Western Baray lies in the distance.

Left: Ak Yum is a temple lying within a large enclosure known as Banteay Choeu. It might have been part of an early capital of Jayavarman II.

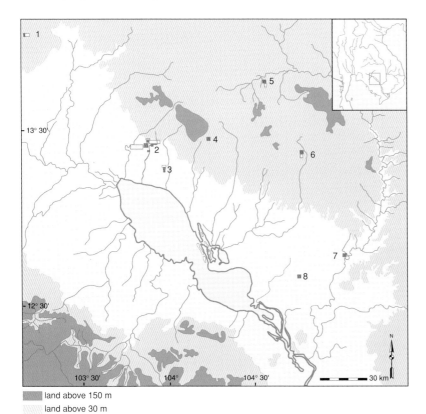

The location of the main sites of Angkor. 1. Banteay Chmar, 2. Angkor, 3. Hariharalaya (the Roluos Group), 4. Beng Mealea, 5. Koh Ker (Lingapura), 6. Preah Khan of Kompong Svay, 7. Ishanapura, 8. Ampil Rolum.

land above 150 m
land above 30 m

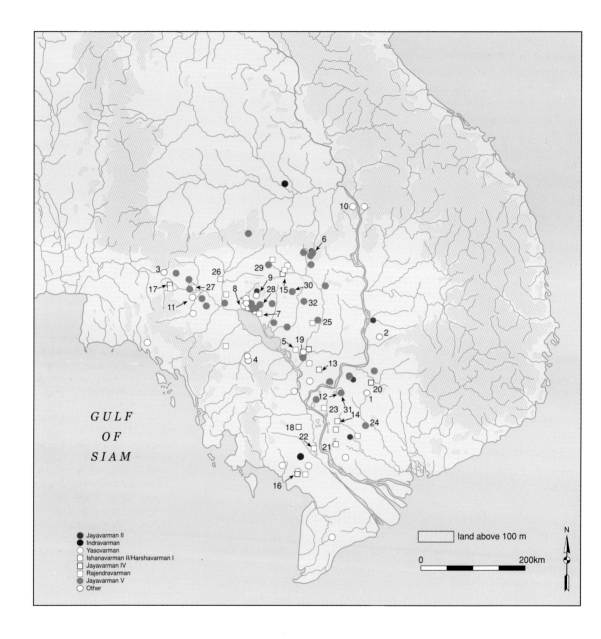

GULF
OF
SIAM

land above 100 m

0   200km

● Jayavarman II
● Indravarman
○ Yasovarman
□ Ishanavarman II/Harshavarman I
□ Jayavarman IV
□ Rajendravarman
● Jayavarman V
○ Other

N

loyal followers and moved progressively towards the northwest. One of his aims might have been to endow his supporters with the rich ricelands of Battambang. Thence, he moved to the northern littoral of the Great Lake, relocating his centre several times from Hariharalaya to Amarendrapura, then up the Kulen Upland and finally, to Hariharalaya again. Tracing these moves archaeologically would be a fascinating exercise. He might have built the brick sanctuaries of Trapeang Phong at Hariharalaya, while there are several early temples beyond and north of the Western Baray which could belong to this episode. The stepped temple of Rong Chen in the Kulen belongs stylistically to this period. It was in that upland that Jayavarman was the centre of a ceremonial consecration in which he was proclaimed the *Chakravartin*, or Universal King. Shadowy as he appears through retrospective inscriptions, Jayavarman II still occupies a central position in the history of Angkor, because he was regarded for centuries after his death as its founder.

Jayavarman II was succeeded by his son of the same name, about whom we know virtually nothing. He was followed by King Indravarman, who was the step cousin once removed of Jayavarman III. Such a remote relationship was compatible with the flexible rules of succession, but to judge from Indravarman's inscriptions, his advent was not peaceful, for "his sword fell upon his enemies, scattering them to all points of the compass". He continued in the former capital of Jayavarman II at Hariharalaya, southeast of Angkor, and was responsible for the construction of a series of temples and a *baray* of unprecedented size and splendour. By abandoning this court, his son ensured the survival of a virtually complete early royal centre to this day. The Indratataka, a central feature of the assemblage, comprised a 3.8 km long bank on an east to west axis with two side banks designed to retain the water brought down from the Kulen uplands by the Roluos River. A contemporary recorded how "he made the Indratataka, mirror of his glory, like the ocean". The water was probably reticulated south to the palace and the two surviving temples, which stand as testament to major architectural advances. Each is surrounded by moats, which in the case of Preah Ko, surround a raised platform which supports six brick shrines. Those on each side of the front row were dedicated to Indravarman's maternal father and grandfather, while the central tower was dedicated to Jayavarman II. Each ancestor's name was linked with that of Shiva. Temples in the second row recalled their respective wives. This conjunction of ancestors with Shiva reflects a cult of royal, deified ancestors which runs throughout the ensuing history of Angkor. Indravarman's inscriptions provide a glimpse of the munificent donations made to the gods: gold and silver vessels, mirrors with gold supports, palanquins, libation vessels, perfumes, fine clothing and the land, workers and animals necessary for the maintenance of the temple and its officiants.

The Bakong temple lies further to the south, and rises above five levels of stone masonry within a moated enclosure. Access incorporated a bridge flanked by sacred *nagas*, snakes which linked

A gilded bronze palanquin fitting gives some idea of the skill of the Angkorian bronze caster. (Height 25 cm).

Opposite:
The distribution of inscriptions for the dynasty of Jayavarman II. 1. Banteay Prei Nokor, 2. Lobok Srot, 3. Sdok Kak Thom, 4. Palhal, 5. Thvar Kdei, 6. Prasat Kantop, Prasat Thnal Chuk, 7. Hariharalaya, 8. Ak Yum, Prei Khmeng, Prasat Kok Po, Prasat Khnat and Phnom Rung, 9. Rong Chen, 10. Wat Phu, 11. Prasat Kuk Pradak, 12. Phum Mien, 13. Tuol Pei, 14. Prah Vihear Kuk, 15. Chok Gargyar (Koh Ker, Lingapura), 16. Phnom Bayang, 17. Nong Pang Puey, 18. Prasat Nan Khmau, 19. Ampil Rolum, 20. Con An, 21. Prasat Anlon Car, 22. Ba Phnom, 23. Kdei Skie, 24. Basak, 25. Ishanapura, 26. Tuk Cum, 27. Phnom Kanva, 28. Banteay Srei, 29. Prasat Komphus, 30. Phnom Mrec, 31. Tuol Prasat.

The Indratataka was the *baray* or reservoir ordered by Indravarman at Hariharalaya. It is seen here during the rainy season.

Preah Ko, the chapel royal of Indravarman at Hariharalaya.

Preah Ko, showing the bull in the foreground after which the site is named. Note the surviving stucco ornamentation over the brick core of the temple.

The central group of temples at Preah Ko. The three towers of the front row were dedicated to Rudravarman and Prithivindradevi, respectively Indravarman's maternal grandfather and father, with the central tower being dedicated to Jayavarman II.

Above right: The massive Bakong temple pyramid at Hariharalaya.

Right: The plan of the Angkor area showing the location of Hariharalaya and Banteay Choeu.

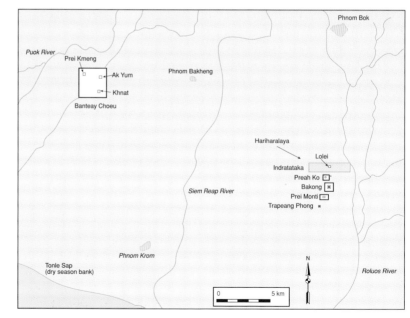

earth with the sacred realm. The temple within was built on an unprecedented scale incorporating huge stone blocks. Although the central shrine has not survived, it evidently contained a *linga* called Indresvara. Such a linking of the king with Shiva indicated that this temple was a centre of reverence for the sovereign whose central shrine was, again, combined with smaller sanctuaries dedicated to his male and female ancestors.

The reign of Indravarman is pivotal because it reveals the energy galvanised through the control of labour in construction programmes and how craft specialists were maintained for the production of opulent offerings. His texts describe how agricultural estates were assigned to provide goods and services to the royal shrines. Although the Indratataka must have retained much water, its function is not fully understood. It would seem likely that it fed the sacred moats and basins within the palace and temple complex to the south, but no contemporary evidence indicates its use in irrigated agriculture. Indeed, Hariharalaya would have been so close to the wet season edge of the Great Lake that there would have been little scope for irrigated fields.

Hariharalaya was not to remain the political centre for long. Indravarman's son and successor, Yashovarman, founded a new capital just to the west, where a low hill known as the Bakheng rises 65 metres above the surrounding countryside. The symbolism of the hill as Mount Meru, home of the gods, was enhanced by the construction of Yashovarman's temple pyramid on its summit to house Yashodharesvara. The Bakheng was located centrally within a large rectangular enclosure, and was to the initiated, a vehicle of deep religious symbolism. Spaced around the central temple tower were a further 108 smaller towers. Filliozat (1954) has pointed out that the perfect symmetry of the plan means that from a central position opposite any side of the monument, only 33 of the towers are visible, a number corresponding to the gods in Indra's heaven. The seven levels of the monument represent the seven heavens. The monument also has cosmic imagery.

The summit of the Bakheng, temple pyramid of Yashovarman at Angkor, provides a view of Angkor Wat in the distance.

Without excavations in the enclosed area of Yashodharapura, it is not possible to be sure whether there was an appreciable urban populace, or, whether on the contrary, the enclosure was reserved for the functionaries whose presence near the overlord was considered necessary. According to Briggs (1951) the interior incorporates up to 800 smaller reservoirs, perhaps for domestic use, which were excavated along the margins of the axial avenues which radiated from the Bakheng out to the city gates. There is some evidence from surface finds of pottery and roof tiles that there was indeed, a residential component to Angkor. Just outside and to the northeast of the city moat, the king set in train the excavation of the Yashodharatataka. This reservoir, the so-called Eastern Baray, covers an area of 7,120 by 1,700 metres and held up to 60 million cubic metres of water. It was fed by the Siem Reap River, which was diverted round its northeast corner so as to feed both the reservoir and the moats of the new city.

Yashovarman also ordered the construction of *ashramas*, or retreats for ascetics. Each contained an inscription setting out the appropriate rules for the conduct of those living within. The distribution of all his inscriptions allows us to appreciate the extent of the area over which he claimed authority. They were sited over a wide area, from Wat Phu in the north down to the Mekong Delta, and west

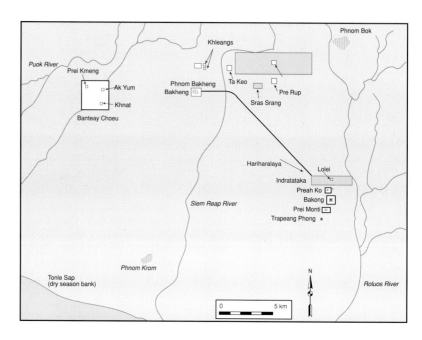

to the coast of the Gulf of Siam. They are also a vital source of information on the state under Yashovarman. We find, for example, reference to a legal system in which fines were graded according to rank. Land tenure and boundaries involved reference to the king, who sent officials into the provinces to investigate on his behalf. The inscriptions refer to *praman*, or administrative districts beyond the capital, and the foundation and endowment of temples. This last procedure would, in due course, increase the quantity of goods provided through taxation, to the court. Such accumulated surpluses were essential for the maintenance of the state, for they provided sustenance not only for the court, but also the army of workers who would have been called upon to construct the state temple of the Bakheng, and the dykes which enclosed the Yashodharatataka. Construction of the raised highway linking the new capital with Hariharalaya would also have taken much labour, while the Indratataka and the island Lolei temple in its midst were also completed during this reign.

Yashovarman's two sons, Harshavarman and Ishanavarman II, have left intriguing inscriptions and small but elegant temples. One text, for example, describes a high-ranking official as the *rajakulamahamantri*, and charged him with exempting a provincial temple from the payment of *vriha*, or a tax. At Angkor, the Baksei Chamkrong and Prasat Kravan temples probably date to these reigns. Harshavarman dedicated the former, a brick shrine on top of steep laterite foundations, to his father, Jayavarman III and Indravarman. The latter incorporates five brick shrines containing bas reliefs of Vishnu. Excavations in February 2001 at Baksei Chamkrong encountered an early brick wall foundation, a clay floor and, below, evidence for occupation during the Iron Age.

The perennial dissent over the succession is well illustrated by the career of Jayavarman IV. He was the grandson of Indravarman

Uncovering a brick wall foundation at Baksei Chamkrong. It may well date to the foundation of Yashodarapura.

Above left: Prasat Kravan at Angkor was dedicated in AD 921. It comprises five brick towers in a linear arrangement, and the unique interior brick bas reliefs depict Vishnu.

Left: Excavations in front of the temple of Baksei Chamkrong in February 2001 revealed prehistoric occupation under an early brick building.

through the female line, whereas Yashovarman and his sons were in the direct male line of descent. Given the long-established inheritence of titles from a ruler to his daughter's son, Jayavarman had a legitimate claim to the throne despite the presence of his cousins in Angkor. He therefore established his own, new capital to the northeast, at a place he called Lingapura. He must have exercised considerable power, because in the space of two decades, he had constructed a splendid complex complete with a central temple pyramid of unprecedented size, and a *baray* which necessitated hewing into the rock. The subsidiary temples at Lingapura incorporate socially illuminating inscriptions which list the workers who toiled to complete this royal centre. They came from many districts, and were maintained by the rice paid through the aegis of provincial temple estates as a form of taxation. Inscriptions set up by the king, or by followers acknowledging his rule, are found as far west as Battambang, then down the Mekong Valley to the upper Delta. One warns that flouting royal taxation demands would see the guilty caged by the local elders and brought to the king for sentence. Another described him as the King of Cambodia, and a warrior whose arrows "fill the eyes of his arrogant enemies with darkness". A third text describes how estate workers were divided into two groups. One

Pre Rup is the temple mausoleum of Rajendravarman. In this view from the top of the temple, Phnom Bok is visible in the distance.

Right: The Eastern Mebon was built by Rajendravarman on an island in the middle of Yashodharatataka, the Eastern Baray. It would have been covered in stucco and radiated across the water of the sacred reservoir.

provided labour during the two weeks of full moon, the other for the darker weeks of the month. Presumably, these people were free to work on their plots when not committed to temple duties.

After a brief interlude under Harshavarman II, son of Jayavarman IV, the court returned to Yashodharapura with the reign of Rajendravarman. The new king was both cousin and uncle of his predecessor. He traced his ancestry in the maternal line beyond Jayavarman II, and described his own mother as a goddess. His inscriptions spare no hyperbole in recounting his military glory and prowess. He located two splendid temple pyramids in the centre and just to the south of the Yashodharatataka, the former now known as the Eastern Mebon, the latter as Pre Rup. Both contained temples which housed *lingas* representing the king linked with Shiva, Rajendravarmesvara in one, Rajendresvara in the other. There were also subsidiary shrines dedicated to royal ancestors including his aunt and predecessor. Beyond the capital, the distribution of Rajendravarman's inscriptions follow closely that of his younger brother Jayavarman IV. We find the king's presence being mentioned in Battambang, Angkor, the vicinity of Lingapura, and down the broad lowlands flanking the Mekong River as far as the upper Delta. That from Ba Phnom in the far south illustrates the relationship between the centre and the frontiers of the state. Here we encounter Mahendradhipativarman, a local grandee whose daughter was a royal consort. He promoted the construction of a series of temples in his area, and opened forested land to agriculture. He was responsible for the building of *barays* and mentioned the presence of canals, and rice field boundaries. A second inscription of this reign also mentions canals as rice field boundaries, and the presence of a brick works. In many respects, these provincial inscriptions provide the essential information on the structure of the state, lacking if one concentrated on the centre alone. A text from Basak, for example, records that the King ordered his *vrah guru*, a high court official, to assure the provision of holy oil, or butter, for temple ceremonies. Two groups of fifteen men and women were detailed to care for the herd of sacred cattle during the two halves of the month, and to ensure that they were properly stabled. Rice production was the key to the well being of the state, and from the rich lands of Battambang, we encounter Viruna, an unfortunate worker who escaped from his assigned foundation. When captured, he had his eyes gouged out and his nose cut off.

Rajendravarman died when his son and successor, Jayavarman V, was only 10 years old. A necessary period of regency allows us to appreciate the high status and authority of senior members of the court. Two brothers, Yajnyavaraha and Vishnukumara, were responsible for the foundation and endowment of the temple complex known as Banteay Srei. The brothers were grandsons of King Harshavarman I, and their meritorious deeds included care for the sick and poor. Jayavarman himself was responsible for a massive temple pyramid now known as Ta Keo, but then called Hemasringagiri, the mountain of golden summits. This, and the nearby royal palace, comprised the court centre known as Jayendranagari, capital of the victorious kings. Ta Keo, like Pre Rup, incorporated five central shrines, but to this day stands uncompleted. This, according to a contemporary inscription, resulted from an inauspicious lightning strike or 'thunderbolt'. The large number of inscriptions dating to this reign again inform us on the titles and duties of central office bearers, and the duties of the agricultural workers employed in fields rigorously defined by boundary markers. There was a chief of corvée labour, inspectors of quality and defaults, chief of the warehouse, the *vrah guru*, a guardian of the bedchamber in the third category. One inscription mentions a court of justice. Mratan Sri Narendrasimha was a *senapati*, or military general. Four princes were gifted land grants by the King, whereupon they founded temples, endowed land and naturally, increased rural production. Transactions in land and personnel involved payments, which were

The brick wall in the foreground probably dates to the foundation of Banteay Srei, but the temple was added to at least twice during its long life.

Ta Keo, the massive temple mausoleum of Jayavarman V, was never completed. It was struck by a thunderbolt or lightning, a bad omen, and work on its construction ceased.

effected in measures of silver or gold, although there was no official form of currency. The extent of the kingdom, to judge from the distribution of Jayavarman's inscriptions, remained centred on the best agricultural land from Battambang to the Mekong, and down to the Delta.

Jayavarman V was the last major king of the dynasty established by Jayavarman II, a dynasty which endured for two centuries. The inscriptions reflect a state centred on the northern shore of the Great Lake, but incorporating Battambang to the west, and the Mekong Valley from the Dang Raek Range to the Delta. The central court was moved on several occasions, most notably to Lingapura during the reign of Jayavarman IV, and succession to kingship was often accompanied by conflict. However, the centre consistently followed the same pattern. There was a state temple containing representations of the king linked with Shiva, and subsidiary shrines dedicated to royal ancestors. Although none has survived, there was a royal palace located nearby. There was a *baray* or reservoir which involved modifications to the natural drainage, not to mention a large labour force. To judge from the available texts, the successive kings were served by a growing number of officials who must have been housed. Some noble families, descended from the followers of Jayavarman II, secured the prerogative to fulfill ceremonial court functions, such as holder of the fly whisk or fan. Succession to these offices followed through the sister's son.

The state exercised political control over an extensive territory which was studded with a growing number of regional temples. These fulfilled religious and economic roles. In the first instance, they tied the centre to the provinces through shared ideology involving the sovereign. The provision of offerings to the deities, which doubtless included local ancestors, accorded a proportion of the merit gained to the king. They also acted as foci for the assembly of surpluses to maintain the upper strata of society. Many inscriptions recount the foundation of temples, aspects of their maintenance, and fine details of land ownership, even down to the location of field boundaries. As far as can be seen, local labour was tied to the temples in terms of providing goods and services. Some groups were required to work for half of each month, others were severely punished for desertion. So surpluses of rice, honey, wax, oil, salt and cloth were taken and deployed to service ritual requirements and the needs of the ruling elite. One aspect of this system involved flexibility in succession to kingship. With the death of Jayavarman V, we enter such a period of dislocation and dynastic change.

The Dynasty of the Sun Kings

We know of three claimants to the throne. Udayadityavarman I was the maternal nephew of Jayavarman V, and was thus probably the legitimate successor, but we know of only two inscriptions which mention his name. Jayaviravarman's ancestry is not known, but he controlled Angkor for a few years after the death of Jayavarman. Two inscriptions northeast of the capital, dated to AD 1003 and 1005, mention the uprooting of boundary markers and, indeed, it was to the east and northeast that we find the early inscriptions of a third claimant, Suryavarman I. Vickery (1985) has undertaken a detailed analysis of this succession, with particular reference to a series of long inscriptions set up by noble families after a period of civil strife. They are at pains to stress their exalted ancestry, but also mention war, the destruction of temples and a countryside laid waste. He has identified the possibility that Suryavarman was a member of the Saptadevakula family, one which recorded descent from the maternal grandfather of Indravarman, and therefore a line stretching even beyond the reign of Jayavarman II. Often described as an usurper, Suryavarman might well have had a legitimate claim to the throne.

Suryavarman's early inscriptions all lie east of the capital, and it is tempting to see in the massive ceremonial centre of Preah Khan of Kompong Svay, his first royal capital. Although some of the temples there are later than his reign, others fall stylistically within his reign period, and one inscription mentions him by name. After AD 1006, however, he appears to have established himself at Angkor and we hear no more of Jayaviravarman. Early in his reign, he required his nobles to take an oath of allegiance, and had both their names and words carved in stone. They promised to offer their lives to the king, never to revere another, nor be accomplices to an enemy. In war, they promised to fight and pledge their lives, and, in peace, to undertake their tasks with devotion and loyalty.

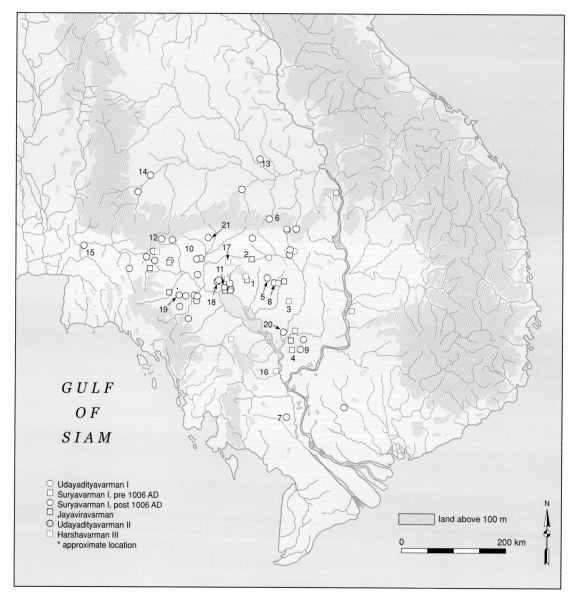

GULF
OF
SIAM

○ Udayadityavarman I
□ Suryavarman I, pre 1006 AD
○ Suryavarman I, post 1006 AD
□ Jayaviravarman
○ Udayadityavarman II
□ Harshavarman III
* approximate location

land above 100 m

N

0   200 km

The distribution of inscriptions of the dynasty of the Sun Kings
1. Prasat Trapan Sno, 2. Prasat Dambok Khpos, 3. Roban Romas, 4. Preah Nan, 5. Preah Khan of Kompong Svay, 6. Preah Vihear, 7. Phnom Chisor, 8. Prasat Trapan Run, 9. Kuk Prin Crum, 10. Nak Ta Cih Ko, 11. Wat Prah That de Tuk Cha, 12. Phnom Sanke Kon, 13. Ban Khamoy, 14. Phimai, 15. Prachinburi, 16. Lovek, 17. Prasat Prah Khset, 18. Vrah Damnap 19. Baset, 20. Phum Da, 21. Prasat Ta Kham Thom.

During a reign which lasted until 1050, Suryavarman greatly expanded Angkor. The central part covered a slightly smaller area than the city of Yashovarman, and was located just to the north of it. The new moats were fed by a diversion of the Siem Reap River. It is also beyond reasonable doubt that Suryavarman had the Western Baray excavated. This is the largest reservoir in the Angkor complex, covering an area of 8 by 2.1 km and able to store up to 70 million cubic metres of water. It was meshed into the existing system by a canal. No temple mausoleum to him is known, but it may well have been destroyed by the later building activity. He also began the construction of the Phimeanakas, a steep temple just north of Yashodharapura, and was responsible for the *khleangs*, an elegant row of buildings east of the Phimeanakas, but of unknown function. Suryavarman I's inscriptions cover the same territory as during the

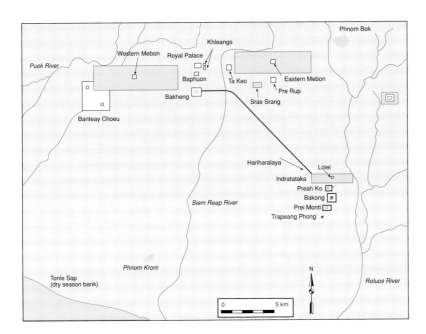

The Western Baray and Baphuon temple mountain were built during the reigns of Suryavarman I and Udayadityavarman II.

previous dynasty, but there are also signs that he extended his domain to the north of the Dang Raek Range into the Mun Valley. Hitherto, this rich low-lying border area was relatively silent, in terms of inscriptions, but may well have sustained a series of independent states. Preah Vihear occupies a ridge top on the Dang Raek escarpment, and from it, one can see south over the plain of Northern Cambodia, and north to the Mun Valley. This temple, known then as Sikharesvara, was one of the major state temples in key parts of the kingdom, and the location, it was said, of miraculous occurrences. Phnom Chisor to the south was also recognised as a key royal foundation. Commanding access to the Delta, this temple still dominates the flat landscape. Elsewhere, there are recurrent signs of recovery from the effects of conflict. In 1012, a loyal supporter was gifted land with the order to return it to its former prosperity. A general was given the land of his defeated enemy, and having founded a temple there, donated the resulting merit to the king. Another general received a land grant, and proceeded to cut back the brambles, clear the forest and found a village. A certain Viravarman purchased land with payments of rice, elephants and gold. He was also given land by the king which had been confiscated from a rebel. The Sdok Kak Thom inscription, however, is the most informative. In it, Sadashiva recorded the history of his lineage. The temple in question contained images of his ancestors, and describes the family land holdings, their boundaries and layout. We learn how reservoirs were built, and properties ravaged in the war were restored to production. Most importantly, the inscription reads as a justification for continued royal approval and support.

Suryavarman was succeeded by his son, Udayadityavarman II. If the great Western Baray was not yet finished, it must have been completed during the new reign, because the island temple in the centre was built in the style of the new king. He also continued with

Viewed from the summit of the Bakheng at sunset, the water of the massive Western Baray is seen in the distance.

Phimeanakas is the chapel royal within the royal precinct at Angkor. Its construction probably began under Suryavarman I, but it had a long life.

Preah Vihear is perched like an eagle's eyrie on the summit of the Dang Raek range. It was a favourite temple of Suryavarman I, and a place where miracles were recorded.

Above right: Looking south from Preah Vihear, the plain of northern Cambodia stretches to the horizon. It would formerly have been dotted with temples. (Courtesy Dr. Nigel Chang)

the construction of the largest temple pyramid yet conceived, the Baphuon. Surrounded by a wall 125 by 425 metres in extent, it is located just south of the royal palace of Yashovarman. The entrance walls of the second of the three stages are decorated with highly proficient bas-reliefs depicting scenes from the Indian epics but unfortunately the central tower, which was probably rendered in gilded wood, has not survived. Two revolts late in the reign of Udayadityavarman record interesting aspects of the organisation and climax of the campaigns. Both were internal rebellions, and each was put down under the direction of the general Sangrama. The booty taken was due to the king, who requested Sangrama to retain it himself. The general then persuaded the king to allow him to present it to the golden *linga* Udayadityesvara, housed in the Baphuon. These insurrections continued during the reign of Harshavarman III, who succeeded his brother in 1066 and ruled until a vassal prince, who to judge from his early inscriptions, probably hailed from the Mun Valley, siezed power.

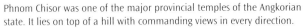

Phnom Chisor was one of the major provincial temples of the Angkorian state. It lies on top of a hill with commanding views in every direction.

The Western Baray is eight kilometres long, the largest at Angkor. The Western Mebon temple lies on an island in the middle.

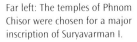

Far left: The temples of Phnom Chisor were chosen for a major inscription of Suryavarman I.

Left: Looking south from Phnom Chisor, one sees a steep flight of access stairs, an entrance *gopura* and the *baray*. Beyond, the flat expanse of the Mekong Delta stretches to the horizon.

Below: The Baphuon is the temple mausoleum of Udayadityavarman II. It was referred to by the Chinese visitor Zhou Daguan, almost three centuries after its completion, as the tower of copper.

The bas reliefs of the Baphuon
are widely regarded as of the
highest quality. They depict
scenes from Hindu epics.

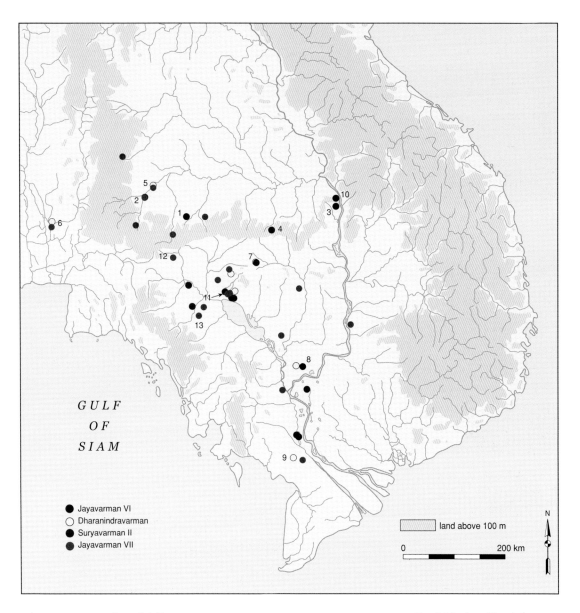

The Dynasty of Mahidharapura

Suryavarman I seems to have attempted to extend his kingdom into the Mun Valley. Perhaps in retaliation, an energetic aristocrat fomented a further episode of warfare over the succession. His claims to the throne were probably followed by a period of factional strife between followers of this northern claimant and those who remained loyal to the legitimate line represented by Harshavarman and his heirs. Jayavarman VI was the first of a new dynasty, that of Mahidharapura. It had two outstandingly active and dominant rulers, Suryavarman II and Jayavarman VII. The former ruled from 1113-1150. He was, according to an inscription from Preah Vihear, the grand nephew of Jayavarman VI. Four years after his accession, according to a second inscription, he "raised corvée labour and dug

The distribution of inscriptions from the dynasty of Mahidharapura. 1. Phnom Rung, 2. Phnom Wan, 3. Ban That, 4. Preah Vihear, 5. Phimai, 6. Lopburi, 7. Phnom Sandak, 8. Yay Hom, 9. Phnom Bayang, 10. Wat Phu, 11. Wat Kok Po, 12. Banteay Chmar, 13. Baset.

During the reign of Suryavarman II, Angkor Wat was constructed just south of the Bakheng.

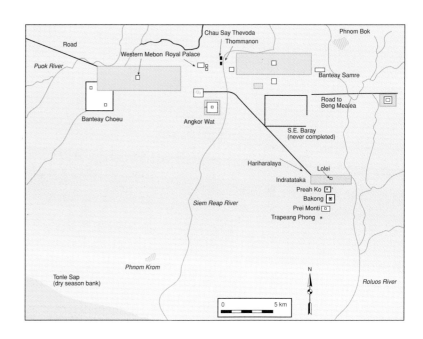

towers and basins". This may not be a direct reference to his greatest masterpiece, known as Angkor Wat, but the construction of this, the largest religious monument known, must have taken the greater part of his reign, and it was probably completed after his death. Suryavarman was a Vishnuite, rather than an adherent of Shiva, and his temple pyramid was placed outside the confines of the central enceinte of the Angkor complex. The scale of the monument represents a quantum change over the temple mausolea which preceded it. The outer moat encloses an area of 195 ha. The moat itself is 200 metres wide, and the monument within links open spaces, walls and courtyards which culminate in the centre with five sandstone towers designed in the form of lotus buds. The sense of space and grandeur is accentuated by immense vistas and the dramatic rise in height of the central lotus tower. Thus a raised avenue 350 metres long links the outer and a second walled enclosure which itself encloses an inner area 340 by 270 metres in extent. Hitherto, the visitor would have crossed a moat and two distinct open areas, the inner one being slightly elevated. The causeway now gave access to a raised terrace surrounded by a roofed gallery. This terrace measures 215 by 187 metres. It in turn gives way to a second, about half the size of the former and finally access was provided to the uppermost third terrace which is in the form of a square with sides 75 metres long. This was surmounted by five towers, the central one rising 65 metres above the natural level of the surrounding terrain.

It is hard to conceive the amount of labour necessary to raise such a monument, given the fact that the stone quarries were located about 30 km away. But its size is not all, for the construction was followed by the chiselling of bas-reliefs on the stone walls. These are the greatest known linear arrangement of stone carving. Those of the outermost terrace extend over 800 metres and are 2 metres high. Many scenes are drawn from the Indian epic literature. In addition,

Above and above left: Angkor Wat, the temple mausoleum of Suryavarman II, is the outstanding architectural achievement of the Angkorian kingdom.

Left: King Suryavarman II, surrounded by parasols, fly whisks and fans.

Far left: The outer gallery of Angkor Wat has the longest continuous series of bas reliefs known. They depict the court of Suryavarman II, battle scenes, images of heaven and hell and most notably, the churning of the ocean of milk to extract the elixir of immortality.

King Suryavarman II, larger than life, is seen seated on a wooden throne. He wears an elaborate crown and pectoral, heavy ear ornaments, armlets, bracelets and anklets. He holds what looks like a dead snake in his right hand, and an unidentified object in his left. A forest of 14 parasols, five large fans and four fly whisks surround him as he receives his ministers. Inscriptions name them. Virasimhavarman offers him a scroll. Vardhana and Dhananjaya hold a hand over their hearts to indicate loyalty and deference. A fourth is described as the inspector of merits and defects.

A royal princess is seen being
carried on her palanquin,
Angkor Wat.

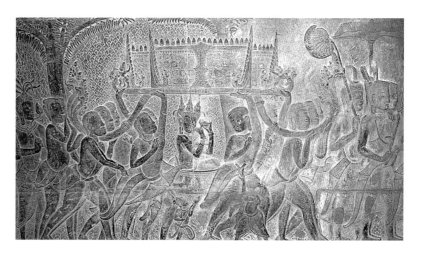

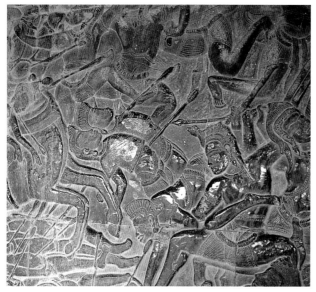

A war scene from Angkor Wat.

Above right: An army on the march.
Disciplined Khmer troops to the
left, irregulars, possibly Siamese
mercenaries, to the right.

Right: The massive moat of Angkor
Wat, seen at dusk.

The Tonle Sap linked Angkor with the Mekong River and ultimately, the sea.

there are depictions of Suryavarman himself, known in death as Paramavishnuloka. He is seen reviewing his armies and giving an audience. We have glimpses of Khmer warfare, one scene showing Jayasinhavarman, general of the troops of Lopburi, seated on the back of great war elephant. This monument, which stands out from all others at Angkor, fulfilled the role of temple to the god-king and as a mausoleum after his death.

The four decades following the death of Suryavarman saw a return to friction over the succession. The weakness of the central authority gave rise to a major military setback when the Chams brought their navy up the Mekong River and across the Tonle Sap to the very gates of Angkor. In 1177, they sacked the city. It was Suryavarman's second cousin, Jayavarman VII, who restored the lineage of Mahidharapura in 1181. He was a Buddhist, soldier and the most active builder of monuments of all the Khmer kings. Indeed, it was during his reign that Angkor approached its final form. Angkor Thom, his new city, was laid out on the cardinal points of the compass, the outer walls being 3.3 km square. Access through five massive gateways involved crossing the broad outer moat. Four gates led directly to the central temple, known as the Bayon. The other gave access to the royal palace, which lay adjacent to the Bayon within its own walls. The bridges crossing the moat are flanked by parallel rows each comprising 54 stone gods who grip a *naga*, a multi-headed snake. The number 54 is highly significant, because the figure 108 is most auspicious.

Angkor Thom and the Bayon have been variously interpreted. Wheatley (1971) projected the image of the gods and demons on the entrance causeways pulling on a snake to incorporate the city as a whole, and the Bayon in particular. He suggested that the *naga* was symbolically twined round the Bayon, the temple mausoleum of Jayavarman VII, which in turn represented the churning pole to produce the elixir of immortality. For one entering the city, the moats would have symbolised the oceans round Mt Meru, the walls the encircling mountain ranges.

Mus (1936) preferred to see in the *naga* balustrade, a symbol of the rainbow, the bridge linking the world of humans with that of the

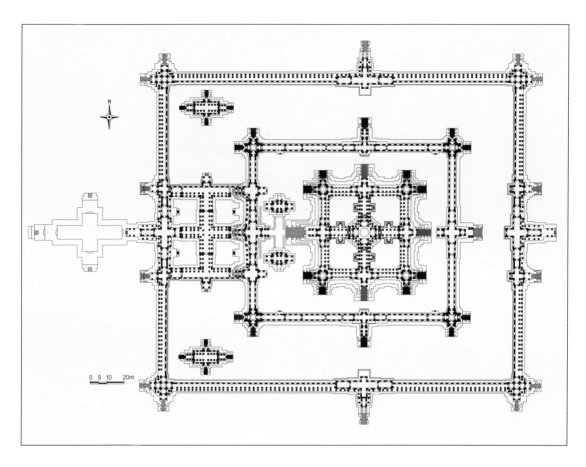

The plan of Angkor Wat, temple mausoleum of Suryavarman II.

The southern entrance to Angkor Thom, flanked by gods and demons holding a *naga* snake.

The Bayon, known as Mahyadri, was finished with huge heads looking serenely out over the kingdom. This enigmatic building was the temple mausoleum of Jayavarman VII.

gods, while Boisselier (1997) has returned to the contemporary inscriptions in seeking the underlying symbolism of the city, stressing that it was designed to represent the capital of Indra. Just as Indra's capital dominated Mt Meru, so the new Angkor would be built in the centre of the kingdom. The Bayon, lying as it does in the heart of the city, is in Boisselier's words, the Assembly Hall of the Gods. It was Indra who cast out the *asuras* from heaven and then by fortunate intercession from a *garuda* after an ensuing battle, repelled their attempt to return. The god then established a permanent guard against any future attacks. We can see these defences represented in the form of the entrance gates to the city, and the 108 guards located on the bridges which span the moat. Close inspection of the gates reveals not only the faces of the kings guarding each cardinal point of the compass, but also Indra himself, riding his three-headed elephant and holding a thunderbolt.

The outer walls of the Bayon are decorated with a series of bas reliefs which for the first time in the history of Angkor depict a wide range of secular as well as ritual and religious scenes. We can see the fine palaces and pavilions in carved wood, and market stalls with people buying and selling. We are taken into the house of a wealthy Chinese merchant, where he is entertaining guests. An army of cooks and waiters prepare food for an alfresco feast on one panel, a woman is seen with her midwives giving birth in another. The army marches, and we can see the camp followers, including a woman and two children accompanying her husband. Two men play chess in a quiet corner, and out on the Tonle Sap, we can see a fishing expedition. The vibrancy of these scenes sharpens our perception of the vigour of life at Angkor, and injects humanity into the surviving stone monuments which include two vast temple complexes constructed beyond the city walls by Jayavarman VII.

The entrance gates to the city of Angkor Thom stand 23 metres high. According to Zhou Daguan in 1296, one of the five stone heads was covered in gold. The gates were closed every night and opened again in the morning. Dogs, and criminals who had had their toes cut off were barred entry.

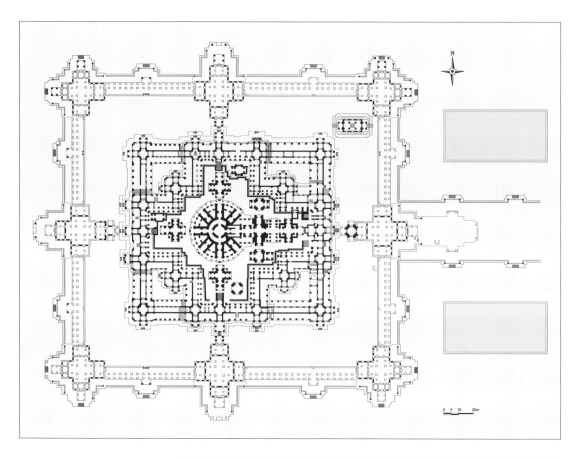

The plan of the Bayon temple, mausoleum of Jayavarman VII.

Cooks prepare meat and fish for a feast, the Bayon.

The bas reliefs of the Bayon incorporate a wide variety of scenes depicting everyday life. Here, we see a family following the army.

Artisans carve stone slabs, the Bayon.

Servants cook and serve rice to an aristocratic feast held alfresco in a forest, the Bayon.

A feast for a wealthy Chinese merchant, resident in Angkor Thom, the Bayon.

Levering stones, probably in building a temple, the Bayon.

Servants prepare food in the lower panel, while grandees are served in a forest setting above, the Bayon.

A forest hunter with bow and arrow, the Bayon.

Fishing on the Great Lake, the Bayon.

A Chinese junk, probably bringing a cargo of trade goods to Angkor, the Bayon.

A close up of feasting. Note the distended ear lobes of the aristocrats being waited on, the Bayon.

Inside a Chinese resident's house at Angkor Thom. Parasols and wine containers hang from the ceilings, the Bayon.

A finely decorated royal barge, the Bayon.

Rajavihara, now known as Ta Prohm, has been left largely as it must have been seen by the first Portuguese, invaded by the jungle and shrouded by trees. The name Ta Prohm, meaning ancestor Brahma, was given to the temple after the local term for one of three statues recovered in 1885 by Étienne Aymonier. He also recovered the foundation inscription, set in place by Sri Suryakumara, the Sun Prince, 699 years previously. The maze of courts, shrines and walls come to life on reading this inscription. We learn that the king wished to have his maternal ancestry highlighted, a lineage rooted in the mythical royal ancestors dating back to well before the time of Jayavarman II. In its heyday, the temple was administered by 18 high priests and 2,740 officials. There were 2,202 assistants and 615 female dancers, while 12,640 people had the right to lodge there. 79,365 people from rural villagers were assigned to supply the temple, which involved mosquito nets, fine cloth, rice, honey, molasses, millet, beans, butter, milk, salt and vegetables. The principal temple housed a shrine for the king's mother, covered in precious gems. There were also 260 statues in the many subsidiary shrines, which were dedicated to the ancestors of highly ranked members of the court. This vast, rich and powerful foundation was responsible for the administration of 102 hospitals built under the orders of the sovereign, and strategically placed across his realm. These, too, called on surpluses generated by the supporting populace. Medicines were made of camphor, coriander, pepper, mustard, cardamoms, molasses, cumin, pine resin, ginger and onions. All these offerings, and the rituals of Ta Prohm itself, were intended to make merit for the salvation of the king's mother depicted as Prajnaparamita, the mother of the Buddha and perfection of wisdom.

The king's father was similarly worshipped at Jayasri, the holy city of victory, now known as Preah Khan. The foundation inscription was written by another royal prince, Virakumara, and records that the temple was raised on the ground where his father the king finally defeated the Chams (Cœdès 1941). The central shrine contained an image of the King's father as Bodhisattva Lokesvara, and was consecrated in 1191. 5,324 villages incorporating 97,840 people were assigned to the upkeep of this vast establishment. They provided resin to light tapers, goats, pigeons, and 645 lengths of white and red cloth to dress the gods. Silk mosquito nets were woven to protect the images,

Above and above right:
Jayavarman VII ordered the
construction of many hospitals
and rest houses. This hospital
is located just south of the
provincial centre of Phimai.

Right: Angkor during the reign
of Jayavarman VII saw many new
monuments, and an entirely new
city of Angkor Thom. The two
major new temples are Preah
Khan and Ta Prohm.

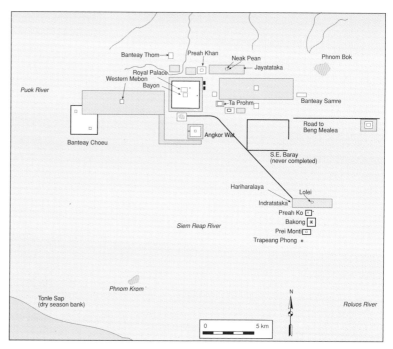

and even a sacred brown cow with gilded horns and hoofs roamed
the complex. We also learn that 23 provincial temples were built
to house an image of the king as Buddha, some of which have been
located as far afield as Central Thailand. Thus Jayasimhapuri is
probably the same place as modern Muang Singh, the Lion City,
in Kanchanaburi Province far to the west.

Jayasri was linked by a landing stage with the Jayatataka,
Jayavarman's new *baray*. It was not as large as the East or West
Barays, but included in the middle an island housing the Rajasri,
or Neak Pean, a temple surrounded by fountains in which pilgrims
could wash away their sins. The king also founded rest houses at
strategic locations along the roads, to house pilgrims. There were
17 on the road linking Angkor with Phimai, the king's ancestral
homeland. Welch (1997) has noted how those on the road south
from Phimai are conveniently placed a day's journey apart. En route,
travellers could visit the remote Banteay Chmar, a sanctuary
dedicated to the crown prince Srindrakumaraputra. He had led a

The entrance avenue to Preah Khan, Angkor.

Above left: Nagara Jayasri (Preah Khan) was built by Jayavarman VII to honour his father.

Left: Like Angkor Thom, the entrance to Preah Khan is embellished with gods and demons holding the *naga* snake.

The hall of columns comprises part of the temple complex of Preah Khan. Here, images of royal and elite ancestors were worshipped in a maze of individual shrines. It was maintained by a huge royal endowment recorded in detail on the foundation stela.

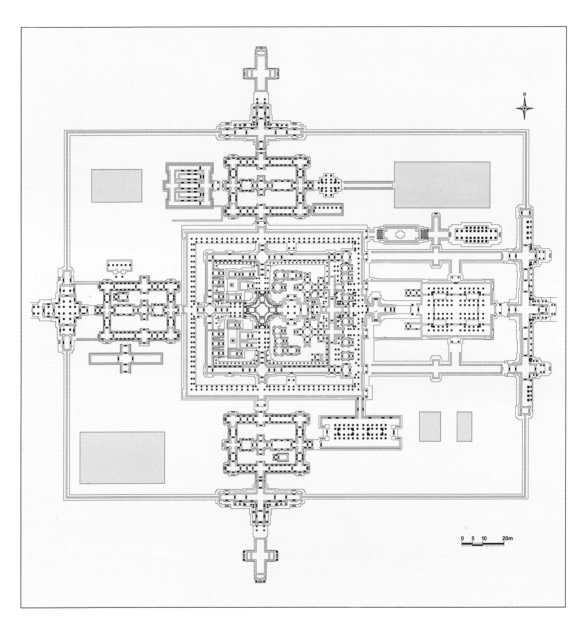

The plan of Preah Khan, Jayasri, a temple mausoleum dedicated to the father of Jayavarman VII.

military expedition to Champa, and predeceased the king. Four of his generals have their own shrines in a complex with bas reliefs rivalling those of the Bayon. As befitted a monument to war heroes, scenes of war against the Chams dominate. We can see land and naval battles in which the Khmer were victors.

As Buddha, guardian and saviour of his people, Jayavarman's building programmes extended beyond temples to include the afore-mentioned hospitals and guest houses. Where necessary, bridges spanned the intervening rivers. These roads doubtless assisted in the transport of goods appropriated in the service of the temples, inns and hospitals. The amount consumed was very great. Thus the 102 hospitals founded by Jayavarman were supplied with 11,370 tonnes of rice provided by 81,640 people residing in 838 villages. In other

The ferocity of a battle between the Khmer and the Chams on the wall of Banteay Chmar contrasts with the tranquillity of the temple ruins beyond.

The Cham navy proceeds to fight the Khmer in a scene at Banteay Chmar, but already casualties lie in the water of the Great Lake.

The Chams are in retreat during this battle in a forest depicted on a bas relief at Banteay Chmar.

The Khmer and Cham navies are locked in hand-to-hand combat. One of the Chams has been grabbed round the throat and is about to be speared. Banteay Chmar.

Rajasri, now known as Neak Pean, lies in the middle of the Jayatataka, the *baray* of Jayavarman VII. The tower in the centre is ringed by two *nagas* with tales entwined, and water from the surrounding pond flows through four figures into their own basin. In one chapel, water spurted through the mouth of an elephant, in the others there was a horse, a lion and a human. The contemporary inscriptions tell us that the complex is a replica of Lake Anavatapta, a sacred Himalayan lake imbued with miraculous curative powers to remove human sins.

The Khmer navy about to engage the enemy. Banners and standards flutter in the breeze. Banteay Chmar.

Above right: A boy contemplates the bas reliefs at Banteay Chmar. The right hand part of this wall was destroyed by Cambodian soldiers, who shipped the carvings to Thailand for sale on the antiquities market in 1998. On this occasion, they were retrieved by the Thai authorities and returned to Cambodia.

As at the Bayon, giant heads gaze serenely from their sanctuaries at Banteay Chmar.

This great bridge over the Chikreng River, east of Angkor, was part of Jayavarman VII's road network.

words, villages with an average population of about 100 people had to supply 13.5 tonnes of rice each in taxation. This would have entailed producing nearly double their own requirements. Such figures provide an insight into the way in which excess production as well as corvée labour was channelled towards the requirements of a state religion which had at its apex, the deified king himself. No ruler after Jayavarman VII, nor for that matter before, galvanized so much energy in the pursuit of monumentality. While Angkor continued as the centre of the state for a further 150 years after his death, there was no further major rebuilding and the ruins of Angkor today reflect the city largely as he left it.

Some insight into life at the capital between August 1296 and July 1297, however, has survived in a report by Zhou Daguan, who visited Angkor with a Chinese embassy. He travelled by boat up the Mekong River and across the 'fresh water sea' (Tonle Sap) to the porterage at Angkor. It is clear that the principal temple mausolea still dominated the great centre. He described the central tower of gold (the Bayon), the tower of copper (the Baphuon) and the royal palace surmounted by another golden tower (the Phimeanakas). The palace was linked by a golden gate giving access to a gilded pavilion supported by stone elephants. These elephants survive to this day as part of the great elephant terrace. The Jayatataka, he said, encircled an island temple, while the eastern lake had in its centre, a bronze Buddha. In this he might have been mistaken, for the Western Baray is known to have had a gigantic bronze statue of Vishnu, rather than the Buddha, in the western Mebon temple. Outside the city confines lay the tomb of Lu-pan (Angkor Wat). Perhaps the most arresting insight, however, is provided by the description of daily life. He noted for example, that there were at least 2,000 servants who lived 'all over the capital'. Their houses were smaller than those of the aristocrats and bureaucrats, and made of poorer materials. He further noted the presence of numerous slaves, some people owning over 100. They could be bought and sold, and were severely punished if they tried to escape. The populace obviously enjoyed religious

One of the Prasat Suor Prat towers at Angkor.

Above right: This terrace lies to the east of the royal precinct of Angkor Thom. It was used in the late 13th century as a reviewing stand for the court.

Top right: The view from the Elephant Terrace at Angkor Thom includes the Prasat Suor Prat, structures of doubtful function. Zhou Daguan reported that those on trial were incarcerated within, their guilt being determined by the degree to which they withstood the ordeal. They may date to the reign of Indravarman II.

festivals and royal ceremonies. We read of a procession centred around King Indravarman III, while the open area beyond the elephant terrace was the scene of parades, firework displays and boar or elephant fights.

To sustain such a concentrated populace, Zhou Daguan noted the cultivation of three to four rice crops a year, using soil enriched by the annual flooding of the lake, but he did not describe any form of irrigation based on the *barays*. He mentioned the importance of the lake as a source of fish, turtles and crocodiles. Infrastructure for transport entailed large oar-propelled boats, and the use of carts, elephants and horses. Merchants had to pay a tax to the administration for a good location in the market. The list of imported goods included silk, ceramics, iron and copper receptacles, gold and silver. Outside the capital, Zhou Daguan referred to over 90 provinces each with a governor and defended centre, as well as villages each dominated by a temple.

Although life at Angkor described by Zhou Daguan suggests prosperity and stability, events were to prove otherwise. We have seen that the state involved a royal dynasty steeped in divinity. The deeds of kings and great officers of state were recorded on stelae carved in Sanskrit. Much wealth was appropriated to maintain the centralised apparatus, not least the means of destruction, the religious rites and the administrative infrastructure. This system came to an end by the mid 15th century AD, though many of its forms survived into the 1970s, and were incorporated and continue in the court rituals of the Thai monarchy. The transition from the Angkorian state to the kingdom of Cambodia based near Phnom Penh was more in the nature of a change of emphasis and location than a sudden collapse. The rise of rivals, particularly the Thai of the Chao Phraya Valley, resulted in the Angkor being prone to predatory attacks. The spread of Theravada Buddhism undermined the centralised authority of the god king in the minds of the people. In the mid 14th century, the Siamese established the kingdom of Ayutthaya where there had formerly been a province of Angkor, and were in constant friction with the Khmer until in 1431, King Ponha Yat abandoned Angkor and established a new capital near the junction of the Mekong and Tonle Sap rivers.

Mabbett (1978) has offered a persuasive analysis of the state apparatus which lay behind the hyperbole of the Khmer inscriptions. He visualises the king as being pivotal in managing the affairs of state, but not absolutely powerful. He had to be versed in the law, religion, tradition and military matters and was the ultimate source of authority in land tenure. His hold on the reins of power was enhanced by his bestowal of patronage, not least in land grants, honorific and administrative posts involving visible status rights and conferring rights to establish religious foundations. Mabbett, however, points out that the system was maintained not by established appointments and bureaucratic procedures, but rather by favour, influence, cliques and sponsorship. It was more effective to retain a hold on the provinces by attracting the devotion of regional landowners and spiritual leaders than by coercion. Alienation of supporters was not good government. The king was every man. He mediated with heaven for the provision of rains, he was available for mediation between individuals over disputes. He consumed the land for taxes, and redistributed them among his retainers and servants. He dispatched his officials to all parts of his kingdom to gather information and undertake his requirements. He patronised the great aristocratic families and in return, relied on their loyalty. The universal ruler occupied the centre, and its outer margins were represented by the ebb and flow of shades of influence. Obeisance, not border posts, defined boundaries.

Taxation

Angkor was sustained by the flow of goods from the large bulk of the population to the major regional temples, and then to the centre. The source of such goods was overwhelmingly from land, the ownership of which was a major source of wealth and power (Ricklefs 1967). The generation of agricultural surpluses to meet tax obligations and maintain a temple community gained merit and achieved prominence. From the earliest campaigns of Jayavarman II, his important followers were rewarded with land. Our understanding of the taxation system which directed surpluses, in the absence of money, towards the centres and upper social echelon is based on a small sample of Sanskrit inscriptions. The Khmer had no currency other than measures of silver or gold, and most dues were paid in the form of primary produce, manufactured goods, labour and merit. The

Fish, probably from the Great Lake, is sold in the market, a scene daily repeated in the area today. The Bayon.

The fish market at Angkor is much the same as it was in 1219 AD.

payment of a proportion of agricultural yields entailed not only intensified production over local subsistence needs, but also a system of assessing due amounts. This required special functionaries, responsible for maintaining land ownership registers, the quality of land holdings and the resultant tax obligations. Some parcels of land were in private ownership, with the king himself having large estates. The ownership of land was also vested in religious foundations but the nature of land tenure among rural communities is less clear. It is possible that a village was assessed for tax rather than its individual members. One way of expanding the tax base was to establish new temples and communities, under which circumstances the payment of goods was deferred until the agricultural base was fully established. Other primary products included honey and wax, sugar, spices, salt, medicines and livestock. The uplands and predominantly wooded areas supplied feathers, rhino horn, ivory, aromatic wood and spices. Each major category was overseen by a particular functionary and his staff, which operated centrally and without needing to consult the local administration.

There were also imposts on manufactured goods, such as cloth, and on goods exchanged in the market place. War-booty, tribute from vassals, fines imposed on criminals and personal assets of a deceased with no heir also augmented treasury receipts. It is clear from several inscriptions that civil works, such as the provision of roads, reservoirs, canals and defensive walls in addition to the most visible of all remains, the temples, were raised on the basis of corvée labour, whereby people worked in part fulfillment of their obligations. Although some religious foundations and their functionaries were exempt from the payment of a tax determined in goods, they yielded to the king a proportion of the merit they earned through their devotions.

The physical assets and corvée labour due to the king were administered by officials in order to fulfil the functions necessary for the maintenance of the state. The strands of political, economic and religious behaviour were interwoven into one fabric. The king and to a certain extent, his close relations were living gods. The temple symbolised the home of the gods. This crucial concept was the motivating force which drove the economy. There was then, an unusually sharp distinction between the court at the centre of the web of activities, and the provinces which sustained it. The former required both ritual and secular administrators. The fundamental change in the organisation of the state issuing from the policy of Jayavarman II saw the establishment of a mystical king which countenanced only one supreme centre. So the regional aristocratic families of Chenla were increasingly drawn into the centre to fulfil the roles of ceremonial and ritual, and their territories were absorbed over time into provinces, known as *praman* or *visaya*, ruled by the overlord's appointees. This was, at least, the theory. In practice, weak central administration was associated from time to time with regional unrest and fissioning.

Carrying containers of rice. The reliefs are the best source of information on wooden buildings at Angkor. The Bayon.

The king was served then, by aristocratic grandees whose positions were inherited and set up within a hierarchy designated by emblems of royal patronage. The crown prince, or *yuvaraja*, was second to the king in order of precedence, followed by the other royal princes. The highest officers of state were accorded a palanquin with gold stretchers and four parasols with gold handles. The lowest in the hierarchy were granted the privilege of a parasol with a silver handle. In the 10th century, Kanbu, an agent of the king, was provided with a grant of land, a gold palanquin, gold cup, a white parasol, another with peacock feathers and a spitoon. The *purohita*, or chief priest, was one of the greatest and most influential positions. Shivakaivalya was *purohita* to Jayavarman II, he and his descendants being given the exclusive right to consecrate a new king. The succession of *purohitas* was through the female line, so Shivakaivalya was followed by his sister's son, Sukshmavindu. This master stroke enabled Jayavarman and his successors to exclude would be usurpers from the means of consecration by confining the office and controlling access to the necessary rituals. In the event, Shivakaivalya's descendants exercised the right until 1050.

The post of *hotar*, or royal chaplain, was not exclusive and more than one could serve contemporaneously. The officers were again chosen from the great aristocratic families, and initial access conferred hereditary rights. The position of *vrah guru*, spiritual adviser to the king, drew upon aristocrats of learning and administrative skill. When Jayavarman VI usurped the throne in 1080, he appointed Divakarapandita as his *vrah guru*. This functionary had previously served Udayadityavarman II and Harshavarman III, and was responsible for the consecration of Jayavarman and his two successors. The role of the *vrah guru* also extended to more temporal matters, not least in the discharge of orders for the donation and demarcation of land. The ministers of state in charge of civil and religious affairs were known as the *mantrin*, with the chief minister called the *rajakula mahamantrin* (Sahai 1970).

The outer wall of the royal palace at Angkor Thom, ringed the centre of the Angkorian administrative system.

In this battle scene from the Bayon, a Cham cavalry officer falls from his horse.

These were the great ministers of state. Below them was a host of other appointments. The *sanjak* was a guard who protected the king's person. The *anak sanjak* protected religious foundations. There was the royal archivist, who maintained the genealogical records and exploits of the king's ancestors. There were the hereditary carriers of the royal fly whisk and fan, pages, and doctors. Further from the royal entourage was the *pratyaya glan*, administrator of the kings warehouses and the chief artisan. Minor officials, known as *sresthin*, attracted a silver handled parasol. The *vyapara*'s role included the fixing of land boundary markers. The *pratyaya* was also an official concerned delineating land for tax purposes.

It is evident that the central administration was most concerned with the registration of land ownership and the fixing of tax levels. Directives and policy were centrally promulgated and reached out through the hierarchy, into the provincial administrative structure. It seems that provinces, each administered by a *khlon visaya*, were units for tax and judicial purposes. *Tamrvac* were those who articulated local provincial affairs with the centre. The individual unit within each *visaya* was the village or *sruk*. There may have been administrative units comprising groups of villages, but this is unclear. The headman or *khlon sruk*, apart from parochial affairs, was ultimately responsible for the payment of goods and services where a community was bonded to the maintenance of a particular temple. Under the reign of Jayavarman VII for example, it was decreed that 3,140 settlements totalling 79,365 people were allocated to sustain the temple of Ta Prohm, and 5,324 settlements incorporating 97,840 people provided the goods and services needed to support Preah Khan. In this manner, there was a direct link between the greatest temples of the land and the broad spectrum of sustaining village communities.

The Means of Destruction

Controlling the means of destruction is a factor isolated by Goody (1971) as central to the maintenance and success of the upper echelon of society. In the Angkorian state, warfare had three principal manifestations. Firstly, there was friction between rivals for central power. It is clear that Jayavarman II subjugated rival princes before establishing himself as supreme monarch on Mount Mahendraparvata. Subsequent episodes of civil war saw conflict between Suryavarman I, Jayaviravarman and Dharinindravarman I. Rajendravarman too, seems to have been involved in subduing regional unrest for according to one of his inscriptions, he "cut off the heads of a crowd of kings". Jayavarman VI took power by force. Second, it was necessary to subdue vassals and appropriate tribute. The state had no fixed boundaries, but rather a waxing and waning of spheres of influence. At its edges were small polities which found it expedient to acknowledge vassal status. At times of a strong central authority, this became an imperative, but a weak and divided administration provided the opportunity to set aside the payment of tribute and to assert a degree of independence. The last and most intensive form involved neighbouring states. There are several instances for example, when the Khmer either attacked their neighbours or were in turn invaded. Such instances rarely resulted in a long term occupation of alien territory. The major powers of mainland Southeast Asia between AD 802-1431 were the Khmer of Angkor, the Chams, the Vietnamese and, by degrees, the Siamese of Sukhothai and Ayutthaya.

The means of waging war during those six centuries were not static, though some features were common throughout. The rulers of Angkor maintained four different types of unit. There were the infantry, the horse cavalry, the chariots and the elephants. Quaritch-Wales (1952) has suggested that the chariots depicted on the Angkor Wat bas-reliefs represent no more than a memory of earlier techniques of warfare. Of the four arms, the most impressive and significant were undoubtedly the war elephants. The Angkor Wat reliefs show them in action as bearers of spear-wielding soldiers. The rather later reliefs from Banteay Chmar and the Bayon show ballistae mounted on the backs of elephants. One man guided the elephant, and it took two to arm and fire the ballista. This technique was probably an innovation of the reign of Jayavarman VII and was, according to Mus (1929), derived from China through Cham intermediaries. One of the Bayon reliefs actually shows soldiers operating their ballista. The elephant was the animal par excellence for dealing with the terrain over which fighting occurred, for providing added height when confronting enemy walls and for its capacity to cross defensive moats. The ruler who controlled war elephants was powerful indeed. Horses by contrast, do not appear to have been so significant, and were probably used by officers in charge of infantry rather than in massed engagements.

Little is known of methods of recruitment or training, nor how long people served. There were permanently appointed generals

In this unusual frontal scene at Angkor Wat, we see the image of a war chariot.

Naval war as depicted at Banteay Chmar involved vicious hand-to-hand combat.

rewarded by land grants, status symbols and booty. Much of the rank and file may well have been raised during periods of need, particularly in the dry season when military activity was favoured and agricultural tasks were minimal. They appear to have been granted tax exemption, provided with food and where possible, with a share of booty. Under conditions of extreme danger to the state, as when the Chams sacked Angkor, even temple servants were pressed into service.

It is recalled that naval warfare was an important consideration, even as far inland as Angkor, since the Mekong was navigable up to the Tonle Sap by ocean going vessels. The late reliefs of the Bayon and Banteay Chmar reveal aspects of naval warfare during the 12th century. Scenes from both sites reveal a naval engagement between the Khmer, who wore loin cloths, and an enemy whose flowered head dresses indicate that they were Chams (Paris 1941). They seem to have used boats as floating fortresses, from which they fought with spears.

The means of destruction are essential to the survival of the state. Here, the Khmer under Jayavarman VII defeat the Chams in a battle scene from Banteay Chmar

Agriculture

The concentration of people at Angkor and the other cult centres, such as Beng Mealea and Banteay Chmar, as well as the need to sustain followers and retainers, made it necessary to intensify food production above the level of subsistence. The Angkor complex and other centres located between the Tonle Sap and the Kulen plateau were favourably placed because the rivers originating in the latter area flow perennially. To a certain extent, this factor alleviated three major problems encountered by rice cultivators there today. First, the area lies in a rain shadow, and the onset and duration of the rains are unpredictable. There is often a short dry season during the critical growing period of late July and August, and during the dry season proper, the long sunny days increase the rate of evaporation. The Tonle Sap, one of the great inland fisheries of the world, alleviated these problems. Rice and fish were the staples. The monsoonal conditions do not make the cultivation of rice outside its natural marshy habitat straight-forward, because the annual quantity of rainfall is variable. It has been suggested that Iron Age and later Funan rice cultivation took advantage of naturally-flooded riverine land. In Bac Bo, the Han Chinese system of plough cultivation was adopted. The Han had by that juncture, developed the technique now universal across the lowlands of Southeast Asia, of creating swampland suited to rice by bunding.

Essentially, this technique involves sculpturing the landscape by creating almost flat rice fields demarcated by raised earthern banks. Natural swampland is mimicked by adjusting the flow of retained rainwater through successive fields and so ultimately to the natural stream or river. This technique is currently imposed on slightly elevated land above natural flood level, so it is usually too dry to risk broadcasting seed in the early weeks of the wet season. Consequently, rice plants are raised in seed beds and transplanted when the fields are prepared. Ploughing was a second major Han innovation. It is much more efficient to plough the soil than to break it with a hoe. One man can bring more land into cultivation than is necessary to support his immediate dependants, thus opening the door to the generation of disposable surpluses. When ploughing, which aerates the soil and controls weeds, is allied with harrowing to break down the clods of soil and provide a creamy soil to receive the transplanted rice, a predictably greater yield is achieved (Hanks 1972). The presence of bunded rice fields is archaeologically attested at Angkor (Pottier 1997). Although no reliefs, nor inscriptions, positively attest to ploughing, it is highly likely that draught animals were used. Indeed, there is a ploughing scene on the reliefs of Borobudur in Java, dated to the late 9th century AD.

One of the essential features of the land bordering the northern margins of Tonle Sap, is that the lake expands greatly with the rainy season. This leads to the deposition of a thin layer of lacustrine silt, but according to Delvert (1961), this is not highly regarded by rice farmers at present. The slope of the land is much more gradual on the southern shore than it is on the northern. Hence, rising floodwaters travel 29 km to reach 14 metres above sea level on the former, but only 4 km on the latter. Currently, several techniques are used for rice cultivation in the area surrounding Tonle Sap. It is possible still 'to beat' wild rice grains into receptacles in a boat. Floating rice, with stalks up to 7 metres long is also grown. It is preferred on the southern edge of the lake because of the gentler flood regime. On the northern margin, floodwaters rise more sharply and if the rate rises higher than about 10 cm per day, the plants cannot keep pace and die. There is some shifting agriculture in fields cut from the degraded deciduous forests, but yields are very low. The most widespread technique involves the bunding of fields, use of animal traction and transplanting. There remains one system peculiar to the margins of the lake, whereby receding floodwaters are trapped behind barrages or 'tanub'. These fields are then cultivated in the early part of the dry season.

The Angkorian state was underwritten by the production of rice to feed the elite, the bureaucrats, specialists and corvée labour force. The number of references to cadastral surveys, assessments of land capability and fixing of tax in kind indicate a central concern for this crucial matter. Royal, synonymous with divine, intervention to counter unpredictable rainfall was one of the hallmarks of Angkor. It is true that Ishanavarman and his predecessors constructed moated enclosures which assured some dry season water supplies for a concentrated populace, but the innovations of Indravarman I were critical. Like his successors, his temple centre was set back above the maximum rise of the flood waters. At Hariharalaya, he had constructed the Indratataka, a reservoir with a capacity of 10 million cubic metres of water. The river Roluos flowed into the northeastern and left at the southwestern corner of the *baray*, whence it was directed through the temple moat of Preah Ko, then on to the double moats of the Bakong.

Angkor itself is located between the valleys of the Stung Roluos and Stung Puok. Its foundation involved the same reworking of the

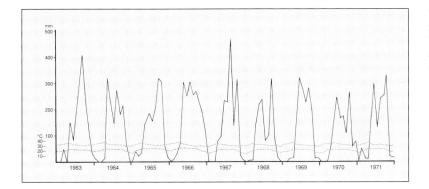

The rainfall at Siem Reap is highly seasonal in duration and amount. There is often a lull in July and August, making rice cultivation difficult to manage.

landscape and imposition of water control as was pioneered at Hariharalaya. The Eastern Baray, or Yashodharatataka, covered 7,120 by 1,700 metres and could store up to 60 million cubic metres. The source of the water was the Siem Reap River. At some point in the development of the Angkorian complex, this river's flow was augmented by the diversion of the Stung Puok along a 4 km long canal. This system established by Yashovarman was greatly expanded by his successors, and Groslier (1973, 1974, 1979) has proposed four major phases. Angkor II was the creation of Suryavarman I, who excavated the Western Baray and linked it by means of a feeder canal with the Yashodharatataka. Angkor III was the work of Suryavarman II, whose temple mausoleum, Angkor Wat, was provided with moats capable of storing five million cubic metres. The final addition came with the new *baray* of Jayavarman VII, which added a futher 10 million cubic metres to the storage capacity.

One of the key questions in any attempt to write the history of Angkor is the role of these great reservoirs. Did kings build them to irrigate rice fields? To have done so would not only have provided them with great wealth, but also with an aura of divine and supernatural power. Yet expert opinion on the issue of irrigation is divided. Some advocate that Angkor was a hydraulic city, located to take advantage of the perennial rivers bringing water from the Kulen Plateau to replenish the reservoirs and feed the rice fields. Others argue against any irrigation on technical and geographic grounds. Since the former school argues that the rise of the Angkor state and, indeed, its decline and abandonment were determined by the success and failure of the irrigation system, it is important to review both sides of the debate.

There are several sources of evidence. Could the quantity of stored water have been sufficient to make any impact upon rice agriculture in the area between their southern dyke and the Tonle Sap? Is there any evidence for a reticulation system? Are there any structures to permit the controlled flow of water from the *barays* into a network of distributaries? Was there sufficient irrigable land to contribute to the amount of rice needed to sustain the populace? One could then seek any reference to irrigation in the inscriptions, whether in terms of named officials or disputes over water. Finally, did Zhou Daguan describe irrigation?

The image of Jayavarman VII looks balefully through the forest at Angkor. Mystery still surrounds the nature of the city of Angkor Thom and the purpose of the great reservoirs.

Groslier (1979) and Dumarçay (1998) have emphasised that the location of Angkor provided the opportunity to control the southward flow of water. The Iron Age settlements in this area are located with respect to the rivers. Banteay Choeu, the first known historic centre, with its temple of Ak Yum was located athwart the Puok River. Hariharalaya commanded the Roluos River, which filled the Indratataka. Yashodharapura, he suggested, was placed to take advantage of the Siem Reap River. This was his first phase of the hydraulic city of Angkor. The second saw the construction of the Western Baray and the third involved the building of Angkor Wat. Groslier even felt that the water in the moat round this temple added significantly to the capacity of the irrigation system. Finally, the fourth city saw the construction of the Jayatataka and city of Angkor Thom. With each stage, the irrigated area expanded.

From the beginning of *baray* construction, Khmer builders regulated the flow of water into canals and moats. The first city of Yashodharapura was crossed by linked canals and water basins. Angkor Thom incorporated stone-lined culverts to take water from interior canals to the moats beyond the city walls. If the *barays* retained irrigation water, where are the outlets and canals leading to the rice fields? None has been found. Groslier responded to this question by suggesting that a channel was excavated outside and parallel with the southern dykes, which filled with water percolating through the dyke. Van Liere (1980) has been shown that this is technically impossible. However, we know that in the *tanub* system of dry season rice cultivation today, distribution channels are re-dug annually. This might explain their absence below the *barays*, but it should be noted that the *tanub* system operates below the maximum height of the flooded Tonle Sap. All the *barays* are positioned well above this limit.

Acker (1997) has given detailed consideration to the area that could have been irrigated, the water requirement, likely yields and the location of the *barays* relative to each other and the land below them. He began with Groslier's own figures, which involved a population estimated (it seems very generously) as 1,900,000 people of which 600,000 were supported by 86,000 ha of irrigated rice fields. In the dry season, a hectare would require 15,000 cubic metres of water. Assuming all the major *barays* at Angkor were full to a depth of three metres, they could have supplied 7,000 hectares. At an optimistic yield of 1.46 tonnes per hectare and annual consumption of 220 kg of rice per capita, the dry season yield would have maintained about 44,500 people, about 2.5% of Groslier's estimated population. This calculation is based only on the amount of water available when the *barays* were three metres deep. It does not take into account the possibility that the *barays* were constantly replenished with water from the Siem Reap River throughout the dry season. There is also the possibility that the reservoirs were used to

Angkor Wat is seen here from the summit of the Bakheng, the temple mausoleum of King Yashovarman.

Left: The huge moat at Angkor Wat was thought by Groslier to have contributed water to the Angkorian irrigation system. Most authorities think otherwise.

supplement water supplies to the fields when there was insufficient rainfall during the wet season. If so, then a further 9,000 tonnes over and above anticipated wet season production could have been obtained, bringing the total irrigated yield to 19,200 tonnes or sufficient to feed nearly 100,000 people.

These figures assume that all the *barays* were being employed simultaneously, a situation theoretically only possible during the reign of Jayavarman VII and his successors. On the other hand, Acker has shown that the reservoirs mask each other from potentially irrigable rice fields. The Yashodharataka could not have irrigated all the potential land below it, because the incised Siem Reap River would have made it impossible.

The inscriptions which mention the Angkorian reservoirs do not describe irrigation. A reference to an estate at Hariharalaya cites the Indratataka as a boundary marker but does not mention water. Another inscription described Yashovarman as the husband of the earth, who filled it with virtue, pleasure and fecundity but the ensuing mention of his *baray* is too damaged to allow its full meaning to be obtained. His foundation inscriptions compare Yashodharatataka to the moon, the source of life sustaining ambrosia. Rajendravarman, it is said, filled the water with his good works, and made it a mirror to reflect his temple. There is also a description of his erecting images in the Eastern Mebon, whose shrines were embellished with stucco. If Jayavarman VII had brought water to the rice fields, it would surely have appeared in his lengthy texts as one of his meritorious acts. Nor do we read anywhere of disputes over water, or of officials charged with its distribution.

Negative evidence does not prove anything, but it is nevertheless intriguing to examine a related context in Sri Lanka, where there was a centralised system of rice irrigation. The first inscriptions which describe irrigation date to the 3rd century BC. The system seems to have begun on a small scale, with each household having a share of

This great statue of Vishnu at Angkor Wat is caught in the dying rays of the sun. Still an object of veneration, it was probably once housed in the central lotus tower of Angkor Wat, and remains a potent symbol of the aura of royal power.
(Courtesy Paisarn Piemmattawat)

the irrigated land. Reservoirs were valued for their fish supply and were used for further cultivation in the dry season. Individual ownership and meritorious gifts of irrigated land to temples began during the first century AD, but it was the invention of the cistern sluice in the second century which opened the path to large scale works. King Vasabha (AD 65-109) constructed 12 reservoirs and the Alisara canal, which took water to distant fields. By AD 150, we read of large, service reservoirs and interlocking systems. In the third century, a huge reservoir 24 km in circumference was completed, and the system expanded to included 12 further reservoirs over the next five centuries. Some were royal property and built by forced labour. Others were privately owned by people known as *vavihamika*, in communal ownership, or were the property of monasteries. The private owners took the *dakabaka*, or water share, a proportion of the two or three crops grown annually on irrigated land. The legal system cited theft of water and fish from irrigation works as offences (Gunawardana 1981). No similar texts exist in Cambodia.

The only eye-witness account of agriculture in the vicinity of Angkor comes from the brush of Zhou Daguan. He wrote that three or four crops a year could be obtained, a statement which supporters of the irrigation theory take as confirmation. On the other hand, Zhou Daguan did not specify that they all came from the same plot. Indeed, with a combination of rain-fed rice fields, the retreating floodwater or *tanub* system, swiddening and floating rice, non-irrigated techniques could bring in four crops at different times of the year.

If the *barays* at Angkor were not used for irrigation, how was rice grown? Aerial photographs have revealed many temple sites associated with small rectangular reservoirs and square plots, all on the same axis (Pottier 1997). These square enclosures are, beyond reasonable doubt, Angkorian rice fields. No such site has yet been dated, but there are strong grounds for suggesting that agriculture incorporated bunded fields for which in an average year, rainfall was sufficient to produce satisfactory returns. The number of references to water buffaloes and at least one possible reference to a plough, suggests that all the ingredients of modern rainfed agriculture were in place during the period of Angkor. There is also, as Acker has pointed out, the possibility that small water tanks could have been used as sources of water in the face of difficult dry spells. If they were dug down below the water table, they would have been constantly replenished as water was drawn off.

The balance of evidence argues against a large, centrally-controlled irrigation system based on the *barays*. This removes the control of irrigation facilities from any explanation for the rise of royal power, or the collapse of the state. What then, was the purpose of the *barays*? If the temples represented Mount Meru, reservoirs would become the surrounding oceans. Their metaphorical role is likewise seen at other major state temples, such as Preah Khan of Kompong Svai and Banteay Chmar. Anyone who has sat in the shade next to a reservoir during April, when the sun burns from a leaden sky, and felt the breeze off the water, will approve of the merit gained by its creator.

Angkor in a wider perspective

General reviews of archaic states tend to concentrate upon intensely studied areas, such as Egypt, Mesopotamia or Mesoamerica. Occasionally, Southeast Asia reaches centre stage for comparative purposes: does it show similarities with better-documented regions? One of several problems with this comparative approach is that there are few authoritative descriptions of the state of Angkor which begin with its deep roots in the prehistoric past, and continue to the abandonment of 1431. Those which do have only paid lip service to prehistory at best, and often present an entirely inaccurate portrayal. George Cœ

The centre of Angkor contains numerous temples. This fine brick complex is known as Prasat Kravan.

dès, after a life time of dedication to the inscriptions, described the indigenous inhabitants, who in effect generated the civilisation of Angkor, as still being in the stone age.

Recent syntheses of the origins of states in other parts of the world have identified several significant variables. Carneiro (1992), for example, has advanced six conditions for the emergence of a state from preceding chiefdoms. They revolve round the power to defeat neighbours and incorporate them into a larger polity, the power to enslave prisoners, take tribute, provide a corps of fighting men and to place one's supporters in control over conquered territory. There is considerable support for these propositions in recent instances of state formation assembled by Flannery (1999). The ritual and physical control of trade is a further variable which recurs in many cases, while Wright (1986) has noted how early stages in state formation are characterised by cycles of different chiefs, the rise and fall of social complexity before the transition to the state has occurred. Marcus (1998) has taken up this theme in her dynamic model, noting the widespread finding in Mesoamerica that archaic states underwent phases of regional dominance and contraction. The Maya, for example, began as a congerie of competing chiefdoms with cyclic rises and falls in power as the centre of gravity switched. In Mesopotamia, the rulers of Susa controlled a state covering a wide area from 3700-3200 BC, but during a later phase, it split into two competing groups (Wright 1998). Is there, underlying these similar patterns, a recurrent difficulty in maintaining inegalitarian social systems?

Although the Maya and Angkor states have from time to time been linked as lowland forest civilisations, there are in fact several basic differences. The latter benefitted from one of, if not the most adaptive and productive grains, rice. The people of Angkor also possessed powerful draught animals, and iron technology. Yet it is still possible to identify a number of consistencies with other emerging states. Even in the late Iron Age, there is some evidence for the crowding of settlements in the favoured low-lying river valleys of the

In 1296, Zhou Daguan described magnificent pageants on this open area fronting the royal palace at Angkor. Formerly the king presided from within a gilded pavilion on top of the massive elephant terrace.

southern Khorat Plateau, linked with a surge in population. The only extensive excavation of one of these sites has shown that iron weapons proliferated, one arrowhead being actually lodged in a man's spine. Steps were taken to control the flow of water well before such techniques were allegedly introduced by Indian traders. With the first Chinese accounts of the Mekong Delta region, we are able to read of wars for territorial gain, the incorporation of other groups into a single polity and placement of a king's relatives over the conquered. Nor should the massive investment in canals linking the delta settlements be overlooked. If modern practice is any guide, these were used for drainage and rapid transport across a marshy landscape. A further widespread feature of early trends towards state formation is drainage and agricultural improvements to maintain the loyalty of followers. This, too, is suggested by an early and important inscription.

Funan, the delta state, probably lasted for two or three centuries before it suffered from a change in international trade routes, and the rise of powerful inland chiefs. The 250 years from AD 550 in the riverine flood plains of the interior saw two diametrically opposing forces at work. The first involved high chiefs, overlords or kings attempting to control land and labour through force and the projection of a sacred persona. This was offset by other local leaders pursuing independence and their own push for regional hegemony. In this context, the cyclic rising and falling of competing overlords echoes similar sequences noted in the Near East and the Americas. Within this period, one does not need to look far to find evidence for growing social inequality. The very names are sufficient evidence. On the one hand, there is the Sanskrit title of a king meaning protégé of the great Indra, and on the other, there are workers with Khmer names meaning dog, stinker, or black monkey.

Within this period of competition and endemic conflict, the inscriptions of Jayavarman I reflect a breakthrough in state formation, with his appointment of state officials and creation of at least three and probably four levels of settlement hierarchy. Yet his successors are only recorded for one generation before the epigraphic record for this dynasty fell silent.

It has been suggested that Maya kings were not greatly concerned with agriculture or its intensification, nor with trade other than that which involved symbols of ritual potency, such as quetzal feathers and jade. This emphasises the importance they attached to religion. The Maya regarded their rulers as the means of communicating with the divine world of the gods and ancestors, and as the symbolic axis of the universe, thus helping us to understand their investment in awe-inspiring temples, symbolically important facades, stelae commemorating accession to rule, genealogies and victories, and concern to control access to symbols of office. On the reverse of the coin, failure of a harvest or a military defeat would soon remove the aura of divinity.

This key issue for the Maya again finds parallels in Angkor. It has been argued that the kings of Angkor did not control a centralised irrigation system based on their undoubted skill in hydraulic engineering. Angkor might have seemed an oriental Venice, but there is insufficient evidence to envisage a kingdom based on irrigated rice. The weight of evidence is more in favour of a decentralised system, in which grandee families controlled labour for the production of rain-fed rice in small bunded fields, supplemented by floating, flood retreat or swidden rice where appropriate. This does not rule out some local and small scale networks of channels to bring water to rice fields if the monsoon faltered, but this is not a royally-inspired hydraulic civilization.

As with the Maya, we are left to ponder how kings maintained their grip on power. Many leading scholars have noted the importance of ritual, emphasising in particular the role of the capital as the symbolic centre of the universe. This is self evident in the inscriptions and architectural remains of Angkor. We can also note the importance of royal sacred power and adherence to *dharma*, the moral law. We find numerous allusions to the divine nature of the king. His name was joined with that of Shiva in the golden *linga* in his temple. In terms of architecture, Angkor is, *par excellence*, the outstanding example of building in the name of majesty and sacred power. The role of the king in interceding with the deified ancestors, and ordering the construction of reservoirs containing temples which literally removed a person's sins and assured a better rebirth, again reflects the importance of ritual authority.

Yet there was a darker side. However many insignia of high status were handed down, however much land was donated, however many roads and bridges were constructed, there was still the problem of controlling distant provinces and court factions. So the civilisation of Angkor joins its peers elsewhere in exhibiting chronic instability in times of central weakness, and a tendency to fragment and contract with outside pressure. Following the death of Jayavarman VII, there was a continuing decline in the projection of central power through construction activity, a contraction of the kingdom's boundaries, ideological changes in favour of Theravada Buddhism and, finally, a series of military defeats at the hands of the Siamese.

Chapter Eight

The Structure of the Past in Southeast Asia

Fifteen years ago, when summarising the predecessor of this book, I wrote that:

"In this study, I have tried to identify images, to seek explanations, and to focus on possibilities. I have not sought answers, but rather to pose questions and propose explanatory structures in the hope that others will tilt at them, knock them over and replace them with better ones." (Higham 1989: 356).

Happily, those hopes have been fulfilled. In virtually every period and major issue, earlier explanations have been set aside by the results of new excavations, and the incorporation of new and detailed scrutiny of older sources of information.

The adoption of rice farming is one of the most critical changes in Southeast Asian prehistory, but this should not obscure the growing awareness of the rich and sedentary coastal hunter-gatherers so clearly illuminated at the site of Khok Phanom Di. In 1986, most research on the origins of rice cultivation centred on identifying a transition from hunting and gathering to agricultural societies within Southeast Asia. Our research at Khok Phanom Di began with the hypothesis that rich, sedentary coastal hunters and gatherers adopted rice cultivation as the environment changed with a falling sea level. The fissioning of resulting Neolithic communities then led to intrusive settlement, which followed the river courses. This proposal foundered on many shoals and is set aside. Intensive research in the middle reaches of the Yangzi River has revealed a long and coherent sequence involving the domestication of rice and establishment of sedentary, village communities. The transition took place during the 10th-8th millennia BC, and covered the same time span as similar developments in the Levant. The examination of many Neolithic settlements in China and Southeast Asia has disclosed a consistent pattern: the further removed from the Central Yangzi Valley, the later the first evidence for rice cultivation.

As this archaeological pattern was crystallising, Renfrew (1987) published a synthesis of archaeological and linguistic data, in which he proposed that the distribution of Indo-European languages can best be understood in the context of the expansion of Neolithic communities from the Near East. A similar conjunction of archaeological and linguistic evidence had been evident in tracing the settlement of the

Opposite:
Neolithic burials in Southeast Asia are very rare and no large cemetery has been excavated. At Ban Non Wat in 2002, part of such a cemetery was discovered, the dead being interred with the head pointing to the north, associated with fine incised and painted pottery vessels.

Bronze Age burials in Southeast Asia are vital in understanding the nature of the social organization. This adult from Ban Non Wat, excavated in 2002, was interred with 47 exotic marine shell bangles, shell beads, and many beautiful pottery vessels.

islands of Melanesia, Southeast Asia and the wider Pacific. These proposals posed a key question: was there a comparable expansion on the mainland of Southeast Asia, which involved those now cultivating rice and maintaining domestic stock?

A vital contribution to this issue came when Reid (1994) identified linguistic evidence on the Nicobar islands linking the major language families, Austronesian and Austroasiatic. The former is dominant in the islands of Southeast Asia, and component languages now stretch from Malagasy to Easter Island. Many scholars agree that its earliest known roots lie in the native languages of Taiwan. The latter is spread widely on the mainland, from eastern India to Viet Nam. The degree of differentiation between related languages across this area suggests a considerable but unspecified time depth to specialists in linguistics (Diffloth 1994). There are cognate words for rice, however, and aspects of its cultivation which link widely-dispersed groups of speakers.

A common origin for both language families would have profound implications, a point stressed by Blust (1996). If, for example, a common ancestral language were spoken by early cultivators of rice, then the expansion of Neolithic communities could explain the present distribution of both Austronesian and Austrasiatic speakers. Blust has proposed that the latter spread into Southeast Asia and India from the upper Yangzi Valley, a movement encouraged and expedited by river transport. It should be added that a parallel expansion from the Yangzi catchment into southern China could likewise have followed the river valleys. No archaeologist with an interest in Southeast Asia could ignore this bold proposal. In my view, the archaeological data available are supportive. We find agricultural settlements being founded in the lower Red River valley, along the course of the Mekong and its tributaries, and in the Chao Phraya Valley. Such an intrusion of rice farmers was, indeed, proposed by Sørensen in 1972. The dates for initial settlement, as far as they are known, are approximately the same with none earlier than about 2300 BC. Most intriguingly, the pottery vessels in many of the sites over a broad area have a similar mode of decoration. The sites reveal extended inhumation graves, and an economy incorporating rice cultivation and the raising of domestic stock.

This proposed intrusive movement of rice farmers stands as a new model, and is just as subject to intensive and critical scrutiny as its predecessor. It is predicted that advances in molecular biology as well as archaeology, will have the potential to refine or replace it. At present, its implications for the hunter-gatherer societies which encountered agriculturalists must be reviewed. We find that few settlements of the enduring and vigorous inland Hoabinhian tradition of hunting and gathering post date 2300 BC. There may, however, have been interaction between inland farmers and rich coastal hunter-gatherer communities. Nong Nor and Khok Phanom Di allow this issue to be explored. At the former, we have no evidence for agriculture, nor for the domestic dog at a site occupied about 2450 BC. Basal Khok Phanom Di dates from about 2000 BC. The virtually identical pottery, bone and stone industries suggest that the first inhabitants belonged to a local maritime hunter-gatherer tradition. According to Vincent (2002), the lowest ceramic industry was replaced before the initial burials were laid down, but it belonged to the same regional tradition. Certainly, the estuarine and mangrove conditions would have been detrimental to rice cultivation, but some of the imported, exotic pottery sherds were tempered with rice chaff. The middle of mortuary phase 3 saw a sharp environmental change in favour of freshwater conditions, and changes in the ceramic industry which hint at increasing specialisation, production and exchange. One possible explanation is that women came into the settlement, perhaps as marriage partners, and introduced new approaches to the ceramic industry. It was also at this juncture, that rice was probably cultivated locally. A return to marine conditions terminated local cultivation, but heralded an extraordinary phase of increased mortuary wealth and ritual linked, it is thought, to the growth in exchange. By about 1500 BC, however, the site was abandoned.

This is a very difficult site to interpret. Was an initial occupation by hunters and gatherers followed by settlement by intrusive agriculturalists? I doubt this because there is no evidence in the first two mortuary phases for agriculture. Were, then, the hunters and gatherers interacting, directly or through intermediaries, with inland farming communities? This seems highly likely, given the importation of exotic, rice-tempered pottery. Were there occasions when the men or women from such farming communities came to Khok Phanom Di as marriage partners? This may have occurred, but techniques to explore this possibility are in their infancy. In any case, the weight of evidence now suggests that the inhabitants of this site, far from initiating an expansion inland, were exposed to intrusive rice farmers with ultimate origins in the Yangzi Valley.

In the first version this book, I concluded that I could not identify an origin of metallurgy while the dates of the early Bronze Age were so ill defined. This issue has been considerably clarified, although there is still no overall consensus. There are two key elements in resolving this contentious issue. On a broad canvas, it is now possible to date the expansion of bronze industries across the steppes into western China. For some time, it has been difficult to explain why the earliest bronze in China came from the far west. Now, however, a western origin is being seriously canvassed. From Gansu, the knowledge of bronze was adopted in the Central Plains and reached an early apogee in the specialist workshops of Erlitou, Zhengzhou and Anyang. The presence of Shang period bronzes and jades in Neolithic contexts in southern China and Viet Nam indicates a possible route for the knowledge of copper and tin alloying to reach Southeast Asia. Serious evidence for bronze in Southeast Asia before the presence of exotic bronzes and jades would thus favour an indigenous origin. Two sites have been widely publicised as providing such early evidence: Ban Chiang and Non Nok Tha. The second key element is the advent of AMS dating. Both sites have proved very difficult to date consistently through conventional means because of doubts over the context of dated charcoal, and contradictory results (Higham 1983). However, the application of AMS dating to the rice chaff employed to temper the clay used in mortuary vessels has shown that bronzes are far later than was first suggested. Indeed, we now have strong evidence for similar bronze artefacts and virtually identical casting technology from Hong Kong and the adjacent

Much time has been spent at Angkor restoring the great temples and putting them in chronological order. In the future archaeology will add enormously to our knowledge of this capital city. Here, a very early brick wall foundation has been unearthed in the precinct of the temple of Baksei Chamkrong.

coast to Central Thailand, and from Yunnan south to the Mekong Delta. It thus seems highly likely that Southeast Asia falls into a pattern in which the diffusion of the knowledge of bronze working crossed the steppes, spread across China and entered first mainland, and then much later island, Southeast Asia. At least partial resolution of the chronological framework for bronze has opened more interesting avenues of enquiry. A series of relatively large excavations has now illuminated the organisational aspects of copper mining and processing, while the social implications of metallurgy can now be placed on a firmer footing.

We do not know whether a knowledge of iron smelting arose locally, or was derived from an external source. Current dating suggests that iron artefacts were probably being forged by about 500 BC, and certainly by 300 BC. While the vigour of the Dong Son Iron Age, and the wealth of the Ban Don Ta Phet cemetery pointed alike to a sharp rise in wealth and social ranking during the Iron Age, the period between AD 1-500 remained little known. It was during these vital centuries, that areas of Southeast Asia beyond the reach of Chinese imperialism witnessed the formation of early states. This void has been filled through the excavations at Noen U-Loke, a site with a sequence covering virtually the entire course of the Iron Age. The energy expended on mortuary rituals during the first few centuries AD illustrates a society which increasingly recognised social status. At the same time, there was an increase in the number of iron projectile points, one of which was embedded in a young man's spine. Excavations in the surrounding banks and channels shows that these same communities were engaged in major hydraulic works designed to retain and control the flow of water round the settlements, some of which were now up to ten times the area of the largest known Bronze Age sites. A new range of exotic ornaments appeared, some of which were locally manufactured. The list includes glass, gold, silver, carnelian, agate and bronze. Iron was also forged into agricultural implements, such as spades, hoes and sickles. It is anticipated that excavations in contemporary contexts in other sites, not least under the great city of Angkor Borei in Cambodia and in Sa Huynh cemeteries, will further enlarge our understanding of Iron Age society on the eve of statehood. This new information allows us to appreciate that maritime trade routes already linked the mainland with the islands, and with India and China, during the late prehistoric period. Rather than supinely accepting foreign traders, the people of Southeast Asia were actively engaged. This proficiency in ocean voyaging might well help explain how they came to occupy distant Malagasy.

The transition to states in Southeast Asia has been a difficult period to evaluate, because it is the point where several disciplines converge. Information is now drawn from inscriptions in Sanskrit, Pali, Mon, Khmer and Cham, from Chinese documents, Indian sagas, art history as well as from archaeology. The notion of 'Indianisation' held centre stage in the writings of the French school. Certainly, local elites chose to worship Indian gods, adopt certain Indian architectural forms and take Sanskrit names. Research over the last 15 years has seriously modified the extent to which Southeast Asian states were indebted to Indian inspiration. New evidence for the technical sophistication and social complexity of late Iron Age societies is one contributing factor to this new appraisal. The second, is a detailed examination of the corpus of inscriptions in the Khmer language by Vickery (1998). Formerly given little prominence in favour of the Sanskrit texts, Vickery has peeled away the Indic veneer, and traced state formation through a series of incremental social changes, linked with worship not just of exotic Hindu gods, but also local, ancestral deities. The rarity of inscriptions from related developments in Champa and the Chao Phraya Valley has vitiated a fuller understanding of the Cham and Dvaravati states, but the basic processes were probably similar.

Vickery (1998) has also provided us with a new appraisal of the origins of the state of Angkor. He has suggested that Jayavarman II was an ambitious and able leader based at or near Banteay Prei Nokor. An inscription put in place over 200 years after his death suggested that Jayavarman had spent some time at Java. This, according to Vickery, probably implies border warfare with the Chams. The King enhanced his power base by a strategic marriage alliance, and moved his followers northwest, to the shores of the Great Lake. From the late 8th century, it is possible to chart the main developments of the Kingdom of Angkor through three dynasties until its abandonment in the 15th century. The foundations of the state were firmly embedded in rice cultivation and the appropriation of rural surpluses, and this basic relationship has led to the supposition that the great reservoirs and water control measures were deployed in order to feed irrigated rice fields. This has been intensely analysed recently. The hydrological variables and geomorphology of the alleged irrigated areas fail to support the irrigation theory. Moreover, the inscriptions are replete with records of disputes over land boundaries, but never mention access to irrigation reservoirs or canals. In this, the corpus of texts contrasts fundamentally with that from Sri Lanka, where irrigation was widespread. It is argued above, that the reservoirs fulfilled a symbolic and religious role. At Angkor, the Kulen Hills and water flowing south were seen as sacred, and each reservoir had its central island temple. Just as the central shrine was built to represent heavenly Mount Meru, so the *barays* and moats are seen as symbolising the encircling oceans. Thus the identification of the sovereign with the gods was a central bonding feature of the Angkorian state which, when viewed in its broader perspective, still faced the problem of factionalism and fissioning.

The growing volume of archaeological activity summarised above has transformed our understanding of the past in Southeast Asia. The early cultures, and by definition the prehistoric people, are thus emerging from the wings to take centre stage in a sequence of innovative changes which lie at the roots of the modern nation states. To understand the prehistoric past is thus to understand in large measure, the cultures of the present.

The past lives on at Angkor. In 1296, Zhou Daguan described King Indravarman riding in procession on his elephants. Here, elephants wait their passengers in front of the great southern gate of Angkor Thom.

References

Abbreviations:

AIB-L Académie des Inscriptions et Belles-Lettres.

AP Asian Perspectives.

APAO Archaeology and Physical Anthropology in Oceania.

BEFEO Bulletin de l'École Française d'Extrême Orient.

BIPPA Bulletin of the Indo-Pacific Prehistory Association.

BSGI Bulletin de la Service Géologique d'Indochine.

BSOAC Bulletin of the School of Oriental and African Studies.

EFEO École Française d'Extrême Orient.

GATIA Gansu Archaeological Teams, Institute of Archaeology

GZAR Guangzi Zhuangsu Autonomous Region

JAH Journal of African History.

JA Journal Asiatique.

JAS Journal of the Asiatic Society.

JMBRAS Journal of the Malay Branch of the Royal Asiatic Society.

JSS Journal of the Siam Society.

KCH Khao Co Hoc (all in Vietnamese).

MEFEO Mémoires de l'École Française d'Extrême Orient.

MSGI Mémoires du Service Géologique de l'Indochine.

MQRISA Modern Quaternary Research in Southeast Asia.

OUSPA Otago University Studies in Prehistoric Anthropology.

PEFEO Publications de l'École Française d'Extrême Orient.

YPM Yunnan Provincial Museum.

Albrecht, G., Berke, H., Burger, D., Moser, J., Muller-Beck, H., Pookajorn, S., Rahle, W. and Urban, n.d. B. Sakai Cave, Trang Province, Southern Thailand. Report on the Field Work 1993.

Agelarakis, A. 1997. Some reconstructions of human bio-cultural conditions during the 3rd and 2nd millennia B.C. in South-East Asia. In Ciarla, R. and Rispoli, F. editors, *South-East Asian Archaeology 1992*, pages 99-117. Istituto Italiano per L'Africa e L'Oriente, Rome.

Alpers, E.A. 1969. Trade, state and society among the Yao in the nineteenth century. *JAH*, 93: 405-520.

An Zhimin, 1998. Cultural complexes of the Bronze Age in the Tarim Basin and surrounding areas. In Mair, V. H. editor, *The Bronze Age and Early Iron Age Peoples of Eastern Central Asia*, pages 45-62. The Institute for the Study of Man and the University of Pennsylvania Museum Publications, Philadelphia.

Anthony, D.W. 1998. The opening of the Eurasian steppe at 2000 BCE. In Mair, V.H. editor, *The Bronze Age and Early Iron Age Peoples of Eastern Central Asia*, pages 94-113. The Institute for the Study of Man and the University of Pennsylvania Museum Publications, Philadelphia.

Argensola, Bartolome L. de 1609. *Conquista de las Islas Malucas*. A. Martin, Madrid.

Au Ka-fat, 1993. An introduction to the spread of various ancient cultures from the middle and lower Yangtze River area to Guangdong region. In Chau Hing-Wah editor, *Collected Essays on the Culture of the Ancient Yue People in South China*, pages 24-33. Hong Kong Museum of History, Hong Kong.

Aymonier, E. 1900-1903. *La Cambodge II: Les Provinces Siamoises*. Paris, Ernest Leroux.

Bannanurag, R. and Khemnark, P. 1992. *Prehistoric burials at Wat Pho Si Nai, Ban Chiang*. FAD, Bangkok.

Barber, E. J. W. 1998. Bronze Age cloth and clothing of the Tarim Basin: the Kroran (Loulan) and Qumul (Hami) evidence. In Mair, V. H. editor, *The Bronze Age and Early Iron Age Peoples of Eastern Central Asia*, pages 647-55. The Institute for the Study of Man and the University of Pennsylvania Museum Publications, Philadelphia.

Barth, A. 1885. *Inscriptions Sanscrites du Cambodge*. Notices et extraits des mss. de la Bib. Nat., t. XXVII, le partie, fasc. 1, Paris.

Bayard, D.T. 1971. *Non Nok Tha. The 1968 Excavation: Procedure, Stratigraphy and a Summary of the Evidence*. OUSPA No. 4.

Bayard, D.T. 1972. Excavations at Non Nok Tha, Northeastern Thailand 1968: an interim report. *AP* 13: 109-43.

Bayard, D.T. 1972a. Early Thai bronze: analysis and new dates. *Science* 176: 1411-2.

Bayard, D.T. 1979. Comment on the linguistic history of mainland Southeast Asia by H.L. Shorto. R.B. Smith and W. Watson editors, *Early South East Asia*, pages 278-80. Oxford University Press, Oxford.

Bayard, D.T., Charoenwongsa, P. and Rutnin, S. 1986. Excavations at Non Chai, Northeastern Thailand. *AP* 25(1): 13-62.

Bénisti, M. 1968. Recherches sur le premier art Khmêr 1. Les Linteaux dits de Thala Borivat. *Arts Asiatiques* XVIII: 85-102.

Bénisti, M. 1970. Rapports entre le premier art Khmêr et d'art Indien. *MEFEO* V.

Bennett, A. and Glover, I.C. 1992. Decorated high-tin bronze bowls from Thailand's prehistory. Glover, I.C. editor, *Southeast Asian Archaeology 1990*, pages 187-208. Centre for Southeast Asian Studies, University of Hull, Hull.

Bergaigne, A. 1893. *Inscriptions Sanscrites de Campa et du Cambodge.* Notices et extraits des mss. de la Bib. Nat., t. XXVII, le partie, fasc. 2, Paris.

Bhumadhon, B. 1987. *The Archaeology of Muang Dongkorn* (in Thai). Amarin Printing Group, Bangkok.

Bloch, M. 1977. The disconnection between power and rank as a process: an outline of the development of kingdoms in central Madagascar. J. Friedman and M.J. Rowlands editors, *The Evolution of Social Systems*, pages 303-40. Duckworth, London.

Blust, R. 1996. Beyond the Austronesian homeland: the Austric hypothesis and its implications for archaeology. In Goodenough, W.H. editor, *Prehistoric Settlement of the Pacific*, pages 117-40. Transactions of the American Philosophical Society 86, Philadelphia.

Boelès, J.J. 1964. The King of Dvaravati and his regalia. *JSS:* LII(1): 99-114.

Boisselier, J. 1968. *Nouvêlles Connaissances Archéologiques de la Ville d' U T'ong.* Bangkok.

Boisselier, J. 1997. The meaning of Angkor Thom. H.I. Jessup and Zéphir, T. editors, *Sculpture of Angkor and Ancient Cambodia. Millennium of Glory*, pages 117-20. Washington D.C: National Gallery of Art.

Bourke, W.W. 1905. Some archaeological notes on Monton Phuket. *JSS* II: 49-62.

Boyd, W.E. 1998. The palaeoenvironment of the archaeological site at Nong Nor In Higham, C.F.W. and Thosarat, R. editors, *The Excavation of Nong Nor, a Prehistoric Site in Central Thailan,* pages 27-86. OUSPA No. 18, Dunedin.

Boyd, W.E., Higham, C.F.W. and McGrath, R. 1999. The geo-archaeology of the Iron Age "moated" sites of the Upper Mae Nam Mun valley, N.E. Thailand. I. Palaeo-drainage, site-landscape relationships, and the origins of the "moats". *Geoarchaeology*, 14: 675-716.

Bray, F. 1984. *Science and Civilisation in China*; vol. 6, *Biology and Biological Technology. Part II: Agriculture.* Cambridge University Press, Cambridge.

Briggs, L.P. 1951. The Ancient Khmer Empire. *Trans. Am. Phil. Soc.* 4 (1).

Bronson, B. 1979. The late prehistory and early history of Central Thailand with special reference to Chansen. In Smith, R.B. and Watson, W. editors, *Early South East Asia*, pages 315-36. Oxford University Press, Oxford.

Bronson, B. 1999. The transition to iron in Ancient China. In Pigott, V.C. editor, *The Archaeometallurgy of the Asian Old World*, pages 177-98. Masca Research Papers in Science and Archaeology, Volume 16. University Museum, University of Pennsylvania, Philadelphia.

Bronson, B. and Dales, G.F. 1973. Excavations at Chansen, Thailand, 1968, 1969: a preliminary report. *AP* 15(1): 15-46.

Buchan, R.A. 1973. *The Three-dimensional Jig-saw Puzzle: a Ceramic Sequence from NE Thailand.* M.A. thesis, University of Otago.

Bui Vinh 1991. Origins of Neolithic pottery centres in Vietnam. *KCH* 1991(4): 1-8.

Bui Vinh 1995. Initial steps on determining areas of distributions and characteristics of stone artefacts of the Ha Giang culture (in Vietnamese). *KCH* 1995(3): 33-45.

Buranrak and Co. 1994. *Report on the Excavation of Non Praw* (in Thai). FAD, Bangkok.

Buranrak and Co. 1994a. *Report on the Excavation of Don Khlang* (in Thai). FAD, Bangkok.

Carbonnel, J. P. 1979. Recent data on the Cambodian Neolithic: the problem of cultural continuity in southern Indochina. In Smith, R.B. and Watson, W. editors, *Early*
Southeast Asia, pages 223-6. Oxford, Oxford University Press.

Carneiro, R.L. 1992. Point counterpoint. Ecology and ideology in the development of New World civilizations, in Demarest, A.A. and Conrad, G.W., editors, *Ideology and Pre-Columbian Civilizations.* School of American Research Press, Santa Fe.

Chang, K.-C. 1986. *The Archaeology of Ancient China.* Yale University Press, New Haven.

Chang, T.T. 1976. The rice cultures. *Phil. Trans. Royal Society of London* B. series 275: 143-57.

Chang, T.T. and Loresto, E. 1984. The rice remains. In Higham C.F.W. and Kijngam, A. editors, *Prehistoric Investigations in Northeast Thailand*, pages 384-5. British Archaeological Reports (International Series) 231: 2. Oxford.

Chau Hing-Wah 1993. Periodization of prehistoric culture of Pearl River Delta Area. In Chau Hing-Wah editor, *Collected Essays on the Culture of the Ancient Yue People in South China*, pages 54-62. Hong Museum of History, Hong Kong.

Cho-Yun Hsu 1999. The Spring and Autumn Period. In Loewe, M. and Shaughnessy, E.L. editors, *The Cambridge History of Ancient China*, pages 545-86. Cambridge University Press, Cambridge.

Choosiri, P. 1998. The human remains from the excavations in the Pasak Valley. In Daeng-Iet, S. and Youkongdee, P. editors, *The Archaeology of the Pasak Valley*, pages 38-66 (in Thai). Fine Arts Department, Bangkok.

Christie, A. 1970, *The provenence and chronology of early Indian cultural influence in Southeast Asia.* In Sarkar H.B. editor, R.C. Majumdar Felicitation Volume, pages 1-14. Mukjopadhyay, Calcutta.

Ciarla, R. 1992. The Thai-Italian Lopburi regional archaeological project: preliminary results. Glover, I.C. editor, *Southeast Asian Archaeology 1990*, pages 111-28.

Centre for Southeast Asian Studies, University of Hull, Hull.

Claeys, J.Y. 1927. Configuration du site de Tra-Kieu. *BEFEO* 27: 469-82.

Claeys, J.Y. 1931. Simhapura, la grande capitale Chame (VI-VIIIe S.A.D.). *Revue des Arts Asiatiques* VII: 93-104.

Clark, J.G.D. 1962. *World Prehistory.* Cambridge University Press, Cambridge.

Cœdès, G. 1924. Études cambodgiennes XVIII. L'extension de Cambodge vers le sud-ouest au VIIe siècle (nouvèlles inscriptions de Chantaboun). *BEFEO* 24: 352-8.

Cœdès, G. 1928. The excavations of Pong Tuk and their importance for the ancient history of Siam. *JSS* 21(3): 195-209.

Cœdès, G. 1931. Deux inscriptions Sanskrites de Fou-nan. *BEFEO* 31: 1-23.

Cœdès, G. 1937-1954. *Inscriptions du Cambodge.* 6 vols. Hanoi: 1937, 1942. Paris: 1951, 1952, 1953, 1954.

Cœdès, G. 1941. La Stêle de Prah Khan d'Angkor. *BEFEO* 41: 255-301.

Cœdès, G. 1947. Fouilles en Cochinchine. Le site de Go Oc Eo, ancien port du Royaume Fou-nan. *Artibus Asiae* X: 193-9.

Cœdès, G. 1958. Nouvelles donnees épigraphiques sur l'histoire de l'Indochine Centrale. *JA* 1958.

Cœdès, G. 1968. *The Indianised States of Southeast Asia.* East-West Centre Press, Honolulu.

Colani, M. 1927. L'Âge de la pierre dans la province de Hoa Binh. *MSGI* XIII: 1.

Colani, M. 1930 Recherches sur le Préhistorique Indochinoise. *BEFEO* 30: 299-422.

Colani, M. 1935. Mégalithes du Haut-Laos. *PEFEO* 25-6.

Corre, A. 1879. Rapport sur les objets de l'Âge de la pierre polie et du bronze recueillis à Som-Ron-Sen (Cambodge) et note annexe sur des instruments en pierre polie et en bronze trouvés aux environs de Saigon. *Excursions et Reconnaissances* (Saigon) 1: 71-91.

Crawford, G.W. and Chen Shen 1998. The origins of rice agriculture: recent progress in East Asia. *Antiquity* 72: 858-66.

Creel, H.G. 1964. The beginnings of bureaucracy in China: the origin of the *Hsien. JAS* XXIII(2): 155-83.

Daeng-iet, S. 1978. Khok Phlap: a newly discovered prehistoric site (in Thai). *Muang Boran* 4(4): 17-26.

Daeng-Iet, S. and Youkongdee, P. editors, 1998. *The Archaeology of the Pasak Valley.* FAD, Bangkok.

Dang Van Thang and Vu Quoc Hien 1995. Khai quat di chi Giong Ca Vo (Can Gio, Thanh pho Ho Chi Minh), (in Vietnamese). *KCH* 1995(2): 3-19.

De Casparis, J.G. 1979. Palaeography as an auxilliary discipline in research on early Southeast Asia. In Smith R.B. and Watson W. editors, *Early Southeast Asia,* pages 380-94. Oxford University Press, Oxford.

de Ribadeneyra, F.M. 1601. *Historia de Las Islas del Archipielago y Reynos de la Grand China,* G. Graells, Barcelona.

Dega, M.F. 1999. Circular settlements within eastern Cambodia. *BIPPA* 18: 181-90.

Delvert, J. 1961. *Le Paysan Cambodgien. Le Monde d'Outre Mer Passé et Présent.* Première Série No.10. École Practique des Hautes Études, Sorbonne.

Di Cosmo. N. 1999. The northern frontier in pre-Imperial China. In Loewe, M. and Shaughnessy, E.L. editors, *The Cambridge History of Ancient China,* pages 885-966. Cambridge University Press, Cambridge.

Diffloth, G. 1981. Reconstructing Dvaravati-Old Mon. In Bhumadon, P. and Na Nakhon Phnom, S. editors, *The Earliest Inscriptions found at Lopburi and Nearby.* FAD, Bangkok.

Diffloth, G. 1994. The lexical evidence for Austric, so far. *Oceanic Linguistics* 33: 309-22.

Dinh Ba Hoa 1998. Dong Son drums found in Binh Dinh, (in Vietnamese). *KCH* 1998(4): 52-65.

Diskul, M.C. Subhadradis 1979. The development of Dvaravati sculpture and a recent find from Northeast Thailand. In Smith, R.B. and Watson, W. editors, *Early South East Asia,* pages 360-70. Oxford University Press, Oxford.

Dobby, E.H.G. 1967. *Southeast Asia.* University of London Press, London.

Domett, K.M. 1999. *Health in Late Prehistoric Thailand.* PhD. dissertation, University of Otago.

Doudart de Lagrée E. de G. 1883. *Explorations et Misssions.* A.B. de Villemereuil, Paris.

Dufour, H and Carpeaux, G. 1910. *Le Bayon d'Angkor Thom.* E. Leroux, Paris.

Douglas, M.T. 1996. *Paleopathology in Human Skeletal Remains from the Pre-Metal, Bronze and Iron Ages, Northeastern Thailand.* PhD. dissertation, University of Hawaii.

Dowling, N. 1999. A new date for the Phnom Da images and its implications for Early Cambodia. *AP* 38(1): 51-61.

Dupont, P. 1943-6. Études sur L'Indo chine ancienne: II la dislocation du Tchenla et la formation du Cambodge Angkorien. *BEFEO* 42: 17-55.

Dupont, P. 1959. L'Archéologie Mône de Dvaravati. *EFEO,* Paris.

Ekholm, K. 1977. External exchange and the transformation of central African social systems. In Friedman, J. and Rowlands, M.J. editors, *The Evolution of Social Systems,* pages 115-36. Duckworth, London.

FAD 2000. *The Fine Arts Department.* The Fine Arts Department, Bangkok.

Filliozat, J. 1954. Le symbolisme du monument du Phnom Bakheng. *BEFEO* 44: 527-54.

Finot, M.L. 1902. Duex nouvelles inscriptions de Bhadravarman 1, roi de Champa. *BEFEO* 2: 185-91.

Finot, M.L. 1903. Notes d'epigraphie V: Panduranga. *BEFEO* 3: 630-48.

Flannery, K. 1999. Process and Agency in Early State Formation. *Cambridge Archaeological Journal* 9(1): 3-21.

Fontaine, H. 1972. Deuxieme note sur le "néolithique" du bassin inferieur du Dong-Nai. *Archives géologiques du Viet-Nam* 15: 123-9.

Fox, J. and Ledgerwood, J. 1999. Dry-season flood-recession rice in the Mekong Delta: two thousand years of sustainable agriculture? *AP* 38(1): 37-50.

Friedman, J. and Rowlands, M.J. 1977. Notes towards an epigenetic model of the evolution of civilization. In Friedman, J. and Rowlands M.J. editors, *The Evolution of Social Systems,* pages 201-76. Duckworth, London.

Garnier, F. 1871. Voyage des Hollandais en Cambodge et Laos en 1644. *Bulletin de la Soc. de Géographie* II-19: 251-89.

GATIA, 1974. Excavations of the remains of Ch'i Chia culture at To-Ho-chuang in Yungching County, Kansu Province (in Chinese). *Kaogu Xuebao* 1974: 29-62.

GATIA, 1975. The excavation of a Ch'i Chia culture cemetery at Chin-wei-chia in Ying-Ching County, Kansu Province (in Chinese). *Kaogu Xuebao* 1975: 57-96.

Geyh, M.A., Kudrass, H.R. and Streif, H. 1979. Sea level changes during the late Pleistocene and Holocene in the straits of Malacca. *Nature* 278: 441-43.

GZAR, 1978. Warring states burials at Yinshanling, Pingle (in Chinese). *Kaogu Xuebao*, 1978(2): 211-58.

Glover, I.C. 1980, Ban Don Ta Phet and its relevence to problems in the pre- and protohistory of Thailand. *BIPPA* 2: 16-30.

Glover, I.C. 1983. Excavations at Ban Don Ta Phet, Kanchanaburi Province, Thailand, 1980-1. *South-East Asian Studies Newsletter* 10: 1-4.

Glover, I.C. 1997. The excavations of J.-Y. Claeys at Tra Kieu, Central Vietnam, 1927-28: from the unpublished archives of the EFEO, Paris and records in possession of the Claeys family. *JSS* 85: 173-86.

Glover, I.C. 1998. The role of India in the late prehistory of Southeast Asia. *Journal of Southeast Asian Archaeology* 18: 21-49.

Glover, I.C., Charoenwongsa, P., Alvey, B. and Kamnounket, N. 1984. The cemetery of Ban Don Ta Phet, Thailand: results from the 1980-1 season. In Allchin, B. and Sidell, M. editors, *South Asian Archaeology 1981,* pages 319-30. Cambridge University Press, Cambridge.

Glover, I.C. and Yamagata, M. 1995. The origins of the Cham civilization: indigenous, Chinese and Indian influences in Central Vietnam as revealed by excavations at Tr Kieu, Vietnam 1990 and 1993 *reference?

Glover, I.C., and Yamagata, M. 1998. Excavations at Tra Kieu, Vietnam, 1993. *Southeast Asian Archaeology 1994,* Vol. 1 P.-Y. Manguin editor, Hull: Centre for Southeast Asian Studies, pp. 75-94.

Glover, I.C., M. Yamagata and W. Southworth 1998. Excavations at Buu Chau Hill, Tra Kieu, Quangnam-Danang Province, Vietnam, 1993. *BIPPA* 14: 166-76.

Goody, J. 1971. *Technology, Tradition and the State in Africa.* Hutchinson, London.

Goody, J. 1976. *Production and Reproduction.* Cambridge University Press, London.

Gorman, C.F. 1971. The Hoabinhian and after: subsistence patterns in Southeast Asia during the late Pleistocene and early recent periods. *World Archaeology* 2(3): 300-20.

Gorman, C.F. 1972. Excavations at Spirit Cave, North Thailand: some interim impressions. *AP* 13: 79-107.

Gorman, C.F. 1977. A priori models and Thai prehistory: a reconsideration of the beginnings of agriculture in Southeast Asia. In Reed, C.A. editor, *Origins of Agriculture,* pages 322-55. Mouton, The Hague.

Gorman, C.F. and Charoenwongsa, P. 1976. Ban Chiang: A mosaic of impressions from the first two years. *Expedition* 8(4): 14-26.

Gorman, C.F. and White, J.C. 1979. Patterns in "amorphous" industries: the Hoabinhian viewed through a lithic reduction sequence. Paper presented at the 44th annual meeting of the Society for American Archaeology.

Gourou, P. 1955. *The Peasants of the Tonkin Delta.* Human Relations Area Files, New Haven.

Groslier, B.P. 1966. *Indochina.* Miller, London.

Groslier, B.P. 1973. *Pour une géographie historique du Cambodge.* Les Cahiers d'Outre-Mer 26: 337-9.

Groslier, B.P. 1974. Agriculture et religion dans l'Empire Angkorien. *Études Rurales* 53-56: 95-117.

Groslier, B.P. 1979. La cité hydraulique Angkorienne. Exploitation ou surexploitation du sol? *BEFEO* 66: 161-202.

Gunawardana, R.A.L.H. 1981. Social function and political power: a case study of state formation in irrigation society. In Claessen, H.J.M. and P. Skalník editors, *The Study of the State,* pages 133-54. Mouton, The Hague.

Ha Van Phung, 1979. In search of relations between Go Mun and Dong Son cultures. (in Vietnamese). *KCH* 29: 43-61.

Ha Van Phung 1995. The find from Hop Minh, Yen Bai, a valuable assemblage of the Dong Son culture (in Vietnamese). *KCH* 1995: 26-36.

Ha Van Tan, 1976. The Hoabinhian in the context of Viet Nam. *Vietnamese Studies* 46: 127-97.

Ha Van Tan, 1977. Excavations at Phoi Phoi (in Vietnamese). New archaeological discoveries in Viet Nam in 1976. Ha Noi.

Ha Van Tan, 1980, Nouvelles récherches préhistoriques et protohistoriques au Viet Nam. *BEFEO* 68: 113-54.

Ha Van Yan 1993. Yazhang plaques in the Phung Nguyen culture sites (in Vietnamese). *KCH* 86: 16-27.

Ha Van Tan 1994 (editor). *The Dong Son Culture in Vietnam* (in Vietnamese). Nha Xuat Ban Khoa Hoc Xa Hoi, Hanoi.

Ha Van Tan 1997. The Hoabinhian and before. *BIPPA* 16: 35-41.

Hanks, L.M. 1972. *Rice and Man. Agricultural Ecology in Southeast Asia.* Aldine, Chicago and New York.

Hanwong, T. 1985. *Artefacts analysis from the Excavation of Ban Thakae, Amphoe Muang, Changwat Lopburi* (in Thai). MA dissertation, Silpakorn University.

Haidle, M.N. 1999. The fragment of a glass bracelet from Krek 52/62 and its implications for the dating of the Mimotian culture. Paper read at a conference on the circular sites of Eastern Cambodia, Phnom Penh, November 1999.

Haselgrove, C. 1982. Wealth, prestige and power: the dynamics of late Iron Age political centralisation in South-East England. In Renfrew, A.C. and Shennan, S. editors, *Ranking, Resource and Exchange*, pages 79-88. Cambridge University Press, Cambridge.

Heine-Geldern, R. von 1932. Urheimat und fruheste Wanderungen der Austronesier. *Anthropos* 27: 543-619.

Higham, C.F.W. 1977. The prehistory of the Southern Khorat Plateau, with particular reference to Roi Et Province *MQRISA* 3: 103-42.

Higham, C.F.W. 1983. The Ban Chiang culture in wider perspective. *Proc. Brit. Acad.* LXIX: 229-61.

Higham, C.F.W. 1989. *The Archaeology of Mainland Southeast Asia.* Cambridge University Press, Cambridge.

Higham, C.F.W. and Lu, T. L.-D. 1998. The origins and dispersal of rice cultivation. *Antiquity* 72: 867-77.

Higham, C.F.W. and Kijngam, A., editors, 1984. *Prehistoric Investigations in Northeast Thailand.* British Archaeological Reports (International Series) 231(1-3) Oxford.

Higham, C.F.W., Kijngam, A. and Manly, B.F.J. 1980. An analysis of prehistoric canid remains from Thailand. *JAS* 7(2): 149-66.

Higham, C.F.W. and Thosarat, R. 1998. *Prehistoric Thailand.* River Books, Bangkok.

Higham, C.F.W. and Thosarat, R. editors, 1998a. *The Excavation of Nong Nor, a Prehistoric Site in Central Thailand.* OUSPA NO. 18, Dunedin.

Higham, T.F.G. 1993. The shell knives. In Higham, C.F.W. and Thosarat, R. editors, *The Excavation of Khok Phanom Di* Volume III (part 1): *The Material Culture*, pages 177-212. Research Reports of the Society of Antiquaries of London No. XLVIII. Society of Antiquaries, London L, London.

Ho, C.M. 1984. *The Pottery of Kok Charoen and its Farther Context.* PhD. dissertation, University of London.

Hoang Xuan Chinh, 1968. *Bao Cao Khai Quat Dot Di Chi Lung Hoa.* Nha Xuat Ban Khoa Hoc Xa Hoi, Ha Noi.

Hoang Xuan Chinh, 1984. The Hoabinhian culture and the birth of botanical domestication in Viet Nam.

In Bayard D.T. editor, *Southeast Asian Archaeology at the XV Pacific Science Congress*, pages 169-72. OUSPA Vol. 16.

Hoang Xuan Chinh and Nguyen Khac Su, 1977. The late Neolithic site of Cau Sat (Dong Nai) (in Vietnamese) *KCH* 24: 12-8.

Hoang Xuan Chinh and Nguyen Ngoc Bich, 1978. *The Excavation of the Archaeological Site of Phung Nguyen* (in Vietnamese). Nha Xuat Ban Khoa Hoc Xa Hoi. Ha Noi.

Holdridge, L.R. 1967. *Life Zone Ecology* (revised edition). Tropical Science Centre, San Jose, Costa Rica.

Hutchinson, E.W. 1940, *Adventurers in Siam in the Seventeenth Century.* The Royal Asiatic Society, London.

Indrawooth, P.1984. Results from the excavation within the ancient town of Nakhon Phathom, Tambon Phra Praton, Amphoe Muang, Changwat Nakhon Phathom (in Thai). *Journal of Silpakon University*, Special Issue, 148-68.

Indrawooth, P. 1999. *Dvaravati. A Critical Study Based on Archaeological Evidence.* Aksonsmai, Bangkok.

Indrawooth, P., Krabuansang, S. and Narkwake, P. 1990. Archaeological study of Ban Krabuang Nok. *Spafa Digest*, XI: 12-20.

Indrawooth, P., Krabuansang, S. and Narkwake, P. 1991. Muang Fa Daed Song Yang: new archaeological discoveries. In Université Silpakon, editor, Récentes Recherches en Archéologie en Thailande: Deuxieme Symposium Franco-Thai, pages 98-111. Silpakon University, Bangkok.

Jacob, J.M. 1978. The ecology of Angkor: evidence from the inscriptions. In Stott P.A. editor, *Nature and Man in South East Asia.* SOAS, London.

Jacob, J.M. 1979. Pre-Angkor Cambodia: evidence from the inscriptions concerning the common people and their environment. In Smith, R.B. and Watson, W. editors, *Early South East Asia*, pages 406-26. Oxford University Press, Oxford.

Jacques, C. and Freeman, M. 1998. *Angkor: Cities and Temples*. River Books, Bangkok.

Jacques, C. Freeman, M. 1999. *Ancient Angkor*. River Books, Bangkok.

Janse, J.M. 1947. *Archaeological Research in Indo-China. Volume 1, the District of Chiu-Chen During the Han Dynasty*. Harvard-Yenching Institute Monograph Series Vol.VII. Harvard University Press, Cambridge Mass.

Janse, J.M. 1951. *Archaeological Research in Indo-China. Volume II, The District of Chiu-Chen During the Han Dynasty. Distribution and Comparative Study of the Finds*. Harvard-Yenching Institute Monograph Series. Vol. X, Harvard University Press, Cambridge Mass.

Janse, J.M. 1958. *Archaeological Research in Indo-China. Volume III, The Ancient Dwelling Site of Dong-S'on (Thanh-Hoa, Annam)*. Harvard University Press, Cambridge Mass.

Jermsawatdi, P. and Charuphananon, C. 1989. Votive tablets from excavation at Wat Nakhon Kosa, Lobpuri (in Thai). *Silpakon Journal*, 32(6): 40-55.

Judd, P. 1973. Irrigated agriculture in the Central Plain of Thailand. In Ho R. and Chapman E.C. editors, *Studies in Contemporary Thailand*. Dept. Human Geography Pub. HG/8: 137-72. Australian National University. Canberra.

Kaewglai, C. 1991. Inscriptions on a Dvaravati silver coin: recent evidence. *Silpakon Journal* 34 (2): 21-7.

Källén, A. 2000. Lao Pakao in the late prehistory of Mainland Southeast Asia. *BIPPA* 19: 93-100.

Karlström, A. 2000. Lao Pakao: an Iron Age site on the Nam Ngum River in Laos. *BIPPA* 19: 85-92.

Kealhofer, L. 1996. The human environment during the terminal Pleistocene and Holocene in Northeastern Thailand: phytolith evidence from Lake Kumphawapi. *AP* 35(2): 229-54.

Kealhofer, L. 1997. Evidence for cultural impact on the environment during the Holocene; two phytolith sequences from the Lopburi region, Central Thailand. In Ciarla, R. and Rispoli, F. editors, *South-East Asian Archaeology 1992*, pages 9-28. Istituto Italiano per L'Africa e L'Oriente, Rome.

Keyes, C.F. 1974. A note on the ancient towns and cities of Northeast Thailand. *Tonan Ajia Kenkyu* 11(4): 497-506.

Kijngam, A. 1979. *The Faunal Remains from Ban Chiang and Its Implications for Thai Culture History*. M.A. thesis, University of Otago, Dunedin.

Kislenko, A. and Tatarintseva, N. 1999. The eastern Ural steppe at the end of the Stone Age. In Scarre, C. editor, *Late Prehistoric Exploitation of the Eurasian Steppe*, pages 183-216. McDonald Institute Monographs, Cambridge.

Knapp, A.B., Pigott, V.C. and E.W. Herbert editors, 1998. *Social Approaches to and Industrial Past. The Archaeology and Anthropology of Mining*. Routledge, London.

Kuchler, A.W. and Sawyer, J.O. 1967. A study of vegetation near Chiang Mai, Thailand. *Transactions Kansas Academy of Sciences* 70: 3.

Kuzmina, E.E. 1998. Cultural connections of the Tarim Basin people and the pastoralists of the Asian steppes in the Bronze Age. In Mair, V.H. editor, *The Bronze Age and Early Iron Age Peoples of Eastern Central Asia*, pages 63-93. The Institute for the Study of Man and the University of Pennsylvania Museum Publications, Philadelphia.

Lai Van Toi 1999. The initial inhabitants of Co Loa (in Vietnamese). *KCH* 1998(3): 39-54.

Le van Thieu 1979. The wild pig and the domestic swine from the site of Hoa Loc (Thanh Hoa) (in Vietnamese). *KCH* 29: 37-42.

Le Xuan Diem 1977. Ancient moulds for casting bronze artefacts from the Dong Nai basin (in Vietnamese). *KCH* 24: 44-8.

Le Xuan Diem, Dao Linh Con and Vo Si Khai 1995. *Van Hoa Oc Eo Nhung Kham Pha Moi*. Nha Xuat Ban Khoa Hoc Xa Hoi, Hanoi.

Lebar, F., Hickey, G. and Musgrave, J. 1964. *Ethnic Groups of Mainland Southeast Asia*. Human Relations Area Files, New Haven.

Leong Sau Heng 1991. Jenderam Hilir and the mid-Holocene prehistory of the west coast plain of Peninsular Malaysia. *BIPPA* 10: 150-60.

Lévy, P. 1943. Recherches préhistoriques dans la region de Mlu Prei. *PEFEO* XXX.

Lévy, P. 1970, Thala Borivat ou Stung Treng: sites de la capitale du souverein Khmêr Bhavavarman 1er. *JA* CCLVII: 113-29.

Linduff, K.M. 2000: Metallurgists in ancient East Asia: the Chinese and who else? In Linduff, K.M. editor, *Beginnings of Metallurgy in China*, pages 1-28. Mellen Publishing, Lampeter.

Loofs-Wissowa, H.H.E. 1967. The Thai-British archaeological expedition: a preliminary report on the work of the first season, 1965-66. *JSS* lv(2): 237-62.

Loubère, S. De La, 1693. *A New Historical Relation of the Kingdom of Siam*. Tho. Horne, London.

Lunet de Lajonquière, E. 1902. Inventaire Descriptif des Monuments du Cambodge. *PEFEO* IV.

Luu Tran Tieu 1977. *Khu Mo Co Chau Can*. Ha Noi.

Lyons, E. 1965. The traders of Ku Bua. *Archives of the Chinese Art Society of America* XIX: 52-6.

Lyons, E. 1979. Dvaravati: a consideration of its formative period. Smith, R.B. and Watson, W. editors, *Early Southeast Asia*, pages 352-9. Oxford University Press, Oxford.

McGovern, P.E., Vernon, W.W. and White, J.C. 1985. Ceramic technology at prehistoric Ban Chiang, Thailand: physiochemical analyses. *Masca Journal* 3(4): 104-13.

McNeill, J.R. 1997. Muang Phet: Quaritch-Wales's moated site excavations re-appraised. *BIPPA*, 16: 167-76.

Mabbett, I.W. 1978. Kingship at Angkor. *JSS* 66(2): 1-58.

Maleipan, V. 1992. Old Stone Age tools at Chiang Saen (in Thai). *Archaeology Journal* 4: 35-43.

Malleret, L.1959-63. *L'Archéologie du Delta du Mekong* 4 vols. EFEO Paris.

Malleret, L. 1959. Ouvrages circulaire en terre dans l'Indochine Méridionale. *BEFEO* 49: 409-53.

Maloney, B.K. 1991. Palaeoenvironments of Khok Phanom Di. In Higham C.F.W. and Bannanurag, R. editors, *The Excavation of Khok Phanom Di Volume II. The Biological Remains (Part I)*, pages 1-134. Research Reports of the Society of Antiquaries of London No. XLVIII. Society of Antiquaries, London.

Manguin, P.-Y. and Vo Si Khai 2000. Excavations at the Ba The/Oc Eo complex (Viet Nam). A preliminary report on the 1998 campaign. Lobo, W. and Reimann, S., editors, *Southeast Asian Archaeology 1998*, pages 107-21. Centre for South-East Asian Studies, University of Hull and Ethnologisches Museum, Staatliche Museum zu Berlin.

Mansuy, H. 1902. *Stations préhistoriques de Samrong-Sen et de Longprao (Cambodge)*. F.H. Scheider, Hanoi.

Mansuy, H. 1923. Contribution a l'étude de la préhistoire de l'Indochine. Résultats de nouvèlles récherches effectuées dans le gisement préhistorique de Samrong Sen (Cambodge). *MSGI* XI(1): 5-24.

Mansuy, H. 1924. Stations préhistoriques dans les cavernes du massif calcaire de Bac-Son (Tonkin). *BSGI* 11.2.

Mason, G.M. 1991. The molluscan remains. In Higham C.F.W. and Bannanurag, R. editors, *The Excavation of Khok Phanom Di Volume II. The Biological Remains (Part I)*, pages 259-319. Research Reports of the Society of Antiquaries of London No. XLVIII. Society of Antiquaries, London.

Maspero, M.G. 1928. *Le Royaume de Champa*. Librairie Nationale d'Art et d'Histoire. Paris and Bruxelles.

Marcus, H. 1998. The peaks and valleys of ancient states. In Feinman, G.M. and Marcus, J. editors, *Archaic States*, pages 59-94. School of American Research Press, Santa Fe.

Meacham, W. 1975. Schofield and Shek Pik in retrospect. In Meacham, W., editor, *An Archaeological Site at Shek Pik*, pages v-ix. Journal Monograph I, Hong Kong Archaeological Society, Hong Kong.

Meacham, W. 1993. New C14 dates and advances in establishing a precise chronology for Hong Kong's prehistory. *Journal of the Hong Kong Archaeological Society* XIII: 115-7.

Meacham, W. 1999. Neolithic to historic in the Hong Kong region. *Bulletin of the Indo-Pacific Prehistory Association* 18: 121-7.

Moore, E. 1986. *The Khorat Khmer.* Ph.D. thesis, University of London.

Moore, E. 1992. Ancient habitation on the Angkor Plain: Ban Takhong to Phum Reul. Unpublished paper.

Mouhot, H. 1864. *Travels in the Central Parts of Indo-China (Siam), Cambodia and Laos* (2 volumes) J. Murray, London.

Mourer, R. 1977. Laang Spean and the prehistory of Cambodia. *MQRISA* 3: 29-56.

Mourer, C. and Mourer R. 1970. The prehistoric industry of Laang Spean, Province Battambang, Cambodia. *APAO* 5: 128-46.

Mudar, K.M. 1995. Evidence for prehistoric dryland farming in Mainland Southeast Asia: results of regional survey in Lopburi Province, Thailand. *AP* 34: 157-94.

Murowchick, R.E. 1986. The development of early bronze metallurgy in Vietnam and Kampuchea: a reexamination of recent work. Paper read at the 2nd International Symposium on the Use of Metals and Alloys, Zhengzhou, 21st-27th October 1986.

Mus, P. 1929. Les Ballistes du Bayon. *BEFEO* 29: 331-41.

Mus, P. 1936. Symbolism à Angkor Thom. Le "grand miracle" du Bayon. *AIB-L* 57-68.

Natapintu, S. 1988. Current research on ancient copper-base metallurgy in Thailand. In Charoenwongsa, P. and Bronson, B., editors, *Prehistoric Studies: the Stone Age and Metal Ages in Thailand*, pages 107-24. Thai Antiquity Working Group, Bangkok.

Natapintu, S. 1997. Current archaeological research in Central Thailand with special reference to the site of Phu Noi, Lopburi Province. Ciarla, R. and Rispoli, F. editors, *South-East Asian Archaeology 1992*, pages 45-56. Istituto Italiano per L'Africa e L'Oriente, Rome.

Natapintu, S. and Phommanodch, S. 1990. *Archaeology in Chiang Rai* (in Thai). FAD, Bangkok.

Ngo Si Hong 1980, Binh Chau (Nghia Binh). A newly discovered Bronze Age site on the central Vietnamese coast (in Vietnamese). *KCH* 33: 68-74.

Ngo Si Hong 1983. The second excavation at Lang Vac, (Nghe Tinh) (in Vietnamese). *KCH* 46: 68-74

Ngo Si Hong 1987. Back to Dong Dau and fresh knowledge of it, (in Vietnamese*). KCH* 1998: 22-35.

Nguyen Duc Tung and Pham Van Hai 1979. The various pollen complexes in the quaternary sediments of the Bac Bo plains (in Vietnamese) *KCH* 32: 34-8.

Nguyen Duy Hinh 1983. The birth of the first state in Vietnam. Paper prepared for Pacific Science Congress, Dunedin, February 1983. Viet Nam Social Sciences Commission Archaeology Institute, Hanoi.

Nguyen Gia Doi 1999. Dieu industry in local background (in Vietnamese). *KCH* 1999(3): 5-24.

Nguyen Khac Su 1995. The Bien Ho culture in Tay Nguyen province (in Vietnamese). *KCH* 1995 7-16.

Nguyen Khac Su and Tranh Quy Thinh 2000. Excavation of Lung Leng site: data and comments (in Vietnamese). *KCH* 2000(1): 15-34.

Nguyen Kim Dung 1990. The lithic workshop at Trang Kenh. *KCH* 1990: 3 64-82.

Nguyen Kim Dung 1998. Nephrite and jadeite manufacturing tradition in prehistoric Vietnam (in Vietnamese). *KCH* 1998(4): 15-22.

Nguyen Kim Dung 2001. *Jewellery from late prehistoric sites recently excavated in South Vietnam.* BIPPA 21: 107-13.

Nguyen Kim Dung, Trinh Can, Dang Van Thang, Vu Quoc Hien and Nguyen Thi Hau 1995. Ornaments from jar burial sites in Can Gio district, Ho Chi Minh City (in Vietnamese). *KCH* 1995(2): 27-46.

Nguyen Lan Cuong 1995. Study of ancient human remains found in Giong Phet and Giong Ca Vo sites at Can Gio district, Ho Chi Minh City (in Vietnamese). *KCH* 1995(2): 20-6.

Nguyen Thi Hau 1995. Giong Ca Vo jar burials (in Vietnamese). *KCH* 1995(2): 47-50.

Nguyen Van Hao 1979. The neolithic in the northeastern region of Vietnam (in Vietnamese) *KCH* 29: 29-36.

Nguyen Viet 1983. The Dong Son civilisation and the foundation of a development rice planting. Paper prepared for the XV Pacific Science Congress, Dunedin, February 1983. Viet Nam Social Sciences Commission, Archaeology Institute, Hanoi.

Nitta, E. 1991. Archaeological study on the ancient iron-smelting and salt-making industries in the northeast of Thailand. Preliminary report on the excavations of Non Yang and Ban Don Phlong. *Journal of Southeast Asian Archaeology*, 11: 1-46.

Niyomka, C. and Adsvamas, D. 2000. Report on the Analysis of Archaeological Finds from Ban Bung Noi, Amphoe Ban Khurat, Buriram Province (in Thai), submitted to the 9th regional office of the Fine Arts Department.

Norman, J. and Mei, T. 1976. The Austroasiatics in ancient South China; some lexical evidence. *Monumenta Serica* 32: 274-301.

Noulet, J.B. 1879. L'Âge de la pierre polie et du bronze au Cambodge d'après les découvertes de M.J. Moura. *Arch. Mus. Hist. Nat. de Toulouse* 1.

Okladnikov, A.P. 1990. Inner Asia at the dawn of history. In Sinor, D. editor, *The Cambridge History of Early Inner Asia*, pages 41-96. Cambridge University Press, Cambridge.

O'Reilly, D.J.W. 1999. *A Diachronic Analysis of Social Organisation in the Mun River Valley.* PhD. dissertation, University of Otago.

Osborne, M. 1966. Notes on early Cambodian provincial history. Isanapura and Sambhupura. *France Asie* 186: 433-49.

Osborne, M. 1975. *River Road to China. The Mekong River Expedition, 1866-1873.* Liveright, New York.

Paris, P. 1929. Anciens canaux reconnus sur photographies aériennes dans les provinces de Ta-Keo, Chao-Doc, Long-Xuyen et Rach-Gia. *BEFEO* 29: 365-70.

Paris, P. 1931. Anciens canaux reconnus sur photographies aériennes dans les provinces de Ta-Kev et De Chau-Doc. *BEFEO* 31: 221-4

Paris, P. 1941. Les bateaux des bas-reliefs Khmèrs. *BEFEO* 41: 335-61.

Paris, P. 1941a, Notes et melanges: anciens canaux reconnus sur photographies aériennes dans les provinces de Takeo, Chau-Doc, Long-Xuyen et Rach-Gia. *BEFEO* 41: 365-70.

Parker, R.H.1968. Review Article: Review of Archaeological Excavations in Thailand Vol. 2, Ban Kao, Part 1. by P. Sørensen and T. Hatting. *Journal of the Polynesian Society* 77(3): 307-13.

Parmentier, M.H. 1904. Les monuments du cirque de Mi-son. *BEFEO* 4: 805-96.

Parmentier, M.H. 1909 *Inventaire Descriptif de Monuments Cams de L'Annam.* Ernest Leroux, Paris.

Parmentier, M.H. 1917. Anciens tombeaux au Tonkin. *BEFEO* 17: 1-32.

Parmentier, M.H. 1918. Dépots de jarres à Sa-Huynh.*BEFEO* 24: 325-43.

Parmentier, M.H. 1918a, *Inventaire Descriptif de Monuments Cams de L'Annam.* Ernest Leroux, Paris.

Parmentier, H., 1927. L'Art Khmèr Primitif. *PEFEO* XXI-XXII.

Patte, E. 1924. Le kjökkenmödding néolithique de Bau Tro a Tam Tao près de Dong Hoi (Annam). *BEFEO* 24: 521-61.

Patte, E. 1925. Le kjökkenmödding néolithique de Bau Tro a Tam Tao pres de Dong Hoi (Annam). BSGI 14(1).

Patte, E. 1932. Le kjökkenmödding néolithique de Da-but et ses sépultures. *BSGI* 19(3).

Pautreau, J.-P. A. Matringhem and P. Mornais, 1997. Excavation at Ban Wang Hi, Lamphun Province, Thailand. *Journal of the Siam Society* 85: 161-72.

Pautreau, J.-P. and P. Mornais, 1998. Le cimetière protohistorique de Ban Wang Hi. *Archeologia* 351: 46-54.

Pearson, R. and Underhill, A. 1987: The Chinese Neolithic: recent trends in research. *American Anthropologist* 89: P807-22.

Pei Anping 1998. Notes on new advancements and revelations in the agricultural archaeology of early rice domestication in the Dongting Lake region. *Antiquity* 72: 878-85.

Pelliot, P. 1902. Mémoires sur les coutumes dur Cambodge, par Tcheou Ta-kouan. *BEFEO* 2: 123-77.

Pelliot, P.1903. Le Fou-Nan. *BEFEO* 2: 248-333.

Pelliot, P. 1904. Deux itinéraires de Chine en Inde à la fin du VIIIe siècle. *BEFEO* 4: 131-413.

Penny, D., Grindrod, J. and Bishop. P. 1996. Holocene palaeoenvironmental reconstruction based on micro- fossil analysis of a lake sediment core, Nong Han Kumphawapi, Udon Thani, Northeast Thailand. *AP* 35(2) 209-28.

Penny, J.S. 1984. Fish in the water and rice in the paddy: contributions to the study of the Southeast Asian Iron Age. Bayard, D.T. editor, *Southeast Asian Archaeology at the XV Pacific Science Congress* pages 152-60. OUSPA Vol. 16.

Péri, N. 1923. Essai sur les relations du Japon et de l'Indochine au XVIe et XVIIe siècles. *BEFEO* XXIII: 1-137.

Pham Duc Manh 1995. First pebble tools of the Late Palaeolithic in South Tay Nguyen (central Highlands) (in Vietnamese). *KCH* 1995(4): 15-25.

Pham Duc Manh 2000 Some recent discoveries about the pre- and protohistory of the Southeastern part of Vietnam. Lobo, W. and Reimann, S., editors, *Southeast Asian Archaeology 1998*. Centre for South-East Asian Studies, University of Hull and Ethnologisches Museum, Staatliche Museum zu Berlin.

Pham Duc Manh & Nguyen Giang Hai 1996. Di chi khao co hoc Bung Bac – Nhan thuc moi (the archaeological site of Bung Bac- new perception (in Vietnamese) *KCH* 1996(3):10-20.

Pham Quoc Quan and Trinh Can 1982. The pirogue-coffins at Xuan La (Ha Son Binh Province). (In Vietnamese). *KCH* 44: 36-50.

Pham Thi Ninh 2000. Recent discovery and excavation of a Sa Huynh culture site on Ly Son Island (Central Vietnam). *BIPPA* 19: 61-4.

Pham Thi Ninh and Doan Ngoc Khoi 1999. The recent discovery and excavation of Sa Huynh culture site on Ly Son island (Central Vietnam) (in Vietnamese). *KCH* 1999(2): 14-39.

Pham Van Kinh 1977. Excavations at Ben Do (Ho Chih Minh City) (in Vietnamese). *KCH* 24: 19-21.

Phommanodch, S. 1991. The past at Thung Samrit at Ban Prasat (in Thai). *Silpakon Journal*, 34: 6-21.

Pigott, V.C. 1998. Prehistoric Copper Mining in the Context of Emerging Community Craft Specialization in northeast Thailand. In Knapp, A.B., Pigott, V.C. and Herbert, E.W. editors, *Social Approaches to and Industrial Past. The Archaeology and Anthropology of Mining.* pages 205-25. Routledge, London.

Pigott, V.C. and Weisgerber, G. 1998. Mining archaeology in geological context. The prehistoric copper mining complex at Phu Lon, Nong Khai Province, northeast Thailand. In T. Rehren, A. Hauptmann and Muhly, J.D., editors, *Metallurgica Antiqua. In Honor of Hans-Bert Bachmann and Robert Maddin*, pages 135-62. Deutsches-Bergbau Museum. Der Anschnitt. Beiheft 8. Bochum

Pigott, V.C., Weiss, A.D. and Natapintu. S. 1997. The archaeology of copper production: excavations in the Khao Wong Prachan Valley, Central Thailand. Ciarla, R. and Rispoli, F. editors, *South-East Asian Archaeology 1992*, pages 119-57. Istituto Italiano per L'Africa e L'Oriente, Rome.

Pisnupong, P. 1992. *History and Archaeology of Si Mahasod* (in Thai). FAD, Bangkok.

Pisnupong, P. 1993. *History and Archaeology of Si Mahasod: Two* (in Thai). FAD, Bangkok.

Pookajorn, S. 1981. The Hoabinhian of Mainland Southeast Asia: New data from the Recent Thai Excavation in the Ban Kao Area. M.Sc. thesis, University of Pennsylvania.

Pookajorn, S. 1992. Recent evidence of a Late Pleistocene to a Middle Holocene archaeological site at Moh

Khiew Cave, Krabi Province, Thailand. *Silpakon Journal* 35(3): 93-119.

Pottier, C. 1997. Élaboration d'une carte archéologique de la région d'Angkor: l'organisation du territoire Angkorien. Manguin, P-Y. editor, *Southeast Asian Archaeology 1994.* Centre for Southeast Asian Studies, University of Hull, Hull.pp. 179-94.

Prishanchit, S., Santoni, M. and Pautreau, J.-P. 1988. Ob Luang. Report on survey and excavation in 1985 (in Thai). In Charoenwongsa, P., editor, *Muang Mae Moh Ob Luang and Ban Yaang Thong Tai*, pages 36-68. FAD, Bangkok.

Quang Van Cay 1995. Archaeological discoveries and study in Than Sa Valley and problem of Nguom industry (in Vietnamese). *KCH* 1995(1): 3-17.

Quaritch-Wales, H.G. 1952. *Ancient South-East Asian Warfare*. Bernard Quaritch, London.

Quaritch-Wales, H.G. 1957. An early Buddhist civilisation in Eastern Siam. *JSS* XLV(1): 42-60.

Quaritch-Wales, H.G. 1969. *Dvaravati. The Earliest Kingdom of Siam*. Bernard Quaritch, London.

Rajpitak, W. and Seeley, N.J. 1979. The bronze bowls from Ban Don Ta Phet: an enigma of prehistoric metallurgy. *World Archaeology*, 11(1): 26-31.

Rattanakun, S. 1992. *The Archaeology of Muang Ku Bua* (in Thai). FAD, Bangkok.

Reid, L.A. 1994. Morphological evidence for Austric. *Oceanic Linguistics* 33, 323-44.

Reinecke, A. 1996. Ohrringe mit tierkopfenden in Sudostasien. *Beitrage zur Allgemeinen und Vergleichenden Archäologie* 16:5-51.

Reinecke, A. 1998. *Einführung in die Archäologie Vietnams*. Linden Soft, Koln.

Reinecke, A., Le Duy Son and Le Dinh Phuc 1999. Zur vorgeschichte im nordlichen Mittelvietnam. Eine Bestandsaufnahme nach vietname sisch-deutschen feldforschungen. *BAVA* 19: 5-111.

Reinecke A. and Lu Duy Son 2000. A newly disovered burial site of the Sa Huynh culture at Go Mun in Central Viet Nam (in Vietnamese). *KCH* 2000(1): 54-75.

Reinecke, A., Le Duy Son and le Dinh Phuc 2000. Ein neu entdecktes graberfeld de Sa-Huyn-Kultur von Go Mun in Mittelvietnam. *BAVA* 20: 43.

Renfrew, A.C. 1972. *The Emergence of Civilisation*. Methuen, London.

Renfrew, A.C. 1984. *Approaches to Social Archaeology*. Edinburgh University Press, Edinburgh.

Renfrew, C. 1987. *Archaeology and Language: the Puzzle of Indo-European Origins*. London, Jonathon Cape.

Reynolds, T.E.G. 1992. Excavations at Banyan Valley Cave, Northern Thailand: a report on the 1972 season. *AP* 31: 77-98.

Ricklefs, M. 1967. Land and law in the epigraphy of tenth-century Cambodia. *JAS* XXVI: 93: 411-20.

Rispoli, F. 1992. Preliminary report on the pottery from Tha Kae, Lopburi, Central Thailand. In Glover, I.C. editor, *Southeast Asian Archaeology 1990*, pages 129-42. Centre for Southeast Asian Studies, University of Hull, Hull.

Rispoli, F 1997. Late 3rd –2nd millennium B.C. pottery traditions in Central Thailand: some preliminary observations in a wider perspective. In Ciarla, R. and Rispoli, F. editors, *South-East Asian Archaeology 1992*, pages 59-97. Istituto Italiano per L'Africa e L'Oriente, Rome.

Rogers, P.R., Leininger, N.W., Mirchandani, S., van den Bergh, J. and Widdowson, E.A., 1995. *Tung Wan Tsai: A Bronze Age and Han Period Coastal Site*. Antiquities and Monuments Office, Hong Kong, Occasional Paper no. 3.

Roveda, Vittorio, Khmer Mythology, Sacred Angkor, 2002. River Books, Bangkok.

Rutnin, S. 1979. A pottery sequence from Non Chai, Northeast Thailand. M.A. thesis, University of Otago.

Sahai, S. 1970, Les Institutions politiques et l'organisation administrative du Cambodge ancien (VI-XIII siècles). *PEFEO* LXXV.

Sahlins, M. 1972. *Stone Age Economics*. Aldine-Atherton: Chicago and New York.

Santoni, M., Pautreau, J.-P. and Prishanchit, S. 1986. Excavations at Ob Luang, Province of Chiang Mai, Thailand. In Glover, I.C. and Glover, E. editors, *Southeast Asian Archaeology 1986*. British Archaeological Reports (International Series), 561: 37-54.

Saraya, D. 1997. Rethinking the historical evolution of Sukhothai. *Muang Boran* 23: 48-57.

Sayavongkhamdy, T. and Bellwood, P. 2000. Recent archaeological research in Laos. *BIPPA* 19: 101-110.

Saurin, E. 1963. Station préhistorique à Hang-Gon près Xuan Loc. *BEFEO* 51: 433-52.

Saxe, A.A. 1971. Social dimensions of mortuary practices in a mesolithic population from Waki Halfa, Sudan. J.A. Brown (editor) Approaches to the Social Dimensions of Mortuary Practices pp. 39-57. Mem. Soc. Am. Arch. No. 25.

Schauffler, W. 1976. Archaeological survey and excavation of Ban Chiang culture sites in Northeast Thailand. *Expedition* 18: 27-37.

Schofield, W. 1975. An archaeological site at Shek Pik. In Meacham, W., editor, *An Archaeological Site at Shek Pik*. Journal Monograph I, Hong Kong Archaeological Society, Hong Kong.

Seidenfaden, E. 1954. Kanok Nakhon, an ancient Mon settlement in North-east Siam and its treasures of art. *BEFEO* 44(2): 643-7.

Shaanxi-ATIA, 1980: Excavations of a Neolithic site at Taosi in Xiangfen, Shanxi (in Chinese). *Kaogu*, 18-31.

Shoocondej, R. 1996. Working towards an anthropological perspective on Thai prehistory. *BIPPA* 14: 119-32.

Shorto, H.L. 1979. The linguistic protohistory of mainland South East Asia.

Smith R.B. and Watson, W. editors, *Early South East Asia* pages 273-28. Oxford University Press, Oxford.

Silpakon University 1980. *Report and a Study of Ancient Culture at Ban Khu Muang, Amphoe Inburi, Changwat Singburi* (in Thai). Department of Archaeology, Silpakon University.

Siripanith, S, 1985. An analytical study on pottery from the excavation at Ban Thakae, Muang District, Lopburi Province. M.A. thesis, Silapakorn University, Bangkok.

Solheim, W.G. II 1968. Early bronze in Northeastern Thailand. *Current Anthropology* 9(1)59-62.

Solheim, W.G. II 1970, Northern Thailand, Southeast Asia, and World prehistory. *AP* 13: 145-62.

Solheim, W.G. II 1972. An earlier agricultural revolution. *Scientific American* CCVI(4): 34-41.

Songsiri W. 1997. Iron-producing communities at the headwaters of the Lamphan River. Muang *Boran* 23: 26-47.

Sørensen, P. 1972. The Neolithic cultures of Thailand (and North Malaysia) and their Lungshanoid relationship. Barnard, N. editor, *Early Chinese art and its possible influence in the Pacific Basin*, pages 459-506.

Sørensen, P. 1973. Prehistoric iron implements from Thailand. *AP* XVI(2): 134-73.

Sørensen, P. 1979. The Ongbah cave and its fifth drum. R.B. Smith and Watson, W. editors, *Early South East Asia, pages* 78-97. Oxford University Press, Oxford.

Sørensen, P. and Hatting, T. 1967. *Archaeological Investigations in Thailand. Vol.II, Ban Kao, Part 1: The Archaeological Materials from the Burials.* Munksgard, Copenhagen.

Southworth, W. 2000. Notes on the political geography of Campa in Central Vietnam during the late 8th and early 9th centuries. Lobo, W. and Reimann, S. editors, *Southeast Asian Archaeology 1998,* pages 237-44. Centre for South-East Asian Studies, University of Hull and Ethnologisches Museum, Staatliche Museum zu Berlin.

Stark, M.T., Griffin, P.B., Chuch Phoeurn, Ledgerwood, J., Dega, M., Mortland, C., Dowling, N., Bayman, J.M., Bong Sovath, Tea Van, Chhan Chamroen and Latinis, K. 1999. Results of the 1995-6 archaeological field investigations at Angkor Borei, Cambodia. *AP* 38(1): 7-36.

Suchitta, P. 1985. Early iron smelting technology in Thailand and its implications. Research conference on early Southeast Asia 25-40. Bangkok, Silpakon University.

Sukawasana, Y. 1996. Recent excavation of Dong Lakon: early moated marine chiefdom in eastern coast of Thailand. Paper read at the 6th International Conference of th European Association of Southeast Asian Archaeologists, Leiden.

Sulaksananont, A. 1987. *The Study of Muang Phra Rot, Amphoe Phanat Nikhom, Chonburi, from Material Culture and Stratigraphy* (in Thai). M.A. thesis, Silpakon University.

Sun Shuyun and Han Rubin 1981. A preliminary study of early Chinese copper and bronze artefacts (in Chinese). *Kaogu Xuebao* 1981, 287-302.

Takaya, Y. 1969. Topographical analysis of the southern basin of the Central Plain, Thailand. *Tonan Aia Kenkyu**: 293-300

Talbot, S. 2000. Notes from the field: an excavation at a Khmer temple in Northeast Thailand. *New Zealand Journal of Asian Studies* II: 162-8.

Tankittikorn, W. 1991. *The Settlement Before Muang Sri Thep.* Fine Arts Department, Bangkok.

Tayles, N.G. 1999. *The Excavation of Khok Phanom Di. A Prehistoric Site in Central Thailand.* Vol. V: *The People.* Research Reports of the Society of Antiquaries of London No. LXI. Society of Antiquaries, London.

Taylor, K.W. 1983. *The Birth of Viet Nam.* University of California, Berkeley.

Theunissen, R., Grave, P. and Bailey G. 2000. Doubt on diffusion: challenging the assumed Indian origin of Iron Age agate and carnelian beads in Southeast Asia. *World Archaeology* 32(1): 84-105.

Thompson, G.B. 1996. *The Excavation of Khok Phnom Di. A Prehistoric Site in Central Thailand.* Vol. IV: *Subsistence and Environment: the Botanical Evidence.* Research Reports of the Society of Antiquaries of London No. LIII. Society of Antiquaries, London.

Tjia, H.D. 1980, The Sunda Shelf, Southeast Asia. *Zeitschrift f. Geomorphologie* NF 24.4: 408-27.

Trinh Can and Pham Van Kinh, 1977. Excavations of the urnfield of Tam My. (in Vietnamese) *KCH* 24: 49-57.

Trinh Nang Chung 1998. Further contribution to the study of the Nguom site (in Vietnamese). *KCH* 1998 (4): 15-22.

Trinh Sinh, 1977. From the stone ring to the bronze ringe (in Vietnamese). *KCH* 23: 51-6.

Trinh Sinh 1996. From experiments of casting of bronze drums (in Vietnamese). *KCH* 1996(2) 42-52.

Turnbaugh, W., Jurmain, R., Nelson, H. and Kilgore, L. 1999. *Understanding Physical Anthropology and Archaeology,* 7th Edition. Stamford.

Van Liere, W.J. 1980, Traditional water management in the lower Mekong Basin. *World Archaeology* 11(3): 265-80

Veerapan, M. 1979. The excavation at Sab Champa. Smith, R.B. and Watson, W. editors, *Early South East Asia, pages* 337-341. Oxford University Press, Oxford.

Veeraprasert, M. 1985. Khlong Thom: an ancient bead-manufacturing location and an ancient entrepôt. Research conference on early Southeast Asia 168-9. Bangkok, Silpakon University.

Vernon, W.W. 1996-7. The crucible in copper-bronze production at prehistoric Phu Lon: analyses and interpretation. In Bulbeck, D. and Barnard, N. editors, *Ancient Chinese and Southeast Asian Bronze Cultures,* pages 809-20. SMC Publishing Inc. Taipei.

Vernon, W.W. 1997. Chronological variation in crucible technology at Ban Chiang: a preliminary assessment. Indo-Pacific Prehistory: The Chiang Mai Papers, *BIPPA* 16: 107-10.

Vickery, M. 1985. The reign of Suryavarman I and royal factionalism at Angkor. *Journal of Southeast Asian Studies* 16(2): 226-44.

Vickery, M. 1998. *Society, Economics and Politics in Pre-Angkor Cambodia.* The Centre for East Asian Cultural Studies for Unesco, Tokyo.

Vincent, B.A. 1984. The analysis of prehistoric pottery from Ban Na Di, Northeast Thailand. Bayard D.T. editor, *Southeast Asian Archaeology at the XV Pacific Science Congress* pages 50-9, OUSPA Vol. 16.

Vincent, B.A. 2003. *The Ceramic industries of Khok Phnom Di.* In preparation.

Vishnu-Mittre 1975. The early domestication of plants in South and South East Asia: a critical review. *The Palaeobotanist,* 22: 83-8.

Vu The Long 1977. The faunal remains from Hang Con Moong (in Vietnamese). *KCH* 22: 19-23.

Vu Thi Ngoc Thu and Nguyen Duy Ty 1978. A tool set for casting bronze from Lang Ca (Vinh Phu) (in Vietnamese). *KCH* 26: 36-9.

Vu Quoc Hien 1991. The urnfield cemetery of Pa Xua, Quang Nam (in Vietnamese). *Vien Bao Tang Lich su Viet Nam. Thong Bao Khoa Hoc* 1991: 167-79.

Wang, Gungwu 1958. The Nanhai Trade. *JMBRA*, XXXI(2): 1-135.

Watson, W. 1979. Kok Charoen and the early metal age of Central Thailand. Smith, R.B. and Watson, W. editors, *Early South East Asia*, pages 53-62. Oxford University Press, Oxford.

Watson, W. and Loofs-Wissowa, H.H.E. 1967. Thai-British archaeological expedition: a preliminary report on the work of the first season, 1965-6. *Journal of the Siam Society*, 55(2): 237-62.

Webb, M.C. 1975. The flag follows trade: an essay on the necessary interaction of military and commercial factors in state formation. Sabloff, J.A. and Lamberg-Karlovsky, C.C. editors, *Ancient Civilization and Trade*, pages 155-209. University of New Mexico Press, Albuquerque.

Weeraprajak, K. 1986. *Inscriptions in Thailand* volume 1 (in Thai). Fine Arts Department, Thailand.

Welch, D.J. 1997. Archaeological evidence of Khmer state political and economic organisation. *BIPPA*, 16: 69-78.

Welch, D.J. and McNeill, J.R. 1991. Settlement, agriculture and population changes in the Phimai region, Thailand. *BIPPA*, 11: 210-28.

Wheatley, P. 1961. *The Golden Khersonese: Studies in the HistoricalGeography of the Malay Peninsula to A.D. 1500*. University of Malaya, Kuala Lumpur.

Wheatley, P. 1971. *The Pivot of the Four Quarters*. Aldine, Chicago.

Wheatley, P. 1983. *Nagara and Commandery*. University of Chicago Department of Geography Research Paper 207-8.

Wheeler, R.E.M., 1954. *Rome Beyond the Imperial Frontiers*. London.

White, J.C. 1982. Prehistoric environment and subsistence in Northeast Thailand. *Southeast Asian Studies Newsletter* 9: 1-3.

White, J.C. 1982a, *Ban Chiang. The discovery of a lost Bronze Age*. University of Pennsylvania Press, Philadelphia.

White, J.C. 1997. A brief note on new dates for the Ban Chiang cultural tradition. *BIPPA* 16: 103-6.

White, J.C. and Pigott, V.C. 1996. From community craft to regional specialization: intensification of copper production in pre-state Thailand. Wailes, B. editor, *Craft Specialization and Social Evolution: in Memory of V. Gordon Childe*. 151-75. University Museum Symposium Series, Volume VI, Philadelphia.

Wichakana, M. 1984. *The Rimsherds from Ban Na Di and their Implications for the Prehistory of Sakon Nakhon Basin*. M.A. thesis, University of Otago.

Wichakana, M. 1991. Prehistoric sacrifices at Noen U-Loke (in Thai). *Muang Boran* 16: 69-79

Wilaikeo, J. 1991a. *The Archaeology of Muang U-Taphao* (in Thai). FAD, Bangkok.

Wilaikeo, J. 1991b. Archaeological work at U-Ta Pao, Chainat Province (in Thai). *Silpakon Journal*, 34(2): 1-20.

Wilen, R.N. 1989. *Excavations at Non Pa Kluay, Northeast Thailand*. British Archaeological Reports (International Series), 517. Oxford.

Williams-Hunt, P.D.R. 1950, Irregular earthworks in Eastern Siam: an air survey. *Antiquity* 24: 30-7.

Wittfogel, K.A. 1957. *Oriental Despotism, a Study of Absolute Power*. Yale University Press, New Haven.

Wolters, O.W. 1974. North-Western Cambodia in the seventh Century. *BSOAS* XXXVII (2): 355-84.

Wolters, O.W. 1979. Khmer hinduism in the seventh century. In Smith, R.B. and Watson, W. editors, *Early South East Asia*, pages 427-42. Oxford University Press, Oxford.

Wolters, O.W. 1982. *History, Culture and Region in Southeast Asian Perspectives*. Institute of Southeast Asian Studies, Singapore.

Wright, H.T. 1986. The evolution of civilisations. In Meltzer, D.J., Fowler, D.D. and Sabloff, J.A. editors, *American Archaeology Past and Future: a Celebration of the Society for American Archaeology 1935-1985*, pages 323-65. Smithsonian Institution Press, Washington DC.

Wright, H.T. 1998. Uruk states in southwestern Iran, in Feinman, G.M. and J. Marcus editors, *Archaic States*, pages 173-97. School of American Research Press, Santa Fe.

Yen, D.E. 1977. Hoabinhian horticulture: the evidence and the questions from Northwest Thailand. J. Allen, J. Golson and R. Jones (editors) *Sunda and Sahul. Prehistoric Studies in Southeast Asia, Melanesia and Australia*, pages 567-99. Academic Press, London.

Yen, D.E. 1982. Ban Chiang pottery and rice. *Expedition* 24(1): 51-64.

YPM, 1981. The Baiyangcun site at Binchuan County, Yunnan Province (in Chinese). *Kaogu Xuebao* 1981: 349-68.

You-Di, C. 1978. Nothing is new. *Muang Boran* 4(4)15-6.

Yuan Jairong and Zhang Chi, 1999: The origins of pottery and rice cultivation in China. *Newsletter of the Grant-in-Aid Program for COE Research Foundation of the Ministry of Education, Science, Sports and Culture in Japan* 2(1): 3-4.

Zhao Zhijun 1998. The middle Yangtze region in China is one place where rice was domesticated: phytolith evidence from Diaotonghuan cave, Northern Jiangxi. *Antiquity* 72: 885-97.

Index

Numbers in bold refer to illustrations.